From Pariah
to Priority

I0029174

SUNY series, Studies in Human Rights

—————

Suzy Lee and Alexandria S. Moore, editors

SUNY series in Queer Politics and Cultures

—————

Cynthia Burack and Jyl J. Josephson, editors

From Pariah
to Priority

How LGBTI Rights Became a Pillar of
American and Swedish Foreign Policy

Elise Carlson Rainer

SUNY
PRESS

Published by State University of New York Press, Albany

© 2021 State University of New York

All rights reserved

Printed in the United States of America

No part of this book may be used or reproduced in any manner whatsoever
without written permission. No part of this book may be stored in a retrieval system
or transmitted in any form or by any means including electronic, electrostatic,
magnetic tape, mechanical, photocopying, recording, or otherwise without the prior
permission in writing of the publisher.

For information, contact State University of New York Press, Albany, NY
www.sunypress.edu

Library of Congress Cataloging-in-Publication Data

Name: Rainer, Elise Carlson, author.
Title: From pariah to priority : how LGBTI rights became a pillar of American and
    Swedish foreign policy / Elise Carlson Rainer.
Description: Albany : State University of New York Press, [2021] | Series: SUNY series
    in queer politics and cultures | Includes bibliographical references and index.
Identifiers: LCCN 2021023969 | ISBN 9781438485799 (hardcover : alk. paper) |
    ISBN 9781438485782 (pbk. : alk. paper) | ISBN 9781438485805 (ebook)
Subjects: LCSH: Sexual minorities—Civil rights—United States—Case studies. | Sexual
    minorities—Civil rights—Sweden—Case studies. | Sexual minorities—Civil rights—
    International cooperation—Case studies. | Human rights—Government policy—
    Sweden—Case studies. | Human rights—Government policy—United States—Case
    studies. | Human rights—International cooperation—Case studies. | Sweden—Foreign
    relations—Case studies. | United States—Foreign relations—Case studies.
Classification: LCC HQ73.73.U6 R35 2021 | DDC 306.760973—dc23
LC record available at https://lccn.loc.gov/2021023969

10 9 8 7 6 5 4 3 2 1

I dedicate this book to my children, Tristan and Sonja Rainer,
as well as to my father, Paul Carlson,
who taught me how to love others.
Thank you to my Swedish spouse, Stefan Rainer,
who has been my love and support for nearly two decades.

Contents

Acknowledgments

I would like to thank the following individuals for their contribution to this research, foreign policy leadership, and/or decades of human rights advocacy: Randy Berry, Daniel Baer, Michael Posner, Daniel Mahanty, Mark Bromley, Todd Larson, Samantha Power, Anne-Marie Slaughter, Anthony Adero, Jessica Stern, Amie Bishop, Katie Hultquist, Julie Dorf, Angeline Jackson, Sören Juvas, Maria Sjödin, Birgitta Ohlsson, Barbro Westerholm, and Helena Westin. Thank you to my brilliant diplomat colleague friends for their wisdom over the years: Saba Ghori, Adrienne Bory, Katie McLain, Karen Chen, Pamela Erickson, Anish Goel, Jessica Lieberman, Aaron Spencer, Dan Mahanty, Stacey May, Deborah Jones, and Hannah Rosenthal. While many others remain anonymous, I am grateful for the important work of many leaders and activists working around the globe, at times in great physical danger, towards a more just and equal world.

I am grateful for the encouragement, support and expertise from many people during this book project. Thank you to SUNY senior acquisitions editor Michael Rinella and SUNY *Queer Politics and Cultures* editor Cynthia Burack for supporting the publication of this book. Phillip Ayoub, thank you for inviting me to conferences and providing your depth of expertise in global LGBTI rights. I am in gratitude to Sabine Lang, Christine Ingebritsen, Dan Chirot, for supporting my research and shaping me as a scholar, as well as Karam Dana at the University of Washington for your mentorship. Thank you to the astute editing work of Kimberly Alecia Singletary from Humanities First, and Sean Butorac at the University of Washington. Thank you to my wonderful research assistants, Sacha Moufarrej and Hope Dorris; I could not have completed the book without your assistance. I am grateful to the stellar network of researchers at the University of Gothenburg Gender and Diplomacy *GenDip* Research Network, especially Ann Towns,

Birgitta Niklasson, Susan Harris Rimmer, and Elise Stephenson. Thank you to Stefano Guzzini, and my cohort in the Department of Peace and Conflict Research at Uppsala University. Nigel Boyle at Pitzer College, whose support helped me earn a Fulbright Fellowship to Sweden, and whose mentorship shaped my diplomatic career. I want to acknowledge a host of colleagues, friends, and peers who graciously supported me personally and professionally to complete this research over the years: Allegra Wiborg, Manuel Guzman, Indra Ekmanis, Dustin Welch, Willa Jeffers, Matthew Crosston, Dylan O'Connor, Lisbet Rodriguez-Perez, Shellwyn Badger, Justin Loustau, Susan Dicklitch-Nelson, Indira Rahman, and David Paternotte.

Conducting international research is costly, and I am grateful for the financial support of multiple organizations to complete this book project: the Swedish Women's Education Association of San Francisco, whose funding enabled original field work in Sweden, and the University of Washington's (UW) European Union Center of Excellence for funding my research to the European Union. Thank you as well to the UW Graduate School and the UW Jackson School of International Studies for travel funds for field work. I also thank the Swedish Women's Education Association (SWEA) of Portland, the American Public University Faculty Research Grant, and the University of Washington's Department of Scandinavian Studies' Synnove Fielding Fund for Excellence for support in the final research, writing, and editing of the manuscript.

Preface

In 2009, on a bright December afternoon in Washington, DC, I sat in Georgetown University's Gaston Hall auditorium waiting for my boss, Secretary of State Hillary Clinton, to deliver her "Human Rights in the Twenty-First Century" speech.[1] This speech was Clinton's first significant public articulation of the Obama administration's vision to reshape the United States' human rights foreign policy. Her policy priorities, and how she would revitalize US engagement in human rights foreign affairs, were not yet known to the wider public.

In 2009, LGBTI rights was not a pillar of American foreign policy. At the time, homosexuality was illegal in more than seventy countries and punishable by death in nine nations.[2] At the same time, there was rapid development of improved laws for LGBTI rights in many liberal democracies. While some progress had been achieved, violence and trauma against LGBTI communities existed in every continent; LGBTI rights concepts were a relatively new issue for public discourse as all states grappled with public policies intended to curb persistent violence toward LGBTI people. Even though the United States had enacted some domestic legal reforms by 2009, American diplomats, including myself, were barred from raising LGBTI rights concerns in diplomatic engagements prior to the Obama administration. Until 2008, the United States worked with other nations seeking to block pro-LGBTI rights reform in the United Nations (UN). American diplomats working in Jordan, Pakistan, or Russia would remain silent when an LGBTI person was stoned to death, disappeared by security forces, killed by their family or a public mob, or jailed for life because of their sexual orientation or gender identity.[3] In the early 2000s, only a handful of Northern European nations addressed LGBTI rights in international affairs.

As Clinton took to the stage at Georgetown University, it was still to be determined how human rights in US foreign policy would be handled under the Obama administration; it was not inevitable that LGBTI rights would become an issue of diplomatic concern. Thus, foreign dignitaries and ambassadors, leaders from the State Department and National Security Council, human rights practitioners, activists, scholars, and university students came to document the speech. I was there as an officer in the US State Department's Bureau of Democracy, Human Rights, and Labor (DRL), the central policy bureau in the State Department responsible for shaping US foreign relations related to human rights policies and programs. My colleagues and I were unsure as to what, if any, changes Clinton would make to address LGBTI rights in US foreign policy. Many of us were career civil servants and had worked for numerous secretaries of state and presidents within both Democratic and Republican party administrations. As a huge portion of American human rights foreign policy is mandated from Congress and outlined under US law, it is bureaucratically difficult to change major policy mandates in the State Department.[4] State Department career personel are familiar with the transition to new administrations and how new leadership can potentially invigorate or, conversely, deprioritize and disengage, or do nothing at all to change human rights foreign policy priorities.

As a US diplomat with human rights as my central focus, I worked on human rights policy and programs across North Africa and the Gulf from 2005 to 2016. Over the years, I met with human rights activists who received protection, both symbolic and logistical, from US embassies. Embassy staff, from entry-level officers to US ambassadors, worked to stop gender-based violence in Jordan, train female lawyers to defend women's rights in Morocco, and conduct dialogue with religious minorities in Egypt, to name a few examples. I worked toward freedom of association in Gulf countries and met with heads of security to advocate for peaceful political participation of ethnic and religious minorities. Six months before the revolution in Tunisia in 2010, I met with journalists and human rights activists in Tunis fighting for a modicum of freedom of expression under the Ben Ali regime. Pulling up his shirt, one man showed me the marks of torture from his government's security forces.[5] I became accustomed to human rights activists showing me the physical signs of abuse they endured under authoritarian regimes.

Always weighing human rights against other national interests, diplomats are mandated to address and report on global human rights issues.

During this time, I also served as senior editor of numerous State Department country reports on human rights practices on the Middle East team.[6] Directed by Congress, these reports are used to inform US bilateral relationships with each country. To draft these reports, I worked to document evidence, triangulating data from local sources and human rights organizations, news media, embassy staff, human rights activists, and other stakeholders across North Africa and the Gulf. Upon collection of evidence of human rights abuses, my colleagues and I would craft strategic recommendations for funding of local human rights groups to address the most pressing human rights abuses. My responsibilities in the State Department also included management of multimillion dollar programs from the State Department grants for Human Rights and Democracy.

At times, US officials leverage their financial influence to address human rights in specific countries, as well as bring political weight to bear to pressure regimes to uphold laws and international human rights commitments. Conversely, at times, diplomats also remain silent. In response to human rights engagement, foreign dignitaries often criticized the US government for meddling in other countries' cultures and domestic affairs. Foreign diplomats in the Gulf would ask me how the United States could criticize issues of torture in other countries when the United States operated the Guantanamo Bay detention camp, a place where external observers charge the US responsible for torture of detainees.[7] US Representative Tom Lantos, the Co-Chairman of the Congressional Human Rights Caucus, described the goals of human rights foreign policy as "closing the hypocrisy gap" from domestic practices to achieving international standards for every country, including the United States.[8] While the United States was criticized for its hypocrisy on human rights standards, at the same time, human rights activists commonly criticized US embassy officials for not doing more to improve advocacy for human rights and democratic freedoms in their countries. Embassies and State Department officials receive requests from individuals and human rights organizations for increased financial support and political intervention.

In the early 2000s, foreign policy leaders in the State Department and other foreign ministries were gaining an increased global understanding of the severity of LGBTI violence and discrimination. Secretary Clinton's leadership team seemed poised to take action on this issue in diplomatic affairs. One seminal moment in Clinton's speech—which left an indelible mark on my professional and academic pursuits—was when she highlighted the human rights situation for LGBTI people in Uganda. She addressed the proposed Ugandan law under consideration in Uganda's Parliament that would criminalize homosexuality and potentially implement the death penalty for homosexual acts. At one point in her speech, Clinton stated, "It is clear that across the world this is a new frontier in the minds of many people about how we protect the LGBTI community."[9] It was a new frontier for us, indeed. Before 2009, we raised concerns in diplomatic dialogues about violence against women, forced labor, trafficking in persons, and religious freedom with our foreign counterparts in Cairo, Tripoli, Rabat, and elsewhere. However, raising LGBTI rights abuses was not part of US embassies' staff agenda. After Clinton's statements, it was clear that our work regarding LGBTI rights in US foreign policy was about to make a complete reversal from the Bush administration and, indeed, from every previous administration. Under the Bush administration, US government officials were directed from the White House to not support new LGBTI rights initiatives in international development programs, multilateral affairs, or LGBTI civil society. During the Bush administration, the killing (often by stoning) of LGBTI people was not an issue of concern in international relations. Beyond the Bush administration, within diplomatic history, it was unprecedented for foreign dignitaries to raise concerns about the treatment of LGBTI people alongside agendas of trade and security cooperation.

However, the diplomatic practice of remaining silent in countries where a lesbian may be punished with corrective rape in South Africa, or a gay man set on fire by a mob in Nigeria, was about to change.[10] Follow-up policy discussions from Clinton's address at Georgetown University focused on how we would carry out the work. Foreign policy leaders deliberated on how to consult with global and local LGBTI human rights advocates. We worked to build networks of civil society groups and identify local and international organizations that the State Department could fund to promote LGBTI rights. For context, diplomats were not instructed to promote same-sex marriage, adoption, or other contemporary issues debated in many liberal democracies at the time. Rather, the work was mainly to address the most egregious issues for LGBTI people, specifically decriminalization of homosexuality and ending violence and the death penalty in countries worldwide. In 2011, the Obama administration formally mandated LGBTI rights to be raised in US diplomatic engagements and incorporated in every US embassy. As each State Department and USAID mission within each country determines annual policy priorities, LGBTI rights is now prioritized in countries across Central Asia, the Middle East, Africa, and in countries with high levels of societal and official violence against LGBTI people.

Promoting LGBTI rights in US foreign policy does not come without its problems. Numerous scholars have pointed to the deep hypocrisy inherent within the United States promoting LGBTI rights.[11] Many foreign leaders have at times criticized LGBTI diplomacy as a new form of colonialism and cultural imperialism.[12] Furthermore, there continue to be widespread negative social attitudes toward LGBTI persons in the United States. In 2009, approximately 40 percent of the American public did not support legalizing LGBTI relations.[13] Data from 2020 show that societal murder of transgender individuals persists at high rates within the United States.[14] Despite progress for LGBTI rights in the Obama administration, former President Trump's cabinet officials were openly homophobic and sought to repeal LGBTI policy reforms.[15] While improvement in some areas has been achieved, violence and discrimination of LGBTI people in the United States continues.[16] Given its domestic human rights shortcomings, the United States was not a predictable global leader on LGBTI equality concerns.

When I began this book project in 2015, after leaving my career in diplomacy, I decided to address the perplexing puzzle of how US diplomacy on LGBTI evolved. Only a few decades earlier, the State Department took part in the "Lavender Scare," a witch hunt that targeted "commies and queers."[17] Hundreds of LGBTI diplomats were fired from their positions in the State Department, Department of Defense, and other security agencies. How then, three generations later, did the State Department, as the central foreign affairs institution of the United States, transform to promote the rights and physical safety of LGBTI people globally? Human rights diplomacy is not conducted in a vacuum; multifaceted national interests are continuously taken into account. Samantha Power, former US ambassador to the UN, documents that even in the face of overwhelming evidence of human rights abuses, including genocide, American and other foreign leaders fecklessly at times remained silent, not willing to jeopardize security cooperation and other national security interests.[18] LGBTI rights abuses are much harder to document and evidence than large-scale genocide, making these abuses difficult to raise in diplomatic dialogue. Additionally, sexual minority rights remain a deeply contested issue in many regions of the world. Would foreign officials prioritize LGBTI discrimination in a diplomatic agenda with strategic nations such as Saudi Arabia or Pakistan, places where LGBTI people are regularly hung and stoned? As such, promoting LGBTI rights in United States foreign policy was not inevitable. Had you asked me in 2008 if I would be allowed to raise LGBTI rights concerns globally as a US diplomat, I would have been skeptical that it would happen in my lifetime. This book seeks to explain the unexpected incorporation of LGBTI rights in US foreign policy.

From Pariah to Priority also seeks to explain the comparative process of integration of LGBTI rights in Swedish foreign policy. This book is a comparative analysis of the process of reforming US human rights foreign policy in contrast with the parallel reforms in Swedish human rights foreign policy. Sweden is a critical case study in the field of LGBTI rights in international affairs. For decades, Swedish leaders and advocates have been a powerhouse in shaping global human rights norms.[19] In the early 2000s, Sweden was the first country in the world to formally incorporate LGBTI rights in its international humanitarian aid and foreign policy.

I have lived, studied, researched, and worked in Sweden and am currently raising two bilingual Swedish children with my Swedish spouse in the United States. I am deeply connected to Swedish culture and society. Given my knowledge of the Swedish political context, dovetailed with original data outlined in the methods section, I am able to critique and compare Sweden's LGBTI rights policies with the United States and global foreign policy agendas. While Sweden has been internationally recognized for its socially progressive policies and acceptance of LGBTI equality, it too has a legacy of discrimination, forced sterilization of transgender people, and inequality.[20] As homophobic policies and social practices endured in Sweden into the 2000s, it was not inevitable that LGBTI rights would become a central foreign policy issue for the country. This book analyzes the policy evolution process in Swedish foreign affairs. It examines Swedish LGBTI advocacy and the very different relationship that exists in Sweden between civil society and the state.

For many human rights advocates, human rights diplomacy is a fallacy; government forces are often the central abusers of human rights around the world. From genocide, to the harassment of journalists, to the arrests of LGBTI individuals, authorities have a monopoly on the power to uphold—or degrade—human rights. Human rights abuses by state actors and security forces tend to be the focal point of news articles and academic research. In 2020, the Black Lives Matter protests in the United States revitalized public discourse on abuse by police toward the Black community.[21] Aside from hypocrisy, many governments simply do not engage in human rights diplomacy. Nations such as China focus their foreign policy exclusively on economic growth, political stability, and security concerns. However, while governments are problematic actors, most foreign policy institutions in liberal democracies engage in human rights diplomacy. Indeed, without governments' engagement on human rights, international standards of human rights would lack accountability and legitimacy in the international system.[22] At times, diplomats save lives and fight to improve human rights conditions in authoritarian regimes. This can manifest through rapid response and emergency assistance funding and programs.[23] By way of emergency assistance, diplomats help human rights activists who acutely fear for their lives, such as an LGBTI advocate in Chechnya, a journalist in Colombia, or a minority religious leader in Libya. Thousands of individuals and civil society organizations across the globe receive funding through government channels to fight for fundamental freedoms. Through long-term, painstakingly sensitive diplomatic work, issues such as female genital mutilation, academic freedom, protection of refugees and freedom of movement, and LGBTI rights are raised in diplomatic engagements.[24] Often conducted through quiet, closed-door diplomacy, the general public and international media often are not even aware of this work. Either for the protection of the individual or because of the political sensitivity of the bilateral relationship, human rights diplomacy is commonly carried out away from the public eye, in high-level meetings. Thus, this diplomatic work remains underanalyzed and largely undocumented in the general press and in human rights literature. A central goal of *From Pariah to Priority* is to shed light on this often opaque process of foreign policy change, specifically by exploring how the unexpected mandate of LGBTI rights evolved to become a major agenda item in modern foreign affairs.

Chapter 1

Introduction

The Genesis of LGBTI Diplomacy and Reshaping International Relations

At Stockholm Pride in Stockholm, Sweden, July 2019, a young Ugandan woman explained to the audience that her Ugandan father knew that she was a lesbian before she did. In reaction, "he came home one night and tried to light me on fire . . . he told me I was going to hell and tried to kill me. . . I fled my country that night and cannot return home."[1] Another Nigerian man at Stockholm Pride in a public forum shared how "a mob broke into my home and killed my partner before my eyes. . . I fled my house out the back door, and barely escaped with my life; I had to leave my country after that day."[2] Uganda and Nigeria are two of more than seventy countries globally that outlaw same-sex relations.[3] The Ugandan President Yoweri Museveni decries homosexuality as "disgusting,"[4] and Ugandan law-makers proposed the death penalty for homosexual acts again in October 2019.[5] In response to Uganda and other countries with official violence and discrimination against LGBTI people, many other liberal democracies began to raise LGBTI issues in diplomatic engagements.[6] Some governments grant asylum to LGBTI persons persecuted in their home countries, threaten to condition foreign assistance funding, or even go so far as severing bilateral relations with a country based on their human rights record. Conditioning foreign assistance based on LGBTI rights abuses, granting asylum based on LGBTI human rights abuses, and raising LGBTI rights in formal diplomatic engagements constitute relatively new issues of concern in international affairs. Lydia Malmedie observes that only since the early 2000s have LGBTI

1

rights issues been considered topics that should be of concern in diplomatic relations and part of European Union (EU) foreign policy.[7] Historically, governments have not addressed domestic human rights practices in other nations. Thus, understood as an infringement on sovereignty, human rights concerns are a relatively new focus of foreign policy.[8] While LGBTI people have been killed, tortured, and stoned to death for centuries in numerous countries throughout the world, leaders in countries such as the United States, Sweden, and other liberal democracies remained silent on domestic affairs related to LGBTI people.

When I worked within the US Department of State, Bureau of Democracy, Human Rights and Labor (DRL) from 2005 to 2016, there were constant internal battles among interagency stakeholders regarding if and when—if at all—to raise human rights abuses with foreign leaders. Raising concerns regarding foreign leaders torturing political dissidents and condemning ethnic or religious violence was taken into consideration with other foreign policy interests, namely security and economic ties to the country. LGBTI persons in Pakistan, Saudi Arabia, Jamaica, and other countries have been beheaded, subjected to corrective rape, and victims of sanctioned mob killings for decades.[9] Yet these specific human rights abuses against the LGBTI community were not part of any diplomatic agenda. After a great diplomatic battle in the United Nations (UN),[10] in 2010 the UN General Assembly's Third Committee approved including the LGBTI populations as a specific marginalized group subjected to global patterns of violence.[11] By including LGBTI populations in UN documentation and other countries' foreign policy agendas, relations between countries can now become predicated on how a country treats this minority group. Conceptualizing LGBTI populations as a specific marginalized group now includes this population in the multibillion-dollar international foreign aid industry. Despite contestation of LGBTI rights, as of 2021 in contemporary foreign relations, governments will now end trade agreements and withdraw foreign assistance to punish foreign governments where societies allow for official and societal violence against LGBTI populations.

This book analyzes how governments advance human rights in diplomacy, specifically concerning LGBTI rights. It examines how and why LGBTI rights became a fundamental doctrine of human rights to be promoted abroad. Specifically, it examines Sweden and the United States as two central players in global LGBTI diplomacy. Sweden's policy adoption of LGBTI rights into its foreign policy was first in the world in 2005. Sweden remains a significant international aid donor. The United States followed suit in 2011 and is the largest player in the sector of human rights and humanitarian aid. Domestically, Sweden exhibits high acceptance rates of LGBTI equality norms.[12] On the contrary, LGBTI acceptance remains a relatively contested issue in the United States. Despite these differences, Sweden and the United States both promote LGBTI rights as part of their broader human rights foreign policy agendas. This book examines the catalysts in each country for institutionalizing the rights of LGBTI populations into their respective foreign policies. The policies of these two countries matter globally; the actions of these two governments, specific policies and programs to support global LGBTI organizations, have been replicated in the EU and UN and impact normative foreign policy around the world.

Through primary and secondary source evidence, *From Pariah to Priority* identifies the central factors for emerging LGBTI foreign policy agendas as nongovernmental organizations (NGO) advocacy; insider government-allied leadership; national interest; transnational activists; and sensitizing international events, namely Uganda's law implementing the death penalty for homosexual acts in 2009. The role of NGO advocacy and social movements in shaping governments' agendas is a focus of this study. Similarly, building coalitions with insider-allies and promoting movement goals toward equality inside the government is also central to this analysis.

As of 2021, approximately sixteen countries incorporate LGBTI rights as a formal aspect of their respective foreign policy.[13] An illustration of this policy is when countries such as Brunei proposed death by stoning for homosexual acts, many leaders within this small group of nations made public statements of condemnation against Brunei officials.[14] These countries also funded urgent assistance to local human rights groups in Southeast Asia. Similarly, at times governments withdraw parts of their foreign assistance in response to another nation's official persecution of LGBTI citizens. In 2017, Egyptian security forces rounded up, harassed, beat, and arrested numerous people presumed to be LGBTI.[15] In response, US Secretary of State Rex Tillerson withdrew "$95.7 million in foreign assistance and withheld a further $190 million in military assistance directly addressing the crackdown on LGBT Egyptians."[16] LGBTI rights diplomacy impacts a host of bilateral agreements, including economic relations. An example in the European context was seen when human rights advocates from countries such as Sri Lanka pressured EU countries and the United States to use the EU trade negotiation process to influence their own country to reform and decriminalize homosexuality in Sri Lankan law.[17]

Promoting LGBTI rights in foreign policy introduces a new set of principles and moral standards that regulate international relations according to emerging human rights norms. LGBTI rights in foreign policy represent the evolution of a principle in human rights that formerly did not impact international affairs. Relationships that were once tenable and acceptable were reevaluated according to the new standards, such as the United States' and Sweden's bilateral relationship with Uganda. Thus, understanding the genesis and reasons for countries to implement a policy is of critical importance to foreign relations.

Evidence in this research is derived from numerous primary sources and academic literature. It is also underpinned by my professional experience working in the US Department of State's Bureau of Democracy, Human Rights, and Labor. For years in this role, I drafted statements from the State Department against human rights abuses across the Middle East, mainly in North Africa and Gulf countries. I worked to craft policy and programs in response to events, such as a nation beheading human rights activists, hanging LGBTI citizens, or stoning women. I conducted diplomatic meetings in Jordan and across North Africa, discussing labor rights, honor killings, torture, and larger human rights concerns. From 2011 to 2016, I served as the senior editor of numerous State Department human rights reports in the Middle East.[18] I also served as a contributing editor to the International Religious Freedom reports and Tracking in Persons reports during this time.[19] This practitioner experience provides the basis for detailed knowledge in this study of how governments document human rights abuses and later respond to state violence through human rights diplomacy.

LGBTI Rights in the Context of International Human Rights

Universal human rights were codified into international law in 1948 with the UN's Universal Declaration of Human Rights (UDHR).[20] Yet how human rights—as arms of foreign policy and its implementation—impact bilateral relations, international norms, and sovereignty is an ever evolving process. Human rights scholar Alison Brysk assesses the central purpose of human rights diplomacy and asserts, "principled states build global governance; they reshape the meaning of sovereignty to implant a slowly emerging legitimacy norm—universal human rights."[21] While human rights are an important aspect of contemporary international relations, the very concept of what is considered to be a universal human right is not static.[22] Foreign policy engagements include the elevation of women's, disability, ethnic, and religious minority rights.[23] LGBTI rights are the most recent set of human rights to be integrated into foreign affairs discourse. Diplomacy is necessary for the actualization of human rights.[24] Diplomats and government actors raising human rights in international affairs institutionalize new norms in government relations.

This books seeks to illuminate the workings of diplomats promoting human rights in foreign countries that are often obscure to the general public. A great deal of diplomatic work is done behind closed doors in what is known as "quiet diplomacy."[25] For example, a country may be enticed to stop discrimination against a minority population through an economic and trade incentive. A group of political prisoners may be released, or widespread arrest of LGBTI advocates may cease as a result of a diplomatic negotiations that include investment for an infrastructure program, for example. Outside observers may not have any idea that seemingly unrelated actions of a government are correlated and that human rights diplomacy has taken place behind closed doors. LGBTI rights is often a politically controversial issue in many regions of the world. At times, quiet diplomacy is the preferred method to gain results while avoiding publicly naming and shaming another nation. Conducting quiet diplomacy may allow foreign government officials to 'save face' and subtly reform their nation's human rights issues while circumventing political and societal opposition in their country. Inherent to the craft of quiet diplomacy is a lack of public documentation, press, or knowledge of results of human rights promotion from efforts behind the scenes. As such, there is not a great deal of press or academic scholarship analyzing quiet diplomacy because outsiders lack access to internal, often classified, workings of foreign ministries. From an insider, practitioner perspective, this book seeks to shed light on the sometimes nebulous process of conducting human rights diplomacy.

The second major gap in academic research on human rights diplomacy is the tension between the state as both a promotor and abuser of global rights. The majority of scholars often focus on governments as one of the central abusers of human rights.[26] Cynthia Burack asserts how the "academic critical humanist left" has unexpectedly become deeply critical and skeptical of US government–funded LGBTI rights promotion, whereby observers may believe the left-wing political spectrum of the United States would be the base of supporters for this issue.[27] On the right-wing side of the political spectrum in many countries there is open opposition to any progressive government policies on LGBTI rights. Scholars often decry the hypocrisy of governments promoting human rights outside their borders when their own countries' human rights record is not perfect.[28] However, no country has a perfect record on gender equality; therefore, promoting LGBTI rights globally will inherently reveal an element of hypocrisy the world over.

Human rights promotion from governmental foreign policy institutions receives much less attention by scholars and activists. And yet it is a pillar of diplomacy that is a multibillion-dollar industry of the international development aid sector. Millions of people's lives globally depend on international donor aid. The aid funding is critical for fledgling LGBTI organizations in the Middle East, Africa and other regions; this aid can provide emergency funding to human rights activists in imminent danger. Foreign governments are sometimes the only source of funding and support for local LGBTI activists. External evaluators of the Swedish government's work documented that in some places the survival of organizations and individuals working on LGBTI human rights is the result of Swedish government financial assistance.[29] In parts of the world where LGBTI equality is violently contested, LGBTI civil society and the existence of civil society organizations are often enabled only by means of foreign governmental support. Yet funding for human rights and democracy is just one aspect of international humanitarian assistance.

Proportionately, the Swedish government funds some of the highest levels for international human rights promotion compared with other governments.[30] Sweden's allocation reflects a higher proportion of Sweden's gross national product (GNP) to foreign aid than any other nation.[31] More than 30 percent of the Swedish International Development Cooperation Agency's (SIDA) programmatic works is allocated explicitly for funding human rights and democracy programs. Human rights are also included indirectly in funding toward cross-sector fields, such as equal access to public health.[32] Sweden's large contribution to international development aid allows for significant influence over norms and policies of the EU and UN institutions, which is discussed further in the Swedish chapter.

In contrast, in 2019–2020 the United States allocated approximately 2.3 percent of its Economic Development and Development Fund toward democracy, human rights, and labor.[33] Yet, in actual numbers, the United States remains the largest humanitarian donor in the world. Humanitarian and human rights donor aid from the United States funds more humanitarian assistance programs than any other country in the world. The work from Sweden and the United States, respectively, has been a critical norm entrepreneurial role and the largest players in the international community. Thereby, Sweden and the United States are important case studies in the general field of international development, specifically for these governments' unique roles in the new aspect of LGBTI diplomacy in foreign policy.

To be certain, Sweden and the United States are not the only influential countries in the new field of LGBTI diplomacy. Other countries have also been critical actors in elevating global norms in LGBTI human rights. Among others, Brazil, the Netherlands, Spain, and Norway have served in pioneering roles in the UN in diffusing global LGBTI equality norms.[34] For example, Brazil's leadership in the UN helped bring international resolutions, bolster NGOs, and set new standards for human rights agendas with regard to LGBTI rights.[35] Multilateral agencies are also engaged in addressing LGBTI discrimination globally. The former president of the World Bank in 2014, Jim Yong Kim, in response to Uganda's proposed death penalty law, stated, "My view is that the fight to eliminate all institutionalized discrimination is an urgent task."[36] There are many global players across sectors of government, nongovernmental organizations (NGOs), private foundations, and multilateral institutions engaged in elevating the global norm of LGBTI rights. This book analyzes two governments among a variety of stakeholders in the emerging field of LGBTI diplomacy.

While humanitarian spending is dwarfed by military expenditures in most countries, *From Pariah to Priority* assesses foreign policy spending on human rights as a new spectrum of diplomatic strategies with growing influence in international affairs. It has only been since the early 2000s that LGBTI populations have been considered by foreign affairs institutions as a distinctly vulnerable group, in need of both human rights protections as well as humanitarian donor aid specifically because of their sexual orientation or gender identity.[37] Further challenges arise in foreign cultural contexts where individuals may not label themselves with the "LGBTI" Western-constructed categories: a woman in Nigeria may have sex with other women but not label herself as "lesbian." Stoum asserts that without using the LGBTI human rights vocabulary, individuals may not be "visible" to foreign ministries or able to acquire donor funds for their community.[38] These categorizations, and the answer as to who is covered by that funding, which populations are deemed deserving of human rights protections, and who counts as true beneficiaries of international human rights funding and programs have enormous implications for foreign relations and international law.

This book addresses how Uganda and other nations with similarly repressive laws have become a central battleground for the conflict between LGBTI equality and anti-LGBTI beliefs. Onapajo Hakeem and Christopher Isike argue that LGBTI rights have become a fault line issue between nations, straining relations between the West and some African countries.[39] This book contextualizes analysis of conditioning and withholding foreign aid based on human rights and examines the potential unintended consequences.[40] At times, conditioning aid can lead to a backlash against the very community these sanctions aim to protect. Thus, withdrawing aid or cutting bilateral ties with another nation based on normative values is a highly contested aspect of modern foreign policy. As seen in the case of sanctioning South Africa's apartheid regime with regard to racial equality, long-standing relations can be called into question based on changes in the international community. These evolving global norms impact how states create military and economic alliances. With shifting norms, LGBTI rights have become an aspect of consideration in international relations.

Global Trends of LGBTI Rights

Scholars recognize the movement for LGBTI equality as one of the most rapid, successful reforms of any social movement across liberal democracies.[41] The pace of some societies transitioning from considering diverse sexual orientation and gender identities as a mental illness to legalizing same-sex marriage was historically swift compared to other human rights movements. However, LGBTI rights are not on a clear trajectory for global acceptance, and some regions in the world move to further restrict basic rights. Phillip Ayoub demonstrates how LGBTI rights are increasingly contested on the world stage.[42] As of 2021, political trends reveal a regression of rights in Africa, Eastern Europe, Latin America, the Middle East, and Russia.[43] Researchers have found a strong correlation between countries that uphold LGBTI rights and those that also adhere to broader democratic values.[44] Julie Dorf, a leading LGBTI advocate, asserts that LGBTI rights can be considered as "the canary in the coal mine," where restrictions on individuals in terms of freedom of association, speech, or expression often start with a crackdown on LGBTI groups.[45] While rapid reforms were made on LGBTI laws and policy in the last few decades especially, these reforms are being called into question in many countries globally.

The dividing line of rights is not a clean division between the Global North and Global South. While laws are rapidly changing globally on LGBTI equality, as of 2021, approximately seventy-two countries still outlaw same-sex relations; eight nations implement the death penalty for homosexuality, including Saudi Arabia and Pakistan; the death penalty is periodically proposed by parliaments in other nations.[46] Russia sanctions state-sponsored violence against its LGBTI citizens.[47] Homophobia is on the rise in Poland and Hungary.[48] On the other hand, in September 2018, India ended the colonial-era ban on gay sex.[49] Transnational activists and

NGOs work in South Africa to influence progressive reforms to local laws.[50] Brazil's foreign ministry was one of the first nations to champion LGBTI reforms in the UN.[51] There is a powerful and influential global movement that works beyond borders for equality in all regions. Brunei, for instance, drew the wrath of the international community when it proposed the death penalty for homosexuality.[52] LGBTI rights are not unique to any continent or region of the world, nor are these rights on a certain linear progression of improvement on any continent.

Human rights diplomacy is not applied evenly across the globe. Some countries that sanction violence against LGBTI people, such as Brunei, garner great international attention; other countries with equally draconian laws draw no attention from the international community at all. As is common with a new law from a small country—as defined by GDP, reputation, and power in the international system—larger powers in the international system are quick to voice harsh condemnation.[53] By contrast, old laws in place for decades in countries such as Nigeria or Pakistan do not draw the same ire. These countries also have more economic and military power to leverage. Saudi Arabia, for example, a powerful economic and security ally of many Western nations, largely gets a pass on human rights criticisms. The US government typically issues only the meekest of statements when the country beheads human rights activists, hangs LGBTI citizens, or stones women.[54] Conversely, if the US government has strained ties with a nation, such as Iran, human rights may be elevated to a central issue of concern to shame the other country.[55] The same human rights abuse does not gain equal attention or response from one country to the next. Human rights abuses can sometimes be completely ignored by the international community. Other times, abuses by a dictator and gender-based violence from a totalitarian regime can sometimes become the justification for military intervention.[56] The importance of the bilateral relationship in economic or security terms is often the key variable for the prioritization of human rights diplomacy.

Countries that have institutionalized LGBTI rights diplomacy take into account the strategic relationship in foreign engagements. The application and implementation of LGBTI diplomacy needs further academic and policy investigation. This book focuses not on the application of LGBTI diplomacy, but rather on the genesis of LGBTI diplomacy. *From Pariah to Priority* uncovers the unexpected institutionalization of LGBTI rights in US human rights foreign policy and the process of policy reform in Swedish foreign affairs agencies.

Swedish and US diplomats work to elevate LGBTI equality as a universal norm. And yet, in the early 2000s, when both nations began internal discussions to reform their respective foreign policy, public opinion toward homosexuality in the two societies varied widely. According to the World Values Survey,[57] at the time of Sweden developing its first LGBTI policies in 2006, Sweden exhibited one of the lowest rates of public resistance against homosexuality; only 4 percent of the population responded that homosexuality was "never justifiable." Comparatively, the United States reported the highest rate of rejection of homosexuality, with 35 percent of the population responding that it was "never justifiable."[58] Yet the two countries began to pursue relatively similar foreign policy goals to promote LGBTI equality around the time of the data collected. *From Pariah to Priority* examines the key factors that influence two countries' foreign policy reforms despite domestic differences of social acceptance of LGBTI equality. It analyzes social movements in each country and the key domestic and international factors that influenced that policy development.

Definition of LGBTI Human Rights Foreign Policy

In this section, I present an original definition of "LGBTI diplomacy." For the genesis of this definition, I use original data collected for this book from interviews, content analysis of policies and programs, participant observation of LGBTI events, speeches, and official documents of diplomatic efforts to promote global equality. I use my diplomatic experience implementing human rights programs in North Africa and the Gulf as a pragmatic basis for how LGBTI diplomacy is conducted, directly and indirectly, publicly and through quiet diplomacy. LGBTI human rights diplomacy is diverse and targets across sectors. Randy Berry, the first US special envoy for the human rights of LGBTI persons, conducted LGBTI diplomacy by meeting with faith-based religious leaders, business partners in the private sectors such as Deloitte and IBM, lawyers and judges, ministers of labor and education, foreign ministries, presidents, and prime ministers, as well as by cementing relationships with NGO leaders and LGBTI civil society organizations.[59] I also piece together academic literature in the fields of human rights and international relations to create this conceptual definition of LGBTI diplomacy. I define LGBTI human rights diplomacy as *global policies and programs with the long-term goal of promoting the social, political, and economic equal rights of LGBTI persons.*

This book uses the UDHR as the foundational document determining international human rights; the UDHR's definition of human rights undergirds this study.[60] As of 2019, the UN defines human rights as "rights inherent to all human beings, regardless of race, sex, nationality, ethnicity, language, religion, or any other status."[61] LGBTI equality is still contested in the UN and not included in the UDHR. Signed in 1948, leaders who crafted the UDHR did not conceptualize same-sex relations as a right. Francine D'amico and other scholars recognize the contemporary challenge that remains in defining LGBTI protections as an international standard.[62] Given that challenge, LGBTI rights are conceptualized according to the internationally recognized Yogyakarta Principles, which cover a range of political, economic, cultural, and social rights as related to LGBTI persons.[63] Beyond marriage equality, global activists are currently advocating for comprehensive reforms for LGBTI equality, such as nondiscrimination in housing, the right to privacy, and protection from medical discrimination.

Human rights in foreign policy aim to globally promote the fundamental principles of human rights as defined by the UDHR and follow-up international human rights treaties. As related to human rights in diplomatic engagement, this book leverages Brysk's definition of humanitarian internationalism as "a variety of cooperative, value-oriented foreign policies. . . values promoted may be labeled human rights, democratization, building civil society, protection of civilians, peace promotion, global humanism, or human security."[64] Human rights diplomacy is the application of human rights norms and principles into a value-based normative foreign policy.

The study of LGBTI rights as they relate specifically to foreign policy is a relatively new field for social science inquiries. Most contemporary studies problematize the application of categorization of gender or sexual identities in international relations norms,[65] in post-colonial contexts, or in diverse cultural contexts. Scholars have called for the need for increased systematic comparisons and further analysis on institutional gender dynamics in diplomacy.[66] Women have long been barred from foreign ministries representing double institutional barrier for lesbians. Known as "the marriage ban," most Ministries of Foreign Affairs required women to quit their jobs if they married. This ban was in place in the US Department of State until 1978. Towns and Niklasson explain how, unlike men, women had to choose between marriage and a foreign-service career.[67] From Turkey to the Netherlands to France to India, married women were removed from service in foreign policy positions.[68] Ann Towns and Birgitta Niklasson provide evidence of the gender disparities in leadership positions globally in Ministries of Foreign Affairs, asserting how gendered patterns in leadership continue to impact power, status, and foreign policy outcomes.[69] Historically, foreign policy agendas have been crafted by heterosexual elite men in most societies, shaping the priorities and agendas from their vantage point.

Academic analyses have yet to create an analytical framework from a diplomatic context to examine LGBTI rights within foreign policy. As such, there is not yet a common definition of "LGBTI-rights diplomacy" in human rights or diplomatic academic literature. Furthermore, from a pragmatic policy perspective, the implementation of LGBTI diplomacy is often carried out indirectly, where programs may support the long-term goal of equality but have the short-term appearance of addressing another issue or human rights broadly. Rule of law or freedom of assembly may be the issues addressed by a program that also seeks to elevate LGBTI rights groups' freedom to assemble and organize. Because diplomats work in places where human rights programs can be risky and even dangerous, manifestations of promoting LGBTI rights are not always directly related explicitly to LGBTI rights. For example, diplomats may work with human rights lawyers to improve general documentation of human rights abuse cases in Lebanon or assist NGOs in expanding their organizational capacity in Kyrgyzstan.[70] The Swedish government funded programs directly toward freedom of expression that also led to the financial support of LGBTI civil society groups working to improve freedom of expression in their country.[71] In Latin America, diplomats and advocacy groups worked to bolster tourism by LGBTI travelers from foreign countries.[72] The long-term goal may include promoting LGBTI equality, but the near-term output manifests as a general human rights development program. In academic analysis, there is a dearth of examination and contextualization of indirect and direct funding from bilateral and multilateral institutions. Burack astutely addresses scholars' pervasive view of the state as a monolithic entity.[73] Burack's 2018 study presents the most comprehensive contemporary examination of US government programs, policies, and interventions for LGBTI people in foreign engagements.[74] She also addresses how many US-based activists lack awareness of US-funded programs seeking to support LGBTI groups globally, which was affirmed in my participant observations for this study. Scholars often document only the most public-facing LGBTI diplomatic programs,[75] ultimately lacking a contextualization of the internal multilayered, direct, and indirect programmatic approach. As Special Envoy Randy Berry asserted, "If police infrastructure is being used to go after LGBT(I) people, you're using resources that could be against terror."[76] Berry notes here that programmatic work may be directed toward police training and general rule of law improvements for the long-term goal of curbing police brutality toward LGBTI individuals. Similarly, in response to violence toward trans Columbians, deputy assistant secretary of the US State Department's Bureau of Democracy, Human Rights and Labor Dan Baer focused diplomatic efforts in Bogotá on general freedom of association. Baer stated, "the Colombian government's protection of freedom of association that allows LGBT advocacy groups and other nongovernmental organizations to operate freely allows it [local groups] to adequately respond to the problem.[77] Bolstering NGOs improves the capacity of LGBTI advocacy organizations, as well as other human rights groups in the country. Indirect programming leads to a conceptual challenge of encapsulating the wide range of diplomatic efforts that work toward the long-term goal of improving LGBTI rights. Given that empirical challenge, for the purposes of this study, I again define LGBTI human rights diplomacy as *global policies and programs with the long-term goal of promoting the social, political, and economic equal rights of LGBTI persons.*

LGBTI diplomacy is often conducted bilaterally. However, influential multilateral policies and programs are an important part of this study. Namely, the flagship multimillion global funding mechanism called the Global Equality Fund (GEF) supports transnational and local civil society groups working to promote the human rights of LGBTI people.[78] Launched in 2011, the fund is managed by the DRL in partnership with co-donors including the governments of Finland, France, Germany, Iceland, the Netherlands, Norway, Sweden, and Denmark, as well as private funders such as the Arcus Foundation; the John D. Evans Foundation; the Norwegian LGBTI Organization; the National Association for Lesbian, Gay, Bisexual and Transgender People (LLH); the MAC AIDS Fund; and Deloitte.[79] The United States and Sweden are the most significant stakeholders for the GEF; Sweden puts immense resources of its international aid toward the Global Equality Fund. The United States manages the GEF for all parties through the US Department of State, thus providing the bulk of human resources to monitor and evaluate the progress of LGBTI programs globally. The GEF supports these global LGBTI programs through:

- Emergency protection of persons or groups against the threat of violence,

- Advocacy against discriminatory laws that criminalize LGBTI status,

- Ending explicit and implicit forms of discrimination in the workplace, housing, education, and other public institutions, and

- Community awareness and support for the human rights of LGBTI persons[80]

These sources, coupled with the original data collected in this book, academic analysis, as well as my diplomatic experience implementing human rights programs, are the basis for the conceptual definition of LGBTI diplomacy. Yet, despite being a multibillion-dollar sector of the international aid realm,[81] human rights diplomacy receives minimal attention from scholars and activists.

Introduction to the US Case

Scholars document how the United States historically lags behind its European counterparts on domestic LGBTI reforms.[82] Despite the slow pace for domestic reform, since the Obama administration the United States has made rapid and unexpected reforms to its foreign agenda. As of 2017, the United States became "an important force and perhaps even the biggest player in international SOGI human rights advocates and assistance."[83] That assistance began in 2011 under the Obama administration, and former Secretary of State Hillary Clinton, when Obama signed a presidential memorandum four days before International Human Rights Day, stated:

> The struggle to end discrimination against lesbian, gay, bisexual, and transgender (LGBTI) persons is a global challenge, and one that is central to the United States' commitment to promoting human rights. I am deeply concerned by the violence and discrimination targeting LGBTI persons around the world, whether it is passing laws that criminalize LGBTI status, beating citizens simply for joining peaceful LGBTI pride celebrations, or killing men, women, and children for their perceived sexual orientation. That is why I declared before heads of state gathered at the United Nations, no country should deny people their rights because of who they love, which is why we must stand up for the rights of gays and lesbians everywhere.[84]

With that memorandum, the United States inaugurated its formal LGBTI human rights diplomacy. US embassies worldwide have since carried out Obama's directive through a host of diplomatic engagements. For example, they host LGBTI civil society actors and government officials at

US embassies to discuss LGBTI rights; publicly participate in host country LGBTI Pride events; raise awareness of LGBTI issues in local media; coordinate with other embassies; support domestic LGBTI outreach campaigns in foreign countries; and include LGBTI equality in their overall human rights foreign policy agendas.[85] These diplomatic engagements continued with the Trump administration, which is analyzed in the final chapter of this book. The US State Department announced in February 2019 that it would continue to work with EU partners and the UN in a global campaign to end the criminalization of homosexuality.[86] This book examines the factors that influenced US foreign policy reform to include LGBTI rights in its official policy.

The US case study chapter traces the policy transformation process of how LGBTI rights became a part of US foreign policy. From the original evidence collected, the chapter reveals the central factors of influence over US diplomatic reform as NGO advocacy; insider government leadership; negative LGBTI rights trends in Uganda and other countries; and the United States' national identity and international reputation. NGO advocacy is a broad term also investigated in this chapter. NGO advocacy has taken many approaches and tactics. This chapter probes mechanisms of direct protest by NGOs against state policies, examining how advocates garnered support from gatekeeper organizations, through which small, newer LGBTI organizations, founded in the early 2000s, gained legitimacy from larger, older organizations. NGO actors also employed direct institutional advocacy where civil society groups conducted sustained, targeted engagement with foreign affairs agencies and harnessed insider governmental allies. Finally, it analyzes the vital and diverse techniques of civil society groups diffusing political opposition to their cause. This confluence of factors led to the overall shift in US diplomatic engagements that included LGBTI diplomacy.

Scholars recognize that foreign policy goals should reflect entrenched domestic social values and mores of a society.[87] The very core of diplomatic work is to represent one's country's culture, ideals, and people abroad. Yet while American ambassadors march in foreign LGBTI Pride parades, the LGBTI equality movement faces powerful opposition at home. Some scholars denote the United States as a late adopter of LGBTI rights in foreign affairs as compared to its European counterparts,[88] while others remain skeptical of the United States' ability to fully implement policies on LGBTI equality.[89] Herein lies the puzzle for this study: in 2011, when the US State Department formally incorporated LGBTI rights into its human rights foreign policy strategy, those rights were far from an agreed-on norm in the United States. According to the Pew Research Global Attitudes Project, in

2013, 37 percent of the US population believed "homosexuality is unacceptable."[90] In 2019, many states continue to ban unmarried couples from adopting, and there is no federal statute addressing employment discrimination based on sexual orientation or gender identity.[91] In 2018, the Human Rights Campaign, one of the most active and powerful LGBTI rights advocacy NGOs in the United States, found that American LGBTI youth were twice as likely as their peers to be physically assaulted.[92] Yet even amid evidence of discrimination against LGBTI populations, the United States began to exhibit unexpected leadership in promoting LGBTI rights abroad in 2011.

Inconsistencies between foreign and domestic policy are not new or unique to the United States. Other countries, such as South Africa and Brazil, elevate LGBTI rights in international affairs, despite severe domestic abuses toward women and LGBTI people.[93] Forsythe posits that a state's foreign policy is "the result of a two-level game in which domestic values and pressures combine with international standards and pressures to produce a given policy."[94] The history of human rights promotion in foreign policy has been rife with controversy and incongruity with dominant American values. To name a couple of inconsistencies, US diplomats have advocated to improve prison conditions in other countries;[95] meanwhile the United States has disproportionately high levels of incarceration worldwide.[96] Additionally, foreign assistance supports ending violence against women globally,[97] while gender-based violence is a significant problem in the United States.[98] These examples indicate that promoting LGBTI equality is not the only inconsistency between the United States' domestic record with its foreign policy. Implementing LGBTI rights in US foreign policy presents a puzzle with regard to domestic levels of acceptance.

LGBTI diplomacy is also an unexpected historical turn given the State Department's open discrimination and persecution of LGBTI employees from the 1950s through the 1990s. Historically, the State Department had an overt policy discriminating against LGBTI diplomats. In the 1950s, during the McCarthy era, the US State Department fired LGBTI diplomats. In 1953, President Eisenhower signed Executive Order 10450, banning homosexuals from working for the federal government or any of its private contractors.[99] At the time, government officials actively sought out and removed "commies and queers" from federal service.[100] David Johnson documents how a "Lavender Scare," the "fear that homosexuals posed a threat to national security and needed to be systematically removed from the federal government," permeated the State Department.[101] The State Department and other federal agencies in the 1950s publicly shamed and fired those suspected of being LGBTI. In the end, approximately 4,380 gay men and women were discharged from the military and about 500 fired from their jobs with the government.[102] Many of these individuals were merely perceived as gay, with little or anecdotal evidence against them. Until 1975, the US federal government could remove a federal employee for "immoral conduct," a euphemism often used for homosexuality.[103] Through the 1980s and into the 1990s, LGBTI diplomats' careers were at risk if they dared to live openly. In fact, LGBTI individuals were prohibited from serving in the State Department until 1992.[104] On January 9, 2017, former US Secretary of State John Kerry issued a formal apology on behalf of the US Department of State for its role in past discrimination against LGBTI employees and applicants.[105] In his apology, Kerry recognized the transformation of the US Department of State from its history of active discrimination to the promotion of sexual minority rights abroad.[106] Specifically, Secretary Kerry highlighted that "in 2015, to further promote LGBTI rights throughout the world, I appointed the first ever Special Envoy for the Human Rights of LGBTI Persons."[107] Kerry's acknowledgment signified a complete reversal of policy toward LGBTI employees within the State Department, as well as a shift making the United States the largest international financial contributor to LGBTI global civil society and programs. As the title of this book suggests, this research investigates how one institution, as seen in the case of the US Department of State, can transition from treating a group of people as pariahs to transition within just a few decades to promote equality globally as a foreign policy priority.

This research traces the process of how repressive laws in the United States, mainly commencing in the 1950s McCarthy era, generated a powerful social movement with the long-term goal of reforming domestic and foreign affairs agencies. LGBTI activists engaged in public resistance toward discriminatory federal policies. Over many decades, advocates cultivated increasing public support and built alliances with LGBTI-allied government insiders. From their position of influence, these government insiders were able to override powerful opponents of LGBTI equality by focusing LGBTI rights diplomacy on extreme violence toward sexual minorities. *From Pariah to Priority* provides original data to uncover how advocates and insider allies employed strategic framing and made LGBTI equality more palatable to even conservative legislators. Leaders who may not support marriage equality will support policies that protect fundamental freedoms, namely preventing people from being killed or jailed due to their sexual orientation in places such as Cuba, Russia, or Uganda. When confronted by the gravity of the problem in many countries, numerous US leaders softened their opposition to certain LGBTI diplomatic frames that centered on ending extreme violence and criminalization, allowing for them to become one of the State Department's mandates.

Uganda plays a central role in explaining how LGBTI rights were institutionalized in the United States and Sweden. In 2009, members of the Ugandan Parliament expressed near-unanimous support for a proposed bill that would have made homosexual acts punishable by death.[108] The Anti-Homosexuality Bill,[109] dubbed by observers as the "Kill the Gays" Bill,[110] was a sensitizing event that spurred a global reaction that became a key factor for institutionalizing LGBTI rights in foreign policy. Most social science research focuses on Americans' role and Christian religious leaders' impact on the Ugandan Parliament in regard to changing their laws.[111] This research argues that in 2009, with the proposal of the "Kill the Gays" law in Uganda, US and Swedish foreign policy institutions were irrevocably changed; without this law, LGBTI diplomacy would not have become institutionalized in these two governments.

Leveraging international relations theories concerning sensitizing events such as the Anti-Homosexuality Bill, this book demonstrates how such events can stimulate discursive renewal to reshape policies.[112] Discursive renewal is explained by theorists who argue that new events can transform public and institutional discourse, triggering a new approach or policy proposal in response.[113] There are numerous countries with the death penalty for homosexuality. These countries had not drawn sweeping international attention for their laws, as was the case with Uganda's proposed law. Discursive institutionalism helps explain how the Ugandan law in particular was a new event that generated societal and political concerns and caused institutional renewal to shape new decision-making regarding LGBTI rights in foreign relations.

Prior to Uganda's proposed law, American diplomats' focus on global LGBTI abuses had been peripheral. Before then, LGBTI issues were addressed indirectly through international development programs related to HIV/AIDS programs and some gender equality campaigns. The proposed draconian Ugandan law inspired international leaders into a new institutional policy discourse and elevated LGBTI rights as a central human rights issue of foreign relations. It also drew international attention and catalyzed an urgent discursive renewal in both the United States and Sweden. In a historic policy decision, both countries conditioned aspects of their respective bilateral aid to Uganda in response to its new anti-LGBTI law. Sweden conditioned its international donor aid by cutting 6.5 million kroner (approximately $928,500) of planned aid to the Ugandan government, while continuing to support local civil society and funding nongovernmental programs.[114] The United States also took a similar approach, with a historic cancellation of a military aviation exercise and a halting of aid to certain other programs, including the Ugandan police force.[115] These actions marked the first time—globally in history—that international donor aid was revamped because of LGBTI human rights considerations.

Conditioning foreign assistance based on LGBTI rights changed global international relations. LGBTI rights abuses are included in negotiations with countries seeking to join the EU, for example. Human rights considerations are included in trade and military agreements with many countries. The Swedish model is used as a blueprint by diplomats in many different nations. In the US case, this practice commenced in 2009 during the Obama administration. Some observers noted that " 'gay rights diplomacy' became a pillar of the Obama administration's foreign policy."[116] With the transition to the conservative Trump administration, many advocates and observers postulated LGBTI rights diplomacy to be removed from the State Department's mandate. However, the Trump administration continued to make aspects of US foreign and military assistance contingent on human rights, including LGBTI rights.

The US case chapter ends with an analysis of the Trump administration and the first few months of President Biden's administration in 2021. Again surprising to most observers, the Trump administration renewed efforts for a global campaign to end criminalization and violence toward LGBTI persons in 2019.[117] It appeared at the time that LGBTI rights diplomacy institutionally survived the first change of administration. In the first year of the Trump administration, the newly appointed Secretary of State Rex Tillerson issued a statement commemorating the International Transgender Day of Remembrance, stating, "The United States honors the memory of the many transgender individuals who have lost their lives to acts of violence."[118] Given the Trump administration's hostility to transgender people's rights, this shocked LGBTI equality advocates.[119] Similarly surprising to observers, in February 2017, after little more than a month in office, Trump administration officials announced that the State Department's US Special Envoy for the Human Rights of LGBTI people Randy Berry would retain his position. Berry had been appointed during the Obama administration in 2015. Political observers noted that keeping "Obama's top gay rights envoy at the State Department stunned LGBTI activists and angered American evangelicals."[120] LGBTI rights in foreign policy have been supported and criticized by both ends of the political spectrum. There are numerous factors, however, that make a mandate within the Department of State difficult to reform or remove. The chapter concludes with providing institutional factors and explanations to the Trump administration's seemingly perplexing actions. Examining a policy's sustainability in foreign policy is important for new human rights advocacy and modern social movements.

LGBTI equality is challenged globally. Like the United States, more conservative governments in places such as Brazil, Hungary, and Poland dismantled aspects of laws and policies for gender equality. Since 2015, the Swedish political climate has also shifted, calling into question the policy sustainability of LGBTI diplomacy in Sweden as well.

Introduction to the Swedish Case Study Chapter

Scholars have deemed Sweden as a "moral superpower,"[121] and "the gold standard,"[122] in human rights foreign policy with regard to how Swedish leaders generate and champion new human rights norms. In 2005, the Swedish government made the historic decision to broaden its human rights foreign policy goals to formally include LGBTI rights.[123] At that time, other countries such as the other Nordic nations, the Netherlands, and Brazil were contemplating similar policies.[124] Since then, the Swedish government has provided financial support to fledgling LGBTI civil society groups to aid their struggle for global equality.[125] On all continents, in countries from Moldova to Uganda, Sweden utilizes its bilateral relationships and leverages its influence in the EU and UN as a large international humanitarian aid donor to end LGBTI human rights abuses.

Central to Sweden's human rights policy is a feminist foreign policy that prioritizes women's rights and gender equality that the Swedish Government considered "prerequisite[s] for reaching Sweden's broader foreign policy goals on peace, security, and sustainable development."[126] Swedish Foreign Minister Wallström explained, "striving toward gender equality is not only a goal in itself but also a precondition for achieving our wider foreign development, and security-policy objectives."[127] The Swedish government openly and vocally promotes human rights, sometimes at the expense of its bilateral relations. For example, it has strained and even eliminated aspects of its bilateral relationship with Saudi Arabia because of gender equality and human rights abuses.[128] LGBTI rights are incorporated into the Swedish government's overall umbrella of promoting gender equality abroad. According to public statements from the Swedish government, "[Swedish] diplomats seek entry points for promoting LGBTI rights in every corner of the globe. Sweden actively works within the UN and EU toward the goal of explicit improvement of laws on LGBTI rights, globally."[129] Most countries hold military and economic alliances as central to bilateral engagement. Prioritizing gender equality is unique in foreign affairs.

Foreign policy institutions around the globe are largely dominated by elite men; the policies generated often reflect this leadership. Several of Sweden's political parties have adopted electoral quotas that require women to comprise a certain number of nominated candidates in an election.[130] Similarly, women comprise nearly half of all parliamentarians and government ministers in the Swedish government.[131] While female leadership does not necessarily lead to improving women's rights, it is a strong indicator that gender issues will be on the agenda.[132] With high levels of female leadership and a legacy of feminist leadership, Sweden prioritizes gender issues throughout government policy.

Sweden has one of the strongest records for upholding LGBTI rights domestically.[133] It was the first country in the world to enact federal anti-LGBTI discrimination policies in the workplace.[134] While strong, Sweden's human rights record is not flawless; gender-based violence and LGBTI hate crimes also persist in Sweden.[135] However, domestically, an overwhelming majority of Swedish citizens support equal rights for all people.[136] This study examines the work of advocates and diplomats to address LGBT discrimination and violence domestically as well as in global venues. The Swedish government and civil society groups have set examples for other governments to follow. Disproportionate to its size, it exhibits a measurable and explicit impact on other nations seeking to commence or strengthen their LGBTI diplomacy foreign policy practices.[137] Bolstered by a strong human rights record at home, Sweden plays a dominant role in promoting LGBTI rights in international affairs.

Sweden plays a prominent role in the international norm diffusion of LGBTI rights. Scandinavians persistently and forcefully raise LGBTI rights in diverse and contentious international forums.[138] Although a small state, Brysk asserts that "Sweden sets the gold standard for human rights foreign policy promotion: funding, sheltering, mediating, and advocating for the full spectrum of human rights, all over the world, for several generations."[139]

International relations scholars theorize that Swedes—and Scandinavians more generally—are "norm entrepreneurs" in the international community.[140] Sweden and other Nordic states have a long history of challenging the human rights status quo and pushing new norms in international relations such as with policy frames related to women's rights in conflict zones and innovative environmental protection policies.[141] Sweden was also the first country in the world to legislate divorce based on irreconcilable differences, and one of the first nations to decriminalize homosexuality in 1944.[142] Scandinavian policies on gender equality, environmental policies, and other emerging social trends have measurably influenced reform toward increasingly progressive LGBTI rights in liberal democracies.

Scholars assert that small and middle power nations conduct human rights diplomacy when they identify the overlap of their states' national interest with global interest and the common good.[143] As Sweden is a small state and vulnerable to global economic and political trends, it is in Sweden's best interest to promote peace. One of the founders of Sweden's modern welfare state, Gunnar Myrdal, asserted, "We are called upon by history and our external conditions to be the advocate of universal interest."[144] Sweden's humanitarian efforts thereby can be explained in part as a small state's "defensive reaction" to the culture of war in Europe.[145] Human rights policies have the end goal of promoting international law, peace, and order to the international system. Thus, while it does not lead to great tangible material gain for Swedes to assist vulnerable populations, such as LGBTI groups in Namibia, that assistance is not provided because of a sense of charity.[146] The Swedish government's actions are an illustrative case study of constructivism determining foreign policy goals.

Human rights foreign policy can be understood as a constructivist form of identity politics. In her comparative study of human rights as foreign policy, Brysk finds that this aspect of foreign policy "defies the realist prediction of untrammeled pursuit of national interest and suggests the utility of constructivist approaches that investigate the role of ideas, identities, and roles as influences on state action."[147] Because of its neutral foreign policy and relative freedom from economic and military alliances, Sweden is able to take stances on human rights that other countries cannot, or do not. Raising issues of LGBTI rights, particularly in countries across Africa and the Middle East, has the potential to jeopardize diplomatic relationships as well as other development programs, yet Sweden consistently champions these rights internationally. In the constructivist theoretical framework, Sweden's constructed national identity as a leader of human rights is a central contributing factor in its evolving foreign policy agenda.

The Swedish case also presents important findings on NGO advocacy and the unique relationship of civil society and government in Scandinavia. Sweden is the location of one of the oldest LGBTI rights organizations in the world. Since its establishment in 1950, the *Swedish Federation for Lesbian, Gay, Bisexual and Transgender Rights* (RFSL) has applied sustained pressure and advocacy to public and government institutions.[148] When faced with political opposition to equality, advocates have honed tactics of publicly naming and shaming specific leaders or political parties. Advocates also strategically employ targeted institutional advocacy efforts that harness insider allied government leadership.

Scholars demonstrate the importance of human rights activists seeking and recruiting allies at the highest levels of government to gain traction for their cause; an insider-outsider coalition for social movements is critical.[149] Swedish LGBTI and human rights groups enjoy comparatively open reception from the government and are able to advocate for policy change within government bodies and institutions. RFSL and civil society leaders are uniquely integrated into Swedish governmental decision-making agencies as related to foreign policies concerning LGBTI human rights. From these sustained advocacy efforts, Swedish government officials turn to civil society leaders as strategic consultants when debating new policy, such as how the Swedish government should respond to Uganda's Anti-Homosexuality Bill.

The 2009 Anti-Homosexuality Bill was a pivotal factor in Sweden's decision to institutionalize LGBTI rights in its foreign policy. Although Sweden began including LGBTI rights in its foreign policy a few years prior, they were still somewhat peripheral in the country's human rights agenda. This book demonstrates that the Ugandan law created renewed discourse among Swedish human rights foreign policy leaders. Similar to the laws impacting American foreign policy leaders, Swedish diplomats described the Ugandan law as an "awakening moment" for government officials and the Swedish public.[150] Others described the law as a "catalyst" for reevaluating their foreign policy priorities in light of severe LGBTI abuses brought to their attention by transnational activists.[151] It took the extreme nature of the Ugandan law to invigorate LGBTI foreign policy discussions in Swedish foreign ministry institutions. The Ugandan law became a lightning rod for the international LGBTI movement's mobilization of government leaders. As a departure from a swath of research about how foreign leaders impacted the Ugandan law, this book analyzes how the law came full circle and served to institutionalize LGBTI rights in Swedish foreign affairs.

The Swedish government decision—subsequently replicated by many other governments—to attach conditions to their levels of aid provided to Uganda on the basis of its LGBTI human rights record was a first in international relations. Making aid conditional based on other human rights and democracy ideals has become a tenet of modern foreign policy. Sweden, other countries, and multilateral institutions such as the World Bank attach conditions on countries based on human rights and democracy standards. If countries do not meet those standards, or violate certain human rights, countries determine, at times, to condition aid.[152] A country's record on torture, prison conditions, women's rights, and trafficking in persons are just a few examples of human rights issues that become connected to foreign assistance.[153] Since 2009, LGBTI rights abuses increasingly have become an international norm to link and condition foreign assistance to a specific country. Policies related to promoting LGBTI rights through foreign assistance and diplomacy have been formulated in the EU, whose leaders are working to develop a comprehensive foreign policy with LGBTI rights guiding collective external relations.[154] Since 2009, conditioning aid has begun to influence bilateral relationships, especially towards African and Middle Eastern nations with repressive LGBTI laws.

The Swedish case study reveals a LGBTI social movement, where organizations are fueled largely by public funding and highly integrated into state decision-making processes. The leading advocacy organization, RFSL, is highly dependent on funding from SIDA.[155] The case study engages with social movement scholarship that contends that too close of a relationship with government partners can pose the risk of social movements becoming institutionalized and agendas neutralized.[156] Social movement theorists argue that integrating with the state, especially by accepting government funding, inherently makes a movement more reformist.[157] Similarly, human rights practitioners and organizations across North America and other parts of Europe exhibit high levels of skepticism toward accepting public funds for their work. Organizational leaders hold that financial support sourced from private funding outside the state will "safe guard objectivity" and enable organizations to contest state policies without a perceived conflict of interest.[158] Furthermore, many social movement scholars argue that organizations that remain outside state structures can more freely make demands of the state.[159] The Swedish model of civil society funding and advocacy tactics challenges these common practices by international human rights groups. Within the key variable of a liberal democracy, where civil society groups are free to criticize their own government, this research makes the case for human rights organizations to reexamine human rights organizations' relationship with the state.

By analyzing LGBTI social movement strategies toward Swedish foreign policy, *From Pariah to Priority* finds that the state model of integration improved Swedish advocates' access and ability to directly influence government policy toward their long-term goals of equality. Even though receiving a majority of government funding, the Swedish LGBTI movement did not become co-opted by the government. Conversely, the data in this book demonstrate that the close institutional advocacy and relationship with foreign affairs offices led to civil society's increased influence over Swedish government policy and funding. The Swedish model challenges a widely feared notion by human rights activists in the United States that government support will hinder their agenda. The case study illustrates that government funding and a close relationship with public leaders will not necessarily undercut a social movement's goals.

Analyzing the successes and failures of the Swedish LGBTI social movement aids other movements in places such as Eastern Europe or Latin America. This analysis also benefits other human rights social movements actively engaged in advocating for the reform of foreign policy goals and provides effective tactics and strategies. The pivotal role of advocacy in foreign policy institutions lends itself to explanations for the process of normative values impacting bilateral relations and broader shifts in the international order.

This case study analyzes the factors that led to Swedish foreign policy reform. The work of Swedish diplomats in integrating LGBTI rights and human rights into foreign relations is still rarely undertaken by other governments in the world. In the EU, Sweden continues to influence the rights discourse in Europe, largely through the forum of EU accession for new member countries. Swedish officials continue to work to define LGBTI rights as an important part of any modern Western democracy that is responsible for upholding principles of equality and minority protections.

The findings in this book demonstrate that early adoption of LGBTI promotion in Sweden was dependent on broad social acceptance, perceived national interest, and an early evolution of the concept of human rights to include sexual minority rights. In Sweden, human rights framing is centered on concepts of fairness and equality. Thus, while the Swedish LGBTI rights movement generated LGBTI norms transnationally, they chose to frame their fight in the domestic context of the welfare state that espouses to care for all citizens and treat them equally. The legacy of solidarity and equality allowed Swedish leadership to enact reforms and rapidly incorporate those rights into government institutions.

Timeline of LGBTI Foreign Policy Developments

Timeline of LGBTI Foreign Policy Developments: Sweden and the United States

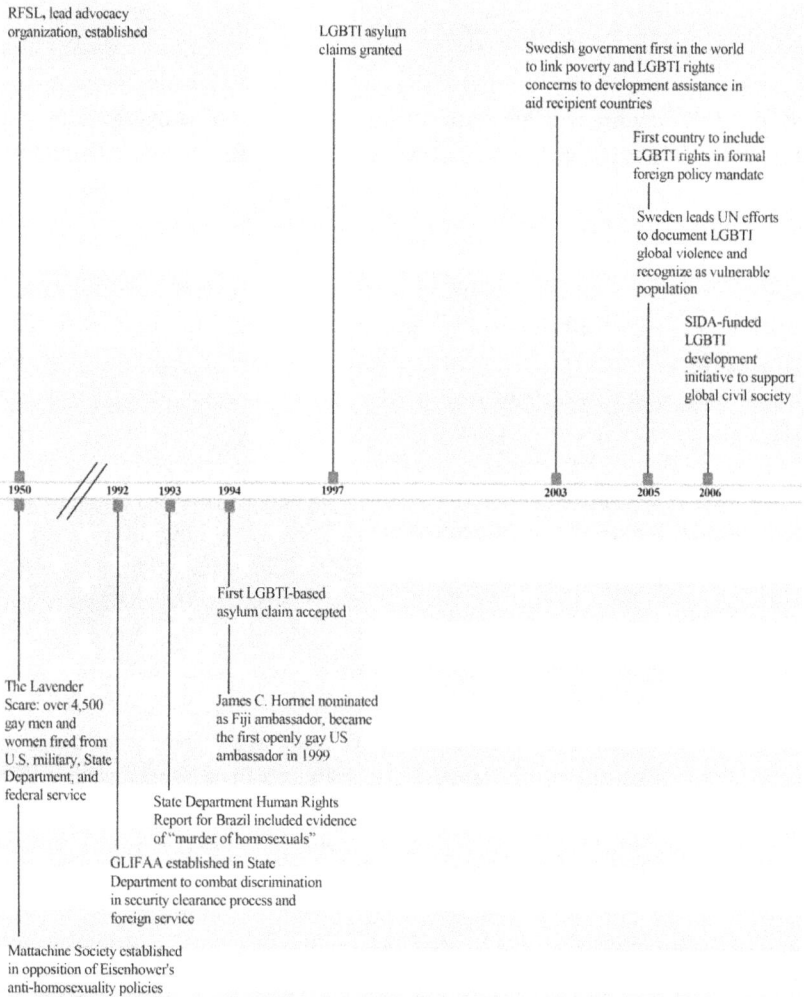

RFSL, lead advocacy
organization, established

LGBTI asylum
claims granted

Swedish government first in the world
to link poverty and LGBTI rights
concerns to development assistance in
aid recipient countries

First country to include
LGBTI rights in formal
foreign policy mandate

Sweden leads UN efforts
to document LGBTI
global violence and
recognize as vulnerable
population

SIDA-funded
LGBTI
development
initiative to support
global civil society

1950   //   1992   1993   1994   1997   2003   2005   2006

First LGBTI-based
asylum claim accepted

The Lavender
Scare: over 4,500
gay men and
women fired from
U.S. military, State
Department, and
federal service

James C. Hormel nominated
as Fiji ambassador, became
the first openly gay US
ambassador in 1999

State Department Human Rights
Report for Brazil included evidence
of "murder of homosexuals"

GLIFAA established in State
Department to combat discrimination
in security clearance process and
foreign service

Mattachine Society established
in opposition of Eisenhower's
anti-homosexuality policies

Uganda proposes the Uganda Anti-
Homosexuality Act (AHA), which
included the death penalty for
homosexual acts, garnering international
attention and condemnation from foreign
governments

SIDA funding levels to support global LGBTI civil society
expand to $1.9 million

Establishment of Rainbow Leaders

Sweden conditions aid to Ugandan
government in response to AHA

Swedish government
becomes one of the largest
international donors to
LGBTI NGOs

| 2009 | 2010 | 2011 | 2012 | 2013 | 2014 | 2015 | 2017 | 2018 | 2019 | 2020 |

Biden elected to office and
recommits U.S. global efforts
The Hillary Doctrine: Trump administration   to promote LGBTI rights in
established global gender   relaunches global   foreign affairs and support
inequality and subjugation   effort to end LGBTI   global LGBTI civil society
of women as threat to U.S.   criminalization
national security

                                         Secretary Kerry apologizes for the persecution
                                         of LGBTI State Department and Foreign
Obama first head of   Service officers during 1950s Lavender Scare
state to address LGBTI
rights in UN General   Tillerson conditions aid to Egypt based
Assembly speech   on treatment of LGBTI Egyptians

                                Secretary Kerry appoints first Special Envoy for the
                                Human Rights of LGBTI Persons, Randy Berry

Secretary Clinton makes   US conditions aid to Uganda, cutting some military and
speech at UN Human Rights   government assistance
Council, proclaiming "gay
rights are human rights"
                                World Bank suspends $90 million loan for Ugandan health care

                                USAID co-sponsors Rainbow Leaders
Establishment of Global Equality
Fund, largest multinational fund in   All U.S. Embassies and USAID missions incorporate
the world to support global LGBTI   LGBTI rights initiatives in their annual Strategic Plans
civil society

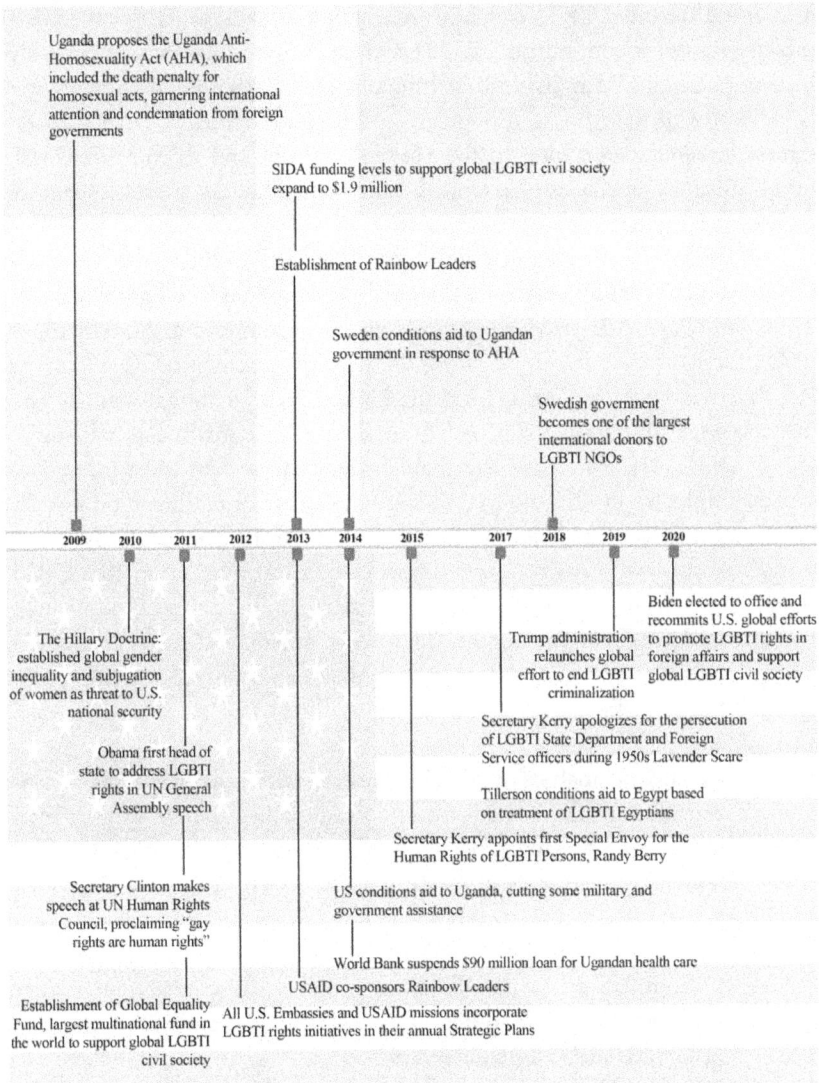

Map of the Book

From Pariah to Priority begins with the US case study. In this section, I draw upon my firsthand experience as an US diplomat, interviews with high-level American foreign policy leaders, and data from US foreign policy institutions. The data are dovetailed with contemporary scholarship of human rights and LGBTI rights in international relations. It opens with a presentation of a conundrum: in 2011, the US State Department formally incorporated LGBTI rights into its human rights foreign policy strategy, yet large swaths of the American population still contest equality. Violence and discrimination remain high in the United States,[160] and as compared with other liberal democracies, the United States ranks low on social acceptance for LGBTI rights.[161]

Given the contestation, it was not expected or inevitable that US foreign policy would incorporate the policy pillar of LGBTI rights in 2011. Thus, the US chapter traces the process of policy adoption of LGBTI rights in US foreign policy by investigating the following factors: NGO advocacy; insider government leadership; and the United States' national identity and international reputation. NGO advocacy is not uniform; social movement tactics are diverse. Therefore, the chapter analyzes the four most influential tactics employed by NGOs to influence policy reform: direct protest by NGOs against state policies, garnering support from gatekeeper organizations, institutional advocacy, and diffusing political opposition to LGBTI rights. Activists continue to employ diverse tactics to maintain LGBTI equality, sustain LGBTI diplomacy in US foreign affairs, and advance LGBTI policy in US foreign policy engagement. American advocates develop strategies to combat opposition to equality globally as well as from their own government.

Following the analysis of NGO advocacy tactics, the US chapter turns to an investigation of the role of powerful insider allied leadership in foreign policy. Individual ambassadors, Secretary of State Hillary Clinton, and influential diplomats applied internal pressure for policy change. From interviews and other primary source data, this research uncovers the unanticipated high levels of internal support within the State Department to commence LGBTI diplomacy from US embassies. Findings indicate the critical role insider diplomats played to reform office and department mandates to include LGBTI diplomacy in US foreign policy.

Finally, the US case study chapter reveals motivation for policy reform in part due to the United States' national identity and human rights record. Data indicate that after the Bush administration, US foreign policy leaders sought new policy frames to renew the US reputation and reengage on global human rights. Leading up to 2011, Obama administration officials asserted that LGBTI rights could be a new frontier for US diplomats to make a distinct change from the previous administration and reclaim the United States' reputation as a country that prioritizes human rights. LGBTI rights diplomacy, therefore, became the flagship policy pillar for America's transformed engagement on international human rights. Thus, national reputation was a contributing factor for policy reform.

Chapter 3 of *From Pariah to Priority* turns the analysis to the comparative case study of Sweden's LGBTI diplomacy. Although Sweden is a small country, it is an enormously high contributor to international aid, a central donor country to the EU, and a top-ten contributor to the UN.[162] Stemming from financial leverage, Swedish foreign policy officials exert measurable influence on norms in the international system. LGBTI rights is a flagship feature of Sweden's foreign policy goals.

Sweden has one of the oldest LGBTI advocacy organizations in the world, RFSL, founded in 1950. Advocates have been working for decades to combat repression and discrimination in Swedish society. Given early contestation, it was not inevitable that Sweden's foreign policy should take up the mantel of LGBTI rights diplomacy. This chapter establishes four major factors critical to LGBTI rights rising to prominence within Sweden's foreign policy: NGO advocacy from LGBTI leaders, insider government allies, repressive laws that sensitized the global movement, and a national self-perception of being a global leader in LGBTI rights.

NGO actors have been pivotal in foreign policy creation and reform in Sweden. Advocates have strategically framed the debate as a human rights issue of equality and fairness under the law, harnessed powerful insider leadership, and publicly shamed top leaders. Sustained NGO advocacy influenced changes to Swedish foreign policy over decades. Swedish advocates have employed varied tactics such as institutional advocacy, public advocacy, diffusing political opposition, and harnessing insider allied leadership. In many other countries, civil society groups are not allowed to be part of policy deliberations, and foreign ministries can be antagonistic toward NGOs.[163] By contrast, Swedish NGO leaders at times serve as strategic advisors to the government on LBGTI foreign policy goals. Swedish advocates documented LGBTI discrimination in housing, employment, and medical treatment as a means of proving that LGBTI populations deserve protections and support equal to what other marginalized groups receive in Swedish foreign aid.

In part from the close relationship of advocates with government officials, LGBTI advocates garnered the support of numerous government leaders who became influential movement allies. Insider allies became critical players in institutionalizing LGBTI rights in Swedish foreign affairs. There are also several prominent diplomats, other members of Parliament, and mid-level agency directors who determined agency funding and agenda prioritization to focus on LGBTI rights abuses in Swedish foreign affairs. Many individuals utilized their positions within foreign affairs institutions to elevate LGBTI rights. *From Pariah to Priority* uses original interview data from contemporary and past Swedish ministers, diplomats, ambassadors, and Swedish representatives to the EU to demonstrate the critical influence of insider allies on the LGBTI movement.

Swedish officials rarely link the development of humanitarian aid and human rights diplomacy to matters of short-term self-interest. Rather, the high levels of international humanitarian and human rights aid are justified by Sweden's fundamental commitment to human rights. In the early 2000s, when LGBTI rights were still a cutting-edge mandate in diplomacy, RFSL leaders used tropes of Swedish national image to convince stakeholders that they should prioritize LGBTI rights in Swedish foreign policy. They emphasized Sweden's national reputation as historically protecting the most vulnerable populations, such as women and children, to convince leaders to bring LGBTI rights abuses into diplomatic agendas.

LGBTI persons in Sweden, the United States, and other countries were once reviled as enemies of the state.[164] In contemporary Swedish politics, LGBTI rights have become a core part of Swedish national identity. Recently, the perceived intertwining of LGBTI equality with the national identity has become a surprising and unexpected rallying cry for right-wing nationalist leaders. *From Pariah to Priority* analyzes how these leaders seek to make a distinction between immigrant groups and perceived contesting Swedish values based on the fault line of LGBTI rights.

One of the distinctive conclusions highlighted in the Swedish case study chapter is the unprecedented integration of civil society's advocacy work in the day-to-day workings of Swedish foreign policy institutions. Diplomats and members of Parliament regularly consulted with RFSL officers regarding LGBTI foreign policy mandates. While some other nations are also open to direct influence from civil society (primarily other Nordic nations), Sweden presents the most glaring exception to the global norm of foreign ministries reticent of direct influence from outside civil society groups.

Chapter 4 analyzes the lasting impact of Ugandan lawmakers on Swedish and US foreign policy leaders. This section investigates the process by which foreign policy leaders conditioned aid based on a country's LGBTI human rights record for the first time in history.[165] The foreign policy decisions surrounding Uganda's proposed death penalty law have left an indelible impact on international relations. Foreign diplomats from the United States, the UK, Germany, Sweden, the UN, and more raise concerns about LGBTI rights abuses at the top levels of government. At the other end of the spectrum, neoconservative evangelicals have made Uganda "ground zero" of their opposition to the social and moral acceptance of homosexuality."[166] Uganda is a global focal point country in the international fight to promote or repress LGBTI rights.

When Uganda proposed the death penalty for homosexual acts in 2009, it triggered an urgent response from world leaders. The law convinced international diplomats of the acute need to address LGBTI rights in their countries' foreign policy. Repressive laws were a sensitizing event for both Swedish and American policy makers. A sensitizing event can motivate discursive renewal and policy reform.[167] Scholarly focus related to international studies and LGBTI rights largely focuses on international donor nations' impact on local LGBTI communities and on power asymmetries of neocolonialism.[168] The central thesis in the Uganda chapter, therefore, is that Uganda's law was a critical event that triggered the institutionalization of LGBTI rights in US and Swedish human rights diplomacy. In the past, ambassadors remained silent on LGBTI right abuses, even in places with public stoning, mob killings, and severe human rights abuses of LGBTI populations. The Uganda law sparked a change to diplomacy by broadening international relations to include considerations of human rights practices toward LGBTI populations.

The Ugandan proposed law solidified LGBTI rights as a fundamental aspect of Sweden's feminist foreign policy, leading to renewed efforts and increased funding. Given the novelty of the incorporation of LGBTI rights in diplomatic engagements, Swedish officials could not be guided by the best practices or policy consultations with other countries. Instead, the Swedish government consulted with leaders of the central LGBTI civil society organization, RFSL. RFSL officers thereby served as strategic advisors for the Swedish government as stakeholders grappled with how to respond to Uganda's proposed law. In turn, RFSL leaders sought local Ugandan LGBTI advocates' perspectives to help draft a strategic policy recommendation for Swedish foreign policy leaders.

Ugandan and civil society partners recommended not cutting aid to Uganda, but rather directing it away from Ugandan government leaders or ministries and instead allocating it to Ugandan civil society. In country contexts, such as Uganda, with low levels of rule of law, high corruption, and rampant state violence against LGBTI people, international donor nations can bypass recipient government agencies and instead fund non-state actors. This diplomatic method seeks to shame and cripple government agencies; it also seeks to empower and assist fledging NGOs.

For the United States, the Ugandan law served as the catalyst for institutionalizing LGBTI rights in US human rights foreign policy. Inculcating foreign aid with normative values is not a new prospect. It took, though, a new extreme event in world politics—as seen through Uganda's "Kill the Gays" proposed law in 2009—to invigorate foreign policy makers to act. The Ugandan law triggered a discursive renewal for US policy makers. American leaders in 2009 asserted that policy discussions transformed an abstract, long-term goal of including LGBTI rights within the State Department's work into an acute, short-term mission to immediately address Uganda's law. The egregious nature of the law sparked a sudden need for a reaction from the State Department and US policy makers. This chapter argues that the Ugandan law proposing the death penalty for homosexual practices was the critical sensitizing event that caused international leaders to reevaluate their foreign policy in relation to human rights. A central outcome of this reevaluation was to condition aspects of foreign aid to Uganda.

This chapter engages with the contested debate regarding foreign aid conditionality. Many low-income countries are largely dependent on foreign aid. Approximately 25 percent of Uganda's GDP comes from foreign aid.[169] International donor aid funds a large portion of Uganda's schools, agricultural sector, health care services and rebuilding of national roads.[170] Terminating foreign funding can lead to significant public health and societal problems. Furthermore, cutting foreign aid with the goal of protecting a specific group, in this case the Ugandan LGBTI community, can lead to a backlash toward that community. Already dealing with societal violence and discrimination, cutting foreign aid can potentially lead to the double victimization of LGBTI populations.[171] However, at times, cutting bilateral ties can lead to long-term systemic change. While local advocates decried the potential detrimental impacts of cutting foreign aid, they also recognized the political influence of foreign leaders condemning Uganda's domestic practices. After the international storm and attention in response to the AHA, the Ugandan government did not pass the death penalty law. Instead, it enacted life imprisonment for homosexual acts. Causal effects of human rights diplomacy are difficult to measure. LGBTI rights are now an issue of consideration for diplomats in negotiating trade and security agreements with countries across Africa, the Middle East, and globally. How diplomats apply political pressure, which tool they use in modern diplomacy—whether funding civil society, ending military agreements, or cutting foreign aid—needs a great deal more scrutiny from scholars.

The Uganda chapter examines the acute reaction of foreign policy leaders in response to the AHA. Paradoxically, many advocates assess that the genesis of the law was from Western homophobic influence, namely American evangelicals. This section of the chapter analyzes the polarizing nature of the American presence in Uganda. Diplomats spread messages of tolerance and fund pro-equality LGBTI civil society organizations; this is in stark contrast with American evangelical groups that established numerous faith-based organizations and funneled millions of dollars into the country to contest homosexuality. Given the contestation among influential portions of the American population, many observers expected the Trump adminis- tration to cease "embracing gay rights" in US foreign policy.[172] The analysis seeks to contextualize the debate of the seeming hypocrisy of LGBTI diplo- macy in US foreign policy. With so many people in the US population contesting LGBTI equality, how can this be an agenda issue for modern US diplomats? The chapter provides context to the conundrum of when foreign policy appears incongruent with domestic practice. American dip- lomats address anti-Semitism, Islamophobia, violence against women, and other challenging societal issues in foreign dialogues. Yet these problems still pervade the United States, Sweden, and other modern democracies. Similarly, LGBTI violence and discrimination still exist in all countries that have formally incorporated LGBTI rights into their foreign policy mandates. Deputy Assistant Secretary of State Dan Baer, one of the drafters of Presi- dent Obama's memorandum commencing LGBTI diplomacy stated, stated:

> I can remember when I started this job, a few years ago, when I would engage on, say, discrimination in employment for LGBT people, and people would say but you still have Don't Ask Don't Tell, so, you know, don't you have this problem too? And there's kind of two answers: one is that, you know, we're working on it, and the second is that, you know, human rights advocacy, particularly within a foreign policy, isn't about saying "I'm perfect, and you should, you should be perfect like me," there's universal standards are something for all of us to aspire to. You don't have to be perfect to support them. Supporting them does mean engaging in good faith and putting hard effort into making your own government more perfect.[173]

Foreign policy officials work in an imperfect world. No country has a perfect human rights record; diplomats work within this context. Since the humanitarian disaster of WWII, addressing human rights is critical for long-term regional and national security interests. While duplicity is to some extent an unavoidable aspect of human rights diplomacy, conducting international relations devoid of human rights considerations is a far more precarious strategy for peace and global security.

Chapter 5 is a theoretical analysis of central arguments in the literature that help to explain how LGBTI diplomacy emerged in foreign affairs. It was not inevitable that LGBTI rights should become a consideration for ambassadors and heads of state. By examining human rights literature, this chapter explores many human rights movements that have failed. It seeks to explain the key factors that led to the global LGBTI equality movement gaining traction in the international community and ultimately coming to be accepted as a human right. As sexual minority rights were not part of the UDHR in 1948, LGBTI advocates worked for decades to change the definition of human rights in international affairs. This section evaluates the importance of gatekeeper organizations, such as Amnesty International and Human Rights Watch, which largely set the international human rights agenda. Social movement literature also helps explain how norms change, methods in which organized groups advocate, mobilize resources, and struggle for recognition based on new human rights standards. LGBTI groups use earlier social movement tactics from the civil rights movement and women's rights movement. This body of work demonstrates how movements crib tactics and interlink social movements. Sabine Lang and other scholars contrast the efficacy of public advocacy, that is, street protests, compared with institutional advocacy, that is, NGOs meeting with relevant government agencies to promote their cause. Social movement actors can come from outside the state, but also within government. This theoretical framework helps explain the significant influence on policy reform of LGBTI diplomats, ambassadors, and civil servants who supported LGBTI equality. Insider allies can allocate resources, change agendas, and use their position of influence within the state to advance social movement objectives.

The theoretical chapter ends with relevant international relations theories. Constructivism is the most salient theory to explain the importance of ideas and identity in shaping foreign political actions in foreign affairs. Numerous respondents in *From Pariah to Priority* asserted "Swedish national values" or "America's place in the world" as a motivating factor to begin LGBTI diplomacy. Upholding their country's national identity, in the case of Sweden, or repairing national reputation, in the case of the United States, was seminal for many leaders. The national identity of a state, and leaders' perceived constructed national interests, are of critical importance to explain policy change. The entire pillar of human rights diplomacy is a departure from traditional diplomatic relations. Leaders, including many past US secretaries of state, believed that it was against the United States' interests to meddle in other countries' domestic affairs. Scholars document the pervasive skepticism of many foreign policy leaders that incorporating human rights into foreign policy would create disorder in the international system, a belief that continues today.[174] However, developing scholarship demonstrates the nexus between human rights, security, and national interests. It is in a state's calculated economic and security interest to promote a stable world.[175] Unstable countries create poor trade and security partners. Therefore, scholars and foreign policy leaders argue that human rights considerations are an imperative component of modern foreign policy.[176] Whether to create a long-term stable world, improve national reputation, or construct a positive national image, international relations theories provide a theoretical framework to this study. Contextualizing these theories serves to explain the complex factors that led to the institutionalization of LGBTI rights in modern diplomatic relations.

Finally, the conclusion chapter is a discussion of the central findings from original data in *From Pariah to Priority*. This section analyzes LGBTI rights diplomacy within the political landscape of the rise of more conservative parties in both the United States and Sweden. The Republican party, led by the Trump administration, and the right-wing Swedish Democrats (*Sverigedemokraterna*, SD) party have taken on the mantle of LGBTI rights in unexpected ways. The United States under the Trump administration continued LGBTI diplomacy and used claims of LGBTI rights abuses against Iran and other political adversarial states. The Swedish Democrats appropriated "Swedish-ness" and national identity to include LGBTI equality. In doing so, they sought to exclude immigrants and other new Swedes. The fight to define national identity in a multicultural society is a central debate in contemporary Swedish political debates and elections. The conclusion chapter examines the work of transnational advocacy networks, advocating across borders to pressure governments and change public opinion. While global opposition to equality in some regions of the world is on the rise, opposition is not new for LGBTI advocates. Civil society groups continue to shift and create new strategies to confront and diffuse political opponents. Similarly, allied leadership and LGBTI social movement actors continue to work within the state to sustain LGBTI rights diplomacy.

Methods and Data Collection

Evidence in this book is derived from a triangulation of data: qualitative interviews with key American and European leaders and decision makers; participant observation of LGBTI rights advocacy events in Sweden, the United States, and EU; and content analysis of government and civil society stakeholders' reports, press releases, speeches, funding priorities, and archived public discourses regarding LGBTI rights in foreign affairs. The research in this book traces the movement's goals and strategies over the past six decades, with a particular focus on 2000–2019. I conducted more than eighty-nine interviews between 2015 and 2019 for *From Pariah to Priority*. In the appendix, I delineate each interviewee's sectoral position, nationality, number of interviews, and location of the interview.

From 2005 to 2011, I was an officer in the DRL, the bureau in the US State Department responsible for shaping international US human rights policies and programs. I worked under two presidents and three secretaries of state, including Secretary of State Hillary Clinton. Secretary Clinton plays an especially important role in this study, as LGBTI diplomacy was largely conceptualized and enacted in the State Department under her leadership. From 2011 to 2016, I served as senior editor of four US Department of State human rights reports to Algeria, Jordan, Oman, and Qatar.[177] Later for this book, I interviewed the leaders responsible for shaping and creating US human rights foreign policy: senior officials; US ambassadors; the first-ever US special envoy for the human rights of LGBTI people, Randy Berry; and numerous other working-level officers within the DRL and State Department.

For the US case study, I conducted in-depth interviews with NGO leaders from the central civil society groups engaged in international LGBTI rights based in the United States. These interviews were primarily with officers from Outright Action International (formerly known as the International Gay and Lesbian Human Rights Commission), the Human Rights Campaign, and the Council for Global Equality. I draw upon participant observation of various US-based events, including the Human Right's Campaign annual conference, various Pride events across the United States, as well as public symposiums regarding international LGBTI rights, such as those at the University of Washington from 2015 through 2019 where international LGBTI activists discussed the struggle for equality.

In Sweden, I conducted interviews with leaders in the government and Parliament, as well as civil society representatives. The interviews were primarily with officers from the Swedish MFA, SIDA, the RFSL, former government officials; and sitting members of Parliament. I used these interviews to trace the evolution and reasoning for incorporating LGBTI rights and norms into multiple branches of Swedish foreign policy offices and divisions.

The annual Stockholm Pride festival is the central point for my participant observation in Sweden. Over the course of a week each year in the summer, organizers gather national and international leaders, civil society groups, foreign diplomats, film directors, transnational activists, political party leaders, and others for political debate and discussions on the movement. Debates and discussions at the festival often include improving transgender rights across the EU, Swedish governmental support to fledgling LGBTI groups in Eastern Europe, far-right nationalism across Europe, political activism in Uganda, and diplomatic engagement on LGBTI repression in Russia and beyond. At Stockholm Pride, I observed presentations by leaders from Amnesty International; Civil Rights Defenders; International Rainbow Cultural Network; International Rainbow Pensioners; the Nordic Rainbow Cultural Workers; RFSL; and numerous other smaller groups over multiple years. Observing public discourse, meeting with key leaders, and conducting interviews on the sidelines has been critical for my research. I used primary source observations from Stockholm Pride in 2015, 2017, and 2019. I use those observations to analyze the current iteration of the LGBTI human rights debate, understand advocacy techniques of local and transnational LGBTI advocates, and map the influential Swedish leaders involved in LGBTI policy formation. While in Stockholm, I also conducted archival research at SIDA and the Swedish Ministry of Foreign Affairs. I collected evidence of original governmental discussions and documentation of historical engagement from civil society with Parliament. I analyzed policy objectives, reports, and evaluations of work done by the Swedish foreign aid agencies from 1990 to 2016 on international LGBTI rights.

With regard to language, I conducted interviews in Swedish and English. The public presentations by top Swedish political leaders and participant observation analysis at Stockholm Pride were almost all conducted in Swedish. I thereby translate quotations into English for this research. I have also collected evidence from Swedish media reports, government documents, and NGO press releases in Swedish, translating the data where appropriate.

Evidence in this book is also derived from primary source information collected at EU institutions in Brussels, Belgium, in 2015. I conducted interviews with key members of the European Parliament's Intergroup on

LGBTI Rights; the EU Committee on Foreign Affairs, Subcommittee on Human Rights; members of the External Policies, Human Rights Unit; and officers of the EU External Action Service. EU foreign policy changes toward LGBTI rights and Sweden's impact on the current debate were the focus in this portion of the investigation.

In Brussels, I interviewed civil society leadership from the International Lesbian, Gay, Bisexual, Trans and Intersex Association for the European Region (ILGA-Europe).[178] As the largest LGBTI rights organization in Europe, and one of the most powerful in the world, ILGA's mandate is to support the development of the LGBTI movement in the EU, Council of Europe, the Organization for Security and Co-operation in Europe. ILGA works to shape a more cohesive, progressive LGBTI foreign policy throughout EU member states.

Chapter 2

The Incorporation of LGBTI Rights into US Foreign Policy

Introduction

In recognition of International Human Rights Day in December 2011, and in a watershed moment for LGBTI rights globally, former Secretary of State Hillary Clinton delivered a speech before the United Nations (UN) Human Rights Council in Geneva, Switzerland, proclaiming:

> Today, I want to talk about the work we have left to do to protect one group of people (LGBTI) whose human rights are still denied in too many parts of the world today. In many ways, they are an invisible minority. They are arrested, beaten, terrorized, even executed. Many are treated with contempt and violence by their fellow citizens while authorities empowered to protect them look the other way or, too often, even join in the abuse[1]

The US secretary of state's acknowledgment that LGBTI people are arrested, terrorized, and executed around the globe by authorities was a defining moment for US human rights foreign policy, as well as the transnational LGBTI movement. As the most powerful nation in the international system, with a global diplomatic impact, the US shift in policy regarding LGBTI rights remains far reaching. As Clinton references, LGBTI people historically were an invisible minority; foreign ministers formerly did not raise concerns of LGBTI abuses in international forums. From this speech forward, US leadership formally joined a handful of other smaller nations in diplomatic recognition of human rights abuses toward LGBTI people globally. The most famous, commonly cited part of the speech came a few moments later when Clinton proclaimed, "Gay rights are human rights, and human rights are gay rights."[2] She concluded by calling for a global consensus to respect the human rights of LGBTI citizens everywhere. With her speech, Clinton signaled to the international community that LGBTI rights would be a priority issue for the United States in foreign affairs. This speech spurred the institutionalization of LGBTI rights into US foreign policy institutions. After her speech, LGBTI issues, like disability and labor rights, gained equal attention in US diplomatic human rights reporting.[3] LGBTI human rights abuses subsequently rose to the top of the human rights agenda for US diplomats in places such as Uganda and Jamaica, where people are threatened by societal and official violence.

Starting in 2011, the US State Department delineated LGBTI persons as a distinctly vulnerable group, thus earmarking international humanitarian and human rights funding for LGBTI individuals and organizations, similar to other minority groups.[4] That delineation has had enormous implications for financial support to LGBTI persons and groups worldwide from international donor aid streams. The Obama administration announced that the United States would use all available tools of American diplomacy, including "the potent enticement of foreign aid, to promote gay rights around the world."[5] US embassy officials worldwide began engaging with LGBTI civil society actors and government officials to discuss local LGBTI rights, raise awareness of LGBTI issues in local media, coordinate with other like-minded embassy officials, and support LGBTI outreach campaigns.[6] Secretary Clinton also enacted numerous LGBTI-friendly policies within the State Department. For example, she granted diplomatic status to LGBTI families, similar to hetero families in the US Foreign Service, who prior to this time did not receive language training or diplomatic protection in an emergency evacuation or natural disaster in foreign countries.[7] Clinton supported the official establishment of the State Department's Gay and Lesbian Foreign Affairs Association and ordered an end to discrimination in the State Department's hiring practices.[8] As the State Department oversees issuing passports for all American citizens, Clinton also changed the policy to allow transgender people to change the gender noted in their passports without proof of gender reassignment surgery. Under Clinton, US consular officers began issuing immigrant visas to spouses and same-sex fiancés of

LGBTI Americans; one recipient of a fiancé visa at the US embassy in London stated, "It's a mind-boggling change after gay couples were treated like legal strangers for the first three centuries of our country's [the United States'] history."[9] As a crescendo to the new internal and external engagement of LGBTI rights in the State Department, in February 2015, Randy Berry was appointed to serve as the first special envoy for the human rights of LGBTI persons.[10] At the time, a special envoy–level official devoted solely to the human rights of LGBTI people was unprecedented in foreign affairs institutions; only a few other governments had similar high-level leadership. Similarly, the United States Agency for International Development (USAID) established a senior LGBT coordinator position and appointed Todd Larson to the role.[11] Thus, American foreign policy institutions bureaucratically changed funding and agenda priorities to include LGBTI rights considerations in diplomatic affairs and international development programs.

Secretary Clinton's words, and the State Department's policy shift to engage on LGBTI rights, were not inevitable given the department's turbulent history with LGBTI rights. Specifically, the State Department's internal policies toward LGBTI employees were openly discriminatory for decades. During the McCarthy era in the 1950s, officials actively sought out, exposed, and fired "commies and queers" from the State Department and other national security agencies.[12] In what scholars refer to as the "Lavender Scare," hundreds of government officials were fired and/or blacklisted from their positions in the State Department, Department of Defense, and broader intelligence community.[13] Scholar David Johnson documents within the State Department that a "fear that homosexuals posed a threat to national security and needed to be systematically removed from the federal government permeated 1950s political culture."[14] Johnson further documents how LGBTI officers would at times be perceived as persons of "perverted morals," and even as mentally ill, implying that LGBTI employees were purported to be at risk for blackmail and extortion from foreign spies "outing" them.[15] Consequently, American leaders argued that LGBTI employees were a security risk and threat to the nation. For decades, LGBTI diplomats were forced to hide their identities for the sake of their careers. Current and retired diplomats recounted for this research that into the late 1990s they risked their careers in the State Department if they dared to live openly.[16] Accordingly, many LGBTI diplomats came to their embassy postings officially single and would not discuss their private lives with colleagues. Historically, the State Department has had an overt policy of discriminating against LGBTI diplomats. Given this discrimination, it was unexpected that the State Department would become a global player in LGBTI rights promotion under any administration.

Puzzle of US LGBTI Rights Diplomacy

LGBTI diplomacy commenced in US foreign policy under the Obama administration in 2011; many advocates assumed the State Department would revoke this policy with the change of leadership to a Republican. Similarly, conservative American faith-based groups expected revoking LGBTI diplomacy to be one of the first actions of the Trump administration, calling for an end of "aggressive policies, such as flying the LGBT flag at US embassies."[17] However, in February 2019, the Trump administration renewed efforts for a global campaign to end criminalization of and violence toward LGBTI persons.[18] This surprising announcement came despite consistent anti-LGBTI rhetoric from the Republican party, as well as domestic rollbacks of progressive reforms, such as formally banning transgender Americans from the US military.[19] This renewed policy directive, however, indicated no plans of the Trump administration to eradicate LGBTI rights diplomacy from US foreign affairs. Herein lies the quandary for this study: Given the historic discrimination of LGBTI people within the State Department, opposition to equality within the Republican party, and large swaths of the American population who oppose LGBTI equality, why and how were LGBTI rights incorporated into US human rights foreign policy? What were the central factors that led to reform of American foreign policy institutions? More broadly, how does this case shed light on other normative values potentially influencing future foreign policy mandates and international relations?

In 2011, LGBTI rights were a contested domestic issue in the United States and globally. The US State Department formally incorporated LGBTI rights into its human rights foreign policy strategy, yet the American public still had not reached social consensus on accepting LGBTI rights as part of the cultural norm. Although US laws and institutions were rapidly changing and incorporating equality policies in some regions of the country, these new standards were contested by a significant number of people and repealed in numerous states.[20] Extreme violence and discrimination against LGBTI people continue to occur at exceedingly high rates within the United States as compared with other countries with similar LGBTI foreign policy. Human Rights Campaign, one of the most influential advocacy nongovernmental organizations (NGOs) for LGBTI rights in the United States, found that in 2018, American LGBTI youth were twice as likely as their peers to be physically assaulted.[21] While US ambassadors march in foreign LGBTI Pride parades, LGBTI rights groups face powerful opposition in the United States. In 2012, one year after the State Department made sweeping changes to US foreign policy, only 46 percent of Republicans believed that gay and lesbian relations should be legal; only 22 percent supported same-sex marriage.[22] These perceptions continue to diverge largely based on political party affiliation and age group; younger Americans on both sides of the political spectrum more readily accept LGBTI equality. However, contestation of LGBTI equality in the United States permeates a large portion of the American population.[23] Compared with other liberal democracies, the US populace exhibits higher levels of antagonism toward LGBTI equality.[24] In 2011, data from the Pew Research Center's *Global Attitudes and Trends* demonstrated that the United States tracked significantly behind other Western European nations' public opinion on acceptance of homosexuality.[25] Similarly, data from the World Values Survey in 2016 indicated that the United States has one of the highest percentages of people providing responses to the survey that "homosexuality is never justifiable," as compared to other industrialized nations.[26] In 2011, the year the United States commenced LGBTI human rights foreign policy, only 51 percent of public opinion supported LGBTI equality.[27] In Clinton's speech in Geneva, she addressed the work of the State Department and US diplomats to build alliances with other governments and civil societies while simultaneously continuing to work toward reform on the United States' domestic record of LGBTI rights. Some scholars assert that the United States will never reach social acceptance levels of LGBTI rights on par with European nations.[28] Tension remains between American attitudes toward homosexuality and US government reforms promoting LGBTI rights internationally.

LGBTI equality remains contested across the globe.[29] It was not inevitable in 2011 that the United States would begin LGBTI rights diplomacy at all. As late as 2008, American diplomats under the Bush administration were directed to support anti-LGBTI states in the UN and deter progressive LGBTI reforms within the UN.[30] Only three years later, the State Department reversed its stance on acknowledging LGBTI rights in foreign relations. The central question for the US case study, therefore, presents the following puzzle: how did the United States, a historically conservative nation on homosexuality, catapult LGBTI rights into one of its central human rights foreign policy agendas?

This chapter uncovers the policy reform process to include LGBTI rights that came about as a result of the following factors: NGO advocacy and transnational activism, insider government leadership, and the United States' national identity and international reputation. Within the first section regarding NGO advocacy, I analyze four of the most effective tactics employed by NGOs to influence policy reform: direct protest by NGOs against state policies, garnering support from gatekeeper organizations, institutional advocacy, and diffusing political opposition to LGBTI rights. NGO actors work around the world with limited human and financial resources. Understanding successful and failed tactics provides lessons for other contemporary human rights social movements. It is therefore important to examine closely the most effective tactics and strategies that influenced foreign affairs institutions.

Following the discussion of NGO advocacy techniques, this chapter examines the role of powerful insider allied leadership in foreign policy. Working from inside the State Department, these leaders circumvented US social critics of LGBTI rights to achieve the inclusion of these goals into US human rights foreign policy. There were countless influential leaders working from within institutions: Ambassador Samantha Power, Special Envoy Randy Berry, Assistant Secretary Michael Posner, Assistant Secretary Tom Malinowski, Deputy Assistant Secretary Daniel Baer, as well as many other influential assistant secretaries, ambassadors, and diplomats. NGO advocacy from outside the government would not have been powerful enough to reform US foreign policy without these influential leaders. The US case study demonstrates a social movement where actors outside of the state effectively worked with allied leaders inside the state to advance movement goals within foreign affairs institutions.

Finally, this chapter reveals how diplomatic motivation for policy reform is in part due to the United States' national identity and human rights record. Coming off the cusp of a tarnished international reputation on human rights under the Bush administration, US diplomats focused on LGBTI rights as a space for the United States to regain ground for the country's global reputation. LGBTI diplomacy was a new frontier policy pillar for the Obama administration's State Department leaders; it was an issue where they could make a clear distinction and departure from the antagonistic policies of the Bush administration. Ambassador Samantha Power recounts that "supporting at-risk LGBTI people in other countries was breaking new ground" where "just a few weeks into Obama's presidency, our administration reversed course" and joined other countries in the UN moving toward pro-LGBTI equality policies.[31] After 2009, leaders in the State Department prioritized human rights in the UN and other international forums, in part to protect the human rights of LGBTI people, in part to construct a new reputation for the United States within the international community.

Human Rights in US Foreign Policy: Definitions and Framework

The United States has some of the most far-reaching foreign policy operations in the world, with a US embassy or consulate present in nearly every nation around the globe. While human rights promotion is a one pillar of this US foreign policy, human rights is only one of many interests driving US bilateral relationships, often dwarfed by military and economic US engagement, both in funding and diplomatic prioritization of efforts.[32] International aid funding historically represents less than 1 percent of the overall US budget.[33] According to one US ambassador, the role of an American diplomat focuses on four key elements: creating jobs for Americans, protecting American citizens abroad, promoting democracy and stability so as to create better trade partners and a stable world order, and working toward nonproliferation of arms and nuclear weapons.[34] Therefore, for many American leaders in foreign policy institutions, promoting human rights and democracy leads to increased stability, which ultimately benefits American economic and security interests.

American leaders often justify human rights promotion not only for altruistic ends of improving foreign people's lives, but also to benefit US national security interests. Political scientists have long asserted a more realist, pragmatic argument in the vein of national security interests for nations to promote human rights diplomacy.[35] Müllerson explains that the violation of human rights is a direct indicator of impending instability; unstable countries are bad for business and threaten the security of other countries.[36] Human rights abuses are often the root of societal conflict. Therefore, human rights diplomacy promises to lead to greater regional and international stability.[37] Furthermore, a stream of literature in international relations recognizes the indirect benefit of international participation in either trade or military interests to the donor country, not just the recipient nation.[38] Reinforcing analysts' assertion that human rights are not often enough justification in and of themselves, American officials in this research echoed scholars' assertions that promoting human rights is in the United States' economic and security interests.[39] In 2019, the State Department summarized the United States' human rights foreign policy as such:[40]

> The Bureau of Democracy, Human Rights, and Labor champions American values, including the rule of law and individual rights, that promote strong, stable, prosperous, and sovereign states. We advance American security in the struggle against authoritarianism and terrorism when we stand for the freedoms of religion, speech, and the press, and the rights of people to assemble peaceably and to petition their government for a redress of grievances.

Human rights diplomacy is one aspect of the larger US foreign policy framework; within the human rights agenda that includes freedom of speech, women's rights, religious freedom, and a host of other human rights issues, LGBTI rights is only one pillar of human rights diplomacy. How, therefore, do US officials articulate LGBTI rights as a direct connection to security and military interests and broader US foreign policy goals? It is of key importance, therefore, to explore the history and motivations for the United States to promote human rights in foreign policy in the first place.

Since WWII, foreign policy leaders have understood that allowing leaders to commit genocide and extreme discrimination of their countries' ethnic and religious minorities can lead to civil conflict and world war. However, it was not until a few decades later that human rights in foreign policy was formally institutionalized into the State Department by US President Jimmy Carter in the 1970s.[41] During his presidency, Carter asserted, "First, we have reaffirmed America's commitment to human rights as a fundamental tenet of our foreign policy. No common mystique of blood or soil unites us. What draws us together is a belief in human freedom."[42] Since the Carter administration, American diplomats have formally promoted free and fair elections, the right for political opponents to organize and run for office, political activists and journalists to freely criticize society, and disability and labor rights, among other issues of concern in the human rights field. Since 1977, the political section of embassies globally is tasked with creating a human rights portfolio and reporting annually on each country's human rights practices, trafficking in persons, religious freedom practices, and labor rights.[43] Human rights reporting and diplomatic engagement with the host country is a required part of each embassy staff's diplomatic work. Depending on the human rights issue, the United States issues a host of responses, ranging from potential sanctions in the case of trafficking in persons, for example, to funding toward programmatic work to address the human rights issue in the country. These reports are required to be submitted to the US Congress annually. Since the inception of the reports, Congress came to rely on the reports as "the most authoritative and complete statement on human rights conditions available."[44] These reports on internal human rights practices inform US congressional and diplomatic engagement, as well as American bilateral relations with each country.

However, while US embassy staffs engage in human rights diplomacy as part of a comprehensive foreign policy agenda, foreign leaders commonly do not welcome discussions of their internal human rights abuses. Human rights discussions are often perceived as meddling in foreign cultures' internal affairs. Leaders in Pakistan, for example, have decried American LGBTI diplomacy in Islamabad as a form of "cultural imperialism."[45] In 2014, the *Guardian* reported on Rauda Morcos, a prominent Palestinian lesbian activist, who criticized US and other Western leaders' efforts to help LGBTI communities as "a patronizing, colonial approach."[46] The Senegalese President Macky Sall in 2013 rejected President Obama's call for African leaders to decriminalize homosexuality and countered in public statements that Senegal had long since abolished capital punishment (whereas the United States still has the death penalty).[47] Anti-colonial and social movement scholars assert the problematic power dynamic in international relations.[48] Queer theory scholars problematize the dominant uniform expression of LGBTI identities in international relations.[49] A body of literature, exemplified by Picq and Thiel, as well as Rahman, assesses how international efforts to promote human rights at times can perpetuate social inequalities and preserve and exacerbate Western power dynamics.[50]

Wealthy countries often set the human rights agenda and use their political weight with more impoverished countries who may want to prioritize other issues, that is, hunger, civil war, and so forth. Ambassadors from non-Western countries try to raise issues of homelessness, gun violence, and universal health care. Commonly, when I was a diplomat and raised a controversial topic such as domestic violence or gender equality, foreign dignitaries often countered about their country's homelessness and lack of universal health care. American and other diplomats articulate LGBTI rights as interconnected to healthy, functioning economies and societies. However, this message can fall short when it is perceived as hypocritical, veiled neocolonialism[51] and wealthy countries meddling in the internal affairs of other cultures.

Given its highly contentious nature, human rights diplomacy can hinder other aspects of US foreign policy and thus be perceived by both foreign leaders, as well as American diplomats themselves, at times as against US interests. For example, host governments have threatened to expel ambassadors for attending the trials of political dissidents, participating in Pride events, or calling for independent monitors of elections.[52] LGBTI rights diplomacy is similar to the diplomatic work of other more traditional human rights pillars; as with all human rights work, it inherently intrudes upon the domestic structures of foreign societies. As one leader stated, advocating for LGBTI rights, similar to other human rights policy, is difficult work: "It makes embassies conduct uncomfortable meetings, and pits other U.S. interests against promoting equal rights; LGBTI rights promotion is not that unique to general human rights diplomacy work."[53] Prioritizing human rights at times strains ties with foreign leaders and nations.

Alongside foreign leaders, human rights diplomacy also draws great criticism from American leaders themselves. Some US ambassadors and lower-level diplomats resist engaging in human rights diplomacy in a foreign country, claiming this work hurts other US national interests. Former Secretary of State Henry Kissinger was a champion of realpolitik and argued that human rights considerations would impair bilateral relations with US allies.[54] In his inaugural speech as US secretary of state in 1973, Kissinger stated, "I believe it is dangerous for us [the United States] to make the domestic policy of countries around the world a direct objective of US foreign policy."[55] Within broader geopolitical realities, it is difficult not to upset sensitive relations with leaders in places such as Bahrain, Kuwait, and Pakistan. Diplomats can become reticent to raise controversial human rights issues to maintain positive relations because of economic or security interests in the region. Internal policy debates remain in US foreign policy engagement regarding when, if at all, to raise human rights issues with foreign counterparts.

Given the risks of human rights diplomacy to other US national interests, why then would the United States engage in it? The compelling explanation lies in the United States' historical, religious, and moral values, best explained through a constructivist theoretical lens advanced by authors such as Brysk, Ingebritsen, and Klotz.[56] Constructivism theory posits that states construct an identity of their nation where ideas and norms shape identity and motivate political action.[57] Material gains are not always at the forefront of a state's interest. While promoting LGBTI rights furthers goals of equality and, potentially, long-term national security, constructivists argue that normative values in international relations are often an aspect of policy constructed from national identity. Klotz posits that norms are not necessarily just a product of economic gains, but rather a fundamental component of the international system and actors' definitions of their interests.[58] Brysk argues that, "at the international level, human rights foreign policy is more than guilt or charity—it is a constructive form of identity politics."[59] US human rights diplomacy is underpinned by an ethos that the United States, especially in comparison with China and Russia, is a moral superpower.

Beginning with the Carter administration, the United States began formally advocating for human rights promotion as a moral, ethical issue for the American people. Roberta Cohen at the Brookings Institute asserts:

> In the 1970s, many Americans felt that the US had reached a moral nadir after the Vietnam War, the secret bombing of Cambodia, disturbing revelations about US military and economic support for police states in the Americas. . . It was felt that America was straying too far from its traditional values and interests and this was affecting America's position in the world. . . . The human rights policy of the 1970s was thus a reaction to a foreign policy largely devoid of ethical considerations.[60]

American leaders historically inculcate perceived American values into the country's foreign policy. President Ronald Reagan, alluding to the biblical metaphor, often referred to the United States as a "shining city on a hill," articulating his belief that the United States should be a moral guide to other nations.[61] The divide from myth and reality of this stance aside, it is important to understand the moral motivations of many American leaders in constructing their national identity by promoting a normative foreign policy. As attitudes and interests change over time, leaders will support foreign policy agendas that do not necessarily lead to economic gain, but rather increase moral standing in international relations.[62] Human rights in foreign policy are partly motivated by American leaders' perceived interest in renewing or upholding the United States' international reputation and moral leadership.

LGBTI FOREIGN POLICY AS PART OF ITS HUMAN RIGHTS POLICY

Drafted in 1948, the UN Declaration of Human Rights (UNDHR) did not include any references to LGBTI rights. At the time, many world leaders perceived same-sex relations as a mental illness. Over the course of the decades, the United States and other nations have incorporated the original tenets of the UNDHR and also added new ones—since LGBTI rights in the early 2000s—to international human rights laws, treaties, and foreign policies.

Similar to labor, disability, and religious minority rights, LGBTI rights have mainly been incorporated into the broader portfolio of human rights policy and programs and diplomatic work. The concept of LGBTI rights is comprehensive and complex and includes the range of tenets outlined in the international Yogyakarta Principles.[63] The State Department's policy centers diplomatic engagement mainly around two issues: ending violence and discrimination of LGBTI people worldwide, and advocating to abolish criminalization of same-sex relations. According to Michael Posner, assistant secretary, Bureau of Democracy, Human Rights, and Labor under Clinton:

> We started out in the international context dealing with violence and discrimination against the LGBT community. Leading with gay marriage is not the place we would start, but we have to recognize how absolutely perilous it is for people in places like Uganda and many other places I visit, I make a point of meeting with the LGBT community. And a lot of them are—you know, it's almost clandestine meetings. Their lives are at risk, so I think you start with the things that they themselves are asking for, and you build out from that.[64]

Diplomats focused not on the burgeoning developments of the complexities of rights and identities as demonstrated in the Yogyakarta Principles, but rather on the most egregious of human rights abuses. Uganda and Iran's death penalty law, or the Kyrgyz Republic's proposed criminalization law, for example, are the center of diplomatic attention.

Modern foreign policy encompasses a wide variety of options and diplomatic responses to human rights abuses, from improving relations to sanctions and cutting ties between countries.[65] In response to a country threatening to kill a human rights advocate, for example, diplomats may issue a statement of condemnation, demarche of a foreign ambassador, or threaten to revoke foreign leaders' visas to the United States. For example, before becoming prime minister of India, Narendra Modi, who was chief minister of Gujarat State at the time, was denied a visa to the United States in 2005 for his role in religious and sectarian violence in Gujarat.[66] Known in international relations theory as a "stick," or punishment for abuses, diplomats also may employ "carrots," or incentives for another country to change actions or policies.[67] Carrots refer to a variety of diplomatic tools to leverage for improvements in human rights. Choosing a carrot or stick is largely predicated on the nature of the relationship between the two countries; tense relations often lead to sticks, that is, US relations with Iran or Venezuela; positive relations can turn into carrots, that is, US relations with Jordan or Morocco. One influential carrot, or leverage tool, to improve human rights globally is through foreign aid and funding local civil society.

The leading global funding mechanism for LGBTI civil society is through the Global Equality Fund (GEF).[68] Support for the GEF comes from numerous governments, multilateral agencies, and private philanthropic organizations. GEF provides assistance to organizations globally to end violence, hate crimes, and discrimination. The "Dignity for All" LGBTI Emergency Assistance Program delivers emergency assistance to NGOs and international advocates facing physical threat or harassment from local authorities in response to their LGBTI human rights work.[69] Some scholars have problematized this fund, and other international LGBTI funding sources, criticizing that, at times, international development funding from Western governments supplants local constructions of sexuality.[70] Conversely, Burack finds many LGBTI human rights defenders looking to this source of funding, and the United States, as an "important force" in international advocacy and assistance.[71] While not without controversy, GEF programs are tailored to each country and cultural context. Policy officers work closely with local LGBTI individuals, organizations, and leaders for program conceptualization, management, and evaluation of the work.

In conjunction with the State Department, the United States' lead foreign policy institution and central humanitarian aid agency, USAID, hosts a variety of funds and develops policies to promote LGBTI rights globally. Since 2011, USAID has included LGBTI rights in its comprehensive international development policy, stating, "At USAID, equal access to foreign aid is not only a matter of human rights, but also critical to holistic, comprehensive and inclusive development. USAID proudly champions Lesbian, Gay, Bisexual, Transgender and Intersex (LGBTI) interests in our policies, practices and initiatives."[72]

Since 2011, USAID integrated concerns specific to LGBTI populations into various rubrics of global health, violence against women, democracy, governance, and beyond.[73] This work continued under the Trump and
Biden administrations with a public-private partnership fund, the LGBTI
Global Development Partnership (LGBTI-GDP).[74] The LGBTI-GDP trains
local civil society organizations in advocacy, peaceful participation in political processes, human rights reporting and documentation, and business
development.[75] Given the history of LGBTI discrimination in foreign affairs
institutions, coupled with continuing inequality in the United States, it
is remarkable for an US foreign affairs organization to champion LGBTI
rights. The next section turns to an analysis of how US-based and international NGOs influenced policy change in US foreign affairs.

NGO Advocacy

Civil society leaders and NGO advocates were critical players in reforming
American foreign relations. Tremblay, Paternotte, and Johnson assert that
the lesbian and gay movement's tactics and history, compared with the
women's or worker's movements, are still poorly known.[76] Some actions
have been public and visible, such as direct public protest, while some are
less publicly visible, such as institutional advocacy and coalition building
of advocate organizations. This section examines the political opportunity
structures and diverse tactics employed by US and transnational advocates
to influence reform.

Direct Protest Against LGBTI State Policies

The most visible tactic of NGOs to reform US foreign policy toward LGBTI
equality norms has been through direct, public protest against state policies.
The US government has a tumultuous history of LGBTI discrimination.[77]
In the United States, activism has often been spurred by discrimination,
violence, and repression. For decades, the public shaming and firing of
individuals suspected of being LGBTI was common practice by the State
Department and other federal agencies. Johnson asserts that during the
"Lavender Scare" the blacklisting, active discrimination, and firing of federal
government employees launched a new civil rights struggle.[78] Under these
policies, 4,380 gay men and women were discharged from the military and

about 500 fired from government jobs in the State Department, Department of Defense, and other government jobs.[79] Extending far beyond the McCarthy era up to 1975, the US federal government could remove a federal employee for "immoral conduct"—which was often a euphemism for homosexuality.[80] US diplomats today still recount how as late as the 1990s, LGBTI diplomats' careers were often at risk if they dared to live openly.[81]

Over the decades, organizations were established in direct protest against antagonistic state policies. Throughout many iterations of the LGBTI movement in the United States, NGOs have used direct activism to protest federal policies. Paradoxically, the policies to discriminate and fire LGBTI people from national security agencies led to organizing and fierce opposition from LGBTI advocates. Organized opposition is a leading factor for ultimately changing the State Department's policy from considering LGBTI persons a pariah within American society to LGBTI rights becoming a priority in US foreign relations. Social movement literature helps explain the processes, strategies, and resource mobilization used by groups seeking to reform public policy over time. In her book *When Protest Makes Policy*, Laurel Weldon demonstrates how protest is often the central tactic for groups and organizations to influence government policy.[82] Weldon establishes how social movements are critical avenues for political representation, especially in the case of excluded and disadvantaged groups.[83] Direct protests are a visible and public manifestation that contests and influences state priorities.

Dovetailed with direct protest, advocates establish formal organizations to collectively make their demands. Protests at times lead to the formal establishment of civil society organizations. According to Tilly and Wood, a core element of social movements is a "sustained, organized public effort making collective claims on target authorities."[84] Similarly, a swath of social movement literature argues that organizations and groups often form in response to experiences of repression and domination.[85] The historical relationship of LGBTI Americans with the US government has been mired in conflict and neglect. Scholars document the mobilization of the American LGBTI movement that occurred in response to the federal firings of LGBTI people.[86] One of the outcomes was the Mattachine Society, a (primarily white, gay, and male) LGBTI organization founded by Harry Hay in 1950.[87] The Mattachine Society's central goal was to combat the Eisenhower administration's policy of firing homosexuals serving as diplomats and changing internal policy that labeled LGBTI individuals as a national security risk.[88] Heather Hines's research demonstrates how "following the Lavender Scare, gay and lesbian societies were created to help combat societally engrained homophobia."[89] In the decades after the McCarthy era, LGBTI activism rose exponentially in open opposition and protest to US federal policies.

Throughout the 1960s, 1970s, and 1980s, LGBTI groups worked to change US perceptions and public policies toward LGBTI rights.[90] During the global HIV/AIDS crisis in the 1980s and 1990s, American advocates mainly used street protests to gain access to and attention from the state, directing tactics against US embassies and institutions to contest the government's agenda domestically and internationally. Americans responded to the government's failure to address the crisis with public demonstrations. One advocate remembered, "Everything we knew was to protest against the government."[91] Public protest was the central tactic of NGOs. An NGO leader involved in four decades of LGBTI activism reflected that in the 1980s, activists acted in "reaction to either the extreme passivism or antagonism from the [US] government."[92] Under the Reagan and George H. W. Bush administrations, antagonistic federal policy stimulated an organized response from LGBTI advocates. Throughout the vast and diverse US movement for equality, advocacy tactics were spurred on by the denial, anger, and frustration advocates have felt from government officials.

Participants in the research for this book stressed that it is difficult to comprehend today (in 2021) the anger and desperation that was felt by members of the community during the HIV/AIDS crisis of the 1980s and 1990s.[93] Interviewees reflected, "We were watching our friends and colleagues die around us; it was a matter of life and death."[94] In the 1980s and 1990s, many HIV/AIDS support groups formed to challenge the US government's denial of the crisis and its lack of funding for HIV/AIDS medication and research.[95] Prior to the Stonewall riots in 1969, there were approximately fifty lesbian and gay groups established in the United States. Within two years, fifty had exponentially increased to 2,500 formal groups advocating for LGBTI reforms (mainly gay and lesbian at the time). In a classic social movement model,[96] the groups began defining LGBTI identity, then identifying political opportunities and publicly advocating for equality. Extensive scholarship examines Stonewall and the US domestic LGBTI movement.[97] The goal of this book is to contribute to the limited scholarship that investigates how LGBTI civil society groups influenced US foreign policy.

During the HIV/AIDS crisis, activists also turned their advocacy efforts toward international institutions to work toward global LGBTI equality norms. Thus, the UN became an important venue for advocates to further their human rights claims. During the George W. Bush administration, LGBTI advocates were motivated by the discriminatory policies from the federal government and organized in response to official anti-LGBTI equality policies. As late as 2008, the United States was not a neutral player on LGBTI rights in the UN. In fact, one foreign policy leader recounted how the United States allied with anti-LGBTI states, such as the Vatican and Gulf nations, to block proposed LGBTI reforms within the UN.[98] In 2008, for example, the United States refused to sign the General Assembly statement when sixty-six other member states in the UN condemned human rights violations based on sexual orientation and gender identity.[99] Many LGBTI advocates, some of whom were former diplomats and US ambassadors, resigned from the State Department in protest.[100] In the early 2000s, when a great deal of social progress within American society had been achieved and continued to gain momentum, it became untenable for some American diplomats to work with the policy directive from the State Department to block reform in international venues. Those hostile policies again drove protest, frustration, and the establishment of civil society groups opposing the State Department agenda at the time.

As a result of frustration and anger about US policy in the UN, leading diplomats and advocates established the Council for Global Equality (CGE) to combat anti-LGBTI policies within international affairs. One of CGE's original founders stated: "We had seen and experienced how our own government, under the Bush administration, undermined LGBTI rights in foreign affairs, especially in international institutions; we thus decided to create the Council (CGE)."[101] Similar to the McCarthy and Reagan eras, the antagonism of the Bush administration motivated LGBTI advocates to mobilize. The same CGE founder asserted that the initial goal was to create an organization with the intent to dissent that the Bush administration was "not even neutral on our rights, they were antagonistic."[102] It was another key moment of charged activism to contest state policies.

Unlike countries such as Sweden, where civil society groups enjoy greater opportunities to build alliances within the halls of government, US-based LGBTI advocates historically orient their advocacy in a position of opposition to state policies.[103] With regard to direct action protests from the street, advocates stressed that before the Obama administration, they only knew how to publicly protest and employ outsider strategies against the state."[104] Public challenge and protest remain the primary tools advocates use to advance LGBTI rights since the origins of the American LGBTI movement.

Building Coalitions, Documentation, and Convincing Gatekeeper Organizations

LGBTI civil society groups formed to combat state policies. Simultaneously, civil society groups began to build coalitions with larger human rights organizations. Establishing these alliances brought political clout and legitimacy to LGBTI rights claims. In the early 1970s, LGBTI rights was a new concept and not yet considered a human right. One advocate recounted how their group of transgender advocates still debated among themselves whether they were mentally ill.[105] To establish their case that this was a human rights issue, fledgling LGBTI organizations first had to rigorously document LGBTI abuses. Human rights abuse documentation served to convince larger gatekeeper organizations of the importance of their cause. Scholars Keck and Sikkink assert that "to be credible, the information produced by networks must be reliable and well documented; to gain attention, the information must be timely and dramatic."[106] At a university presentation Amie Bishop, a senior researcher with Outright Action International, stated, "If there is no documentation and no measurement, then we don't exist."[107] Amnesty International (AI) and Human Rights Watch (HRW) are considered "gatekeeper" organizations because they serve to define the scope of international human rights norms.[108] As two of the most reputable and established human rights organizations in the world, the agendas of AI and HRW have a significant influence on the setting of new human rights norms. Clifford Bob and others have found that AI and HRW fundamentally define what is considered universal in the international human rights discourse.[109] Foreign policy leaders engaged in human rights look to Amnesty, HRW, and other large international human rights organizations to set the human rights agenda. Scholars have noted that the initial steps for the creation of a new category of human rights are for advocacy groups to make their case, frame their policy goals, then set policy agendas to focus on that new right.[110] LGBTI leaders and groups advocated at length for AI and HRW to place LGBTI rights within the broader framework of internationally recognized human rights.[111] Initially, in the 1970s, AI and HRW were amenable to the idea of collaboration, but were hesitant because of the lack of documented evidence regarding LGBTI abuse and discrimination globally.

Documentation of LGBTI abuses was critical to convincing gatekeeper organizations to include LGBTI rights in the broader international human rights agenda. In the 1970s, LGBTI persons were largely a hidden minority, and there was a near complete lack of documentation globally

concerning LGBTI rights discrimination. Human rights scholar and practitioner Jo Becker asserts that human rights groups must be able to document abuses to gain broader legitimacy of their grievance and further the
movement.[112] Similarly, scholars analyze failed and successful human rights
campaigns and argue that the documentation of abuses, especially bodily
harm, is essential.[113] In places such as Uganda, Indonesia, or Russia, a person could be killed for merely identifying as LGBTI, making it exceedingly
difficult to even consider publicly reporting violence against them due to
their sexual orientation or gender identity.[114] Despite the risks, advocates
began collecting evidence of specific cases and abuses. One LGBTI leader
interviewed for this book stated: "Human rights work is essentially documentation work; [in the 1970s and 1980s] we had to prove human rights
abuses were happening around the world in order to be accepted."[115] Because
of the critical need for systematic documentation, LGBTI groups focused on
gathering systemic evidence of abuses against LGBTI individuals in places
such as Russia, Peru, and Brazil.[116]

  Clear documentation of homophobic and transphobic abuse was, and
continues to be, difficult for LGBTI rights groups. Referencing descriptions
of homosexuals during the 1950s Lavender Scare, Johnson describes how
much of the newspaper coverage "was cryptic, resorting to coded language
that must be carefully interpreted by historians."[117] Similarly, Toops documents how in the 1950s, US senators referred to lesbians as "unmention-
ables."[118] Euphemisms for homosexuality were common in the United States
and remain common in many countries. In Turkey, for example, authorities
arrest LGBTI persons on charges of misconduct, such as "disturbing public
order," in response to their political activism.[119] Given the often oblique
language of targeting LGBTI groups, LGBTI advocacy groups and researchers continue to face challenges documenting global human rights abuses.
Despite this challenge, LGBTI advocacy groups and researchers tracked cases
of police raids on gay establishments, harassment of university students,
public instances of beating and torture, and arrest of activists.[120] Advocates began presenting evidence and proof of global LGBTI rights abuses
based on sexual orientation to HRW and other prominent members of the
human rights community.[121] The combined efforts of activist groups engaging with powerful human rights gatekeeper organizations, such as AI and
HRW, became integral to coalescing the international LGBTI movement.
As of 2021, policy pillars of both AI and HRW specifically address international LGBTI rights discrimination.[122] Through systematic documentation
of human rights abuses and strategic coalition building, LGBTI activists

effectively integrated and expanded their agenda within broader human rights mandates.[123]

During the international HIV/AIDS crisis, the LGBTI movement garnered international allies and gained international visibility. International coalitions with local organizations in Uganda, South Africa, and Tanzania beginning in the 1990s largely focused on HIV/AIDS prevention. According to advocates reflecting on their current transnational networks, "many LGBTI transnational partnerships with African groups that exist today were generated from building coalitions during the global HIV/AIDS crisis in the 1990s."[124] Advocates have built coalitions around the HIV/AIDS crisis in Europe, Africa and across the globe to address health, international humanitarian aid, and LGBTI rights more broadly.

One of the Council for Global Equality's (CGE) initial goals in the early 2000s was to create a coalition of powerful players including AI, HRW, Human Rights Campaign, and other organizations to target US foreign affairs agencies. Although CGE is a relatively small organization with few full-time staffers, it has had an enormous impact on the State Department. According to one current US diplomat, "we would go to meetings with [CGE] and HRC, HRW, and Amnesty all would be at the same table; all of these top organizations would present to us a unified goal."[125] As Clifford Bob asserts, by building coalitions with broader organizations, LGBTI groups gain critical access to the political institutions they seek to change.[126] Coalitions of human rights groups worked to articulate LGBTI rights to US diplomats, introducing them to the already accepted international human rights framework. Many modern diplomats within the State Department were accustomed to promoting human rights abuses as defined by the UN, namely stopping violence, torture, and killing of other minority groups from authorities.[127] One US foreign policy leader stated: "It was a natural progression of our human rights policy; certain people, by virtue of their birth are discriminated against and marginalized. It had been understood for decades prior to our policy that LGBTI equality was part of fundamental rights."[128] A coalition of organizations effectively advocated foreign affairs leaders to reform their human rights diplomatic agenda and include considerations for LGBTI rights.

Targeted Institutional Advocacy

Institutional advocacy encompasses the vast political action of groups to influence institutions, including lobbying, lawsuits, and press conferences.[129]

Sabine Lang defines institutional advocacy as "the attempt to influence decision making by gaining some degree of insider status in institutions or in
organizations that initiate, prepare, legislate, or execute policy."[130] She identifies the hallmarks of those strategies as NGOs securing access and building
relationships within a government body, demonstrating that institutional
advocacy, rather than public demonstrations or other displays of public
discontent, can be more time and cost-effective for NGOs.[131] Institutional
advocacy often comes in the form of consistent and persistent meetings
and interactions of social movements' actors with key governmental interlocutors. These meetings and actions rarely make headlines and often are
not reported on in the mainstream media. In contrast to public campaigns
that are often expensive, monopolize limited resources, and have limited
effectiveness, NGOs can choose more targeted advocacy. This form of advocacy represents a critical avenue for resource mobilization of the LGBTI
movement. Targeted institutional advocacy is often less in the public eye.
However, this method of NGO advocacy was essential for reforming US
foreign policy.

Institutional advocacy efforts toward foreign affairs agencies began
when advocates started to focus their resources on assisting asylum claims
of foreign individuals facing violence and persecution based on their sexual
orientation in the 1980s and early 1990s (gender identity came later in
asylum policy).[132] The first LGBTI-based asylum claim was granted by the
US government in 1994 under the Bill Clinton administration.[133] Since the
formation of the Department of Homeland Security, asylum claims are adju-
dicated outside the State Department by civil servant adjudicators within
the Department of Homeland Security. Homeland Security officials rely on
information about human rights abuses detailed in the State Department's
annual report on human rights for each country. The reports document
each country's specific domestic human rights abuses based on a host of
factors: religion, disability, gender, among others.[134] For example, editors of
the State Department (including me from 2005–2016) often knew from
local human rights groups in North Africa that gay men were persecuted,
subjected to family and societal violence, and sometimes forced to leave
the country under this threat of violence. (We often had very little evidence or documentation at the time of the treatment of lesbians, bisexuals,
transgender, or intersex people.) We thus attempted to corroborate specific
cases and triangulate the data with local and regional human rights groups,
human rights advocates based in Washington, local capitals, and newspaper
reporting. We documented this growing body of evidence in the reports

under the section *Societal Abuses, Discrimination, and Acts of Violence Based on Sexual Orientation and Gender Identity*. As the State Department reports are used for US asylum cases, they have international legal ramifications. These reports help document who is persecuted around the world and thus who can claim asylum in many countries based on international law. Over time, these reports have increasingly included documentation of persecution of LGBTI individuals.

The victory of this first case in the early 1990s caused advocates to realize that the State Department's annual human rights reports were a critical tool for institutional advocacy. Advocates realized the importance of encouraging the State Department to document LGBTI discrimination as a distinct human rights abuse. US courts and legal advisors reference those documents as official US policy. Thus, advocates began a period of strategically targeted advocacy aimed at the State Department's Bureau of Democracy, Human Rights, and Labor (DRL). The DRL is the bureau responsible for drafting those reports for Congress and the public, documenting global human rights abuses, and crafting US human rights policies and program goals. LGBTI rights were hardly mentioned prior to the early 1990s. As the first accepted LGBTI-based asylum claim was in the courts, several reports began to include limited information on LGBTI concerns, such as the human rights report on Brazil in 1993:

> There continue to be reports of murders of homosexuals. Sao Paulo newspapers reported that 3 transvestites were murdered on March 14; other reports claimed 17 transvestites were killed in the first three months of 1993. One military policeman was charged in the March 14 killings and was awaiting trial at year's end. Homosexual rights groups claim, however, that the vast majority of perpetrators of crimes against homosexuals go unpunished.[135]

A section of the State Department's human rights report was established to specifically document "Acts of Violence, Discrimination, and Other Abuses based on Sexual Orientation and Gender Identity."[136] In part through targeted institutional advocacy efforts, the State Department began systematic reporting and detailed documentation of LGBTI abuses globally. The US government, with diplomatic presence in Brunei, rural China, and every country in Africa, has the institutional capacity to document abuses in all parts of the world, and remains required to do so by the US Congress.[137] A representative of an LGBTI advocacy organization, who was involved in the initial meetings in the late 1990s and early 2000s to convince State Department officials to include LGBTI abuses, argued that in 2016, "There is now no better global compilation of LGBTI rights than these reports. . . . No other NGO has the capacity or does the extensive global outlook like these reports."[138] Unlike NGOs with smaller budgets or smaller governments, the US government and diplomats in each embassy are tasked with collecting LGBTI abuse evidence annually. Accordingly, international advocates recognize that the State Department annual human rights reports have become critical documentation of global LGBTI abuses.[139] Although consistency and depth vary by embassy and country report, the State Department human rights reports have become one of the most comprehensive resources for advocacy against global LGBTI abuses.

By way of institutional advocacy efforts, officers became increasingly familiar with NGO staff and expertise. Thereby, US government officials consulted activist groups for their expertise and sought advice for new policies. Since 2011, CGE officers and advocates from other LGBTI advocacy organizations have served as a conduit between the State Department and local and transnational groups for the reporting and documentation of LGBTI human rights abuses. A senior-level US diplomat who worked on the State Department's annual human rights reports recalled: "Many of us were not knowledgeable about LGBTI rights when we were given the mandate to focus on them. . . the Council for Global Equality called us to offer their assistance and help us gain competency on these issues."[140] CGE officers continue to provide critical documentation of global LGBTI human rights abuses for diplomats to record in the annual State Department reports. Beyond the reports, CGE provides strategic consultations on country-specific issues of LGBTI abuses and works with key personnel in the State Department.[141] The State Department's relationship with CGE represents a significant transition from its history of routine firings of LGBTI diplomats to becoming what some advocates recognize as one of the most important international clearinghouses for global LGBTI rights abuses documentation. Under the Trump administration, CGE's did not cease institutional advocacy, but rather continued to work with "allies within the federal civil service, Congress and civil society to demonstrate the value and positive impact of inclusive foreign and development policies."[142] With the transition to the Biden administration in 2020, CGE leaders work with interagency US government leaders and call for an increased prioritization of human rights and gender equality in US foreign policy, as well as for

US leaders to restore the countries leadership in support of global LGBTI equality.[143] Strategic, targeted institutional advocacy from NGOs changed US foreign policy agendas to focus on LGBTI rights abuses.

CGE applied targeted institutional advocacy strategically in their appeal to senior State Department officials to appoint a new special envoy for the human rights of LGBTI people. Leaders in CGE, and across the advocacy community, recognized the need for a specific office and leader within the State Department to address LGBTI rights abuses globally. Advocates raised this issue in multiple meetings, policy briefs, and engagements with foreign policy leaders.[144] This goal was realized in 2015 when Secretary of State Kerry appointed Randy Berry to serve as the US special envoy for the human rights of LGBTI persons.

When the conditions of governments are receptive, advocates dedicate their time and resources toward garnering influential allies. In line with Lang's assertion of NGOs employing institutional advocacy,[145] American LGBTI advocacy groups have strategically sought the support of influential allies within the halls of US foreign policy institutions. In Thoreson's examination of transnational LGBTI activism, he argues that NGOs have a defining power to "construct, promote, and institutionalize" new LGBTI human rights norms.[146] Similarly, Joachim demonstrates that access to institutions and the agenda-setting process is "pivotal for NGOs to enable them to introduce their problems and solutions and to convince policymakers of both their significance and their validity."[147] NGOs changed their tactics depending on how well they were received by the federal government. Scholars argue that actors must adapt to policy environments, specifically by adopting new agendas, strategies, and mobilizing techniques.[148] Under Republican leadership, LGBTI NGOs have been largely shut out of the halls of power, leading those organizations to use street protests and more highly visible advocacy tactics. Conversely, NGOs have changed tactics under the last two Democratic administrations, which have exhibited more openness to LGBTI equality, and thus more openness to advocates' policy recommendations. During this time, officials accepted meetings with NGOs more often, consulted with NGOs in an advisory role, and provided more overall political opportunity structures for targeted institutional advocacy. NGOs choose the tactic of advocating within, and targeting specific institutions, when it is more beneficial than protest tactics.[149] Government officials during the Obama administration were increasingly receptive to LGBTI rights claims, creating political openings for new advocacy methods. Thus, NGOs were able to more strategically conduct targeted institutional advocacy. LGBTI advocates worked to influence decision making within US foreign policy institutions by acquiring strategic advisor status. They documented abuses and proposed policy changes within the State Department. Advocates leverage the relationship with civil servants and career diplomats to continue their work regardless of the administration in power, changing tactics and initiating creative means to diffuse political opposition.

STRATEGIES TO DIFFUSE POLITICAL OPPOSITION

In the face of opposition, advocates have generated diverse tactics to oppose hostile leaders and discriminatory policies within American foreign policy institutions. The United States is home to some of the world's most active and well-funded NGOs promoting LGBTI rights and equality. Conversely, it is also a country that hosts powerful organizations whose mission it is to combat and oppose LGBTI equality.[150] Funded centrally by private religious groups, there are numerous US-based evangelical organizations, in particular, that remain opposed to LGBTI equality.[151] Focus on the Family, Concerned Women for America, and the Family Research Council are a few of the most influential organizations.[152] As of 2019, when LGBTI diplomacy continued taking shape at the State Department, 71 percent of white American evangelicals believed same-sex relations are wrong.[153] Many American congressional leaders have, and continue, to openly oppose LGBTI equality.[154] In light of this powerful contestation, advocates of LGBTI equality developed varying strategies to diffuse both anti-LGBTI opposition groups as well as antagonistic national political leaders in Congress from blocking LGBTI rights reform in foreign affairs.

One central venue where advocates circumvented hostile American leaders was within the UN. Activists from various human rights groups and organizations seek consultative status in the UN as a mechanism to shape the international human rights agenda.[155] Consultative status is the highest status granted by the UN to an NGO and allows advocates access to key leaders, opportunities to take part in policy discussions within international forums, enhanced international legitimacy for their cause, and an ability to influence the human rights agenda. The UN has not historically granted consultative status easily or evenly to international human rights groups.[156] NGOs must invest significant time and human resources, sometimes over many years, to achieve consultative status. In 2010, OutRight Action International sought to obtain formal consultative status in the UN's Economic and Social Committee (ECOSOC).[157] As of 2019, OutRight Action International remains "the first and only U.S.-based LGBTIQ human rights organization to obtain consultative status with the United Nations Economic and Social Council (ECOSOC)."[158] A key part of OutRight Action International's successful bid was to address and oppose political opposition from leaders within its own country, specifically oppositional Republican leaders within Congress.

Two influential congressmen, Republican Congressmen Chris Smith (R-New Jersey) and Trent Franks (R-Arizona), opposed OutRight Action's bid for consultative status. They led a campaign to oppose OutRight's formal recognition in the UN. Smith and Franks co-drafted a letter claiming that the "preservation of the rights of freedom of expression and freedom of religion require that (OutRight) undergo further review in the standard review process."[159] Smith and Franks joined forces with Islamic governments to oppose OutRight's bid for consultative status.[160] In response, OutRight officers mobilized. They sought support from a host of allied US and global leadership and organizations that supported their bid, including from influential leaders such as John Kerry, who was then-chairman of the United States Senate Foreign Relations Committee, as well as leaders from other LGBTI-friendly UN member nations. OutRight also garnered allies within the office of UN/AIDS. Finally, although an unusual appeal from an organization from the global north, OutRight beseeched support from LGBTI organizations located in the global south. Groups in Brazil and Argentina vocalized support for American-based OutRight Action International.[161] Thus, it was an illustrative case of the importance of transnational advocacy networks bolstering advocacy efforts across traditional regional divides. In the end, OutRight gathered more than 160 leaders and organizations in support of their bid for consultative status in the UN. Colum Lynch in *Foreign Policy* asserted:

> In previous years, American conservatives like Smith, backed by the White House and the Vatican, exercised enormous influence on social matters at the United Nations. But the letter from Smith and Franks appeared to have backfired, awakening Congressional leadership that has grown decidedly more liberal during the past two years.[162]

OutRight's ability to combat powerful leaders and organize allies in opposition to these leaders affirms the pattern noted by scholars that LGBTI equality and coalition building in some cases can emerge from backlash and opposition.[163]

The antagonistic forces from within Congress became a focal point for action from international leaders. Social movement scholars find that official backlash for equality can lead activists to "find resonant frames, build internal solidarity, and win allies—even when social movement resources are minimal."[164] Obtaining consultative status was key to the group's international advocacy. Circumventing powerful US congressmen was an important tactic for achieving that status. Through their role in the UN, OutRight Action International holds governments accountable for human rights violations, raises concerns of LGBTI people on the agenda at the intergovernmental level, and hosts global LGBTI delegates participating in strategy and advocacy meetings with UN staff and government representatives.[165] Importantly, they are able to influence the entire global human rights dialogue.

Another critical tactic LGBTI advocates have used is to strategically frame their issues. While opposition to LGBTI rights remains robust in the United States, the level of opposition varies. Some conservatives oppose same-sex marriage, yet do not condone the killing or jailing of LGBTI people. Short of material resources, scholars stress the importance of effective strategic framing for NGOs to legitimize their issues.[166] When working with some conservative leaders, advocates carefully crafted and framed their message, stressing the terminology of "fundamental freedoms" for LGBTI persons globally, rather than "LGBTI rights" in certain venues. The term "fundamental freedom" is largely associated with Republicans and American conservatism.[167] Focusing on fundamental freedoms, rather than "rights," harkens closer to a conservative political ethos, covering the topics of freedom of assembly, expression, and association. Scholar Christina Kiel demonstrates the idea that civil society groups can effectively graft issues to existing norms possessing political salience for a particular audience.[168] The central issue NGO leaders repeatedly stressed was that when addressing opposition forces in the United States, they found that "we can disagree about marriage equality; but no one believes people should be stoned or beheaded due to how they were born."[169] Advocates stated for this research that Republican support for protections of LGBTI people from being killed in places such as Jamaica and Uganda became a "safe place" for them to stand politically on the issue.[170] While it was politically untenable for some leaders to support marriage equality, many conservative leaders began to agree that violence against and killing of LGBTI people was wrong.[171] Focusing on the worst forms of discrimination and abuse against LGBTI people globally was, and remains, the central tactic used by advocates to counter political opposition to LGBTI human rights diplomacy. Raising awareness about human rights activists killed in Iran or jailed in Cuba neutralized opposition. In 2009, some Republicans joined the Congressional LGBT Equality Caucus.[172] The elimination of hate-motivated violence, domestically and globally, was a central mission of the Caucus.[173] Advocates calibrated discussions with conservative leaders away from controversial topics of same-sex marriage or gender-neutral bathrooms. Instead, they framed the issue on life and death, thus garnering some conservative support for an American focus on LGBTI rights abuses globally. Focusing on finding common ground on basic human rights represents a key strategy to buttress the longevity of LGBTI diplomatic policy.[174] Ayoub demonstrates that LGBTI advocates in global contexts choose different frames that resonate best within their organizations' cultural and national context.[175] Concentrating on the worst forms of discrimination and violence toward LGBTI people were two issues where advocates garnered consensus and diffused political opposition.

With LGBTI issues framed in terms of fundamental freedoms, conservative leaders were more willing to engage on human rights abuses with historic adversaries of the US government. Human rights policy is thus applied in an unequal world.[176] Within human rights institutions, the agenda is inculcated with racial and income power dynamics between states that often disadvantage lower-income, non-white, former colonial nations.[177] In the US context, leaders at times lambast a country for a human rights abuse with an adversarial government, whereas they will remain silent on the same human rights abuse from an ally nation.[178] For example, Cuba became a country for leaders to highlight and criticize LGBTI human rights abuses. Conservative Cuban-American leaders, for example, began to include LGBTI discrimination as one of the many human rights grievances of the Castro regime. Human rights advocates and leaders who denounce the actions of the Castro regime can become the heros/heroines of the Cuban-American community in Florida, the home to many Cubans who fled the Castro regime.[179] LGBTI rights became incorporated into the overall US foreign policy dialogue with the Cuban government.[180] Non-strategic or non-allied countries are thus a softer target for the US government to criticize human rights abuses. When the Trump administration announced the relaunch of the "global effort to end criminalization of homosexuality," observers noted that leaders first highlighted the hanging of a young gay man in Iran, "Trump's top geopolitical foe."[181] Taking into account strategic international relations also made addressing LGBTI rights in foreign affairs more tenable for hawkish, or even oppositional conservative US leaders.

Insider Allied Government Leadership

In tandem with activists working toward reform from outside the government, insider allied leadership and decision makers within US foreign policy institutions were instrumental to LGBTI policy reform. Burack contends that LGBTI rights in US foreign policy "emerged from within executive branch agencies, in coordination between civil servants and civil and human rights activists outside of government."[182] Developing literature demonstrates the critical coordination between insider bureaucrats and outsider activists for policy change.[183] Furthermore, insider government allies have been historically overlooked in social movement analysis, yet can play a critical factor in changing policy from within the halls of government.[184] Far more than nominal allies of LGBTI equality, some career civil servants, diplomatic advisers, ambassadors, and interagency leaders served in central roles leading to the inclusion of LGBTI rights in US foreign policy.

Internal leaders, as well as numerous ambassadors serving worldwide in US embassies, took key leadership roles drafting new LGBTI diplomacy policy, especially between 2009 and 2011.[185] Prior to this time, LGBTI rights concerns were part of peripheral considerations chiefly addressed by the State Department's Office of Global Women's Issues and Bureau of Democracy, Human Rights, and Labor. Leaders and officers in regional bureaus, such as the Bureau of Near East Affairs (NEA) and the Bureau of South and Central Asian Affairs (SCA), traditionally are more reticent to raise human rights concerns and generally conservative to policy change. However, NEA and SCA desk officers also began raising awareness of human rights abuses and violence against LGBTI individuals in places such as Lebanon, Egypt, Iraq, Afghanistan, and Pakistan. The work became formalized and streamlined in US embassies globally when Secretary Clinton's leadership team drafted an internal State Department cable to all US chiefs of missions. This cable outlined specific mandates and a host of tools for each embassy to tailor for suggested programs and diplomatic efforts for each country to improve LGBTI rights.[186] Daniel Baer, deputy assistant secretary of the Bureau of Democracy, Human Rights, and Labor, was a lead drafter of the cable and stated:

> I helped Secretary Clinton write the cable that she sent to all ambassadors actually, a year before she gave her famous speech. . . In her first year as secretary she sent a cable out to

every U.S. ambassador around the world and said, gay people, LGBT people are part of our human rights work. And you should treat the human rights of LGBT people as you would any other human rights issue and this is now part of your portfolio.[187]

With this cable, and further official communications from the State Department headquarters, LGBTI rights were no longer an abstract issue of concern. Institutionally, LGBTI rights became on par with all other embassy human rights work. From this directive, embassies received decisive instructions to create implementation plans to address LGBTI abuses in their host countries.

The implementation of foreign policy manifests differently for each region and country. US embassies create an annual *Mission Strategic Plan* that outlines US priority goals in each country.[188] Embassy staff work closely with local civil society groups and human rights activists to generate a strategic plan for the country. One central author of the cable said it was inspired by a question a US ambassador asked Clinton: "Are we allowed to work on [LGBTI rights] now?"[189] The ambassador was poised to begin LGBTI diplomacy upon receiving the go-ahead from headquarters. That same ambassador shared with Clinton's central team in Main State that embassy staff felt "hindered by the previous administration during the Bush years" on this issue, and felt the time was right for diplomatic engagement with the host country on LGBTI rights.[190] USAID's senior LGBT coordinator Todd Larson noted that he did not meet widespread opposition to his mandate; he stated, "I am, rather, working with a team of committed and experienced folks to guide and focus an institution which is already very committed to LGBT(I) inclusion in how it operates both internally and externally."[191] Deemed by some scholars as "professional feminists"[192] in the case of the women's movement, officers and bureaucrats were influential actors for movement organizing within local, state, or federal government.

This research demonstrates that implementation and reform requires a commitment from all working levels inside US foreign policy institutions. In 1992, for example, a group of State Department employees founded Gays and Lesbians in Foreign Affairs Agencies (GLIFAA) to serve as a voice protecting gays and lesbians from discrimination. Originally GLIFAA worked to combat the State Department's official discrimination of LGBTI people in the security clearance process.[193] Beyond the security clearance,

GLIFAA members worked for years from within the Department to reform discriminatory bureaucratic practices toward LGBTI employees.[194] Special Envoy Berry referenced that when he formerly served in Uganda in the 1999, he submitted a draft of the Uganda human rights report to the State Department headquarters. The report referenced hardships experienced by the LGBT community. However, DRL officers at the time rejected these changes; Berry recalled that, "[r]eport editors in DRL at the time removed the material, indicating that this didn't fall within our concept of human rights at that time. Now, DRL is the engine that drives our efforts."[195] Special Envoy Berry discussed the important changes from within the State Department over time: "I entered the Foreign Service just after the policy under which FSOs could lose their security clearances due to sexual orientation effectively ended. That had meant basically losing your job if you came out. . . I believe the department mirrors the much broader evolution on equality and treatment of the LGBT community that has occurred in the country during recent years."[196] Other line officers recounted that before the official orders were dispatched from Washington, some embassy staff asked permission to initiate LGBTI diplomacy.[197] Upon convening a meeting of US officials across agencies to brainstorm how to integrate LGBTI rights in foreign policy in the National Security Council, Ambassador Power recounts: "I've never seen such a beaming bunch of government officials in my life."[198] Committed career civil servants were important actors at all levels working to push progressive LGBTI reforms in international forums. These officers, and a host of actors, engaged quickly in the UN in 2014 to stop the Russian-led vote to strip same-sex partners in the UN of benefits.[199] In a vast bureaucracy, institutional changes have transitioned internally over the years through work from all levels of officers to carry out new policy directives.

While there was personal commitment from many working-level officers, making LGBTI rights a human rights priority was not immediately embraced by all career diplomats. There were, and remain, personally conservative diplomats who resisted the inclusion of LGBTI rights into official policy or human rights dialogues. Most of these individuals claimed that it hindered US diplomatic relations; however, many also disagreed personally with the policy move. There were some reported cases of ambassadors, chiefs of missions, and some leaders in US embassies who openly opposed raising LGBTI rights with their host government. At one point, a leader in a high-level meeting of ambassadors congregating in Washington asked "if

they would then need to paint the U.S. embassy pink?"[200] Others asked if
flying a rainbow flag during local Pride events was a requirement and/or
sufficient for their embassy to recognize equality.[201] Officials in Washington
said they felt at times that they had to tell diplomats to "climb down from
the rafters; they felt we were asking them to do something that is impossible."[202] Some directors expressed hostility to a potential requirement to
raise LGBTI rights abuses. However, resistance seemed to be the exception,
not the rule. Interviewees reported that Washington, for the most part,
did not need to apply pressure on American embassy personnel to begin
LGBTI diplomacy.

Given the often slow nature in general of US foreign policy change,
coupled with the history of LGBTI discrimination within the State Department, one may expect a high level of resistance from foreign affairs institutions to implement LGBTI rights diplomacy. Burack notes a perception
by some outside LGBTI advocates and scholars of a "simplistic conceptualization of the state," or monolithic black box government that acts
as a single unit.[203] However, perhaps surprising to some activists, in this
research, internal officers and diplomats did not raise significant battles
among leaders and officers against the policy within Main State. This may
be due to the hierarchical nature of the State Department that leaves little
room for questioning policy changes from above. It may also be due to
diplomats observing severe LGBTI abuses in countries where they served
and consequently perceiving that the US should be raising the issue in
human rights dialogues.[204] A frequent sentiment from respondents was the
high level of support for LGBTI diplomacy within the State Department
at all levels.

While US diplomats at times have the political and financial power
to raise LGBTI rights abuses, they can be hesitant to do so because of
a variety of factors. Furthermore, diplomats traditionally tread carefully
with their host country counterparts, thereby avoiding uncomfortable or
unwanted discussions about internal reforms. Human rights diplomacy is at
times at odds with other national interests and impedes bilateral relations.
Raising LGBTI rights in places such as Gambia or Namibia often is not a
welcome diplomatic dialogue. US Ambassador to the UN Samantha Power
describes promoting LGBTI rights internationally as walking a fine line:
statements from Obama and other Western leaders often were met with
counteraccusations that they are " 'imperialists' foisting their values on traditional cultures."[205] Recommending legal or social reforms on any human

rights front can be met with open hostility, with governments deriding such diplomacy as mere meddling from Western powers in their domestic affairs. Not unique to the United States, governments such as South Africa that inculcate normative values into foreign policy are sometimes charged with "exhibiting a morally duplicitous and ideologically rudderless foreign policy" with regard to humanitarian interventions.[206] Accusations of abridgement of sovereignty are challenges faced by many foreign leaders when raising LGBTI rights concerns.

However, recent scholarship finds that at times, high-level diplomatic efforts can improve the lives of LGBTI persons at the grassroots level.[207] As Ambassador Power also notes, "We took our cues on whether to speak out publicly or engage governments behind the scenes from LGBT activists."[208] Given the complexity of raising human rights in international relations, one would expect a fairly high level of resistance from diplomats taking on yet another potentially difficult human rights agenda item. The evidence culled from interviews, however, revealed a more nuanced progression in attitudes among embassy staff to pursue an LGBTI inclusive diplomatic agenda. According to a senior US official, "The level of engagement from our embassies has far out-paced our expectations in Washington. . . Embassy staff have been tackling the issues, planning events, utilizing and requesting funds towards this goal from headquarters—work Washington had not even requested they carry out!"[209] Insider government officials across agencies responded that, for the most part, State Department officials did not need to be given orders to carry out the new directive.

Although strong opposition to commencing LGBTI diplomacy was not a central issue of concern within the State Department, implementation was. There was much less discussion of why they were engaging in LGBTI rights diplomacy and much more emphasis on how it would be carried out. Interviewees asserted that the most difficult policy discussions were not about whether the State Department should conduct LGBTI diplomacy, but about how it should be implemented. To address questions and concerns with implementation within the State Department from various embassy staff, an internal Task Force was created that provided global implementation strategies and recommendations.

The Task Force comprised diplomats serving in US embassies glob-ally, including in Africa and the Middle East, as well as officers serving in the State Department's headquarters in the regional and functional bureaus in Washington.[210] The Task Force recommended diplomatic approaches to address LGBTI rights in contentious countries. For example, the group generated recommendations for indirect approaches of diplomats to cultivate contacts and potential allies in progressive law schools or universities to promote the rule of law. While this type of approach had the long-term goal of promoting equality, the short-term optics and impact of a program such as this would be to assist independent courts and bolster democratic institutions. According to one diplomat, the key theme became simple and powerful: "The law is important for more than just the law. It sends a message for who counts and who does not."[211] In countries where same-sex relations are illegal, the task force recommended policies to work with human rights lawyers and courts, with the long-term strategy of legal reform.

The Task Force initially debated whether or not the United States should prioritize the so-called "worst offender countries" that criminalize and kill LGBTI people, or the "moveable middle,"[212] such as Vietnam or Venezuela, and countries that have demonstrated progress toward human rights and have more potential to build partnerships with transnational LGBTI civil society. Describing the humanitarian crisis created by the worst abusers, a leader overseeing the work of the Task Force in 2011 pointed out a "natural magnetism" toward focusing on worst offender countries.[213] LGBTI rights diplomacy is conducted worldwide; however, places that criminalize homosexuality or enforce the death penalty receive the lion's share of top US diplomatic engagement. Leaders felt it was natural to gravitate toward countries where the human rights needs were most acute. The pragmatic program ideas generated by the Task Force of both indirect and direct approaches alleviated some of the anxiety of hesitant diplomats concerned about raising LGBTI rights in contentious countries. Ultimately, the group decided to focus acute, emergency funding on the worst-offender countries while still providing funding for long-term change in "moveable-middle" nations. The Task Force also served to crystallize an abstract policy goal before 2011 into an applied toolbox of pragmatic policy options for American diplomats globally.

Insider allies are sometimes the linchpin in determining both policy reform and its actual implementation overseas. Many diplomatic leaders talked of their own personal convictions about equality. In a dramatic moment in 2011, Ambassador Samantha Power recounts in her book that before President Obama's UN General Assembly speech, she attempted to add a reference about LGBTI rights abuses in the world and for world leaders to respect LGBTI rights. However, her addition was rejected by Obama's speechwriting team several times.[214] She pushed numerous times, to no avail. For context, LGBTI rights were still very controversial among many UN member states in 2011, and it would be unprecedented for an American president to mention this topic in the country's annual speech to the UN General Assembly. The night before Obama's speech, Ambassador Power waited in the hotel lobby where Obama's staff was staying and "began a light jog" toward a senior staffer, to encourage once again the inclusion of recognition of LGBTI rights abuses in the speech.[215] The next morning, Power found a "Happy Birthday" message in her inbox from one of Obama's advisors informing her that a reference to LGBTI rights would be included in Obama's speech that day. In doing so, notably, "President Obama became the first sitting head of state to advocate for gay rights in the UN General Assembly."[216] This is an example of when outside observers may attribute a message solely to Obama, lacking an examination of the complex group of players who create policy and foreign policy messaging. Personal motivation of foreign policy leaders engaged in LGBTI rights in international affairs sometimes is known, sometimes is not. The actions of many influential leaders at the time led to important institutional changes pushed from within government. With regard to the feminist movement, scholars Holly McCammon and Amanda Brockman assert that as "institutional activists strategically shifted governmental arenas and adapted their mobilization and discursive strategies to these arenas, they were able to dismantle policy-specific barriers that impeded their goals."[217] Under the Trump administration, solely listening to the rhetoric of the president and his handful of top advisors could cause outsiders to miss the vast work that continues within USAID and the State Department, UN, and other international venues to promote LGBTI rights globally. In a large bureaucracy, mechanisms for assistance continue for the support of LGBTI civil society groups through the funding of small grants, protection of international activists, and capacity building of local NGOs.[218] Rather than focusing on the handful of people at the top of any government, it behooves activists to gain a more in-depth understanding of the vast nature and breadth of work within foreign affairs agencies.[219]

Another key internal leader and ally emerged in February 2015, when Randy Berry was appointed as the first special envoy for the human rights of LGBTI Persons. This was the highest-level diplomatic position in the US government's history appointed specifically to promote LGBTI rights.[220] Similar to the special envoys for monitoring and combating anti-Semitism or international disability rights, Special Envoy Berry's position was established in the State Department for a senior-level diplomat to address a specific issue worldwide. The special envoy position has both symbolic and pragmatic power. It is symbolic in that it represents the commitment of the United States to put forth diplomatic capital and resources toward LGBTI rights. This position is also pragmatic in that there is an identified leader to spearhead LGBTI diplomatic dialogues with foreign leaders, a focal point office to gather information and documentation of LGBTI rights abuses, and a team of personnel to identify policy and funding priorities to support global LGBTI civil society. With the establishment of the special envoy's position and office, leaders throughout the State Department and in US embassies across the globe were able to direct questions, resources, and documentation regarding LGBTI rights abuses toward the special envoy office. Special Envoy Berry, officers on his team, numerous officials in DRL, US leaders in the UN, the National Security Council (NSC), and USAID served as insider government allies to further global LGBTI rights.

In international relations, actors matter.[221] A leader's worldview, life experience, ethnicity, professional background, religious beliefs, and political perspectives can make a significant impact on policy. The Pew Research Center Social Trends and Demographic report illustrated that in 2013 LGBTI Americans held Clinton and Obama as among the top five public figures in advancing LGBTI rights in the United States.[222] Ambassador Power describes how global activists saw Obama as "uniquely situated to advocate for gay rights, as he could draw on America's long struggle for civil rights—and our own country's slow progress toward LGBT rights—as he explained the importance of equality."[223] Similarly, drawing on her work on children's rights and women's equality, it was Secretary Clinton's personal conviction about LGBTI equality that led her to become a fierce advocate in international forums.

Clinton supported LGBTI equality long before her leadership in the State Department. Her passion comes from her broad belief in equal rights for all, regardless of any background. One colleague of Clinton's asserted that as Clinton is a staunch woman's rights advocate, "Clinton sees LGBTI rights as a progression of gender rights."[224] Similar to top leadership in the Swedish government, Clinton perceived LGBTI equality as a sort of next phase of the women's movement. Clinton's colleagues pointed to her experience working on children's rights, religious beliefs, and deep sense of human dignity as foundational influences on her decisions regarding LGBTI policy. Data from this research indicate that without Obama and Clinton, whose leadership dovetailed with the confluence of other factors addressed in this book, LGBTI rights diplomacy would not have become institutionalized in US foreign policy.

As soon as Clinton became secretary of state in 2009, she began top-down directives that signaled LGBTI equality was going to become a flagship issue of her leadership in the department. Banaszak illustrates how powerful, determined leadership, acting with conviction from within the government, is a critical variable in social movements; it is the link between the behavior of a few individuals and their influence over policy change.[225] Secretaries of state often rely on officers and diplomats down the chain of command to provide talking points and recommendations. By contrast, Clinton's speechwriters reported that when it came to public remarks, meetings, and briefings on LGBTI concerns, she mainly wrote her own talking points. A member of her inner circle stressed that especially in the early days of the department-backed policy, "Clinton laid out the argument and how she wanted things framed."[226] This is novel because many top foreign policy leaders depend on senior advisors to help craft foreign policy on a particular issue. If an ambassador or an assistant secretary is not personally invested in a particular trade negotiation, for example, specific foreign policy goals are often formulated by lower-level officers, who are much more familiar with the country or issue. By contrast, Clinton generated remarks and policies regarding LGBTI diplomacy largely motivated from her personal conviction.

Two years before her defining speech in Geneva in 2011, Clinton changed the internal policies of the State Department to impart equal benefits for LGBTI staff and their family members for the first time in State Department history.[227] For diplomats, attaining official partnership status can be a life-or-death determination. In emergency situations, such as a coup d'état in a foreign country or a hurricane, only official members of the diplomat's household would be evacuated and brought into the protection of a US embassy. Numerous diplomats asserted that the extension of benefits to all employees, led by Clinton, was an important milestone for equality in the State Department.[228] These internal policy changes were lauded by the advocacy community and were a watershed moment for LGBTI diplomats in the State Department.[229] LGBTI diplomats could not serve openly in the State Department until 1992. Modern-day American diplomats still remember the repression of LGBTI employees only a few decades ago. In 2015, an American diplomat shared how before Clinton's leadership, she never would have believed she would be able to live openly as a lesbian and serve as an American diplomat in her lifetime.[230]

The internal changes Clinton made as secretary of state influenced US diplomats' sense of legitimacy to begin external global LGBTI diplomacy. One lesbian officer described the internal policy change as a critical moment for her and other LGBTI colleagues: "It signaled to us that that we were considered equal members of the Department; we then felt empowered to begin incorporating LGBTI rights with integrity into our policy agenda."[231] Her sentiment was echoed in the press. *The Daily Beast* reported, "To those who worked and advocated at the State Department for LGBTI rights, the moves in 2009 set the tone for a very pro-LGBTI State Department. . . Clinton advanced things for LGBTI State Department employees, but her impact was much greater in terms of setting a global policy agenda. . . We have never had a champion before in this arena."[232] One State Department employee thanked Clinton, stating, "This is the first time in my 24.5 year career that I have seen this type of support. I appreciate all the hard work you have done in the short time as Secretary of State."[233] Clinton's actions of internal reform helped to legitimize her reforms for external foreign policy promoting LGBTI rights in global contexts.

Some critics may claim that Clinton's policy decisions in 2011 were a political calculation to gain future votes as a presidential candidate in 2016. One official opined, "Of course any decision cannot be politically futile, in any decision you are making a political judgment: is this something you are willing to stand for, even with the potential of fallout?"[234] Conversely, interviewees suggested that Clinton's strong stance on LGBTI rights could have hurt her politically. Statistical polling illustrates that by and large, LGBTI people are liberal and vote heavily for Democratic candidates.[235] Her reforms in the State Department likely would not have won her many more votes than she did not already have as the Democratic presidential candidate. NGO leaders similarly assessed that it seemed that Clinton made the determination for LGBTI equality in the State Department fairly early on; they asserted that Clinton's motivation likely was political, as well as a real conviction that it was the right thing to do.[236] Notwithstanding political motivations, Clinton established quickly that LGBTI rights were going to be one of the legacy issues from her tenure as secretary of state.

Although Secretary Clinton was instrumental in changing State Department policy, she was criticized by the right wing for her activist foreign policy,[237] and from the left wing for her late conversion to LGBTI equality.[238] Furthermore, Clinton's foreign policy speeches related to LGBTI rights are decried by some as infused with homonationalist rhetoric.[239] What many scholars take as an assumption is that LGBTI rights were an inevitable topic for the diplomatic agenda. Many lack a sense of diplomatic history, of what is traditionally raised in foreign relations, what is taboo, and how unlikely it was for LGBTI rights to become an issue for international relations at all. *From Pariah to Priority* in part argues that although there are problematic aspects of Clinton's leadership, without her directional role on this issue, LGBTI would not have become formally institutionalized within the State Department.

One of the most striking points derived from multiple NGO respondents in *From Pariah to Priority* was that they recognized that their work depended on Clinton's leadership reforming from within. One may expect internal diplomats, but not necessarily outsider activists, to recognize her leadership and unique championing of LGBTI issues. In American history, NGO leaders often exhibit an adversarial relationship with government actors.[240] NGO activists recognized Clinton's important influence. Advocates repeatedly stressed that "Without Clinton's and other top foreign policy leaders' support, U.S. foreign policy would not have shifted to include LGBTI rights."[241] Clinton's powerful position over US foreign policy directives served as a critical game changer to US foreign relations. Similarly, advocates emphasized that had all things been equal—same funding, same year, same public opinion, and so forth—without Secretary Clinton's leadership from her position of power, US foreign policy would not have changed. Activists noted that, hypothetically, with the same time frame but a different US leadership, the United States most likely might have stayed silent on Uganda's so-called "Kill the Gays" law.[242] In advocates' own assessment of their roles, they believe their lobbying efforts and strategies would not have been sufficient to change US foreign policy without key insider allied leadership championing the movement's goals.

Similar to Clinton, Obama was a crucial player in commencing LGBTI diplomacy in US foreign policy. In 2012, *Newsweek* magazine called Obama the "first gay U.S. President," referring to Obama's personal transformation and evolution on LGBTI rights.[243] While not initially supportive of marriage equality, Obama eventually began supporting same-sex marriage and overall equality. In 2011, the White House issued a Presidential Memorandum, "International Initiatives to Advance the Human Rights of Lesbian, Gay, Bisexual, and Transgender Persons,"[244] which outlined guidelines and goals for LGBTI equality in the United States throughout all federal institutions. Under Obama's leadership, the Executive Branch, and specifically the State Department, enacted sweeping reforms to address LGBTI rights in international affairs. As the US's first Black president, activists remarked

that "Obama understood gay rights through a minority rights framework."[245]
Multiple leaders interviewed in the State Department and from Obama's
inner circle remarked that Obama came to understand LGBTI equality as
a logical extension of the civil rights movement.[246]

An opportunity for Obama to make a stand on LGBTI rights in his
foreign engagements, albeit in a politically tense diplomatic venue, came in
2013 during his travels to Senegal. On the day after the US Supreme Court
ruled the Defense of Marriage Act (DOMA) unconstitutional, Obama was
in Senegal's capital, Dakar.[247] In Dakar, Obama remarked on the Supreme
Court ruling, praising the decision as

> [. . .]not simply a victory for the LGBTI community, it's a victory
> for American democracy. I believe at the root of who we are as
> a people, who we are as Americans is the basic precept that we
> are all equal under the law. We believe in basic fairness. And
> what I think yesterday's ruling signifies is one more step towards
> ensuring that those basic principles apply to everybody.[248]

Obama communicated LGBTI rights to the Senegalese audience as a personal civil rights issue that he was prepared to defend despite condemnation
from some quarters of American society. During his later press conference
with Kenyan President Uhuru Muigai Kenyatta, Obama affirmed that Kenya
should not discriminate against people based on their sexual orientation:

> If you look at the history of countries around the world, when
> you start treating people differently, not because of any harm
> they're doing anybody but because they're different, that's the path
> whereby freedoms begin to erode. . . . As an African-American
> in the United States, I'm painfully aware of the history of what
> happens when people are treated differently under the law.[249]

For Obama to reference the painful history of inequality as a Black person
in the United States, he was able to further alliances of equality movements
globally. He bridged the fight for LGBTI equality to the importance for
any society to treat all people equally.

Obama raised LGBTI equality issues in diplomatic dialogues with
Kenyan leaders. Kenyan LGBTI activists such as Eric Gitari of Kenya's
National Gay and Lesbian Human Rights Commission advocated for
Obama to address LGBTI right as a "unique opportunity—a president

with Kenyan heritage who can call people here brothers and sisters. It's a rare chance for the issue to be raised this way, to show that it's not a 'foreign issue.' "[250] However, some Kenyan activists worried about Obama's potential "preachy tone" and the importance of recognizing human rights problems in the United States. Nevertheless, they expressed that Obama raising LGBTI equality and international recognition was vital to their work.[251] Conversely, local African leaders bristled at Obama's open support for LGBTI rights. Kenyan President Kenyatta later responded that "Obama should know that gay rights are Western. When in Africa he should value our rights."[252] Paradoxically, those leaders did not take into account the fact that Obama's father is Kenyan, instead focusing their criticism on Obama's words as illustrative of Western leaders trying to impose their cultural values on African societies. Researchers from the Namibia and South African contexts demonstrate how some leaders across West and sub-Saharan Africa decry LGBTI rights as "un-African," while at the same time there are robust local and regional LGBTI equality advocates working toward equality.[253] A battle remains globally for how regions and cultures have or will come to identify LGBTI rights as either a "threat" or conversely a new aspect of one's culture.[254] Diplomats and heads of state clash in diplomatic engagements on both sides of this argument.

Raising LGBTI equality in Dakar, Nairobi, and other capitals in East and West Africa was unprecedented at the time for a US leader. A host of programs and new policies follow in the wake of any presidential visit. President Obama's diplomacy in countries such as Kenya led to financial and political support of local LGBTI civil society. US financial assistance helped fund local groups to register as formal civil society organizations and to formally establish new local advocacy organizations. Obama and other foreign policy leaders provided political clout for domestic advocacy. One Kenyan activist argued, "When the Kenyan president said [LGBTI rights abuses] was not an issue in this country, in response to President Obama's words . . . that was when our lobbying started for equality."[255] In this case, similar to opposition from the government in the United States, the antagonism of the Kenyan president toward his own LGBTI Kenyan community backfired. LGBTI organizers felt emboldened by Obama's words and used a new influx of international funding to formally organize and lobby for LGBTI equality.

Over the course of Obama's tenure as US president, elevating LGBTI rights abuses in his diplomatic engagements had significant global impact. Obama's "personal engagement" on the issue with Brazilian President Dilma

Rousseff led to the establishment of the Organization of American States for monitoring LGBTI rights in Latin America and later a Special Rapporteur on LGBTI rights.[256] Obama's leadership led to international focus on equality, establishment of civil society groups globally, and increased international donor funding for LGBTI populations.

Obama's diplomatic attention to LGBTI groups did not come without problems, however. Backlash and increased discrimination toward local LGBTI groups in Liberia and other countries rose after Western leaders raised LGBTI rights on foreign tours.[257] Ending foreign aid may also pose the risk of double discrimination or backlash against local LGBTI populations.[258] They may be blamed by their compatriots for drawing the ire of the West on their country while they are already experiencing societal discrimination based on sexual orientation or gender identity. Whether addressed through quiet diplomacy or by publicly shaming leaders, best practices for how to address LGBTI equality globally without the unintended result of hurting local populations are still debated. Whether resulting in increased backlash or support for local organizations, when global leaders raise LGBTI rights, they create a palpable wave of domestic and international attention to the issue.

In the case of US foreign policy reform toward including LGBTI diplomacy, insider government allies within the government were key players in changing institutional agendas. Robert Tsai demonstrates that presidential aides are critical in characterizing new social conditions on which rights are made; they articulate, disseminate, and model institutional support for a new right.[259] A host of diplomatic leaders within the various State Department headquarter bureaus, as well as US ambassadors around the world, were poised to reform ebassy internal human rights policies. From working-level officers to the secretary of state and US president, government allies were able to make reforms from their position of power inside foreign affairs institutions. LGBTI diplomacy was a new frontier for the United States' international diplomatic engagement that also served to change the country's international reputation.

The United States' National Identity and International Reputation

This chapter analyzes the central factors that led to the inclusion of LGBTI rights into US foreign policy. First, it examines the tactics of NGO advocacy: direct protest, building coalitions, targeted institutional advocacy, and strategies to diffuse political opposition. The case study then studies insider allied government leaders, from working-level diplomats to the highest levels of leaders within the State Department, and President Obama's role in shifting US foreign policy. Finally, this chapter examines the role of the United States' reputation. Reputation and national identity were important factors for foreign policy leaders to change US foreign policy. Evidence from interviewees for *From Pariah to Priority* demonstrated that institutionalizing LGBTI diplomacy was one way for leadership in the Obama administration to cast a new light on US foreign policy for the international community after the Bush administration.[260]

Addressing the United States' tarnished global human rights reputation was an immediate priority of the Obama administration. During the George W. Bush presidency, the United States' international reputation in human rights was severely damaged. The invasion of Iraq,[261] abuses at the Guantanamo Bay detention camp,[262] mistreatment of prisoners in Abu Ghraib,[263] defunding of global reproductive rights,[264] and campaigns against LGBTI rights all damaged the United States' global reputation. Ilan Peleg identifies foreign invasion, a militarized foreign policy, and coercive democratization as the legacy of the Bush administration's foreign policy.[265] Scholars note the importance of the United States' leaders being driven by a need for moral rehabilitation and to rebuild the national reputation.[266] The Guantanamo Bay detention center became central to the narrative of the United States as an abuser of human rights globally.[267] US foreign policy officials lost a great deal of ground and clout in the international community. Directing the closing of the Guantanamo Bay detention center was Obama's first official action as president.[268] Following this action, leaders in the National Security Council and State Department conducted internal meetings to deliberate new policy opportunities to reengage on global human rights.

LGBTI rights emerged in these deliberations as a politically timely human rights issue for a new administration to engage with globally. Interviewees asserted that LGBTI rights were a new frontier for foreign affairs officials to focus on and regain lost ground on the United States' national reputation in human rights.[269] Samantha Power and other foreign policy leaders advised a complete reversal on LGBTI policies from the Bush administration.[270] Elevating LGBTI rights into foreign policy was a way for Obama's administration to differentiate itself from the preceding administration and take a new leadership role in the global equality movement.

Analysts asserted that Obama believed LGBTI rights was an area where the United States "can get it right."[271] Women's rights, religious freedom, and freedom of expression were concepts that had been raised in diplomatic engagements for decades. By contrast, raising LGBTI rights in foreign affairs had never been done by American diplomats. Michael Posner, former assistant secretary of the Bureau of Democracy, Human Rights, and Labor, stated, "Rather than stand in the sidelines, America has decided to get in."[272] By taking on such a new and still controversial topic, leaders in the Obama administration made a complete shift from their predecessors on LGBTI rights, in part to redefine the United States' global reputation.

Some scholars criticize the appropriation of LGBTI rights in conceptualizations of national identity, charging that Obama and other top leaders exhibited a form of homonationalism. Jasbir K. Puar's 2007 *Terrorist Assemblages*,[273] in Puar's updated analysis in 2018, from the US context, homonationalism is a "dual movement in which certain homosexual constituencies have embraced [US] nationalist agendas and have also been embraced by nationalism agendas. . . homonormative ideologies replicate narrow racial, class, and gender national ideals."[274] Puar's analysis can be seen through the lens of how the LGBTI community, once a pariah population and formally banned from the State Department, became the focal population to predicate foreign relations and bilateral affairs with countries such as Uganda. Furthermore, Miriam Smith assesses the trend of homonationalism among some Western leaders as a "form of nationalism in which the recognition of LGBTQ rights is used to promote a particular version of the nation."[275] The interviewees in this study affirm the sentiment that Obama administration leaders sought a new version of America's reputation; LGBTI rights became an area for them to reinvigorate America's reputation on addressing human rights. However, evidence in this book does not affirm Puar, Smith, and other homonationalism scholars' assertion that Obama administration officials chose to elevate LGBTI rights to diffuse criticism for the states' actions in oppressing others. By contrast, analysis based on data in this research shows that the new administration was motivated by a strong sense of shame during the Bush administration; out of this shame, leaders sought to act on a new issue that was not battered by previous leaders and reestablish the United State's commitment to human rights in foreign policy.

Officials have attributed the United States' international reputation on human rights as a contributing motivation for Clinton's seminal speech in Geneva in 2011. One officer stated that they decided on this moment to launch the LGBTI policy because it was "not so early that it would be marginalized and not take root, however, early enough to show bold leadership by the U.S. . . . [W]e were setting the course for the rest of the world to follow, that many of the rest of the world leaders were newly and increasingly supporting."[276] Assistant Secretary Posner remarked, "I feel great, also, about the—putting the LGBT issues on the global stage. I was with Secretary Clinton in Geneva when she gave, really, a landmark speech saying that LGBT rights are human rights. A number of countries have now—governments have come to us and said, we want to do what you're doing."[277] After Clinton's speech, two foreign ministers from other wealthy donor countries initiated contact with top US leadership within the State Department.[278] A US leader recalled that one of the foreign ministers asserted, "Now that the U.S. has laid down a marker on [LGBTI rights], what can we do to support it from our government?"[279] Other countries immediately and publicly supported LGBTI rights after Clinton's speech and the subsequent US policy that was enacted. A senior US official assessed that the United States gave a number of like-minded governments "the latitude to take [LGBTI rights diplomacy] to the next level. . . We realized we created the space for some of the countries who had not yet taken a bold initiative, to make a stand with us; it opened the doors for numerous other governments."[280] Ayoub demonstrates that LGBTI advocates choose different frames, largely connected to messaging around national values.[281] US officials looked to LGBTI rights in international affairs as a new platform to redefine the United States' reputation and commitment to human rights in foreign policy.

Conclusion

This chapter analyzes how LGBTI rights became an issue of diplomatic engagement in US foreign policy. The State Department is a highly bureaucratic institution, where a great deal of policy is mandated by long-standing laws and regulations. It is difficult to make rapid sweeping policy reforms.[282] Thus, it is important to analyze the key domestic and global factors that influence policy change.

This chapter investigates how NGO advocates employed varying tactics to motivate US foreign policy changes on LGBTI rights. Domestic contestation of equality impacted foreign policy orientation less than would have been expected, especially when looking at scholarship on the trajectory of other social movements.[283] The specific efforts of NGO advocates to reform US foreign policy were identified as direct public protest against state policies, coalition building with large human rights gatekeeper organizations, targeted institutional advocacy, and strategies to diffuse political opposition to LGBTI rights. NGOs, in a strategic advising role, assist the US government in its capacity to gather knowledge and documentation of global LGBTI rights. In turn, the government has become one of the central sources of information used by international LGBTI advocates.

This chapter also evaluates the strategic role of insider allied government leadership. Individual ambassadors, Secretary of State Hillary Clinton, desk officers, and individual diplomats applied internal pressure for policy change. As with most human rights issues, some leaders were reticent to raise LGBTI issues in US diplomatic engagements. However, high levels of internal support within the State Department was an unexpected finding in this research. For ambassadors to express willingness and a sense of urgency to raise LGBTI human rights issues was unanticipated and a factor that ultimately impacted the institutionalization of LGBTI diplomacy. Obama and Clinton came to conceptualize LGBTI rights as the next frontier of the minority rights and women's rights movements, challenging inequality in society. In her speech in Geneva, Clinton presented LGBTI rights as on par with all of the human rights pillars, laying the foundation for them to be integrated into official policy moving forward. These leaders were partly motivated to renew the United States' global reputation in international human rights.

The United States' national identity and reputation played a role in institutionalizing LGBTI rights in US foreign policy. Obama administration officials expressed an acute desire for leaders to assess and realign the United States after previous backsliding on human rights. Diplomats deliberated how the United States would regain its reputation as a player in global human rights dialogues. The confluence of these factors led to the evolution of the State Department's human rights foreign policy. The State Department, once a discriminatory organization that routinely fired LGBTI employees, treating them like social and professional pariahs, just a few decades later became a key source of global documentation of LGBTI discrimination and LGBTI rights diplomacy.

The fight for LGBTI equality, as well as its contestation, is not specific to any one country or continent. Advocates play an influential role in building international coalitions and work for the globalization of LGBTI equality.[284] Similarly, other governments came before the United States in raising the issue of LGBTI rights abuses in their foreign aid policies. Sweden was the first country in the world to formally address LGBTI rights within its foreign policy mandate. The next chapter is a comparative analysis of the central factors that led to Sweden's pioneering work in LGBTI diplomacy.

Chapter 3

Sweden's Pioneering Role in LGBTI Diplomacy

Introduction

In contemporary international affairs, Sweden is a global leader in championing LGBTI rights in diplomatic relations and supporting LGBTI human rights organizations. For example, the Swedish government supported Moldovan activist Andrei Colioglo, who received death threats from his community and anti-LGBTI Moldovan authorities as a result of his work fighting for equality in his country.[1] Because many countries such as Pakistan, Gambia, and Jamaica codify discrimination and state violence in national laws,[2] Swedish foreign policy leaders raise the issue of LGBTI rights during diplomatic engagements. In 2005, the Swedish government became the first national governing body in the world to formally institutionalize LGBTI rights in its foreign policy agenda.[3]

Incorporating LGBTI rights into foreign policy measurably changed international relations. Sweden's initial actions continue to influence the entire realm of foreign policy and international development. Raising LGBTI rights in diplomatic dialogue with other countries where homosexuality is illegal may jeopardize other security or trade interests and the overall bilateral relationship with the nation. Nevertheless, LGBTI rights are incorporated into Sweden's overall international aid development programs. From Indonesia to Vietnam, Sweden provides global financial support to fledgling LGBTI civil society groups to aid their efforts toward LGBTI equality.[4]

Though Sweden is a small nation of approximately 10 million people,[5] Sweden's LGBTI rights policies in international affairs have become a
blueprint for policy makers in the United States and other powerful nations.
Sweden spearheaded the international response to Uganda's Anti-Homosexuality Act (AHA),[6] dubbed by observers as the "Kill the Gays" Bill,[7] starting
in 2009. Through the mechanism of EU accession requirements, Sweden
and other pro-LGBTI equality EU member states have had a palpable effect
on the reforms of new EU member states toward LGBTI equality. Sweden
also leads in its asylum adjudication for LGBTI people, granting asylum
to individuals from around the world based on their sexual orientation and
gender identity. Sweden's progressive asylum policy has resulted in numerous
international advocates from Nigeria, Russia, and Indonesia gaining asylum
in the country. Stockholm thus has become a global center of international
LGBTI leadership, serving as a base for the transnational LGBTI movement.
Often working in concert with other countries, especially other Nordic
nations, Swedish foreign policy leaders will stake human rights concerns as
on par or above other bilateral interests in international relations. Unlike
most other nations' foreign affairs institutions, human rights are incorporated into Sweden's national security strategy. This chapter analyzes the central factors that led Swedish leaders to incorporate LGBTI rights into their
official diplomatic work.

Central Factors That Led to Sweden's LGBTI Diplomacy

The evolution of Sweden's policy to incorporate LGBTI rights into its foreign policy cannot be attributed to one factor. Rather, a host of events and
factors, sometimes working in tandem, brought about these policy reforms.
There were four major factors critical to LGBTI rights rising to prominence within Sweden's foreign policy: NGO advocacy from LGBTI activists,
insider government allies, repressive global laws that spurred the movement,
and a national self-perception of being a global leader in LGBTI rights.

In Sweden, LGBTI activists are mainly united by one large organization, the Swedish Federation for Lesbian, Gay, Bisexual and Transgender
Rights (RFSL).[8] RFSL officers are integrated into foreign policy debates
to such an extent that government officers sometimes seek out RFSL staff
before turning to their own internal colleagues within the Swedish Ministry of Foreign Affairs. NGO advocates globally interact with their governments differently according to political opportunity structures.[9] Officers in

the Swedish International Development Cooperation Agency (SIDA) and the Swedish Foreign Ministry (*Utrikesdepartementet*, UD) are exceptionally receptive to briefings and policy recommendations from NGOs. Over the decades, Swedish advocates have largely chosen methods of direct advocacy as well as targeted institutional advocacy to state their claims to foreign policy leaders. LGBTI advocates harnessed transnational activist networks and used lessons learned from other social movements to shape new human rights norms. NGO advocates worked to develop allies within the government. Furthermore, many LGBTI civil servants worked within agencies and institutions toward policy change. Insider allies made lasting change from their positions of power in the government. While Sweden does not have one central leader championing the LGBTI issue, the Swedish case is hallmarked by the ways its leadership buttressed direct advocacy to influence government reform.

Additionally, Uganda's repressive laws were a sensitizing event for Swedish policy makers. A sensitizing event can stimulate discursive renewal.[10] When Ugandan lawmakers proposed the death penalty for homosexual acts in 2009, it triggered the decision to make LGBTI rights a central focus of both Swedish and US human rights diplomacy.[11] The AHA brought the LGBTI movement into the international spotlight and solidified LGBTI rights as an important pillar of Swedish foreign policy.

Finally, Sweden's construction of its national identity as a global humanitarian superpower motivated inclusion of LGBTI rights diplomacy. Evidence from civil society and government leaders in *From Pariah to Priority* addressed how Sweden's global reputation as a defender of human rights was an important driver for their work. The national reputation of Sweden as a human rights leader permeates advocacy efforts and government actions. Anna-Maria Sörberg demonstrates how activists have broadly worked to formulate and solidify LGBTI rights as a new foundation for Sweden's national identity.[12] Fear of shaming or loss of reputation and desire to remain a global force on human rights influence Swedish foreign policy decisions.

SWEDEN'S HISTORY AS A HUMAN RIGHTS LEADER GLOBALLY

Global leadership on human rights policies is not a new phenomenon for Sweden. The country has a historic legacy of generating human rights policies that are followed by other nation states. Sweden was the first country in the world to introduce freedom of the press in 1766.[13] It was also the first country to allow couples to divorce for any reason in 1915.[14] Sweden pioneered work on climate change policies that were subsequently adopted by EU-level institutions.[15] In 2018, Swedish teenager Greta Thunberg inspired a global movement of youth activism to address climate change.[16] As related to LGBTI rights, Sweden was the first country in the world to legislate against LGBTI discrimination in the workplace.[17] In 1972, Sweden was the first country to allow people to change their legal gender.[18] Sweden has an extensive track record of being the first country to establish various human rights norms, policies, and laws.

Despite its small population size, Sweden is Europe's largest per-capita donor of foreign aid, making it one of the largest donors of international development aid in the world. Compared proportionately with most other international donor nations, including the United States, in 2018, for example, the government of Sweden spent approximately four times more of its GDP on international development aid annually.[19] Sweden is also a large contributor to the EU, influencing EU institutions as one of the highest contributors to international aid.[20] Annika Björkdahl exhibits that Swedish entrepreneurship in the United Nations (UN) helps the country shape global norms, asserting that through "norm entrepreneurship as a foreign policy strategy, small states may be able to 'punch above their weight' in international politics."[21] High funding levels and extensive diplomatic presence across international institutions allow Sweden's foreign policy leaders to exert enormous normative influence in the EU, UN, and other international forums.

Sweden incorporates its domestic norms of LGBTI equality goals into its foreign policy goals. In 2015, Foreign Minister Margot Wallström asserted, "Our values on LGBTI issues should direct the management of our international aid."[22] Scholar Jens Rydström expounded that the imbedded concepts of equality and fairness in Scandinavia create an ideal ground for advocacy of tolerance and inclusion of sexual minorities.[23] The Norwegian scholar Tina Stoum finds that Scandinavians perceive their countries as tolerant, benevolent nations and "legitimate promoters" of LGBTI rights whose citizens are sexually liberated and wish the same for others.[24] Brysk asserts that "[a]t the international level, human rights foreign policy is more than guilt or charity—it is a constructive form of identity politics."[25] Humanitarian promoter nations are usually open societies with strong human rights traditions domestically, where leaders leverage a narrative of their nation as a human rights promoter in their foreign policy.

Changes in domestic policy were the foundation for changes in Sweden's orientation internationally. In 1944—earlier than most countries—

Swedish lawmakers revoked legislation that made homosexuality a criminal offense. In 1950, RFSL was founded, making it one of the oldest still-active LGBTI rights organizations in the world.[26] RFSL's original goals were three-fold: provide a safe place for lesbian and gay people to meet, educate society on homosexuality, and integrate homosexuality into mainstream society and government policy. Swedish and international leaders began working with transnational activists for universal health care and for more broadly defining LGBTI equality as a human right. The Swedish government was one of the earliest and largest donors to the World Health Programme on AIDS in the late 1980s and early 1990s.[27] In the late 1990s, the Swedish Ambassador Jan Nordlander was one of the original international leaders to raise and connect LGBTI rights with human rights issues in international fora.[28] While LGBTI discrimination was, and remains, an issue in Sweden, espe-cially for individuals living with HIV/AIDS,[29] Sweden was a front-runner to link health and human rights internationally. Swedish foreign policy leaders advocated for a greater international response to the HIV/AIDS crisis.[30] In 1998, Hans Ytterberg was appointed the first EU Ombudsman Against Discrimination Based On Sexual Orientation.[31] The Swedish government subsequently sent Ytterberg to the UN, where he became one of the first international leaders to voice the need for antidiscrimination protections based on sexual orientation.

A transformative moment for LGBTI rights in the EU came when Swedish leader Thomas Hammarberg assumed the chairmanship of the Council of Europe Commission for Human Rights in 2009. Under his purview, the Council of Europe issued a policy report on sexual orientation and gender identity rights in the EU.[32] Only a few governments at the time formally addressed LGBTI rights in foreign affairs. That document offered new recommendations on issues such as discrimination based on gender identity, conditions for the right to a legal sex and name change, access to health care for transgender people, and other contemporary policy discussions across EU member states. It was one of the first transnational documents to assess the status of LGBTI rights across Europe and provide country-specific policy recommendations. In 2015, interviewees in *From Pariah to Priority* cited this report as having a sustained impact on the LGBTI transnational movement.[33] A leader of RFSL's youth movement stated in 2015, "This report (from 2009) was a transformative document for the EU, Council of Europe, and international LGBTI activists. . . . After the report was published we were able to use the evidence to create specific recommendations for each country."[34] From health care norms to workplace discrimination and legalities on changing identity documents, this report, and subsequent policy discussions, influenced the norms and policies in other EU nations. Under the auspices of Swedish leadership, Hammarberg's report and agenda-setting role ushered in early prioritization of LGBTI rights in the Council of Europe.

In 1998, Stockholm hosted EuroPride. This event catapulted Sweden onto center stage of the European and global LGBTI movement. Since 1977, an annual "Homosexual Liberation Day" took place in Stockholm.[35] Prior to 1998, the day was a small gathering of activists working mainly toward domestic change focused on their local communities. EuroPride 1998, however, changed the Swedish movement into a global one. It set the stage for Stockholm to begin annually hosting LGBTI activists and leaders from all over the world. According to one activist, "From that year [1998] onward, the Stockholm Pride Festival shifted from simply being a party to being a week-long public political discussion forum."[36] Lesbians and non-white gay men especially emphasized the importance of Stockholm Pride becoming a resource and organizing focal point for the worldwide political movement.[37] More than a celebration, though celebrating Pride was an important aspect of the event, activists shaped Stockholm Pride to become a critical time to highlight grave issues, both domestic and foreign.

Annually at Stockholm Pride, Swedish political parties, government, and private sector leaders attend and discuss the status of the domestic and global movement. Prime ministers, members of Parliament, ministers of the government, and other leading Swedish officials participate in public discussions during Pride. Even conservative party leaders, such as Ebba Busch Thor and the Christian Democrats, regularly attend Stockholm Pride events.[38] Notably, Sweden's military commanders participate in Pride and march "for LGBT[I] rights in the capital's Pride parade and actively seek to recruit LGBT[I] personnel in order to increase diversity in the ranks."[39] The development of Sweden's security sector leaders, historically highly homophobic institutions, marching in Stockholm's Pride parade is remarkable. Leaders from police departments, and other security agengies articulate more than acceptance; they give speeches during the Pride march to actively demonstrate the inclusion and equality of LGBTI people in their institutions. Pride week has become a national event for solidifying and establishing new national LGBTI norms.

However, since 2014, Stockholm Pride has also become a place of schism from the far right-wing political party, the Swedish Democrats (SD; *Sverigedemokraterna*). In 2014, Stockholm Pride's press secretary Maria

Paulsson publicized that the Swedish Democrats, led by Jimmie Åkesson, were to be excluded from participating in that year's events and festivities, making the political party the only organization to be banned. RFSL blocked the SDs mainly because of their racist and xenophobic political platform. RFSL leaders also emphasized the intersectionality of race and LGBTI issues, and explained the need to protect all Pride participants.[40] In response at the time, Åkesson expressed no interest in attending Stockholm Pride, regardless of the ban.[41] The political right wing and left wing clash in contemporary Swedish politics and national identity over how LGBTI rights aligns with Swedish values. Nevertheless, Sweden's reputation, and its ability to champion LGBTI rights internationally, is a key theme of Stockholm Pride.[42] This annual event provides a platform for national and international advocates to influence Swedish foreign policy.

Sweden's Contemporary Foreign Policy

There are several Swedish governmental agencies responsible for carrying out the mandate of LGBTI diplomacy: the Swedish International Development Cooperation Agency (SIDA); the Swedish Foreign Ministry (UD); and the Swedish Migration Agency (MV).[43] In the beginning of the 2000s, these agencies began addressing LGBTI rights concerns. Initially, SIDA indirectly began LGBTI international development work by providing access to HIV/AIDS health care in global health programs to vulnerable populations in some African nations. The Swedish Foreign Ministry formally included LGBTI rights in its human rights foreign policy framework, and the Swedish Migration Agency called for Sweden to begin legally accepting LGBTI asylum claims in the early 2000s. Within Swedish government institutions, there are multiple platform agendas influencing Sweden's foreign policy development. LGBTI rights promotion is a specific component of a feminist foreign policy that represents a progression of the core values of gender equality that challenge gender norms and social hierarchies.

Sweden's Human Rights Foreign Policy

Compared with most nations in the international system, Sweden distinctly prioritizes human rights in foreign policy. Karin Aggestam and Annika Bergman-Rosamond establish the distinctive quality of a normative orientation within Swedish foreign policy mandates, informed by ethical considerations of global justice and peace.[44] The Swedish government stands out for its comparatively high budget levels of foreign aid earmarked specifically for democracy, human rights, and supporting civil society.[45] It is much more common for countries to maintain trade and economic development as central foreign policy goals, rather than through perceived normative values. In contrast, China, Russia, and other influential players in world affairs hold a more pragmatic approach to foreign policy, often devoid of normative values, and thus sideline human rights.[46]

In contrast with realist scholarship, human rights scholars argue that neglecting human rights is both bad for business and detrimental to international stability.[47] Scholars contend that struggles over land rights, religious or ethnic discrimination, the lack of political freedom, and beyond can spark civil unrest and wars.[48] Thus, the international community has a vested interest in addressing domestic human rights practices in other nations. In 2015, the Swedish Minister for International Development Cooperation, Isabella Lövin, asserted, "Human rights are the focus of [Sweden's] foreign policy. It is intended for human rights to be on par with security policy and all of our other international relations."[49] As Sweden is a small state and thus vulnerable to global economic and conflict trends, Swedish leaders articulate that it is in Sweden's best interest to promote peace. One of the founders of Sweden's modern welfare state, Gunnar Myrdal, asserted, "We are called upon by history and our external conditions to be the advocate of universal interest."[50] Sweden's humanitarian efforts thereby can be explained in part as a small state's "defensive reaction" to the culture of war in Europe.[51] Human rights policies have the end goal of promoting international law, peace, and order to the international system. Yet still, the prioritization of human rights in Sweden's foreign policy, as the most important foreign policy mandate articulated by one of the country's top leaders, is distinctive. For many other governments, the primacy of human rights fluctuates.[52] Post WWII, Sweden has been a consistent advocate of human rights in the international system.

SWEDEN'S FEMINIST FOREIGN POLICY

Central to Sweden's human rights policy is its prioritization of women's rights and gender equality in what the Swedish government has deemed a "feminist foreign policy."[53] It was the first nation to formally institutionalize an explicitly feminist foreign policy in 2014.[54] That year, former Foreign Minister Wallström stated, "Striving toward gender equality is not only a goal in itself but also a precondition for achieving our wider foreign development, and security-policy objectives."[55] Aggestam and Bergman Rosamond evaluate how "Sweden's feminist foreign policy has pursued a head-wind agenda, which reflects a readiness to confront contestation in global politics."[56] Swedish leaders are often met with opposition and reproach from other foreign leaders when they try to raise gender equality and LGBTI rights in diplomatic forums. At the time, no other country placed gender equality at the primacy of its foreign policy goals.

Wallström demonstrated the power of Sweden's feminist foreign policy in Saudi Arabia in 2015. When a major arms deal was up for renewal between the two countries, Wallström ended the decade-long military agreement.[57] Wallström condemned Saudi Arabia's unequal treatment of women, corporal punishment for bloggers, and death penalty for homosexuality.[58] Saudi Arabia is perceived as a key ally in the Middle East, and therefore diplomats remain reluctant to criticize the kingdom.[59] Because of the kingdom's financial power and oil monopoly, few governments have taken action to censure Saudi Arabia's human rights abuses. Sweden is a rare country "willing to take the risk" to publicly condemn Saudi Arabia's human rights abuses.[60] It was a strong demonstration of what Abdul Karim Bangura denotes as Sweden's history of "putting morality over profit."[61] As opposed to keeping gender equality on the periphery or not raising the issue at all with a politically strategic country such as Saudi Arabia, as is practiced by most other governments in the world today, Swedish foreign policy leaders elevated human rights as a central bilateral issue. In this case, Wallström placed gender equality as a more important national interest than security cooperation. It was a rare moment in international relations for a small country, albeit a wealthy nation, to stand up to a large, politically powerful country such as Saudi Arabia based upon the praxis of human rights.

Human rights diplomacy is controversial and can lead to negative repercussions between nations. The backlash against Wallström's decision was severe and swift. She received criticism for ending the military agreement across the Arab world. The day the deal was ended, Saudi recalled its ambassador from Stockholm. The United Arab Emirates also recalled its ambassador from Sweden. Saudi Arabia organized the fifty-seven–member-state Organization of Islamic Cooperation, along with the twenty-two member states of the Arab League, to protest the "flagrant interference" in its domestic affairs.[62] Saudi Arabia further punished Sweden by declining business visas and not renewing current visas for Swedish citizens residing in Saudi Arabia. This decision cost Sweden millions of kronor in military sales, as well as diplomatic political capital across the Gulf region.

Wallström's decision to speak out against Saudi Arabia's lack of gender equality and human rights abuses also came with controversy domestically. Leading Swedish business and military advisors challenged the decision, charging that it threatened their credibility as a trade partner throughout the Middle East region.[63] This case in diplomatic affairs illustrates the difficulties, and potentially severe repercussions, of governments and leaders who choose to stand for human rights globally. Regardless of the backlash, Wallström's outspokenness demonstrated how Sweden, at times, prioritized human rights above other state interests.

Swedish diplomats have promoted LGBTI rights—and human rights in general—to such a degree that they have jeopardized bilateral relationships and other foreign policy priorities. For example, in 2012, the former Swedish ambassador to Belarus Stefan Eriksson attended the local trials of democracy activists in Minsk, including LGBTI advocates who were calling for increased freedom of association and assembly for LGBTI people, as well as generally protesting for the improved human rights of Belarussian people under Lukashenko's regime. Human rights and democracy are severely repressed in Belarus under President Alexander Lukashenko, who has been in power since 1994.[64] Given Lukashenko's long consolidation of power, it is difficult for diplomats and human rights activists to influence human rights reform in the country. For foreign diplomats, and an ambassador from an EU nation, to attend trials of political opposition leaders can draw great ire from a local government. In doing so, Ambassador Eriksson risked other Swedish interests, such as trade partnerships between Swedish and Belarusian companies. Eriksson was subsequently deemed persona non grata by the Belarusian government and expelled from the country. Sweden followed suit and denied entry of the new Belarusian ambassador to Sweden and revoked the Swedish residency of two Belarusian diplomats.[65] Expelling a country's ambassador is a serious action in diplomatic affairs. The two countries risk undermining trade relationships, collaborative agreements within the EU region, and security negotiations. Sweden's willingness to jeopardize its diplomatic interests in Belarus represents Stockholm's readiness to risk other national interests for the sake of human rights.

Sweden's LGBTI Foreign Policy

LGBTI rights are institutionally incorporated into the framework of Sweden's feminist foreign policy. Swedish officials assert that LGBTI rights are a critical component of their gender equality policies domestically and in foreign affairs.[66] At Stockholm Pride 2015, Swedish Minister of International Development Lövin declared, "If a country oppresses half of its population [women], the society cannot move forward. . . . Similarly, LGBTI rights, the rights of the child, disabled, etc. . . . enabling equality for all is a critical part of freedom and democratic development."[67] Lövin extended the LGBTI rights policy, committing SIDA to fully integrate LGBTI rights into all international development goals. She argued, "We include LGBTI rights in our dialogues along with other human rights pillars . . . and look at how we can integrate LGBTI into every engagement."[68] Her statement is unprecedented for a foreign policy leader in that it implied that, as the head of the agency, Lövin would place the full force of the institution's influence on promoting LGBTI rights. Additionally, it conveyed the depth of the commitment of the Swedish state to LGBTI rights as a strategic issue in international affairs. Lövin declared further in 2015, "All [Sweden's] foreign policy is centered in a 'rights-based' policy. Promoting LGBTI rights is part of our comprehensive policy to all our relations."[69] Swedish foreign policy leaders thus elevated LGBTI rights to become a cornerstone of their engagements with foreign governments in international affairs.

In December 2003, the Swedish Parliament adopted Sweden's new policy for global development (PGD), which stated, "The rights perspective focuses on discriminated, excluded and marginalized individuals and groups. . . . People must be able to enjoy their rights regardless of sex, age, disability, ethnic background and sexual orientation."[70] This was the first time sexual orientation was formally incorporated into SIDA's global work as presented to the Swedish Parliament. In 2003, SIDA commissioned an independent study on the link between sexual orientation and gender identity, poverty, and development. It was the first report of its kind in the world issued by an international aid donor government to link poverty and development concerns specifically to discrimination against LGBTI populations. The report was later used by transnational activists and foreign diplomats to shape emerging LGBTI diplomatic policy of other nations.

Swedish development offices were some of the first to report officially on the missing dimension of "sexuality" in democracy and human rights international work.[71] In 2005, the Swedish government commissioned a study for SIDA to begin support for LGBTI rights and then created an action plan for promoting LGBTI rights in Sweden's international aid.[72] SIDA connected sexual minority concerns to its broader international development strategies. LGBTI discrimination became an official agenda topic incorporated into policies and programs related to gender equality, reproductive rights, and global health (namely with HIV/AIDS programs). General human rights and democracy promotion indirectly incorporated LGBTI rights as well. For example, included in the rubric of human rights/ democracy promotion's *Freedom of Expression*, 11 percent of funding has gone toward LGBTI rights and activist groups since 2009.[73] Bureaucratically, this would be recorded as human rights and freedom of expression funding, however, it also has the indirect; long-term goal of LGBTI rights promotion. A significant portion of Sweden's human rights foreign funding goes toward supporting LGBTI civil society organizations throughout the world. The International Lesbian and Gay Association (ILGA), Outright Action International (formerly IGLHRC), and ARC International are just a few of the many international organizations that receive financial support from the Swedish government. In turn, those organizations provide small grants to local LGBTI civil society organizations worldwide. SIDA is one of the largest international donors to LGBTI NGOs and civil society organizations.[74] The Swedish government also supports LGBTI work in international bodies such as the Office of the High Commissioner of Human Rights and the International Court of Justice.

The first SIDA-funded LGBTI-specific development project initiative began with a small budget of 0.6 MSEK ($74,238.54) in response to the 2005 action plan.[75] By 2013, SIDA support for eleven specific LGBTI initiatives had ballooned to 15.7 MSEK ($1,942,672.47).[76] Funding and programs have only expanded since then, and SIDA runs country-specific and regionally focused programs promoting global LGBTI rights.[77] While SIDA has identified target regions and areas such as Vietnam and Uganda, it also raises LGBTI rights comprehensively across bilateral and multilateral relationships globally. In partnership with RFSL, SIDA sponsors targeted programs such as the Indonesia and Uganda projects and a global program called Rainbow Leaders, cosponsored with other international donor agencies.[78] Rainbow Leaders is one of the world's largest and most comprehensive LGBTI activism training programs, which equips activists with the skills and experience to manage and sustain their organizations within harsh sociopolitical environments through curricula focused on international law, logical framework development, fundraising, and empowerment. To illustrate the substance of one of the programs SIDA sponsored in collaboration with the EU and the RFSL, the Eastern Coalition For LGBTI Equality is a program implemented in several countries (Armenia, Azerbaijan, Belarus, Georgia, Kosovo, Moldova, Serbia, Ukraine, and Russia) that supports nascent LGBTI organizations.[79] The project supports coalitions between movements in former Soviet states, helps activists combat anti-LGBTI legislation, and builds organizational capacities within those countries. For example, SIDA has supported GenderDoc, Moldova's only LGBTI rights activist organization, since 2010, primarily through funding of information initiatives and activist training; SIDA's financial support of GenderDoc reached about SEK 5 million ($494,500) between 2018 and 2020.[80] The agenda of the Policy Action Plan focuses on raising awareness of LGBTI human rights and supporting local civil society.[81] Independent analysts find that civil society organizations are increasingly financially dependent on external, foreign sources of funding, such as SIDA.[82] In an initial evaluation of its work, SIDA, in consultation with local partners, concluded, "In some countries, the survival of organizations and protection of [LGBTI] activists is a result of the Swedish support."[83] Human rights organizations working in authoritarian states often lack human and financial resources. SIDA plays an integral role in capacity building for many of these international LGBTI civil society organizations.

While SIDA takes the institutional lead on LGBTI rights programming for the Swedish government, the Swedish Foreign Ministry (UD) is the lead agency for the country's central diplomatic engagements. Swedish diplomats formally raise LGBTI rights in exchanges and dialogues with foreign governments. Diplomats are directed to advocate for LGBTI rights in high-level negotiations, promote reform of anti-homosexuality laws, and support fledgling LGBTI foreign civil society groups.[84] Funding mainly comes from Stockholm, through UD and SIDA's general budget, but also occasionally from the Swedish embassy in specific countries, such as Croatia and Russia.[85] Direct embassy funding is indicative of a diplomatic country team prioritizing LGBTI rights as a critical bilateral priority. Minister Lövin reasoned, "We include LGBTI rights and human rights in our anti-terrorism guidelines, pillars of protecting minority rights, and our whole comprehensive political engagement."[86] The Swedish Foreign Ministry's inclusion of LGBTI diplomacy with anti-terrorism mandates is exceptional. In other government foreign policies, anti-terror guidelines are often unrelated to human rights or are addressed in separate negotiations.[87]

Considerations for LGBTI violence outside the country is also incorporated into Swedish asylum laws. Sweden amended its law in 1997 to accept asylum claims for "homosexuals who feared persecution."[88] Sweden is one of a growing number of countries—Canada, the United States and the UK, among other nations—where foreign nationals can claim asylum based upon claimants' sexual orientation and gender identity.[89] The Swedish

Migration Agency (MV) is the lead institution to adjudicate those cases.[90] Since 1997, the MV has created comprehensive analysis tools for adjudicating LGBTI asylum claims.

Claiming asylum based on sexual orientation is exceptionally difficult to prove. Unlike other asylum claims, such as discrimination claims based on ethnicity, religion, or political affiliation, where the claimant likely would have documented evidence of violence or persecution, or an asylum officer can physically see that the person belongs to a minority group, LGBTI persons often lack evidence to support their asylum claim.[91] LGBTI persons seeking asylum often come with no formal evidence of ever having had a same-sex relationship; often, no photographic or other evidence exists because documenting a same-sex relationship could get them killed or jailed. For example, as many gay teens and adults in Sweden regularly take photos, selfies with friends and partners, start families, and marry same-sex partners with ample photos, there are witnesses, observers, and evidence to demonstrate their relationships. This is in contrast with youth and adults claiming asylum from Turkey or Nigeria, where they can be arrested for public affection of a same-sex partner or revealing transgender identity, let alone take pictures evidencing a relationship. With respect to asylum, LGBTI people can be considered an "invisible minority" for two reasons: first, compared with other minority groups, there is often no outward distinction, and second, in many cultures, LGBTI people have worked their whole lives to keep their sexuality invisible to their community for their safety.[92] As evidence is hard to produce for LGBTI individuals seeking asylum, Swedish officials have the difficult task of adjudicating the veracity of the claim.

There is great international controversy about the misuse of asylum claims, mainly as a ruse for channeling economic immigrants.[93] Especially since the immigration crisis in 2015, the rise in asylum claims have overwhelmed most EU agencies. Worse still, globally some individuals connected to terrorist organizations have gained refugee status and manipulated the asylum process.[94] The connection between terrorism and asylum is the focus of great political debate and contemporary research. Scholars Markus Rheindorf and Ruth Wodak demonstrate how right-wing parties especially exaggerate threats from immigration and refugees for political gain.[95] Researchers establish that political parties and the media manufacture fear in many societies to grow support for anti-immigration policies.[96] Yet still, Swedish officials must remain cognizant that in the immigration process, some claimants will disingenuously claim asylum based on sexual orientation. To that end, Sweden's asylum officers are trained as specialists to adjudicate

LGBTI asylum claims. Swedish officials travel to prevalent asylum-seeking countries to learn more about their cultural context and LGBTI rights in the country. For example, in 2015, the MV funded asylum officers to travel to Uganda and Nigeria to assess LGBTI asylum claims and further understand the complexities of living as an LGBTI person in those societies.[97] Their daunting task is to analyze the country data and understand the person's story and cultural context to make a decision on the validity of the asylum claim.

However, the MV is a government bureaucratic agency with failings. In a public forum at Stockholm Pride 2019, newcomers to Sweden discussed—albeit anonymously for their safety—the obstacles of the MV and asylum process.[98] Individuals shared their experiences of not understanding the process and not being believed by Swedish officials. Often coming from countries with corrupt governments, it is difficult for many to share their story openly and trust government officials.[99] Giorgia Matheson's 2019 research comparing the Swedish and Italian adjudication processes for LGBTI individuals fleeing from war indicates a highly problematic process where applicants report confusion and lack of control over their application experience that ultimately, for some, leads to new experiences of state oppression.[100] When examining the asylum seeker perspective parallel to the challenges of the Swedish government official needing evidence for the claim, adjudicating asylum cases for LGBTI individuals is rife with difficulties for both the applicant and officer. In a 2017 interview with Radio Sweden, immigration lawyer Silas Aliki—who opened Sweden's first legal firm focused on LGBTI asylum seekers—spoke about the uniqueness of the burden of proof LGBTI asylum seekers face: "For LGBTI people, a big thing is credibility. . . You have to be a 'credible' lesbian, gay or trans person."[101] In a seminar during Stockholm Pride 2019, Aliki provided further detail on this burden of proof, especially in the context of trans asylum seekers: "No official documents match the trans experience, leading to issues with credibility of seekers."[102] Significant political, social, and bureaucratic challenges remain for Sweden and other countries willing and able to accept asylum seekers based on LGBTI violence and discrimination.

One result of MV's asylum policy is that Stockholm has become an international hub of global LGBTI activist leaders living in exile. The country hosts high-profile international LGBTI leaders from places such as Belarus, Chechnya, Iran, Russia, and Turkey, among other nations. Sweden is an oft reported country for LGBTI persons globally to seek resettlement because of Sweden's reputation as a place for LGBTI equality. Jon Binnie and Christian Klesse document a person seeking to leave violence and discrimination in Poland stating, "I myself wanted to leave (Poland), to Scandinavia, to Sweden. . ."[103] Sweden's asylum policy has led to collaboration of global LGBTI leaders and activists, fostering a base for the intellectual, transnational LGBTI movement.

Analysis of Key Factors Influencing Swedish Foreign Policy Reform to Include LGBTI Rights

NGO Advocacy; Targeted Institutional Advocacy

The first and arguably most influential factor for reforming Sweden's foreign policy was NGO advocacy, and specifically targeted institutional advocacy from LGBTI influential civil society groups. Since its founding in 1950, RFSL leaders have strategized long- and short-term targeted action plans for domestic and Swedish foreign policy reform. Their organization's ultimate goal, as described by one former leader of the organization, was "to make LGBTI rights a part of the general structure of the Swedish foreign ministry's (UD's) global human rights portfolio."[104] A human rights international development officer at SIDA remembered, "RFSL came knocking on our door stating, 'You must work on LGBTI rights; it is an important work that our country cannot ignore.' RFSL was instrumental in changing our [SIDA's] policy agenda."[105] Consistent and persistent activism over decades from Swedish civil society organizations, and in particular RFSL, was, and remains, a critical factor for Swedish policy reforms on LGBTI rights.[106] Through targeting institutional advocacy efforts, Swedish advocates worked for decades to shape the agenda of SIDA and the Swedish Foreign Ministry to prioritize LGBTI diplomacy.

Swedish civil society groups primarily focus their advocacy efforts on institutions with key relevant government leaders, rather than public demonstrations on the streets. Institutional advocacy is conceptualized here from Lang's work as the attempt to influence decision-making by gaining some degree of insider status in institutions or organizations that initiate, prepare, legislate, or execute policy change.[107] According to a former president of RFSL, "Our general strategy was to advocate to politicians and government ministers—to conduct poignant and targeted meetings with key officials."[108] In 1987, the Swedish Parliament funded RFSL to educate the public, political parties, and government leaders about the critical concerns of global LGBTI rights. That strategy also included creating awareness campaigns and educational seminars concerning the importance of LGBTI rights in humanitarian aid, the detrimental effects of discrimination from HIV/AIDS and other societal stigmas, and the potential role Sweden could play in raising LGBTI rights as human rights internationally.[109] Hosted and funded by the Swedish Parliament, RFSL led an annual seminar for education and awareness. Diverse topics addressed in the 1980s and 1990s covered topics such as LGBTI health care needs, the diversity of sexual orientation and gender identity, same-sex partnership laws, international adoption, and asylum. Advocates were brought into Swedish institutions not just to lobby their case, but also to educate members of Parliament (MPs), public health officials, diplomats, and other public leaders on global LGBTI rights.

Swedish LGBTI civil society was integrated into the policy debate of commencing a feminist foreign policy and LGBTI diplomacy at its inception. As Pia Laskar documents, from about 1995, RFSL's parliamentary lobbying for a "broader homosexual citizenship (including fundamental rights such as decriminalization of homosexual acts, the right to organize, etc.) in aid recipient countries expanded and focused on countries in Africa."[110] Human rights advocacy scholar Jo Becker emphasizes the importance of civil society gaining access to the political institutions that advocacy groups seek to change.[111] Over time, RFSL became the lead conduit organization for the Swedish government on LGBTI rights.

In the early 2000s, SIDA's core work focused on combating war and poverty and improving women's rights. RFSL lobbied SIDA to look at LGBTI rights as a unique aspect of post-conflict concerns. RFSL's staff brought activists from war-torn countries, such as Sierra Leone, to SIDA to raise the issue of sexual violence during war. The activists informed Swedish officials about the distinct needs of the LGBTI community in postwar reconciliation methods, theretofore unaddressed by SIDA's international development work. RFSL and others changed the Swedish government's agenda by providing evidence that LGBTI rights were linked to general development and thereby were a critical need in the development of international programs.

RFSL's consistent message was that LGBTI groups are impacted in war, through public policy, and by foreign aid in distinctive ways. While advocating for the institutionalization of LGBTI rights in Swedish foreign policy, advocates would stress to government officials that "SIDA was neglecting an important group of marginalized populations."[112] One interviewee explained that the governmental knowledge and awareness of LGBTI violence and discrimination around the world was limited because "old-timer employees prioritized other issues of development."[113] For example, groups for people with disabilities and ethnic and religious minorities often have specific programs and funding in international development programs to address their needs. It took RFSL many years of institutional advocacy to explain to Swedish foreign affairs officials how LGBTI populations' needs were not being met by existing international development programs.

Initially, some SIDA representatives responded with skepticism. However, through consistent institutional advocacy, civil society groups were able to make the case for the importance of addressing LGBTI rights in Swedish foreign policy. Advocates recounted that officers would ask them, "Why should we support this fringe group? How are they different, and why do they need to be identified as a separate group?"[114] RFSL officers worked to document how LGBTI people were vulnerable to homelessness, joblessness, violence, marginalization, and poverty specifically because of their sexual orientation and gender identity. Thereby, LGBTI populations were insufficiently addressed under existing foreign policy mandates and international development programs at the time. RFSL conducted initial targeted institutional advocacy of political party leaders and MPs who, while at times reticent adoptees, recognized that the government lacked data and knowledge on the link between LGBTI rights and international development. In 2003, as a result of pressure from advocates, members of the government directed SIDA to study the link between sexual orientation and gender identity as connected to poverty and development; SIDA subsequently published a report of its findings based on a systematic analysis of global studies on the intersectionality of poverty and sexuality.[115] Swedish advocates worked to document LGBTI discrimination in housing, employment, and medical treatment as a means of proving that LGBTI populations deserve protections and support equal to what other marginalized groups receive. The final report recognized that existing development pillars such as global health, women's rights, and education did not sufficiently address the distinct needs of LGBTI populations in terms of discrimination and marginalization in employment, health services, housing and beyond. The marginalization and vulnerability of LGBTI populations in Indonesia, Mozambique, Namibia, and Vietnam, for example, were not previously addressed by international donor agencies. According to SIDA at the time, "Few studies and reports examine the relationship between poverty and the denial of sexual rights."[116] The Swedish government, using the documentation and expertise of RFSL advocates, was one of the first official foreign ministries in the world to make this link correlating poverty and LGBTI discrimination.

The report continues to be used by advocates and government officials in Sweden, the United States, and other countries.[117] In 2015–2018, interviewees for *From Pariah to Priority* working within the EU, UN, and United States referenced data from this original Swedish government report: they used evidence from the Swedish government to lobby their own governments and other international organizations.[118] US-based advocates used evidence from Swedish civil society groups and SIDA reports to lobby the US State Department on the need for LGBTI diplomacy and funding for LGBTI-specific international development programs. Swedish advocates and government officials laid the foundation for global advocates to argue the imperative of addressing LGBTI discrimination in global poverty eradication efforts. Research developed by think tanks, scholars, and policy institutes continue to conduct follow-up research to this report.

Establishing the causal relationship between a country's economic development and LGBTI discrimination is an enormous undertaking. Contemporary analysis and large-scale global data from the Williams Institute provide evidence that the GDPs of Brazil, India, and other nations are decreased because of official discrimination, demonstrating the impact LGBTI discrimination has on a country's economy and overall development.[119] Scholars assert the critical work of collecting evidence and documentation of human rights abuses to influence policy change.[120] Foreign ministries require evidence of discrimination and marginalization to be moved to change policy priorities.

As in any large institution, drafting a report does not necessarily translate into immediate policy reformation. Civil society leaders attested that SIDA's report in 2003 did not lead to satisfactory bureaucratic changes soon enough.[121] After the report was completed, advocates did not want it to languish within the Swedish foreign affairs agencies, nor did they let it. When they observed a lack of immediate action from state officials to reform programs according to the report's recommendations, advocates turned to leading politicians in [Parliament].[122] In an advocacy loop within their own government, those politicians directed the executive branch of government—mainly SIDA officers—to create an action to reform Swedish global development policy according to the report's findings and recommendations. Those recommendations led, in part, to the overall institutionalization of LGBTI rights in foreign affairs agencies in Swedish foreign policy institutions.

RFSL has intricately interwoven its work into the broader Swedish government's agenda. One SIDA human rights officer asserted, "My colleagues at SIDA and I realized early on that RFSL is an important organization for Sweden and also the global LGBTI movement. It is an organization that has pushed the development of LGBTI rights globally. Therefore, Sweden has an important knowledge base; we have developed expertise on this issue."[123] The integration of RFSL with Swedish government agendas has only increased with time. According to a government human rights officer at SIDA, "RFSL helped us because at first we didn't have experience, networks, or training on the issues . . . they were a part of our internal discussions."[124] Furthermore, interviewees asserted that, at times, SIDA officers treated the entire organization of RFSL almost as a wing of the government. Similarly, government officials regarded RFSL staff at times as colleagues. Seeking recommendations from civil society for foreign policy formation, as found to be the case in Sweden, is not common practice in other countries.

As a result of targeted institutional advocacy, RFSL and others became well-known in the halls of power in the Swedish government. Accordingly, RFSL used that relationship to become strategic advisors on government policy on LGBTI rights in Swedish foreign relations. In 2015, the Swedish Justice Minister Morgan Johansson recognized how RFSL became instrumental in increasing the expertise of his agency, the Swedish Migration Agency.[125] That same year, the Migration Agency requested expertise from RFSL to help civil servants better understand violence against transgender persons in target countries. Those civil servants adjudicate asylum claims based on sexual orientation, and their knowledge of violence against LGBTI people and norms in other societies is imperative to their work. RFSL advised officers and completed a comprehensive report on international violence against transgender people, which resulted in increased capacity of Swedish government asylum adjudicators. That collaboration increased the migration board's expertise when reviewing cases. Also that year, Minister Johansson allocated 10 million kronor ($1.2 million) for more research on LGBTI violence around the world.

Swedish LGBTI advocates served as important strategic advisors while conducting institutional advocacy in the government agencies they sought to reform. For instance, in the early 2000s, the Swedish embassies globally received a directive from Stockholm's SIDA headquarters to commence LGBTI diplomacy. However, embassy officials did not receive country-specific directives on how the Swedish government would implement LGBTI diplomacy locally. At the time, some embassy officials contacted RFSL civil society leaders to help devise a country plan for Swedish diplomatic engagement on LGBTI issues.[126] According to one leading advocate, "The [Swedish] government does not expect you to be quiet."[127] The government allows, and even encourages, advocacy from inside its halls or by way of public advocacy. Swedish advocates serve as strategic advisors for specific policy formation and generation of new program ideas.

High levels of integration of civil society within a foreign policy institution is exceptional from an international perspective. Many other governments often treat their local NGOs with antagonism and often try to obstruct their work.[128] On a global scale, civil society groups are rarely allowed access inside foreign affairs institutions, especially during policy deliberations. In authoritarian states, governments often work to silence civil society organizations and even at times physically threaten and arrest human rights activists.[129] The Peruvian and Chinese governments, for example, do not allow transparent access into the policy deliberations of their respective foreign policy apparatus.[130] In countries where state support dominates civil society, the government can control the agenda, and authorities can make overt and covert attempts to shut down organizations.[131]

When I worked with NGOs across North Africa, covert government officials would often attend quarterly meetings of human rights advocacy organizations; everyone in the room would often know there was an undercover government representative present, listening to their conversation, and later documenting the meeting results. Advocates knew the government could shut down their work and arrest them at any time if they were too critical of state policies. Even in many liberal democracies, at times it can be hard to gain access to foreign ministries or secure meetings with top diplomats, and foreign ministries tend to be much more closed to civil society. In the United States and other nations, civil society groups often face closed doors or even hostility to collaboration if they run counter to the leading political party's agenda. The US State Department or the British Foreign Office do not conceptualize officers of Human Rights Campaign or Amnesty International, for example, as integral experts on American or British foreign policy. In many countries, foreign ministries are either closed to civil society or antagonistic to human rights advocacy.

By contrast, RFSL and Swedish civil society organizations have exceptional access and influence over Swedish foreign policy formation. In Tiffany Jones's comparative work on transgender advocacy in the UN, Jones finds, "Some Northern countries had in place (such as Sweden since 1950) clear-cut NGO structures allowing community representation which stimulated the prioritization of funding for transgender themes from the community itself over time."[132] Remarkably, Swedish interviewees spoke of the two organizations, SIDA and RFSL, one governmental and one nongovern-mental, almost interchangeably.[133] RFSL's advocacy and persistent presence in society and government engagements have led to a blurring of lines between government actors and civil society in shaping new foreign policy goals. Advocates in Sweden serve as consultants and integrated advisors on developing LGBTI diplomacy goals.

NGO Public Advocacy

Advocates in Scandinavia historically do not make demands of the state through large street protests. Instead, they tend to put immense efforts into public awareness campaigns, live public debates, and cultural events that are open to the public. Mustola and Rydström provide a historical analysis of Sweden's domestic transformations, tracing Scandinavia's transformation from a region that once outlawed homosexual activity to becoming "pro-gay Scandinavia."[134] They argue that public awareness campaigns, including high-profile court cases, led to an increased public awareness of the existence and prevalence of homosexuality. Public visibility and public awareness campaigns mainly in the 1970s and 1980s led to a shift toward support for equality in public opinion and government policies.

Stockholm Pride is the central annual flagship event for LGBTI activists in Sweden.[135] Organized by RFSL, the Stockholm Pride Board, and other transnational LGBTI advocacy groups, Stockholm Pride is the single largest annual event—including entertainment, politics, and sports—in all of Scandinavia. Stockholm Pride 2018 had "60,000 participants and 600,000 spectators."[136] Over time, the event has become a global nexus for the creation of new LGBTI human rights norms. It has become the leading public advocacy event to raise awareness about equality in Sweden and globally. Organizers gather national and international leaders, civil society groups, foreign diplomats, film directors, transnational activists, political party leaders, and others to attend and publicly discuss the status of the international movement.

During Stockholm Pride, discussions across Swedish media outlets, television programming, and businesses permeate all aspects of public life. For one week, the duration of Stockholm Pride, the entire city becomes inundated with rainbow flags, music, art, images, and other references to Pride. High-end department stores such as NK hang rainbow banners in their locations. Starbucks offers rainbow coffee cups. Public Swedish city buses fly rainbow flags on their mirrors.[137] Unlike Pride festivals around the world that center on a parade and focus more on a celebration of LGBTI identities, alongside the celebration, Stockholm Pride is an influential week-long public political forum that brings together thousands of activists and thought leaders from all over the world for public discourse. Taking place in the center of Stockholm, public discussions cover torture practices in Chechnya, reparations for transgender people forcibly sterilized in Sweden and across Europe, ending official violence against LGBTI people in Iran, political asylum for international activists, and Swedish governmental support of fledgling LGBTI groups around the globe.[138]

Swedish activists also learn from the many international advocates who attend Pride events across Sweden from South and North America, Asia, and across Europe. Hailing from Brazil, the Netherlands, Nigeria, and other nations, activists discuss best practices and contemporary needs of their equality movement within their own country and internationally. Advocates engage in public discourse regarding successes and lessons learned from the Swedish LGBTI movement and offer insights for newer movements in places such as Armenia and Belarus. Lang defines public advocacy as NGOs "tailor[ing] their communication toward mobilizing, synthesizing, and amplifying citizen voices."[139] During Stockholm Pride, global activists discuss how best to mobilize resources within Sweden and across borders. This was exemplified during a seminar at Stockholm Pride 2019 titled "Our Spaces, Our Rights: Eastern Europe," in which the panel facilitator focused the discussion with Eastern European activists on a key question: "What can we do in the global North to help support activism?" Panelists repeatedly emphasized the need for transnational pressure in support of their LGBTI rights movements.[140] Another seminar, "Rainbow Riots India," introduced attendees to the work of Swedish activist Peter Wallenberg, who has collaborated with the Dancing Queens, an LGBTI dance group in India, and rapper Tropical Marka, in using artistic mediums for activism.[141] The magnitude of Stockholm Pride contributes to an overall impact on general political opportunities on the national level.[142] Advocates generate and update movement goals as well as amplify their collective demands to Swedish government leaders and members of Parliament.

Advocates from other more conservative European societies seek Swedish and other Northern Europe LGBTI networks to aid them in their cause. Reflective of Keck and Sikkink's "boomerang theory," international activists have, at times, circumvented their own leaders, looking to Swedish and other European powers to apply pressure to their own governments.[143] During Pride, advocates also have the opportunity to admonish Swedish leaders for not stressing LGBTI rights more with other EU leaders. A prominent Portuguese activist noted, "Sweden and Dutch leaders should do more. . . we are members of the same [European] union and cannot accept inequality. . . we need more political pressure from your governments."[144] In the face of resistance from their home government, they called for continued pressure from outside governments to influence change domestically. Pride events around Sweden are an annual opportunity for global advocates to generate and update movement goals, as well as amplify their collective demands to Swedish government leaders and members of Parliament.

Stockholm Pride is one of the most dynamic LGBTI political manifestations in the world. For a comparison, in other countries Pride marches do not gather such high proportions of the population or raise issues of international or foreign policy. Researchers occasionally criticize the evolution of the Pride parade from a protest march to a tourist attraction in many cities. In many liberal democracies, Pride celebrations are centered on a one-day parade. They tend to be more oriented as a party and celebration. For example, surveys of participants at Dublin pride have referred to Pride as a "place of fun"; the popularity of this public opinion shows that many assume there is no longer a need for an "angry march," which may be reflective of the politics of the host country and public consensus on whether Pride is seen as a national or international event.[145] In 2017, activist Peter Tatchell wrote a letter to the Pride in London committee, expressing concerns regarding the event: "What began in 1972 as a protest for LGBT rights has now become an overly-commercialized, bureaucratic and rule-bound event, which too often reflects the wishes of the city authorities, not the LGBT community."[146] Pride events across the United States do not have as much of a political focus as in Sweden; if politics and policies are discussed, they are mainly regional or domestic. Speakers often facilitate discourse regarding civil rights within the United States and diverse queer identity.[147] Government leaders at times inform audiences and discuss evolving health care policies and regulations from the Department of Health and Human Services (Ministry of Health).[148] However, foreign policy is rarely a highlighted topic in US pride events. Pride celebrations globally tend to focus on domestic policy and individual experiences related to sexual orientation and gender identity.

A former leader within the organization of Stockholm Pride made clear that the organizers of Stockholm Pride in the early 2000s did not want the events to center on a giant party; while celebratory, they also wanted Stockholm Pride to focus on domestic and international political movement goals of fighting for equality.[149] For example, the backsliding of LGBTI rights in Poland and Hungary is of great concern to Swedish advocates, both from a sense of international solidarity and also because of the close proximity to Sweden. Regression of rights across the EU could influence Swedish borders in the future. Therefore, it is in advocates' and government officials' interest to engage in international affairs and evolving standards of equality across the continent and globe.

The solidification of LGBTI equality within European identity is often a central focus of seminars at Stockholm Pride. At Stockholm Pride 2015, Moldovan activists directly attributed internal reforms in Moldova on LGBTI rights to Swedish leaders' advocacy and EU human rights requirements for Moldova's accession into the European Union.[150] According to one advocate in the same panel, "Our politicians have had to focus and publicly discuss LGBTI rights due to pressure from countries like Sweden and other nations in the EU."[151] A body of scholarship analyzes the idea of "Europeanness" correlated with LGBTI rights and how this normative shift across the continent has led to policy changes in newer EU member nations.[152] Safia Swimelar documents that in places such as Serbia and Croatia, concerns about acceptance for membership into the EU directly influenced domestic politics to support same-sex marriage and other societal norms.[153] A representative of the International Lesbian and Gay Association (ILGA-Europe) in Brussels referenced EU accession as the single most important leverage point for the LGBTI movement in the EU region: "With these 'carrots and sticks,' advocates have been able to realize a great deal of reforms because countries want so badly to be in the EU and be considered 'European.' "[154] Swedish leaders and advocates have played a key role in prioritizing LGBTI human rights in EU policies. This role is both debated and promoted during Pride events throughout the country.

In places such as Belarus and Russia, repression from authorities does not necessarily depend on a group promoting LGBTI rights, but rather that the group is organizing politically in the first place. Activists have found that restrictions on individuals in terms of freedom of association, speech, or expression often starts with a crackdown on LGBTI groups.[155] According to one activist, "In Minsk, repression is not unique to us trying to organize a Pride parade, but rather relates to all public events, as they are all forbidden."[156] Moldovan representatives at Stockholm Pride recognized that their work is first and foremost about LGBTI rights, but also broadly aimed toward a goal of promoting human rights more generally in their society and globally. One advocate shared further, "We are working towards overall democratic development in our country."[157] One leading activist from a former Soviet state asserted, "Any NGO dealing with human rights issues in the former Soviet Union has problems; they go after us all."[158] In Stockholm Pride 2019, a transgender panelist from Russia stated that "issues for the trans community remain invisible," especially because "laws that restrict organizing into NGOs inhibit mobilization and outreach," and anti-propaganda laws restrict any education about LGBTI rights to the public.[159] In response, community mobilization has gone underground in Russia, and many activists are trying to work with the medical community to provide transition services. In many Eastern EU countries demonstrations are not allowed, regardless of the issue. Freedom of association and expression for all individuals and groups generally are highly regulated across Eastern Europe.[160] Thus, activists stated that NGOs are actively building coalitions with other human rights groups and activists, such as women's rights and disability rights groups, to gain strength against their respective governments. In this way, LGBTI groups seek and organize with other democracy activists to push for general human rights reforms in their countries.

Coalitions of transnational networks and human rights groups influenced the initial LGBTI movement in Sweden and its sustainability in Swedish foreign policy and international business practices. Transnational activists' public advocacy and discourse remains an important factor for the sustained durability of LGBTI rights in Swedish institutions. Allying with the global movement has helped Swedish advocates keep the issue a top priority in Sweden's foreign policy. Scholars have shown that transnational actors can leverage international networks to further their cause.[161] A current manifestation of transnational networks' influence is the fact that Swedish companies' corporate policies often reflect the human rights values of Swedish society.

Public advocacy goes far beyond government bodies, and advocates across Pride events direct their efforts toward business and private companies. Corporate social responsibility business strategies are mechanisms for companies to articulate commitments to labor rights, environmental practices, and other normative standards.[162] LGBTI civil society leaders pressure companies such as IKEA, H&M, Scandia, and others to include LGBTI equality in their corporate social responsibility platforms.[163] These business platforms, in theory, commit companies to inclusive hiring and nondiscriminatory workplace practices, even in corporate international satellite offices where LGBTI discrimination may be codified within local laws. In Poland, for example, the Swedish-based company Scandia hosted and funded a local training for diversity in its Warsaw offices.[164] These types of trainings occur within the context of growing anti-LGBTI sentiment in Poland: regional officials and politicians have declared their cities and regions to be "LGBT-free zones," where the LGBTI community has been deemed "unwelcome."[165] Despite local contestation, some Swedish businesses actively support Pride festivals across Eastern Europe, Latin America, and more, visibly connecting their brand to the international equality movement.[166] During public events, advocates have the opportunity to address and challenge business leaders on their corporate practices, both in theory and practice, pushing toward upholding LGBTI equality in the workplace.

Advocates have publicly highlighted how the corporate practices espoused by headquarters in Stockholm are not always followed in practice in foreign offices. IKEA, along with most multinational Swedish-based companies, has an explicit policy of nondiscrimination and equality for all workers.[167] However, advocates publicly hold IKEA leaders to account, charging that there is little follow-through with their internal policy. For example, IKEA's annual catalogue has been a source of contention among transnational activists. Illustrative of this controversy was its 2013 catalogue, when IKEA removed a lesbian couple, photographed in their London home with their child, from the Russian version of its catalog. This action created global backlash, exemplified by a staged "kiss-in" by LGBTI advocates at the IKEA located in Brooklyn, NY.[168] As IKEA spokesperson Ylva Magnusson explained to the *Wall Street Journal*, "One of the conditions we have of running our business is that we have to follow the law in the markets where we operate."[169] Magnusson referenced Russia's ban on "homosexual propaganda" or the advertisement of "nontraditional sexual relations."[170] Similarly, in 2012, IKEA removed pictures of women from its Saudi Arabian edition of its catalog because of local societal norms of excluding women in pictures. In both examples, the company adhered to local discriminatory practices, prioritizing the interest of corporate profits over LGBTI and gender equality practices, and not adhering to its own stated company values of diversity and inclusion. When companies diverge from their expressed labor practices of promoting equality in Sweden and abroad and do not uphold these mandates in practice, it can lead to global backlash and negative consequences for the company. Much improvement has been made in promoting LGBTI rights in its global business policies: in stark contrast to IKEA's actions in Russia in 2013, on May 16, 2019, the company published an online post showing support for the LGBTI community. This public company statement led to an unsupportive social media response from an IKEA employee in Poland. After the employee refused to take down his posts he was fired. An IKEA representative explained that his post "could affect the rights and dignity of LGBT+ persons."[171] Although enforced unequally, many multinational companies realize following through on equal treatment of all employees and labor standards is good for both the company's international reputation and bottom-line profits.

Similar to some Swedish-based companies, Swedish diplomats sometimes balk at challenging other powerful nations on LGBTI rights, even though Swedish foreign policy is supposed to prioritize gender equality. In the Russian case in 2013, activists criticized Swedish diplomats who were initially reticent to raise LGBTI rights with Russian leaders. In response to activists challenging IKEA's decision, Swedish diplomats stated that raising LGBTI rights too strongly in Russia "may hurt other Swedish interests."[172] Transnational activists found that company representatives and diplomats were equally nervous to stand up to Russia and risk "provoking the country too much, as it affects our other relations."[173] Swedish officials initially pulled back their human rights agenda in the face of market forces. Transnational activists, however, did not allow business transactions with foreign interests to win quietly. Instead, advocates publicly shamed IKEA as well as Swedish diplomats' feckless role in this instance for not standing up for LGBTI rights. The Russian IKEA catalogue controversy sparked a debate and direct action from Swedish and transnational LGBTI networks that contributed to reform of IKEA's multinational policies.

Developing literature examines the role of transnational corporations in contesting, as well as adopting, LGBTI-equality aligned business practices.[174] Similarly, researchers question the authenticity of business efforts and uncover "pinkwashing" hypocritical business practices.[175] The concept of pinkwashing, synthesized, can be understood as a broad range of appropriating LGBTI rights for corporate profit, for example, a rainbow flag on coffee cups at a café during Pride. Pinkwashing can also denote empty promises of equality policies that are not followed through in practice, or touting company or government policies on LGBTI issues while potentially ignoring or perpetuating other race, class, or environmental injustices.[176] Corinne Blackmer asserts that the State of Israel practices pinkwashing when celebrating its LGBTI policies, all the while attempting to conceal discriminatory practices toward Palestinians.[177] Similarly, corporations may tout their progressive LGBTI employee practices while downplaying their detrimental environmental impact in manufacturing. Many governments and private companies strive toward increasing equality policies; however, for a variety of motivations, they may not follow through on these claims, or they seek LGBTI equality policies to downplay other negative practices of the company or state. When companies or foreign leaders are reticent to uphold equality domestically or abroad, at times advocates turn to the strategy of diffusing political opposition.

NGOs Strategies to Diffuse Political Opposition

From outside Sweden's borders, observers may mistakenly believe there is a lack of resistance to LGBTI equality within the country due to high levels of public support for LGBTI equality. Indeed, some interviewees and participants from outside Scandinavia doubted the importance of examining Sweden's human rights record or analyzing opposition to LGBTI equality in Sweden, largely because of the false perception that Sweden has achieved full gender equality. That perception renders silent the gender-based crimes that occur in Sweden. Public opinion data from 2018 reveal that 93 percent of the Swedish population was "highly supportive of gay and lesbians' right to live their lives as they wish."[178] However, there is no country in the world yet free from gender-based violence. Scholars such as Hans Rosling illustrate how Swedish media continue to underplay and underreport gross domestic violence in Sweden similar to other counties.[179] During Stockholm Pride 2019, transgender asylum seekers publicly shared their experience of discrimination and violence while residing in Sweden.[180] One trans woman recounted their public assault on a street in Stockholm during broad daylight while a Swedish guard inside a building stood by, watched, and did nothing to help or stop the attack.[181] Transgender discrimination and violence are reported and documented in many sectors of Swedish society.[182] Sexual assault remains a significant problem that is documented to have increased over the last few years across the Swedish population.[183] LGBTI discrimination remains in Sweden, albeit evolving. As cultures and societal norms change over time, advocates develop various strategies to address contemporary political and societal needs.

Like most modern LGBTI movements, advocates' message of equality was initially rejected by some Swedish officials. During the HIV/AIDS crisis in the 1980s and 1990s, HIV-positive people (mostly documented as gay men at the time) were largely denied access to health care. Medical professionals reported that they were dying from cancer rather than HIV/AIDS, even when the cause of death was HIV/AIDS. Jonas Gardell's television series *Don't Ever Wipe Tears Without Gloves* recollects Sweden's often

forgotten dark past of mishandling the HIV/AIDs health crisis.[184] Gay men
were commonly stigmatized in society and the workplace, ostracized from
families, often denied such rights as attending the funerals of loved ones,
and could not get adequate health care for HIV/AIDS. Discrimination
against the Swedish LGBTI community persisted well into the 2000s and
continues in contemporary Swedish society, especially for those living with
HIV/AIDS.[185] While official legislation supports same-sex couples, studies
of LGBTI access to employment and housing show disparities in opportunities and lower wages based on sexual orientation or gender identity.[186]
Thus, although laws and societal norms are generally improving in Sweden,
LGBTI people at times continue to face legal and societal discrimination
throughout their lives including in employment, housing, and health care.

Over the decades, Swedish advocates for equality faced societal and
institutional opposition. Therefore, strategies of advocates adapted over time
to confront and diffuse opposition. Strategic framing was a critical component of diffusing opposition. LGBTI rights cover a wide range of diverse
issues. Significant power dynamics were at play from within political parties
and outside government in civil society. For example, in 1989, the Christian
Democratic Party (KD; *Kristdemokraterna*) strongly objected to Sweden's
proposed same-sex registered partnership law. The Swedish government
debated to enact a new same-sex partnership law that year. One leader
of the movement recalled, "Christian Democrats believed that homosexual
marriages would break the whole ground for family law to pieces. . . . If
homosexual marriage was accepted they [the KDs] believed there would no
longer remain any rational reasons not to accept polygamy."[187] The KDs
and other conservative groups historically fought to keep traditional family
structures.[188] LGBTI advocates worked hard to change these biases and
break down perceptions that equated same-sex partnerships with polygamy.
Domestically, institutional and public advocacy focused on educating the
public and government officials about queer identity and sexual orientation.

With regard to foreign affairs, advocates diffused skeptics' doubts by
initially focusing on grave human rights abuses of LGBTI people internationally. Addressing human rights abuses presented the most urgent need
of the LGBTI community globally and was the most politically palatable.
By focusing on platforms such as ending the imprisonment and killing of
LGBTI people, rather than perceived faith-based issues such as marriage or
adoption, advocates were able to gain a consensus among political parties.
Thereby, the approach of focusing on violence against LGBTI populations
manifested in reforms to Sweden's asylum laws.

Asylum for LGBTI people provided an important bridge between the leading political parties and the adversarial leaders in the early 1990s.[189] When advocates raised the dire human rights situation of LGBTI people in other countries, the Christian Democrats unexpectedly embraced ideas in Parliament to accept asylum seekers based on persecution due to their sexual orientation. An advocate recalled that this change came about because "Christian Democrats may have disagreed with different definitions of family, but they did not want people to be killed because of their sexual orientation."[190] The party ultimately shifted parts of its platform on LGBTI foreign policy, supporting LGBTI-friendly asylum policy proposals in Parliament "because they felt Sweden needed to protect people that are being most persecuted abroad."[191] Thus, after consolidating political support across the political party spectrum, in 1997 Sweden's asylum law was amended to include protection for asylum seekers who, because of homosexuality, feared persecution.[192] The KD's platform change due to grave human rights abuses for LGBTI foreign population made incremental changes for domestic reform an easier task. Framing and focusing advocacy on foreign violence toward LGBTI populations led to the softening of opposition to LGBTI policy reforms within the country.

Along with strategic framing, advocates used the strategy of public shaming to diffuse political opposition. In 2003, RFSL leaders used their organizational influence and public shaming to oust the most powerful Swedish diplomat, Jan Karlsson. At the time Karlsson served as the top government official of the triumvirate of the Swedish Foreign Ministry, SIDA, and the Migration Agency. In a SIDA-hosted conference regarding Sweden's international development work, a key topic of the conference was considerations for sexual orientation in Sweden's international development programs. Karlsson mistakenly believed his microphone was turned off and muttered, "Now all these gay questions need to come to an end!"[193] His comment was interpreted by Swedes as derogatory and close-minded, shedding light on his personal view that LGBTI rights concerns in foreign affairs were trivial. For Karlsson to express belittling regard for the work, not only within the privacy of his home or personal office, but at a SIDA conference no less, was extremely problematic for LGBTI advocates.[194] Furthermore, as one of Sweden's top foreign policy leaders at the time, his words carried enormous weight about his leadership over Swedish foreign policy. In 2003, advocates had gained a great deal of public support and institutional allies for the importance of Swedish foreign aid to address LGBTI violence and discrimination. The very next day, RFSL called for Karlsson's immediate resignation. His gaffe ignited a slew of media shaming reports in national news outlets and a public discussion on the value of LGBTI diplomacy in Swedish international development work. Sören Juvas (né Andersson, as seen published in the statement) was the head of RFSL when Karlsson made his statement. Juvas and other advocates spearheaded the calls for Karlsson's resignation. In the wake of the controversy, Karlsson resigned from office.[195] From this experience, leading advocates at the time "realized we had the political clout to call for his resignation. This experience still gives us power today: leaders fear getting a bad reputation or negative comments from RFSL."[196] Bringing down one of Sweden's top foreign policy leaders was no small feat, and it bolstered RFSL's political capital in the country. Interviewees in *From Pariah to Priority* still referenced this exchange with Karlsson and RFSL from 2003 more than a decade later. One advocate asserted that from this experience the "fear of public shaming continues to hold some government officials accountable from openly opposing LGBTI policy reform."[197] Publicly shaming political opponents was a powerful tactic that brought down a central foreign policy leader and continues to silence and diffuse political opposition.

Along with intermittent resistance from civil servants within the government, societal opposition to equality and nontraditional family structures surfaces annually around Stockholm Pride. According to a SIDA official, "Conservatives in society start harassing us before and during the Pride parade. . . There are homophobic groups who question our policy and international programs at SIDA on LGBTI rights."[198] However, officials and advocates believed those groups are disorganized and comprised of fringe individuals.[199] Since 2015, however, the political landscape in Sweden dramatically changed in the country, giving rise to the right-wing Swedish Democrats party (SD; *Sverigedemokraterna*).

The right-wing Swedish Democrats party has a fluid platform on LGBTI rights; at times challenging progressive gender norms, at times defining "Swedishness" based upon support for LGBTI equality. While established in the late 1980s, the SD gained popularity after Sweden accepted an unprecedented number of immigrants from Syria, Iraq, Afghanistan, and other Muslim nations; approximately 130,000 immigrants came to Sweden in 2015 alone.[200] Coming from neo-Nazi roots, SD leaders frame speeches around fear of immigrants, and their central campaign is an anti-immigration platform.[201] Kehl argues that emerging right-wing leaders co-opt LGBTI rights frames "to produce themselves as the true protectors of LGBTI rights in Sweden."[202] While the party platform continues to evolve, the SD's central conservative campaign agendas revolve around law and order, curbing immigration, reversing multiculturalism, cutting taxes, increasing military spending, and promoting traditional family structures.[203] Tobias Hübinette and Catrin Lundström find the racist policies of the SDs play on the fear and anger of Swedish voters, especially working-class white Swedish men, with the passing of "good Sweden."[204] After the 2018 general elections, the Sweden Democrats gained 17.5 percent of the votes during the Swedish general elections. Consequently, with this success, they became the third-largest party in the Riksdag (Swedish Parliament).[205] The SDs are unequivocally against immigration and want to overhaul the country's asylum policy that would include asylum claims based on LGBTI discrimination.[206] The Swedish Democrats' main political platform is one of anti-immigration, but they also espouse a heteronormative family structure and originally threatened to change the face of resistance to LGBTI norms in Sweden.[207]

The Swedish Democrats, however, are not easily classified as a traditional right-wing anti-LGBTI political party calling for the return of traditional gender roles. In fact, its political platform can be explained, in part, by the contemporary political phenomenon of homonationalism. In the Swedish context, Anna-Maria Sörberg's book from 2017, *Homonationalism*, addresses how LGBTI issues are appropriated and become a focal point for the nationalist movement in Sweden and across Europe.[208] Platforms of right-wing leaders solidified against "foreign and backward" immigrants perceived to be anti-LGBTI rights.[209] New immigrants, many of whom are Muslim, are assumed to be anti-LGBTI by the leaders of this populist party. SD leaders capitalize on those assumptions, claiming that LGBTI Swedish people "live in fear of hate crimes from foreigner migrants coming from homophobic, honor-bound, oppressive cultures."[210] The Swedish Democrats demonstrate homonationalism as they espouse xenophobic and racist claims, deploying assumptions that being against immigration is in the interest of protecting Swedish values and LGBTI equality. Katharina Kehl, for example, exhibits how this assumption is manipulated in nationalist discourses, marking new migrants, refugees, or Muslim groups as racial "Others" and outside Swedish society.[211] The SDs' anti-immigration stance would further hinder or halt asylum claims based on LGBTI discrimination internationally. More broadly, in a global context, Jasbir Puar argues that homonationalism intertwines national identity with queerness, whereby political powers manipulate and appropriate LGBTI rights to justify racist and xenophobic claims.[212] As LGBTI rights have become a central political issue in the majority of liberal democracies, political leaders have used LGBTI rights as the defining point to separate East/West, North/South, religious/secular modern democratic societies.

Leading political parties in the Netherlands, Sweden, and other nations have come to intertwine national identity with LGBTI equality. Researchers assert that "to be homosexual and tolerant has become synonymous with being Dutch. . . According to that logic, a white Dutch person cannot be homophobic."[213] Populist leaders articulate an assumption that tolerance of LGBTI persons and rights are a symbol of a progressive, modern society. Francesca Romana Ammaturo asserts a "dichotomy between tolerant and intolerant countries" permeates modern political politics across Europe.[214] This trend among politicians exemplifies the exploitation of human rights concepts such as the rights of minorities and freedom from discrimination to justify explicit exclusion of others who do not support LGBTI equality. Cristian Norocel's research illustrates how Sweden Democrats leader Jimmie Åkesson has reinterpreted the Swedish concept of "Folkhem" (peoples' home) to justify frames from the Swedish radical right as modern, all the while reinvigorating heteronormative masculinities.[215]

Contemporary LGBTI advocates and scholars and international Pride events work to combat the current trend of homonationalism. Many activists are horrified that political parties are using LGBTI rights frames as justification for exclusion of refugees.[216] RFSL criticizes the SD platform in public venues and issues public statements against the group. RFSL wrote a statement in 2016 against SD leaders' criticism of local city governments for paying tax money toward Pride events, calling for an end of municipal funds to support an "exhibitionist public event for people with an extreme need to show off their naked bodies."[217] The SDs publicly challenge state support for Pride events and other LGBTI rights programs. In Stockholm Pride 2019, RFSL organized several seminars focused on this topic of LGBTI rights and Swedish identity, including Sweden and homonationalism, LGBTI equality and Islam, and xenophobia and LGBTI Rights in Sweden.[218] One (anonymous) Swedish activist at Stockholm Pride 2019 expressed anger about politicians co-opting the LGBTI movement to exclude and denigrate newcomers to Sweden; in her mind, the LGBTI rights movement is "fundamentally based upon equality."[219] Other international activists recognize how polarizing LGBTI rights and immigration renders null the thousands of global LGBTI refugees and intersectional identity of some migrants.[220] Many nationalist parties across contemporary Europe engage in an "anti-gender" campaign.[221] Some nationalist parties, especially in the Netherlands, Sweden, and other Northern European countries, have appropriated LGBTI equality as a central part of their national identity in opposition to new immigrants.

At the same time, advocates contend with very low acceptance rates of LGBTI equality by many migrants and refugees entering the country.[222] At Stockholm Pride 2019, several LGBTI asylum seekers, specifically from Nigeria and Uganda, described their experience of trying to find community with other Nigerian and Ugandan migrants and refugees, but being met with animosity and discrimination within their immigrant community by other Nigerians and Ugandans in Sweden.[223] One asylum seeker succinctly summarized his experience in Sweden's Nigerian community: "I'm still living the same life I was in Nigeria."[224] To meet this need, RFSL provides public outreach and educational awareness resources about LGBTI rights for newcomers to Sweden. The RFSL Newcomers program provides counseling services and support to LGBTI asylum seekers who are still suffering discrimination in Sweden.[225] Their services include information about rights, legal support when filing a police report, and secret sheltered living. Swedish LGBTI advocates grapple with how to address LGBTI biases held by some immigrants to the country, educate and engage with newcomers to the country on LGBTI equality norms, and help to extricate LGBTI rights from a populist, xenophobic framework that is contrary to their core human rights work toward equal rights for all people.

Insider Allied Government Leadership

Leaders of the Swedish LGBTI movement came from both outside civil society leadership as well as from progressive insider government leaders. However, scholars often overlook bureaucrats or insider government representatives as social movement actors. Lee Ann Banaszak defines "insiders" as collective or individual actors located inside state institutions.[226] She argues that insiders within government, or individuals in places of power and influence, represent a critical factor in social movements.[227] The influential role of insider allies within government was critical for the Swedish foreign ministry to institutionalize LGBTI rights in Swedish foreign affairs.

As Pia Laskar documents, one of the results of RFSL's lobbying was garnering allies within Swedish Parliament, especially leaders within the Liberal Party (*Folkpartiet; L*).[228] Early on RFSL's "ears in the parliament were members of the liberal party (Folkpartiet); the liberals (Folkpartiet leaders) pushed the issue that aid would be conditional to promote rights for 'gays and bisexuals.'"[229] Laskar's demarcation is notable regarding Folkpartiet leaders becoming the "ears" of RFSL in Parliament. Liberal party leaders became allies of RFSL and in turn pushed for incorporating LGBTI considerations in Swedish foreign aid from within government.

The link between the behavior of a few individuals and their influence over policy change is critical in many social movements.[230] Notable Swedish leaders inside government of focus in this analysis are Birgitta Ohlsson, Mona Sahlin, and Barbro Westerholm. These leaders are representative of Swedish leaders from within government who have shaped and propelled the movement from their positions of influence. There are also several other prominent diplomats, other members of Parliament, and mid-level agency directors who determined LGBTI rights abuses in Swedish foreign affairs to be a necessary focus for agency funding and agenda prioritization. Many individuals used their positions within foreign affairs institutions to elevate LGBTI rights.

Early inroads into LGBTI rights were brought into Swedish government discussions though the Swedish health care system under Barbro Westerholm's purview of the Swedish National Board of Health and Welfare (*Socialstyrelsen*). On September 26, 1979, Sweden repealed the classification of homosexuality as a disease and mental illness. In original data for this research, Westerholm recalled that the change was not made overnight; rather, it was born from her and other governmental leaders' direct consultations with LGBTI groups.[231] In the lead-up to the mental health decision, LGBTI advocates organized a public protest outside the Swedish National Board of Health and Welfare. Their central demand was ending the designation of their sexuality as "diseased." In response, Westerholm walked out of her office and met advocates on the street to listen to their demands and speak with them publicly.[232] Looking back on her decision more than forty years ago, Westerholm reasoned that "Love cannot be regarded as a disease; neither between heterosexual couples nor between homosexual ones."[233] Having the head of a government agency willing to talk and listen to advocates creates an important political opportunity for institutional change. Banaszak asserts that "Favorable location within the bureaucracy of the state is especially powerful in its ability to create lasting influences on policy and praxis."[234] Westerholm's stance led to other reforms to provide LGBTI people with equal access to health care, which later became elevated into a global health issue with the onset of the HIV/AIDS crisis. This change in distinction also reformed Sweden's military apparatus; it lifted the ban of LGBTI personnel from military service due to previous medical regulations.[235] From changing the country's health care sector, Swedish Armed

Forces, and public awareness about homosexuality, Westerholm's leadership in Swedish public policy led to sweeping changes throughout the country.

With insider allies, LGBTI issues were propelled to even greater policy prioritization. Mona Sahlin, the leader of the Swedish Social Democratic Party from 2007 to 2011, Swedish Minister for Integration Issues, and former Deputy Prime Minister of the country, has been an influential ally and supporter of LGBTI equality for decades. From the highest levels of government, Sahlin has engaged on gender equality laws related to prostitution, human trafficking, and LGBTI equality.[236] She is a regular speaker at Stockholm Pride; in 2015, she asserted that "At the end of the day we are contesting a male norm."[237] Originally active in the women's rights movement, Sahlin explained to a Stockholm Pride audience that LGBTI equality was to her a natural extension of women's rights.[238] Sahlin and other like-minded female leaders explained they originally became involved in LGBTI rights advocacy because they were questioning all gender norms and societal hierarchies.

Sahlin also uses her political clout to fight for LGBTI equality outside Swedish borders. In 2015, she stated, "We can change countries such as Russia and others in the EU. LGBTI rights should become a self-evident part of international human rights. . . . We don't want to accept the situation how it is now."[239] Sahlin's words are notable: "we can change countries," and not "accepting" discrimination internationally, denote a high level of influence and confidence from a Swedish leader, especially aimed toward the large, powerful nation of Russia. Sahlin's assertion that Swedish foreign policy can influence norms outside Sweden, even in large nations such as Russia, indicates a high level of commitment to LGBTI global equality from Swedish leadership. Sahlin's words also embody what Emil Edenborg and Christine Agius signify as a process of gendered bordering, where feminist Swedish foreign policy is pitted against a Russian masculine security profile and a gendered power relationship between the two countries.[240] Leaders such as Mona Sahlin advocate for gender equality to be a forefront issue in Swedish foreign policy.

Another instrumental ally within Swedish government was Birgitta Ohlsson, a member and former leader of the Liberal Party. Interviewees across sectors in *From Pariah to Priority*, including respondents from RFSL, Stockholm Pride presenters, civil servants in SIDA, EU officials, and American advocates, recognized Birgitta Ohlsson as a key leader over many years in the fight for LGBTI equality in Sweden and globally.[241] Ohlsson does not come from the vantage point of an activist, but rather as member of Swedish Parliament and an EU representative. During her leadership, Ohlsson participated in Pride marches across the Baltic countries, at times facing physical threats for her participation. At a Baltic Pride march in 2013 in Vilnius, Lithuania, marchers were pelted with eggs.[242] As the crowd threatened violence, Ohlsson marched at the front of the demonstration. As a Swedish member of Parliament and Sweden's European Union Affairs Minister, Ohlsson used her official diplomatic protection to shield Pride participants. Per diplomatic international norms, local authorities are required to provide security for foreign diplomats; Lithuanian police were required to protect Minister Ohlsson. Many counterprotestors threatened violence and were arrested by authorities. Ohlsson later stated, "It shows that we need to march until eggs aren't thrown anymore and people can march peacefully."[243] Ohlsson was pregnant at the time, which, for many advocates, added political gravity to Ohlsson's willingness to stand for equality in the face of potential personal risk. In reference to Ohlsson's work at Stockholm Pride 2015, a representative from the Nordic Rainbow Cultural Workers, an international LGBTI group based in Sweden, stated, "Bold leadership from hetero-people and politicians has been transformative for our movement; they offer legitimacy and at times provided critical leadership."[244] Ohlsson and other Norwegian, Dutch, and foreign diplomats all similarly provided protection for local LGBTI advocates to march relatively unharmed through the streets of Vilnius. From their respective positions of influence, they also brought international press and media attention to the situation for LGBTI activists in the Baltic region.

When representing Sweden and the European Union, Ohlsson asserted LGBTI equality as part of European values. To a Lithuanian crowd in 2010, Ohlsson declared, "Today we are marching for freedom, today we are marching for equality, today we are marching for Europe . . . that we would never accept homophobia taking over our streets."[245] In Belgrade 2012, upon the official banning of Belgrade Pride, Ohlsson warned Serb officials that their resistance to Pride marches and LGBTI rights may "complicate Serbia's path to EU membership."[246] This thinly veiled diplomatic warning was not taken lightly by Serbian officials, many of whom coveted EU membership. It put Serbia and other potential EU member states on alert that the normative value of LGBTI equality is a critical component of EU negotiations. Katja Kahlina finds that LGBTI equality promotion resonates with pro-EU political elites in countries such as Croatia and Serbia.[247] However, Kahlina also conversely documents how concepts of sexual citizenship and connecting to the EU can produce an "othering" effect of EU-skeptical leaders and thereby at times bolster resistance to struggles for sexual equality.

The connection of LGBTI equality with European identity remains debated across the continent. However, Swedish and other allied-member EU states have made LGBTI rights a key negotiation point between EU nations. As Kevin Moss asserts, "tolerance of gay people became a litmus test for attitudes towards EU accession."[248] From her influential diplomatic position, Ohlsson used both carrots and sticks to cajole her foreign counterparts to change. In international relations, carrots and sticks refer to incentives and diplomatic punishments for countries to reform.[249] She worked to transform potential resistant leaders into LGBTI equality allies in other European government. In situations where those leaders were not allies, Ohlsson used her role to warn European nations that failure to protect Pride participants, freedom of association, freedom of speech, and other human rights are inconsistent with European values. In a 2012 Swedish government press release, in response to Serbia's ban on Pride that year, Ohlsson stated, "Pride parades serve as a litmus test for freedom and human rights.[250] She and other EU leaders have held LGBTI rights as the central measure for progress of nations seeking EU accession. As such, Ohlsson has been an influential advocate, using the power of her office as a Swedish government official and EU representative to promote equality across the European continent.

Members of Swedish Parliament have worked to convince and change reticent leaders throughout the Swedish government. According to a principal advocate, civil society leaders recognized that their advocacy efforts toward changing other government agencies were buttressed by influential parliamentary leaders: "Initial pressure on government institutions came from (Swedish) politicians who gave specific directives for the government's foreign policy agenda to shift."[251] The advocate's point here exposes the opposing points of view, within foreign policy institutions of the same government, views that are not necessarily apparent to the public. In any government, leaders in any one agency, congress, Parliament, or a human rights bureau may be required to negotiate internally, and negotiate hard. These internal battles in the United States, Sweden, and other countries are often conducted behind closed doors, as much of foreign policy deliberations are classified. Bitter battles are sometimes waged between directors, civil servants, or ambassadors within the same government representing different policy interests. As these debates are seldom public information, they are rarely studied or analyzed. Thus, investigation of divergent policy perspectives is often lost to outside researchers and the public. Officers or parliamentarians representing foreign trade deals or negotiating foreign weapons sales may try to silence their colleague counterparts in the human rights wing of the government. Illustrative of this internal conflict, an interviewee noted, "Some diplomats initially saw this work (LGBTI diplomacy) as potentially jeopardizing the country's [Sweden's] other diplomatic priorities."[252] When met with resistance from SIDA or the Swedish Ministry of Foreign affairs officers, Swedish MPs would at times be the key players to hold these government representatives accountable. Swedish MPs would insist SIDA and the MFA increase funding and prioritization of LGBTI rights in Swedish foreign policy. Similarly, at times SIDA officers fought for LGBTI prioritization within agencies as well. Contemporary Swedish government leaders provided critical leadership to the movement from inside the state.

The influential role of insider government allies can be the critical factor in achieving policy reform. Since the 1990s, numerous MPs, civil servants, and leaders throughout Swedish government have pushed for increased prioritization of LGBTI rights in Swedish government affairs. According to a SIDA representative, "It was not hard to convince a critical mass at SIDA that this was important to do. We accepted and took on this policy easily and quickly."[253] Below the headlines and leaders who make public speeches in the press, there are dozens and hundreds of civil servants working worldwide in embassies to implement human rights diplomacy.

Internal allies also worked to highlight the issue of LGBTI abuses in multilateral venues. As LGBTI rights reforms became increasingly prominent in the Swedish domestic sphere, key supporters emerged, such as Jan Nordlander, the Swedish ambassador for human rights from the Department for International Law, Human Rights and Treaty Law Ministry for Foreign Affairs.[254] Nordlander, himself gay, connected LGBTI rights with other, more traditional, human rights issues and spearheaded the debate in the EU and other international venues. While Nordlander's perspective has become the norm, placing transgender rights on par with other human rights issues such as torture, labor rights, and the rights of children was new thinking in 1989.[255] Same-sex relations at the time were still largely taboo in many international fora.[256] Similarly, in 1999, Swedish leaders became vocal advocates of LGBTI rights abuses to other UN leaders. Sweden sent Hans Ytterberg, the country's first Ombudsman to Combat Discrimination Based on Sexual Orientation, to the UN.[257] Ytterberg became a vocal proponent for the UN to promote global reforms on antidiscrimination protections based on sexual orientation and equal rights for other minorities. The Swedish case demonstrates numerous powerful leaders from within government who, once convinced of the importance of LGBTI equality, made reforms from their position of influence. Eventually advocates and allies succeeded in making LGBTI rights more than just a policy matter and elevated it to become part of the fabric of Swedish national identity.

SWEDEN'S NATIONAL IDENTITY AND INTERNATIONAL REPUTATION

Swedish leaders' perception of their country's place in the world as a protector of and leader on human rights was a key factor in the early institutionalization of LGBTI human rights foreign policy. In Brysk's global comparison of human rights diplomacy, she denotes Sweden as "the gold standard" based on the country's efforts to stand for human rights in foreign policy.[258] Anna-Maria Sörberg documents the new trend of contemporary Swedish leaders and LGBTI advocates alike asserting that LGBTI rights has become an integral pillar of Swedish national identity.[259] The national identity of Sweden as a human rights leader permeates advocacy efforts and contemporary Swedish foreign policy.

Equating LGBTI rights with Swedish national identity has become the common vernacular of political party leaders. Even the Swedish Christian Democratic Party (*Kristdemokraterna*; KD), the political party initially resistant to LGBTI social reforms, has come to connect LGBTI equality with national Swedish values. Ebba Busch Thor, leader of the Christian Democratic Party, participates in annual Pride events. She articulates her political party's support for LGBTI equality on the grounds of a human rights–focused national identity framework. At Stockholm Pride 2016, Busch Thor declared, "Defending LGBTI rights is a self-evident expression of Swedish values."[260] The KD party historically blocked or contested all major LGBTI reforms in Sweden, but over time made a complete policy reversal of its platform on LGBTI equality, in part based on Sweden's evolving national identity.

Foreign policy goals traditionally reflect entrenched domestic social values and morals.[261] However, the construction of national identity is always in flux.[262] In contemporary Swedish politics, mainstream political parties have now made "Swedish values" and national identity congruent with human rights and LGBTI equality. In reference to giving international development aid to a country such as Namibia, one Swedish SIDA government official stated, "We have no reason to help a country like Namibia; we do it because it is important for the world community."[263] The Swedish officer implied that a low-income sub-Saharan African nation presents little economic or security interest for Swedish citizens. And yet Swedish officials are willing to allocate millions of Swedish crowns toward the country's human rights development.[264] Swedish officials do not necessarily link development humanitarian aid and human rights diplomacy to their short-term self-interest. Rather, the high levels of international humanitarian and human rights aid are often justified by Sweden's human rights identity.

Vocalizing LGBTI rights abuses in foreign affairs has become a central part of Sweden's international reputation. Jonathan Mercer argues that a state's reputation can have an enormous influence on leaders' action and state policies: "reputation is central to a state's security," both in the perceived as well as real actions of what other nations believe a state will do.[265] Part of Sweden's global reputation is that of a nation that prioritizes human rights and gender equality. Katarzyna Jezierska and Ann Towns assert how gender equality has become an integral aspect of Swedish "nation branding."[266] Promoting LGBTI rights internationally is carried out in part because of Swedish leaders' perceptions of themselves and their role as leaders on human rights in the international community. Swedish leaders distinctly do not make an economic or strategic security argument toward funding human rights. By contrast, representatives of other international donor agencies often justify and articulate international development aid as an integral part of their long-term national security strategy.[267]

Improving gender equality in Botswana or advocating for the equality of LGBTI persons in Gambia leads to almost no tangible material gain for Swedish citizens. Thus, it is hard to argue that the motivation for LGBTI diplomacy comes from an economic (i.e., a realist) international relations theory. So why would the Swedish government, with the support of the Swedish public at large, fund programs in remote locations around the world? The theory of constructivism helps explain Swedish government actions. Many scholars recognize Sweden's identity as a human rights superpower as a carefully constructed identity.[268] Swedish identity as a protector of human rights has salience for the Swedish public. Brysk identifies the motivation for development aid as part of Sweden's national identity: "Swedish taxpayers bankrolling African refugees are not just trying to be better human beings—they take national pride in expressing their identity as Swedes . . . acting globally builds national identities as 'Swedish volunteers.' "[269] Scholars recognize that states pursue foreign policy agendas to bolster their reputation and promote a positive image abroad.[270] Swedish leaders' willingness to provide funding toward countries whose national development does not have bearing on Swedish interest is expressed as being for the sake of the common universal good.

Evidence in this research found that both civil society leaders and Swedish government representatives identified promoting LGBTI equality as increasingly part of Swedish global identity. During Stockholm Pride in 2015, Minister for International Development Cooperation Isabella Lövin explained Sweden's leadership role: "We have strong domestic policies for protections of equal rights for all people, we are not former colonizers, we provide aid to countries for the long-term, and human rights is at the forefront of Swedish policies domestically and abroad."[271] Sweden remained neutral in both World Wars and has a strong domestic human rights record. Compared with other former colonizing European nations, Sweden leaders recognize that the country has a better reputation and thus more clout to play a leadership role in principled foreign affairs.

The construction of a national identity connected to being a global leader on women's and gender rights has become part of how government officials, civil society leaders, and Swedish laypersons communicate their national values. The Swedish foreign ministry holds that "Sweden considers it legitimate to react and call attention to violations of these rights, since oppressed people—precisely because they are oppressed—seldom have the opportunity to assert their interests."[272] Using its relative wealth and position of influence as a global aid donor, the Swedish government is able to assert its values internationally. Across Western Europe, LGBTI rights have become the defining feature of modern European societies. Ayoub examines how advocates have sought to define a "Europeanness" that includes democratic principles of equality and tolerance for all minority groups, including LGBTI populations.[273] In modern Latvia, a newer EU member nation, Dace Dzenovska determines "Europeanness" perceived by Latvians as an "adherence to the principles of human rights and tolerance."[274] Tova Andersson demonstrates that "[t]he inclusion of a homonormative homosexuality becomes an important factor for the construction of Sweden as an open and tolerant nation. . . . The national sense of community is formed through interaction between national symbols and symbols of the LGBT(I) community."[275] Activists and government leaders alike have begun to equate Swedish reputation as a symbolic, as well as tangible, supporter of global LGBTI equality.

One of RFSL's early strategies was to equate LGBTI equality with foundational tenets of a modern, democratic society. Advocates stressed the need for policies to reflect and uphold equal rights for all citizens, including all minorities under Swedish and international law.[276] Ayoub reveals similar traits across EU transnational advocates; demands are often framed within a European discourse by correlating LGBTI equality with democratic responsibilities of EU member states.[277] RFSL leaders similarly contended that LGBTI rights violations were no different from discrimination against other, more established minority groups. Advocates hold that it is in the national interest to uphold LGBTI rights diplomacy in Sweden's foreign policy while simultaneously addressing LGBTI discrimination domestically.

One assumption for the progression of the Swedish LGBTI movement's shifting focus from local to global forums could be that as Swedes felt they were achieving LGBTI equality at home, they turned their attention to the international stage.[278] However, advocates emphatically refuted this idea, arguing that LGBTI rights have not been fully secured in the country.[279] Rather, Swedish activists express solidarity with LGBTI persons globally and advocate for their governments to provide aid and support to other LGBTI movements as they simultaneously work toward equality at home.[280] During Stockholm Pride debates, concern regarding Sweden's international LGBTI advocacy arises often in the form of questions such as "Is this self-righteous or arrogant of our country to tell others how to change their culture?" or "Do Swedes feel they have figured it out at home, and are therefore now addressing the rest of the world?"[281] Activists responded that their international work was a way to demonstrate unity with other transnational movements. One advocate stated, "It is not in our interest to state that everything has been completed in Sweden on equality, because that would not be true; we still have problems with discrimination in this country."[282] They assessed that highlighting the grave problems that remain in the global sphere, as well as domestic national solidarity on the issue, help maintain LGBTI rights as a focal point for Swedish institutions.

While LGBTI abuses and discrimination persist in Sweden, it has one of the strongest domestic records for upholding LGBTI rights. Observers have described Stockholm as the "pink capital" of the world, asserting how LGBTI rights have become part of Sweden's global reputation.[283] Pink capitals are hallmarked by LGBTI-friendly arts, music, sports, and political and cultural events that openly celebrate LGBTI equality.[284] Strand and Kehl, in their 2019 analysis of ad campaigns from the Swedish Armed

Forces, find Sweden messaging as "performative enactments of a gender-exceptional nation," thus implying that Swedish authorities capitalized on Sweden's national identity with LGBTI equality.[285] Julia Lagerman chronicles the perspectives from Swedish city officials, staff, and other personnel surrounding Pride events in Sweden as "defining human rights as a Swedish national trait and a tourist commodity."[286] Reaching an annual crescendo during annual Pride events across the country, Swedish leaders across public and private sectors explicitly articulate to domestic and foreign audiences the connection of LGBTI rights with their national identity.

A former top leader of RFSL asserted that taking on the controversial topic of LGBTI rights in places such as Uganda and Jamaica "fit[s] well with Sweden's view of itself as protector of minority rights."[287] As human rights are articulated by officials at the forefront of the foreign policy agenda, activists expressed confidence that "Sweden will take the fight for human rights when other countries will not."[288] One may expect this type of comment to come from a government spokesperson, possibly inflating their government's stance on human rights. Notably, this came from a civil society leader, purporting the country's reputation for taking a strong stance on human rights globally. The national identity of Sweden as a human rights leader permeates advocacy efforts and government actions. LGBTI theorists have found that in other countries around the world, such as Poland and Slovenia, LGBTI rights have been articulated by political leaders as a "threat" to their national identity.[289] By contrast, Swedish activists and government leaders have worked for decades to mold the Swedish identity and citizenry to support domestic and international policies that promote protections for all people.

In the early 2000s, when LGBTI rights were still a cutting-edge aspect of modern diplomacy, RFSL leaders used tropes of Swedish national image to convince stakeholders of the importance of the issue. In interviews for *From Pariah to Priority*, they recalled meeting resistance by some embassy officials who were initially "embarrassed to take up these issues, asking, 'Should Sweden really stand for these issues?' "[290] RFSL countered this reluctance by emphasizing Sweden's national reputation as historically protecting the most vulnerable populations, such as women and children, and championing human rights issues when other countries stayed silent.[291] RFSL made it clear that Swedish foreign policy leaders had a responsibility to promote equal rights in twenty-first-century diplomacy. Retaining a positive reputation and standing in the world can become a motivating factor for policy change.

Homonationalism and the Fight to Define National Identity

Intertwining LGBTI equality with Swedish national identity has unexpectedly become a rallying cry for recent right-wing nationalist leaders. Across
Europe, leaders seek to make a distinction between who fits into "the nation"
based on the fault line of LGBTI rights.[292] These parties shifted from once
protecting traditional family values to "so-called modern Western values,
including LGBTI rights.[293] Contemporary right-wing Swedish political leaders claim new Muslim immigrants are a threat to LGBTI equality, Swedish
values, and national identity.[294] In 2015, Sweden accepted more refuges per
capita than any other European country.[295] A 2020 Brookings Institution
report found many Swedes joined the Swedish Democrat party after the
2015 immigration crisis, reporting "some Swedes perceive that being too
'different' can threaten the equality that the 'people's home' relies on."[296]
Some LGBTI Swedes themselves have also begun to vote for the Swedish
Democrats out of support for secular Sweden.[297] Research from polling data
across Europe and in Sweden reveals " 'sexually modern nativists' have the
highest likelihoods to vote for populist radical right parties.[298] Voters from
across political parties in Sweden began to vote for the Swedish Democrat
party because of a perception of protecting Swedish national identity.

As LGBTI rights become solidified into the ethos of national identity,
it is further institutionalized into foreign policy institutions. Sweden continues to be one of the highest contributors to international LGBTI civil
society. In a 2020 Brookings Institution report, Danielle Lee Tomson notes
that the humanitarian efforts of Sweden are a point of national pride and
marker of Swedish identity.[299] Swedish Democrats wanted to offer significant aid to Muslim refugees, albeit in their countries of origin. Rather than
inviting so many people into Sweden, Tomson documents Swedish voters'
desire to continue humanitarianism efforts "that satisfy Swedish values of
peace, tolerance, and humanitarian efforts—just on other territory."[300] While
steeped in xenophobic perceptions, in the perspective of the right wing
of the Swedish political spectrum, human rights aid is articulated as an
important aspect of Sweden's foreign affairs work, as long as these policies
do not bring increased immigration to the country.

No culture is static. Societies, hierarchies, in-group, and out-group
dynamics are ever evolving. With the increase of immigration into European nations, there is a robust discourse in Sweden and across Europe to
define what it means to be "Swedish" and/or "European." There is a swath
of literature that seeks to identify central factors of national identity and

building group identity.[301] How language, religion, and ethnicity factor into modern society are key aspects of defining group identity. Can an individual be Muslim, or a non-Swedish speaker, or disagree with LGBTI equality, and still be considered Swedish? Micheletti asserts that in 2019 Sweden is "reassessing its national goals, political culture, and collective identity.[302] Some LGBTI Swedes, as well as hetero liberal secular Swedes, fear the backsliding of hard-won domestic human rights. Contemporary scholars have found the concept of "European sexual nationalism" increasing in popular national sentiments since 2015.[303] The battle to define national identity to include tolerance and equality, as well as multiculturalism and plurality, takes center stage in contemporary political debates and elections.

Conclusion

One of the central assertions of this chapter, and the importance of the Swedish case study, is to examine how a political movement founded in this small country in northern Europe is often replicated throughout the world. LGBTI youth in Seattle, São Paulo, Rome, Istanbul, and beyond are influenced by policy changes in LGBTI human rights norms in Sweden. Transnational advocates have used Sweden's laws on divorce, abortion, and transgender rights as a blueprint for their own policies and legal proposals for reform in their countries.[304] Swedes produce a host of entrepreneurial social domestic reforms, from family policy to health care restructuring, that are replicated in other countries and regions.[305] On an international scale, many progressive policies originate in Sweden and Scandinavia and are later replicated in other parts of the world by other LGBTI rights groups or other human rights movements. What happens in Sweden, and human rights policy reforms in this small country, matters globally.

Laws and policies enacted in Sweden, for better or worse, have a global ripple effect. Across the spectrum of rights, from trans medical access to ending the death penalty, Sweden is often first in multilateral engagements to raise new international human rights norms. Sweden's security sector, a sector that is often a bastion of homophobia in other countries, was the first to openly conscript and employ openly gay individuals.[306] Sweden was the first country to officially institutionalize a feminist foreign policy. SIDA was one of the first international donor agencies to establish the relationship between sexual orientation and gender identity, poverty, and development and implement Swedish foreign aid accordingly.

Swedish leaders articulate LGBTI diplomacy as a part of gender equality and critical to their national security interests. Elevating human rights
as equal to, or greater than trade and security interests is distinctive in
the international system. Yet no country is able to prioritize human rights
in foreign relations at all times. However, by and large, data demonstrate
that Swedish leaders' statements and policy directives demonstrate that top
leadership is willing to place LGBTI rights as an institutional priority. From
lower civil servant ranks to ambassador and minister levels, there is a depth
of commitment within the Swedish government to LGBTI rights as a strategic issue in international affairs.

Early adoption of LGBTI promotion in Sweden was dependent on
broad social acceptance, a critical mass of public support, perceived national
interest, and an evolution of the concept of rights. Tracing the path of policy
change leads to the influential factors that led to the institutionalization of
LGBTI rights in Swedish agencies. This chapter identifies the key factors
that influence Swedish foreign policy institutions to incorporate LGBTI
diplomacy: NGO advocacy, both targeting institutional advocacy and public
advocacy; insider government allies; and a framing of the national identity
of Sweden as a global leader in LGBTI rights.

NGO advocacy of civil society groups, especially one powerful organization, namely RFSL, historically has been included in foreign affairs
decisions. RFSL was rapidly integrated into the knowledge base and inner
workings of SIDA. SIDA officers conceptualize RFSL's work and knowledge
base as part of their own Swedish government's expertise. RFSL's direct advocacy influenced political leaders to evaluate the government's agenda and
recognize how the unique needs of LGBTI populations were not addressed
in Sweden's former international development mandates. RFSL wove its
work into the broader Swedish government's agenda, and it has become a
critical component of increasing the institutional capacity of the Swedish
government's expertise on sexual minority rights. Civil society leaders were
invited into Swedish foreign policy deliberations. They positioned themselves
as a knowledge base and consulting organization for the government's new
policies. RFSL's expertise on LGBT issues has come to be equated with the
Swedish government's expertise on the global movement.

Advocates linked LGBTI strategies to best practices of other domestic and international social movements, such as activism to end racial and
gender discrimination. Those movements reframed the international human
rights discourse, which, in turn, realigned domestic and foreign policy institutions. As with other domestic policy changes, at times Swedish LGBTI

advocates were met with harsh criticism and resistance. Activists were able to diffuse critics with multiple advocacy strategies, including influential public shaming campaigns. Activists also focus specifically on the gravest international human rights abuses to diffuse domestic opposition.

This study contributes to social movement scholarship that rarely highlights the importance of allies and social movement actors from within the state. Insider allied government leadership concerned with LGBTI equality worked from their position of influence inside government. Many influential leaders drew upon their earlier engagement with the women's rights movement. They quickly realized that LGBTI equality was a clear extension of women's rights that continued to fight patriarchal norms in the country. There is a wide consensus within the government and Parliament that LGBTI rights should be a fundamental human right. Powerful diplomats, ambassadors, and political leaders enabled LGBTI rights to become elevated at the highest policy levels. Leaders in Parliament were important to coax some historically hesitant diplomats to embrace LGBTI rights. Their influence was a critical factor in foreign policy reform.

The Swedish state's identity as a global leader in human rights also underpinned the institutionalization of LGBTI rights in Swedish foreign affairs. Swedish political leaders have used tropes of Swedish national identity as a champion of human rights to institutionalize LGBTI diplomacy. Sweden has long been recognized as a "moral superpower," although this status has been called into question over debates related to COVID-19, immigration, and homonationalism.[307] Scandinavian countries are acutely aware of, and take pride in, their international reputation for tolerance and global human rights leadership. Stockholm Pride became a hub for the international LGBTI movement and a part of Sweden's public commitment to equality. Current leaders on both the right and left wing of the political spectrum espouse LGBTI rights, albeit for different political goals. The unexpected political merging of this issue serves to sustain and further institutionalize LGBTI issues in government agencies.

In the next chapter, the analysis turns to trends in other regions of the world that are backsliding on LGBTI rights, especially Uganda. The country's Anti-Homosexuality Act (the AHA, or the "Kill the Gays" law) highlighted LGBTI rights as an important issue in foreign policy. It was a sensitizing moment for Swedish officials to reevaluate their foreign policy, strengthen the LGBTI rights pillar, and condition aid for the first time based on LGBTI rights. Thus, the Ugandan AHA further institutionalized and prioritized LGBTI rights in Swedish diplomacy.

Chapter 4

Uganda's "Kill the Gays" Law

A Global Sensitizing Event

Introduction

In February 2014, Ugandan President Yoweri Museveni stated: "Homosexuality is unnatural, disgusting, and not a human right."[1] Museveni made the remarks after signing the Uganda Anti-Homosexuality Act (AHA) into law, a bill that punished homosexual acts with life imprisonment. Dubbed the "Kill the Gays" law by international press, the AHA garnered the attention of human rights activists and foreign policy leaders from around the world.[2] The law has undergone many revisions: in 2009, Ugandan lawmakers originally proposed the death penalty for homosexual acts.[3] This chapter argues that the proposal of Uganda's first AHA in 2009 was a critical sensitizing event that triggered the decision to institutionalize LGBTI rights in US and Swedish foreign affairs institutions. Prior to the international debate over the AHA, foreign diplomatic concern with LGBTI rights in diplomatic affairs was minimal. Top foreign policy leaders within former US Secretary of State Hillary Clinton's inner circle of advisors asserted for this research how the urgency of the Ugandan proposed law catapulted LGBTI rights in a concrete policy idea within the State Department.[4] They reported that the prospect of people dying at the hands of authorities under this new law, solely for being LGBTI, created a sense of urgency for foreign policy leaders.[5] Without the Ugandan law, LGBTI rights diplomacy may have taken years longer to materialize within foreign governments' policy agendas. In the annual rollout of the State Department's human rights reports in 2010, Assistant Secretary of State for Democracy, Human Rights, and Labor Michael Posner recognized violence against Ugandan LGBTI people from local authorities as one of the most significant human rights concerns in the world.[6] While Sweden was already formally conducting LGBTI diplomacy by the time of the proposed law in 2009, the AHA catapulted LGBTI issues to become a Swedish foreign policy priority. This law exemplifies how significant world events create new political opportunities for foreign policy leaders to institutionalize new policies.

The Ugandan case fixed the international spotlight on LGBTI rights and became the event that drove lasting institutional change in human rights foreign policies. It caused international leaders to reevaluate their foreign policy in relation to human rights. In what scholars deem as "discursive renewal," a sensitizing event can trigger changing discourses and become the driving force for institutional change.[7] Wiering and Arts define a sensitizing event as a circumstance "that can cause institutional renewal and shape the ideas and plans for future decision-making."[8] Based on this definition, sensitizing events can stimulate discursive renewal and lead to the reshaping and creation of human rights foreign policy.

In this case, the proposed AHA legislation catalyzed a new discourse in foreign policy institutions. The emerging normative value of LGBTI equality had not previously impacted bilateral relations. Discursive institutionalism helps explain how a global event can create opportunities for leaders to rethink and reassess policy agendas around an emerging issue.[9] It sheds light on how an issue is discussed, perceived, evaluated, and ultimately addressed over time. Stassen, Smolders, and Leroy put forth a framework of discursive institutionalism as "the concept that new, sudden events can change the public discourse, or reposition it into a new focus."[10] An extreme, draconian new law can sometimes serve to shock public audiences and spur government representatives to act. Uganda is measured by the Global Barometer of Gay Rights (GBGR) as an "active persecutor" of homosexuals,[11] and the AHA spurred a global reaction powerful enough to mobilize foreign governments to change their human rights foreign policy priorities. This chapter examines how Uganda's AHA prompted the decision to make LGBTI rights a central focus of US and Swedish human rights diplomacy. It also analyzes the process by which, for the first time in history, foreign policy leaders conditioned foreign aid based on a country's LGBTI human rights record.

Following the passage of the AHA, the Swedish and US governments (along with a handful of other northern European nations and the World Bank) proposed cutting foreign aid to Uganda. The purpose of conditioning aid is to apply pressure on a foreign government to change laws and policies. Scholars Doucouliagos and Paldam define conditioning foreign aid as predicating the allocation of foreign aid from one country to another, based on the recipient's fulfillment of certain political, economic, or social requirements.[12] In a similar way, Selbervik explains conditioning foreign aid as "an expression of the donor's strategic and/or economic interest."[13] Currently, foreign international donor aid supports the rebuilding of Uganda's agricultural, educational, health care, and national infrastructure.[14] The Ugandan government relies heavily on development assistance for approximately 25 percent of its annual budget, ranking Uganda as the thirteenth largest aid recipient nation worldwide.[15] While at times foreign leaders condition aid to pressure political reform, the complexities of conditioning international aid may have unintended consequences.[16] For context on international development aid, the most vulnerable people in the lowest-income countries are the primary beneficiaries of foreign aid projects, including clean water wells, housing, and food.[17] Potential harm in cutting foreign aid can come to vulnerable populations that depend on this funding, such as food aid for malnourished children and those who depend on health care facilities funded by foreign governments.[18] Removing this aid can threaten the survival of already marginalized populations. In 2014, Sweden funded approximately $10 million (approximately 70 million Swedish Crowns) of the $250-million annual foreign aid budget to the Ugandan government. Swedish funding supported women's sexual and reproductive health and research in the country.[19] In response to the AHA, Swedish leaders threatened to cease Swedish international donor aid. By cutting aid, Ugandan citizens, including the LGBTI community, may lose housing, health care, and potentially direct cash transfers. Cutting foreign aid, even if it is for the long-term purpose of improving human rights, can have significant short- and long-term consequences for recipient country populations.

In diplomacy, all foreign donor aid is conditional. While cutting aid wholesale is rarely done, making foreign aid conditional on political reform is common. I often worked on negotiations throughout North Africa that would provide a specific country with economic investment predicated upon local governments improving human rights policies. For example, before receiving US military jets, a country would need to improve its prisons to meet international standards. Similarly, another nation would have to agree to stop harassing its religious minority community in order to continue a trade deal with US partners. As seen in the case of India, the State Department will revoke visas to foreign leaders who are responsible for violence against ethnic minorities.[20] Sometimes donor governments include human rights concerns within a comprehensive aid package for a broad range of programs local leaders would like to support, yet lack the funds. For example, Piotr Lis finds that countries may receive foreign support to fight terrorism while also receive funding for the promotion of governance, education, and social capital.[21] Foreign policy leaders regularly use the tool of foreign aid to influence domestic practice and improve human rights and democratic practices. What was new in this case in Uganda was that LGBTI rights were at the center stage. While aid is often conditional, frequently outside the public eye, this was the first time that governments used their foreign donor aid explicitly and publicly to work and try to improve LGBTI human rights practices.

Despite this economic dependency on foreign aid, Ugandan leaders scorned US, Swedish, and other foreign leaders for their support of LGBTI rights. President Museveni declared to Western leaders that they do not want "gay aid."[22] One Ugandan official stated: "I feel disgusted with foreign countries like Sweden that are trying to intimidate Uganda. . . Ugandans should guard our own cultural and social values."[23] Ugandan Pastor Ssempa decried Obama: "Obama, even if you do not give us money for medicine for our people, to hell with that money, we would rather die, but die in dignity."[24] Moreover, the stakes are high for local LGBTI Ugandans when international aid donors propose to cut aid. Ending foreign aid may also pose the risk of double discrimination or backlash against local LGBTI populations.[25] They may be blamed for drawing the ire of the West upon their country, while already experiencing societal discrimination.

Formal public conditioning of aid that demands immediate human rights reform in a host nation is rare. Furthermore, threatening to cut international aid based on human rights is an exceptional act because it requires breaking ties with a nation and elevates normative values as the central bilateral issue between countries. The internal debate of policy implementation and incorporating human rights as part of the United States' national interest is often contentious. Some diplomats continue to argue that promoting human rights hurts other US interests. As Ambassador Samantha Power notes, "convincing the American national security apparatus to incorporate concern for human consequences into our dealings with other countries would never be easy."[26] American foreign policy officials often do not regard human rights as a key US strategic interest. Yet the Ugandan AHA proved a rare case in international relations where US, Swedish, and other foreign policy leaders reacted swiftly and strongly by placing human rights as a primary issue of foreign policy concern.

Though the Swedish government was already actively conducting LGBTI rights diplomacy when the Ugandan AHA was proposed in 2009, the bill served as a driving force to further prioritize and institutionalize LGBTI rights in Swedish foreign policy. It established LGBTI rights as a key human rights issue for Swedish leaders and the society at large. Swedish media regularly reported on the status of the Ugandan law, and human rights conditions for LGBTI Ugandans, even though there is little cultural or historical connection between Sweden and Uganda. Swedish civil society organizations formed to help people living with HIV/AIDS in Uganda. Despite the fact that many other countries implement the death penalty or imprisonment for homosexuality, Uganda swept the attention of the Swedish public. Swedes and northern European LGBTI networks placed a strong focus on Uganda in their agendas and activism. This law launched LGBTI rights into the international spotlight. International relations surrounding this bill measurably changed the nature of foreign affairs because of new normative considerations such as LGBTI rights.

Human rights abuses generally receive peripheral attention in diplomatic affairs. In the past, world leaders would have neglected to respond publicly to LGBTI rights abuses by Ugandan President Museveni's regime. Human rights are a relatively new policy priority in international relations. According to Keck and Sikkink, "as recently as 1970, the idea that the human rights of citizens of any country are legitimately the concern of people and governments everywhere was considered radical."[27] Incorporating human rights in foreign policy remains a widely debated policy agenda that some leaders decry is an infringement on sovereignty.[28] Some foreign leaders criticize LGBTI diplomacy as a new form of colonialism and cultural imperialism.[29] For instance, after Obama's visit to Jamaica, in diplomatic dialogue with Jamaican leaders, Obama raised the importance of upholding LGBTI rights. In response, one local journalist noted that, "many Jamaicans thought the visit demonstrated blatant cultural imperialism and a sneaky attempt to impose on Jamaica the LGBT(I) philosophy of marriage and family."[30] Other opponents of LGBTI rights have rallied with signs, "No, to U.S. buggery export!"[31] Conversely, local LGBTI advocates welcomed Obama raising LGBTI rights concerns with Jamaican leaders. Angeline Jackson, the executive director for Quality of Citizenship Jamaica and a survivor of sexual assault, reaffirmed the importance of foreign leaders raising LGBTI rights in Jamaica for the physical protection of lesbian advocates like her.[32] Randy Berry, the State Department's special envoy for the human rights of LGBTI persons, and Todd Larson, USAID's senior LGBTI coordinator, met with Jamaican advocates to listen to their concerns, discuss the universality of human rights for everyone. These leaders offered US political and financial support for their cause in Jamaica. Local LGBTI advocates welcomed the visit and asserted that the political support from these foreign leaders helped them gain traction on LGBTI rights within their country.[33] Scholar Kyle James Rohrich argues, "In World War LGBT, the series of cultural proxy wars to influence a country's geopolitical alignment . . . one man's freedom fighter is another man's cultural imperialist."[34] An embassy official noted raising LGBTI rights in the country was "part of a broad engagement on a variety of issues ranging from economic development and security cooperation."[35] From Jamaica, Uganda, and other countries in the world, over the past decade, LGBTI rights have become part of comprehensive diplomatic dialogues. Despite local controversy, foreign leaders have moved LGBTI right from the peripheral to a central issue of diplomatic dialogue.

Incorporating gender equality into diplomatic dialogue with countries is a new, controversial issue in bilateral relations. Sex and gender are recent considerations within US foreign policy, mainly gaining traction since the early 2000s. Valerie Hudson and Patricia Leidl analyze "The Hillary Doctrine," which highlighted the lack of global gender equality and subjugation of women worldwide as a significant threat to US national security.[36] Hudson and Patricia Leidl demonstrate how correlating gender discrimination with national security is a departure from historic foreign policy norms. The incorporation of LGBTI rights into foreign policy is a further expression of prioritizing gender equality as a national security issue and shift in international relations.

Many countries worldwide behead, stone, torture, and imprison LGBTI citizens.[37] Yet Uganda has become a central battleground for the global equality movement. International media report Uganda as "highly conservative and a dangerous place to be openly gay."[38] There are reports of death and violence in the country, where Ugandan LGBTI activists are killed for their work.[39] In 2019, LGBTI activist Brian Wasswa was murdered in Uganda. In response, Frank Mugisha, the executive director of Sexual Minorities Uganda (SMUG), stated that when "members of Parliament call for . . . the reintroduction of the 'anti-gay' law, they are responsible for this increase in vulnerability in the LGBTI community."[40] Further, Neela Ghoshal, senior researcher at Human Rights Watch, contended that "every few months . . . a Ugandan politician threatens to revive the 'kill the gays' bill and 'it brings them the political notoriety they want.' "[41] The local Ugandan LGBTI community is often the target of political attacks from the country's leadership.

Uganda's notoriety on LGBTI rights abuses did not come only from global supporters of equality. There also was a considerable presence of for-eign religious leaders vehemently opposed to LGBTI equality, namely Amer-ican evangelical pastors, before the proposal of the AHA. Noting the many different stakeholders on the ground in Uganda, Kristen Cheney reports how "neoconservative evangelicals have made Uganda 'ground zero.' "[42] While many Western diplomats promote LGBTI equality, American Christian Evangelical organizations have simultaneously exerted influence over Ugan-da's policy regression. As of 2014, approximately 20 percent of all NGOs in Uganda are faith-based, evangelical organizations.[43] Local Ugandan leaders hosted Lou Engle, an American evangelical leader from Kansas City, as a special speaker for a Ugandan political rally and prayer service in 2009. At this rally, he equated homosexuality with "witchcraft" and "corruption," among other "evils."[44] He also asserted: "I believe Uganda has suddenly become ground zero. . . God brought you to make a statement and stand for righteousness."[45] On the other side of the spectrum, US-based TV star Neal Gottlieb flew to Uganda, hiked to Uganda's highest peak, Mount Stanley Margherita Peak, and planted the rainbow flag to protest Uganda's criminalization of homosexuality.[46] From Los Angeles, Stockholm, Berlin, and beyond, global activists, news outlets, diplomats, and evangelicals look at Uganda as a global focal point for defining, defending, or resisting LGBTI rights.

Religious opposition to LGBTI equality is not new—the location for evangelical activism however is.[47] While Christian conservatives may be losing battleground opposing LGBTI rights in industrialized nations, they increasingly look to lower-income countries to attack those emerging rights.[48] Brysk finds that in Uganda, "ironically, [evangelical leaders] reflect the imposition of a rival fundamentalist universalism rather than a defense of an indigenous identity."[49] Labeled the "Western gay lobby" by Ugandan evangelicals and political leaders, as well as those in other African nations, a swath of vocal political actors resist LGBTI rights.[50]

International civil society, as well as evangelicals coming from Western nations, had a measurable impact on the Ugandan Parliament generating the initial AHA bill. The influence of different Western actors advocating for both the promotion and the persecution of LGBTI people is connected to aspects of Uganda's colonial history. Uganda's colonization by Britain began in the 1860s.[51] The British government ruled with political and economic power over the region and implemented legal codes that included criminalization of homosexual relations.[52] While Uganda gained independence from Britain in 1962, these legal codes remained. Contemporary Ugandan policy mirrors this colonial legacy.

Ugandan LGBTI civil society leaders have long been fighting against foreign influence as well as sustained domestic LGBTI discrimination. Upon the proposed legislation of the AHA, Ugandan LGBTI activists Frank Mugisha, Pepe Julian Onziema, and Kasha Jacqueline emerged as leaders for the Ugandan LGBTI community.[53] They traveled internationally to bring the severity of the law, and violence against their LGBTI Ugandan community to the attention of the international community. These civil society leaders took to the world stage to recognize the plight of Uganda's LGBTI community, but also to warn of the negative consequences of ill-conceived foreign aid or diplomatic efforts to stop the AHA. Pepe Julian Onziema, the program director of Sexual Minorities Uganda, spread awareness about the severity of the proposed law, but also explained how cutting aid would increase "LGBTI persons' vulnerability to both non-state and state-sanctioned homophobia."[54] To illustrate the concern of conditioning foreign aid, more than fifty organizations based in African countries published a statement in line with Onziema's concerns.[55] This statement reasserted how the reduction of foreign aid can negatively harm LGBTI people and increase their vulnerability as a marginalized social group, primarily because of increased anti-LGBTI violence and persecution. This coalition further criticized Western governments for not consulting with the affected population before making decisions to cut aid to Uganda. At the same time, representatives from governments in Ghana and Nigeria made retaliatory remarks, saying that "aid donors could keep their money."[56] These perspectives from both Ugandan LGBTI activists and leaders of African countries clashing with Western governments highlight the complexity of the situation in Uganda. The many existing stakeholders have vastly different objectives, and the discussion of foreign aid lands squarely in the center of this debate. This tension exists alongside the reality that implementing such strong diplomatic actions, such as terminating bilateral aid, may lead to systemic societal change. In terms of Uganda's AHA, cutting aid arguably led to the suspension and reform of this law.

Transnational activists were the central actors bringing the new law from Uganda to the attention of foreign governments. When prominent Ugandan LGBTI activist David Kato was murdered, New York–based advocacy organization Outright Action International released a statement strongly condemning his attackers highlighting the "grave safety and security dangers confronting the Ugandan LGBT community and those working in defense of human rights."[57] Keck and Sikkink argue that transnational advocacy networks generate new ideas, norms, and systems for norm implementation.[58] Because of transnational activism, LGBTI organizations across the globe were the first to become aware of the violent discrimination against LGBTI persons in Uganda. From their respective locations across the globe, they lobbied their own governments to put pressure on the Ugandan government. International activists, in turn, credit the local Ugandan LGBTI population for harnessing transnational networks and bringing Uganda's practices to the international spotlight.[59] In this way, transnational networks can embolden domestic advocacy. Ayoub illustrates how transnational activists help establish domestic LGBTI concerns as a human right, resulting in successful policy diffusion across borders.[60] A key advocacy method for policy diffusion is to also ally with other social movements. Transnational advocacy networks allow groups to document global abuses and develop policy recommendations for foreign relations. While other countries, such as Nigeria or Indonesia, receive little international attention for killing LGBTI citizens, Uganda is the focal point for diplomats and citizens alike in the United States and other countries to defend LGBTI rights. The AHA in Uganda created discursive renewal for global human rights foreign policy leaders, especially in the United States and Sweden.

The Impact of the Ugandan Law on Swedish Foreign Policy

The Ugandan Anti-Homosexuality Act in 2009 propelled LGBTI rights to become a critical component of Swedish foreign policy. Although the Swedish government began including LGBTI rights in its diplomatic dialogues a few years prior to Uganda's proposed law, those rights still were peripheral to Sweden's human rights foreign policy agenda. The Ugandan law was a critical moment of awareness for the Swedish public. One Swedish international development aid officer asserted that "the Ugandan law received an enormous amount of coverage in Swedish press. It awakened a public, and the average citizen, about how dire LGBT(I) rights are in many parts of the world."[61] Similarly, Katarina Jungar and Salla Peltonen document the immense coverage of the Ugandan AHA in Swedish daily newspapers that sparked gay liberation discourses in Sweden.[62] According to another official from the Swedish International Development Cooperation Agency (SIDA), "Uganda's law was an eye opener for lots of politicians . . . it was definitely a catalyst for Sweden and many other governments to address LGBTI rights in their foreign policy, and pay attention to it as an important human rights issue."[63] A sentiment shared by top Swedish foreign policy leaders and observers was that without the Ugandan law, LGBTI rights would have remained a component of Sweden's foreign policy and international aid, albeit a marginal foreign policy issue of concern. In 2014, Swedish finance minister Anders Borg traveled to Uganda and commented on the trip that "We have to, in our aid strategy, ponder how we can remain active but still in a clear way point out that this is unacceptable legislation."[64] Remarkably, the head of a country's foreign investment strategy recognizes here that a normative principle, that is, LGBTI rights abuses, may render trade investment "unacceptable" to the Swedish bilateral relationship. It took the extreme nature of the Ugandan law to invigorate LGBTI foreign policy discussions in the Swedish public and government institutions.

Prior to this time, no country previously made LGBTI rights abuses a primary issue of bilateral concern in their formal foreign policy mandates.[65] Given the novelty of the incorporation of LGBTI rights in diplomatic engagements, Swedish officials could not be guided by the best practices, or policy consultations with leaders from other donor countries. Therefore, it was initially unclear how Sweden would, and should, respond within its overall bilateral relations with Uganda. Thereby, Swedish foreign policy leaders looked to domestic LGBTI advocates for strategic recommentations. Swedish diplomats and aid workers worked with leaders of the central Swedish LGBTI civil society organization, the Swedish Federation for Lesbian, Gay, Bisexual and Transgender Rights (RFSL). RFSL advocates found themselves in the center of an international firestorm to respond to this law. There was an extreme sense of urgency, with people's lives at stake. In a significant moment of policy change, RFSL officers served as strategic advisors to the Swedish government, as all stakeholders grappled with how to respond to Uganda's proposed law.

In helping to draft a strategic policy recommendation for Swedish foreign policy leaders, RFSL leaders sought out consultations with local Ugandan LGBTI advocates. Ugandan LGBTI groups expressed that they did not necessarily want to be singled out as the primary human rights issue in the country; freedom of assembly and association, freedom from arbitrary arrest and detention, and press freedom were many issues of concern impacting all human rights groups. They communicated to Swedish advocates, as well as other foreign activists and diplomats, the need to form a united coalition to advocate for overall improved human rights.[66] Freedom of association is an important human rights concern for many advocacy groups in the country. Many Ugandan LGBTI organizations in Uganda are not formally registered because of safety concerns. Even by participating in unregistered or informal associations, members fear harassment from authorities and violence.[67] Ugandan activists conveyed a desire to improve human rights and democracy in the country across many human rights concerns. By listening to LGBTI Ugandans' needs, Swedish civil society representatives incorporated the need for increased capacity and protection of NGOs into Swedish foreign policy recommendations.

Local Ugandan representatives also emphasized the importance of coalition building with other human rights groups, as well as increasing capacity for documentation of human rights abuses. Social movements gain strength when connected with other social movements with similar goals.[68] LGBTI organizations and individuals sought partnerships with local women's groups, journalists/media associations, and other democracy organizations. Building coalitions helped strengthen civil society numbers and capacity; it also was a tactic to provide political cover, protecting LGBTI people and groups from being singled out by government officials.

Documenting abuses is vital for legitimizing a human rights cause.[69] Recording abuses is also critical for individuals seeking asylum in another country. As Nicole Laviolette reports, sexual minorities have the same evidentiary burden as other asylum applicants; however, existing country documentation often fails to provide the evidence that LGBTI asylum seekers need to support their claims.[70] The Ugandan government often denies the existence of homosexuals in the country.[71] Despite this denial and persecution, if given the choice, many LGBTI Ugandans would not opt to leave their country; rather, they want to improve human rights in their homeland.[72] However, those who do in fact leave often face the problem of arriving to Sweden, Canada, or other foreign nations that accept LGBTI asylum seekers without sufficient documentation of persecution for their asylum claim based on sexual orientation. Whether intending to stay in Uganda or leave the country, advocates attempt to systematically document their abuses. Yet documenting specific abuses is often difficult to do in repressive, authoritarian regimes. Media outlets are often controlled by the government.

Independent sources either do not document LGBTI abuses or fear reprisal for publishing articles on the topic. Thereby, similar to other human rights groups working in the country, LGBTI groups work to increase capacity in their ability to document LGBTI abuses. From coalition building between civil society, to building capacity to document human rights abuses, Swedish leaders spent time garnering best practices and tactics recommended by Ugandan LGBTI leaders.

Advocacy organizations such as RFSL recognize that sexuality and identity are immensely diverse globally. The vast expanse of human sexuality is a complex topic that RFSL leaders continue to espouse and teach to the public in community events in Sweden and around the world.[73] Similarly, homophobia, violence, and discrimination manifest in countries in a variety of ways; advocates thus address them differently. According to Frederik Nilsson, ombudsman and head of administration for RFSL in 2013, "the aim is to make international activism sustainable and locally-driven rather than to go into places like Uganda and tell them what they need. . . We always use consultative methods and it keeps us updated and connected to the peoples' realities."[74] The NGO holds the practice of surveying members' views and garnering a collective response from local populations. For example, RFSL's "Rainbow Leaders," an international activism training program, upholds a consultative approach, where local leaders set priorities and identify the most critical needs for their community.[75] In RFSL's international work, advocates attempt to have local community leaders set policy recommendations, trainings, and programmatic agendas tailored specifically to the local societal needs.

Swedish advocates apply Swedish democratic mechanisms to their internal policy structures when generating policy recommendations. RFSL provides its partner organizations with consultative opportunities in RFSL's engagement in meetings at the United Nations (UN) and other international venues. Frederik Nilsson remarked how each of the 7,000 LGBTI community members of its organization "can text or contact us at any time to voice their views on what we are or should be doing or text us during a congress if they can't be there."[76] In reflecting on RFSL's internal member consultative practices, Nilsson "linked these methods to a long history of socialist government in Sweden and "networked structures with connectivity going 'up' and 'down' from people to leaders and leaders to people . . . so in a way people are the leaders."[77] RFSL holds a local, community, people-led approach when conducting policy advisement. Even with this intention, Christine Klapeer documents the "colonial constructions" experienced at times by recipient nations of Swedish civil society and foreign aid.[78] At times, local populations respond that they perceive foreign input to reflect that nation's agenda, not necessarily local priorities. Therese Brolin's study analyzes the bilateral relationship between stakeholders in Sweden and Uganda, noting how at times, "Swedish development actors have different ways of describing the problem they intend to address with the results agenda, leading to misunderstandings over the implementation of the agenda and the effectiveness of the development co-operation."[79] International donor agencies are often located in faraway countries with different cultures and traditions than aid recipient nations. As human rights norms are often steeped in local cultural practices, it is difficult for foreign agencies to rectify abuses in local communities without strong input from local communities.

RFSL's international work is undergirded by the ethos that the needs of the community are best understood and served by local leaders of their community. As such, they consult with Swedish government officials and encourage Swedish leaders themselves to meet with local LGBTI advocates. When the Swedish finance minister, Anders Borg, traveled to Uganda in 2014, with the purpose of increasing Swedish investment opportunities in the growing East African economy, at the start of the visit, Borg met with local Ugandan LGBTI activists.[80] The finance ministers of other countries would mainly focus on meetings related to trade and foreign investment on diplomatic trips; it is exceptional for a finance minister to meet with human rights activists at all. Normally government leaders are siloed; military leaders meet with foreign security officials, finance ministers meet with foreign trade partners, and so forth. It is uncommon for trade officials to meet with human rights advocates, and further still to make public overtures that foreign investment may be predicated on a human rights issue in the country. Borg's meeting with local Ugandan activists helped his team incorporate human rights considerations into Sweden's East African investment strategies. A SIDA representative noted that while the Swedish government thoughtfully developed its foreign policy toward Uganda, "other governments react in a clumsy way—they create policies without talking to Ugandan NGOs."[81] RFSL, and Swedish government officials, challenge the norm from previous decades of foreign aid, mainly by having Swedish leaders across sectors actively consult with human rights groups and create structures and processes to let local advocates provide strategic recommendations on how best to allocate Swedish foreign aid.

In attempting to maintain a local-led agenda when faced with the challenge of responding to Uganda's AHA, RFSL representatives contacted

their Ugandan and East African organizational partners for Ugandan perspectives on the best way for Swedish foreign aid to support LGBTI rights
in Uganda. Ugandan civil society leaders, in communication with Swedish
NGO partners, raised serious concerns regarding Sweden cutting aid to their
country.[82] Instead, they lobbied to have the Ugandan people receive the same
levels of foreign assistance, albeit funneled through different channels. This
diplomatic method seeks to shame foreign government leaders and cripple
the government agencies they lead while simultaneously empowering and
assisting fledging NGOs in the country.

In the end, the Swedish government followed RFSL's recommendation. SIDA and the Swedish MFA shifted the delivery of international
development aid away from public Ugandan ministries and governmental institutional recipients and reallocated the development funds to local
civil society.[83] One Swedish activist reflected on the difficulty of generating
RFSL's policy recommendation to the Swedish government in light of the
Ugandan law:

> At first we did not know what to recommend to our govern-
> ment. . . Cutting aid is a very risky proposition. . . Ultimately,
> we decided to recommend our government should channel
> money through local NGOs, rather than its traditional govern-
> ment-to-government funding of aid.[84]

RFSL leaders therefore recommended to the Swedish government to increase
funding and assistance to local Ugandan civil society organizations.[85] In this
case, the Swedish government made the historic decision to support LGBTI
rights by removing parts of its funding from the Ugandan government, and
instead turned its diplomatic efforts and funding toward local Ugandan civil
society groups. The Swedish government made the decision to stop working with Ugandan governmental institutions, and SIDA stopped funding
Uganda's justice sector programs. As opposed to cutting aid entirely, Sweden removed approximately SEK 6.5 million ($994,000) of planned aid to
the Ugandan government and reallocated its funding to nongovernmental
programs in the country.[86] This represented a diplomatic precedent for a
country to formally condition aid based on the praxis of LGBTI human
rights abuses.[87]

The leveraging of international aid as a strategy to promote human
rights continues to be contested. Activists in aid-receiving countries have

criticized the "aid conditionality" approach, describing that it "undermines another right, namely the right to development."[88] Sweden's response to the Ugandan AHA exemplifies the consequences of aid conditionality: as Ugandan president Yoweri Museveni signed the bill into law in 2014, the Swedish government changed is foreign policy toward the country and revamped its bilateral aid during the following aid period, as a way to incentivize LGBTI rights reform. Ugandan activist Val Kalende, however, warned that "African LGBTI activists know too well what the consequences of aid cuts would be—especially the backlash against LGBTI people."[89] Edwin Sesange, director of the African LGBTI Out and Proud Diamond group, also remarked on this approach: "Aid in various forms helps all ordinary Ugandans, including LGBTI people who we are campaigning for. Therefore the consequences of not being able to access those services financed by foreign aid will directly impact gay, lesbian, trans and bi Ugandans' wellbeing."[90] With these complexities of who benefits from international donor aid, Swedish foreign policy leaders indicated that Swedish aid to Uganda would still be disseminated to Uganda, but for the specific use of supporting maternal and child health and promoting sustainable economic growth and employment.

Foreign aid allocation to civil society—rather than traditional government-to-government financial support—is a relatively new tool in diplomatic practice. In 2014, Swedish Foreign Affairs Minister Margot Wallström stated, with regard to Sweden's new feminist foreign policy that year, "I have also declared that our foreign policy will be solidly based in civil society."[91] Dietrich argues that the practice of bypassing funding from government ministries and instead engaging and funding local civil society organizations can be effective for human rights goals.[92] International NGOs' shaming of governments' human rights abuses influences donor governments to redirect funds to non-state aid delivery channels.[93] Foreign aid donor nations may pull their funding from local government ministries for a variety of reasons: corruption, lack of institutional capacity, or to express condemnation of official human rights abuses. Joseph Wright's research exhibits a growing concern among foreign policy officials that allocating foreign aid to authoritarian states may enable dictators to hold on to power longer.[94] Through funding non-state actors instead, foreign governments are not necessarily led to pulling foreign aid away from the local population. Swedish leaders thus still shame the Ugandan government and condemn state violence at the highest levels of government without cutting off all foreign aid to the Ugandan people. In this case, Ugandan and East African partners recommended not cutting aid to Uganda, but rather directing it away from Ugandan government leaders or ministries and instead allocating it to Ugandan civil society.

The Ugandan law sparked official responses from foreign policy leaders; it also generated a great deal of attention and activism from LGBTI advocates. During the last few years of Stockholm Pride, many activists specifically pointed to how Uganda, once obscure to most Swedes, has permeated the Swedish public space as a focal point for diplomatic and transnational LGBTI activism. For example, Uganda forbids a Pride celebration anywhere in the country. In response, advocates in Stockholm and Amsterdam recognize a proxy "Kampala Pride." In 2015, according to a Dutch leader speaking at Stockholm Pride in reference to Uganda, "no matter what governments do not accept, at this point, it is an international movement with support and allies across borders. They cannot stop us."[95] Swedish civil society groups seek to address human rights issues in Uganda and work with local LGBTI Ugandan populations. For example, Swedish LGBTI activists founded a Swedish based nonprofit organization, "In Lube, in Uganda."[96] This Swedish-based NGO addresses the concern that lubricant (lube) is illegal in Uganda. Access to lube is a health issue, as using lubricants during sex can help prevent condoms from breaking or tears and help decrease one's risk of transmitting HIV/AIDS.[97] For each tube of lube Swedes purchase through the website, the organization donates one tube of lube to a local Ugandan. As the website is only in Swedish, the assumption is that the clientele is mainly for the Swedish public, or limited to Swedish speakers.[98] Clients "get a bottle of lube and at the same time help the LGBTI movement in Uganda," where the founders call on Swedes to support a "more open world filled with love."[99] There are many countries in the world where homosexuality is illegal, many with the death penalty. Gambia, Pakistan, and other countries with laws that are as draconian as Uganda's laws. Yet these other countries are rarely discussed in the Swedish press, nor are they the focus of civil society. In the aftermath of Uganda's law and the high levels of media attention to the LGBTI movement in Uganda, Swedes and global LGBTI networks have placed a strong focus on Uganda specifically in their agendas and activism.

Amnesty International, one of the leading human rights organizations in the world, made Uganda a central focus of its advocacy, also in response to Uganda's AHA. The Swedish Chapter of Amnesty International (AI) sent representatives to Uganda in 2015 for a fact-finding trip after the law passed. Amnesty officers analyzed the social impact of the AHA, which extended to family and friends of LGBTI individuals. Part of the particularly nefarious aspect of the AHA was that it criminalized not just the LGBTI person, but also anyone who "aids" or "abets" another person to "engage in acts of homosexuality" is liable for up to seven years in prison.[100] This could lead to family members housing a relative and then being charged as an "accomplice" in "promoting homosexuality."[101] The law also included a "three-year prison term for anyone who, knowing of the existence of a homosexual, failed to turn him or her over to the authorities."[102] One of AI's central conclusions was that violence toward LGBTI people increased significantly because of the law.[103] An AI representative presented that year at Stockholm Pride and asserted that "even the proposal of the law was like the state-sanctified violence."[104] Whether carried out by authorities or societal mobs, state-sanctioned violence can lead to a ripple effect of increased violence and lack of human security for persecuted groups.[105] Amnesty's representatives documented stark levels of increased violence, discrimination, and social stigma against LGBTI Ugandans after the proposed bill. The representatives also affirmed that Uganda's law was a catalytic factor to stimulate the global LGBTI equality movement.[106] In their public presentation at Stockholm Pride 2015, they reasoned that the draconian nature of the Ugandan law brought LGBTI human rights abuses to global human rights advocates.

For decades, human rights advocates tried to raise LGBTI rights abuses to the attention of international leaders. They documented severe violence toward LGBTI individuals in Brazil, Russia, Indonesia, and other countries where LGBTI people are subjected to extreme violence. There were even discussions in the early 1990s of Swedish leaders who considered linking foreign aid to a country's human rights practices, including LGBTI abuses. In 1991, for example, the president of RFSL at the time, Tobias Wikström, recommended that SIDA officials condition foreign aid to Cuba based on the "conditions for homosexuals."[107] That same year, Wikström also recommended similar action toward Nicaragua, after Nicaragua passed a draconian ban against homosexuality. RFSL advocated at the time for SIDA foreign aid to include the ban "in the assessment of the extent to which Nicaragua met the democracy conditions that Sweden's aid policy is now based on."[108] While it was recommended to incorporate considerations of abuses to homosexuals with foreign aid to Central America and the Caribbean in the 1990s, the policy was not institutionalized. Despite earlier recommendations, until the AHA in Uganda, advocates did not gain significant traction on linking LGBTI abuses to conditional foreign aid. Prior to the Ugandan law, advocates had not succeeded in changing foreign policy priorities to address these abuses.

Unlike these earlier cases, Swedish government officials articulated the AHA law in Uganda as severe enough that it threatened a long-standing bilateral relationship between the two countries. Leaders across sectors of the Swedish government, including those in trade and finance, elevated the new norm of LGBTI rights to surpass other Swedish foreign interests. It took the extreme nature of the Ugandan law, change in public attitudes, as well as persistent action from global advocates to change foreign policy agendas. While inculcating foreign aid with Swedish normative values is not a new prospect, it took a new, extreme sensitizing event in world politics to invigorate Swedish policy makers to act and formally address LGBTI rights in Swedish foreign policy.

The Anti-Homosexuality Act's Impact on US Foreign Policy

By comparison with Sweden and other industrialized nations, the United States traditionally takes a more realist approach in its foreign policy. It is well documented in international relations literature that the United States often prioritizes security in foreign relations above all other national interests, including human rights.[109] Therefore, an unexpected turn of events caused LGBTI rights to become incorporated into US bilateral relations with Uganda.

In response to the AHA in Uganda, internal discourse in the State Department transformed from nebulous proposals of promoting LGBTI rights generally to concrete action for how the United States would specifically combat the Ugandan law. A member of Secretary Clinton's inner circle assessed:

> Uganda gave the world a specific example of how critical this issue was as a fundamental human right. With this law, promoting LGBTI rights was no longer an abstract policy area, but rather gave leaders a specific example of what we would be targeting.[110]

US officials attested that State Department policy deliberations were focused not on whether the United States should raise LGBTI rights generally in diplomat affairs, but rather "how are we going to defeat this law?"[111] A high-level US government official asserted that the law became "a focal point for leaders to address these issues; heads of the Africa Bureau, Bureau of Democracy, Human Rights and Labor (DRL), Trade, USAID, and Department of Defense (DOD) began deliberating how the United States comprehensively was going to revamp its international development aid and military assistance to try and stop this law."[112] Engaging military officials from the DOD, in concert with American foreign aid assistance representatives at USAID and foreign policy leaders within the State Department, for the collective goal of stopping the death penalty for LGBTI people in a foreign country was unprecedented.

Discussions regarding the development of LGBTI diplomacy were ongoing before the Ugandan law, but had yet to take shape or significantly influence bilateral relations. In another case instance, the State Department's human rights report of the Kyrgyz Republic in 2011 documents "the practice of lesbians and/or their partners being raped by their own family members as a punitive measure or as a so-called method of 'curing' their homosexuality."[113] Human rights advocates document the situation in Jamaica as: "to be gay in Jamaica is to be dead."[114] In places such as Jamaica and the Kyrgyz Republic, where societal violence against the LGBTI populations remains severe, internal State Department discussions were underway for how diplomats could address human rights issues in a specific country. Yet there was not an urgent focus on the issue. Amid abuses throughout many countries, one of Clinton's advisors recounted that, before the Ugandan AHA, it was difficult to get traction on the issue inside the State Department.[115] Julie Dorf, senior adviser to the Council for Global Equality, remarked, "In an ironic and unfortunate way, the intensity of the homophobia surrounding the 'kill the gays' bill in Uganda has helped raise awareness within the State Department, within Congress and within the international community more generally on the global impact of LGBT(I) discrimination and abuse."[116] The Ugandan AHA became a lightning rod for US foreign officials to address LGBTI human rights within diplomatic efforts.

Furthermore, LGBTI rights abuses are often one of many human rights concerns. Many nations that oppress LGBTI people also jail political prisoners, have high levels of trafficking in persons and forced labor, and discriminate against ethnic and religious minorities.[117] Foreign policy officials have the task of debating where and when to raise human rights in bilateral relations. Once human rights issues are possibly included as an agenda item between a US official and their foreign counterpart, US policy leaders then have a further challenge to decide which human rights issues to raise. These internal meetings are often heated and contentious. It is a grim task to determine which human rights abuses are worse, which abuses merit foreign attention, and which ones do not make it onto the agenda of diplomatic dialogues.

The policy objective to address LGBTI rights by US embassies was still in early formation; Obama had recently come to power in 2009 when Ugandan lawmakers proposed the AHA. With the change in US administration, it was a critical time of broader reevaluation of US foreign policy. Michael Posner, former assistant secretary of state for the Bureau of Democracy, Human Rights and Labor, explained that under Secretary Clinton's leadership, the United States was able to provide "a very full-throated support for LGBT(I) rights" along with concrete measures.[118] Diplomats had not yet been given any specific direction regarding if, or whether, to incorporate those issues into their mission's strategic plan.[119] Each year, embassy teams and officers in Main State generate a strategic plan, tailoring US policy goals uniquely to each country. The "Integrated Country Strategy" takes into account all US foreign policy interests, including security, trade, poverty, human rights, and economic relations for each country. Officers representing these varied interests debate and then create a strategic plan for US policy priorities and set mission goals and objectives.[120] Before the Ugandan law, annual strategy meetings included human rights and, only on sporadic occasions in some countries, human rights issues related to LGBTI abuses. Discussions on LGBTI equality did not occur evenly in every embassy, even in places where local violence was acute. There was only a generalized dialogue, mainly in Washington, about how the United States would address LGBTI rights globally. Uganda's lawmakers provided a specific law for human rights policy makers to target. State Department leaders asserted that their policy discussions were transformed from an abstract, long-term goal of including LGBTI rights in the State Department's work to an acute, short-term need to specifically address Uganda's law.

While Obama officials expressed urgency to react to the law, it was not initially clear how the State Department, and US foreign policy institutions, would respond. Diplomats deliberated internally on potential policy reactions, drawing from a myriad of options in the modern human rights diplomatic toolbox.[121] For instance, foreign policy officers can choose to respond to human rights concerns with immediate condemnation, closed-door diplomacy, long-term programmatic support and funding for NGOs, or conditioning aid, to name just a few of several potential policy options. A significant portion of the work of the Bureau of Democracy, Human

Rights and Labor (DRL)—the bureau in the State Department responsible for shaping international US human rights policies and programs—is to react to immediate global human rights abuses and events. DRL develops rapid response and emergency assistance programs to intervene to ensure the safety of human rights defenders in spaces where such activism is restricted and repressed.[122] DRL additionally supports and assists journalists and the media in improving government accountability and democratic transparency, among other human rights. Daily, DRL officers respond to issues such as violence against minorities in Libya or stoning of women in Saudi Arabia.[123] Responses depend on the case and context, as well as the bilateral relationship between the two countries. Reactions can include an official statement of condemnation, a demarche of the foreign nation's ambassador to the State Department, or long-term programmatic funding to address structural changes in the country.

One of the most sustained tools to support human rights diplomacy is through funding civil society and providing long-term support for structural changes to the rule of law, democracy, and human rights practices in foreign countries.[124] For example, DRL programs seek to bolster civil society organizations working to increase transparency within their countries through the Global Anti-Corruption Consortium initiative. Further illustrative funding distributes local grants for inclusive voter campaigns to increase political participation of minority groups.[125] Initially, policy discussions within the State Department debated how the Human Rights and Democracy Fund and other US embassy funding could support long-term efforts of civil society in Uganda. However, this was quickly deemed not fast enough to address the acute needs of human rights defenders in the country, who may be put to death under the AHA.

Upon the proposal of the AHA, foreign policy leaders began to consult with Ugandan interlocutors for local input on how to address the severe human rights situation while simultaneously not putting local advocates in jeopardy. US leaders Randy Berry, special envoy for the human rights of LGBTI persons; Michael H. Posner and Tom Malinowski, both former assistant secretaries, Bureau of Democracy, Human Rights, and Labor; Daniel Baer, deputy assistant secretary; and Todd Larson, USAID's senior LGBTI coordinator, all recognized the important ethos of "do no harm" when working with local activists on human rights. Assistant Secretary Tom Malinowski stated, " 'Do no harm' is *the* most important principle guiding our efforts, which are shaped in consultation with local communities."[126] Further, Assistant Secretary Michael H. Posner highlighted:

> We have to recognize how absolutely perilous it is for people in places like Uganda and many other places I visit, I make a point of meeting with the LGBT community. And a lot of them are—you know, it's almost clandestine meetings. Their lives are at risk, so I think you start with the things that they themselves are asking for, and you build out from that.[127]

While generating a new foreign policy mandate, foreign policy leaders consulted with local NGOs, asking them their advocacy priorities, all the while cognizant of the danger they were in. Special Envoy Berry traveled to Uganda and met with local LGBTI organizations, such as SMUG Executive Director Frank Mugisha. In response, Mugisha stated, "We welcome the visit. . . It is a clear indication that the US government is strategically working to support LGBT rights globally. We feel the visibility is good because it creates dialogue and keeps the issues on the agenda, among the issues discussed was working with our government to advance LGBT rights."[128] Similarly, Assistant Secretary Michael Posner and Deputy Assistant Secretary Daniel Baer traveled to Uganda to meet with Ugandan civil society leaders. They discussed the issue of NGO registration and harassment from government officials. In a press statement, Posner asserted, "A society's commitment to human rights can often be measured by how it protects the most vulnerable or unpopular persons within it. As we raised the protection of all Ugandans, including LGBT Ugandans, with government officials today, we did so on the basis of making sure that universal rights are protected for all people, and we will continue to do so."[129] Diplomats also consulted with regional African LGBTI organizations, mainly located in Tanzania, as well as international LGBTI organizations to discuss how to support their work. Reflecting on continued efforts toward LGBTI diplomacy, Special Envoy Randy Berry explains, "Through small grants, our network of embassies and consulates is able to provide targeted support to grassroots organizations working to promote and protect the human rights of LGBT(I) persons."[130] Global advocates worked with foreign diplomats to craft an international response to the AHA and to support LGBTI civil society.

Very quickly, however, after the proposed law in 2009, it seemed apparent to policy makers that long-term work supporting civil society would not be strong or rapid enough to stop the AHA. Statements of condemnation and human rights dialogues seemed to have little impact on Ugandan leaders. In 2012, one Ugandan official claimed, "if giving us mosquito nets, ARVs, and malaria medicine involves us embracing sodomy, and giving the way to Sodom and Gomorrah, then we would rather die in dignity than live in dishonor."[131] This response showed that long-term programming to support the human rights of LGBTI people would not be sufficient. US and other foreign policy leaders deliberated over stronger policy options, namely cutting foreign aid to Uganda or conditioning aid in exchange for improved human rights practices.

The strongest, most severe reaction to a human rights event in modern diplomacy is the conditioning of bilateral aid. One country, namely the donor nation, may find the human rights practices of the recipient nation untenable with their national values. While rare, at times normative prin-cipals are prioritized over market forces, as seen in the case of apartheid South Africa, and the international community may cut ties with a country to pressure reform.[132] Conditioning international aid based on human rights is an exceptional act because it requires severing ties with a nation. Before the AHA, severing ties with another nation based on LGBTI rights had not been done before in international relations.

As the conditioning of US donor aid based on laws against homosexu-ality had never been done, senior US officials found themselves in unknown diplomatic territory. Advocates were also initially unsure as to how to pro-ceed. There was first a consultative process for US officials to deliberate over a policy response. Similar to the process in Sweden, US officials accordingly sought the consultation of influential US-based civil society groups. A lead-ing activist at the time acknowledged that "conditionality based on LGBTI rights was a brave new world, and no one really knew the right answer."[133] Human rights organizations and diplomats often try to have a local-led, consultative approach with local LGBTI organizations before recommend-ing policy directives to Washington. Frank Mugisha, executive director of SMUG, asserted that in Uganda, "the U.S. government follows *our* lead before taking action on our behalf."[134] Formerly, foreign aid institutions in the 1970s and 1980s entered local communities with agendas largely man-dated by capitals. After decades of evaluations establishing that sustainable change is generated from local-led initiatives, modern diplomatic best prac-tice is to consult with local stakeholders. Burack remarkably documents in her field research that "every U.S. government official I spoke to gave this principle of listening to and following the lead of local LGBTQ activists as the first principle of SOGI (sexual orientation and gender identity) human rights assistance."[135] As a departure from international development aid prac-tice in the 1970s and 1980s, modern diplomats work under the assumption that programs led by locals will be more effective and sustainable. Since the

2000s, most human rights democracy programming is not determined in Western capitals, but rather in consultation with local civil society groups in that country. According to Outright Action International, rights organizations work with a "long history of productive and trusting relationships with grassroots LGBTIQ communities worldwide, [serving] as a bridge between local communities and high-impact external levers of power."[136] US-based advocates consulted with local Ugandan organizations, LGBTI advocates in Kampala, and civil society groups in neighboring East African nations. As some LGBTI Ugandans reside in Tanzania and Kenya, there are important advocacy networks between these communities. The result of consultations with civil society groups at the time was divided, with some groups and advocates supporting conditional aid and others strongly opposing it.[137] Advocates and diplomats alike were conflicted on the best response: should the United States unleash its strongest condemnation yet towards LGBTI rights abuses, maintain the status quo, or even conduct quiet diplomacy to advocate Ugandan leaders to change the law? Heated and contested debates were underway within the advocacy community, State Department, and National Security Council.

Ultimately, officials decided to strongly condemn Uganda's proposed law and to condition aspects of the United States' bilateral relationship with the country. This manifested as discontinued and redirected funds for certain programs involving the Ugandan Police Force, Ministry of Health, and National Public Health Institute. US response also prevented entry into the United States of certain Ugandan officials involved in serious human rights abuses, including against LGBTI individuals, as well as cancelled plans to hold US military-sponsored aviation exercises in Uganda.[138] The White House similarly cancelled military cooperation with the Ugandan defense force and halted aid to the Ugandan security sector, among other actions.[139] In response to the AHA, the United States also suspended $4 million in a cooperative agreement between the US Centers for Disease Control and the Ugandan Ministry of Health.[140] This was new precedent for US foreign policy institutions to assume this type of hard-line stance to another nation's human rights abuses toward the LGBTI community.

While unprecedented in diplomatic history, that year the United States mirrored the actions of other governments, including Sweden, the Netherlands, Denmark, and Norway to condition its bilateral aid to Uganda in response to the passage of the 2014 AHA.[141] Furthermore, the World Bank suspended a $90 million loan that was to be allocated to the Ugandan health care system.[142] Thus, US leaders joined a small but powerful group of international donor nations in shifting international relations to elevate a new normative value of LGBTI equality in foreign affairs.

One of the central debates in human rights literature is whether human rights conditioning of foreign aid leads to human rights improvement. Conditioning aid with the goal of improved human rights is widely contested in scholarly literature and foreign policy discussions.[143] There is evidence on both sides of the debate. A body of scholars provide empirical evidence of correlation between conditioning donor aid and the long-term effect of improving human rights. Carnegie and Marinov evidence that making aid conditional to improve human rights can produce positive outcomes in the domain of democracy and human rights, largely dependent on the relationship of the donor and recipient nation.[144] Conditioning aid sends a strong signal to the foreign government to reconsider the law and take LGBTI rights seriously.[145] It may be a shock to the economic system in the recipient country that catalyzes a response from local leaders. Fear of ostracism and retribution from the international community may lead to action. Suspending foreign assistance is one of the strongest symbols in international relations. Gabriella Montinola finds that under certain political conditions, conditioning aid can be an effective strategy for promoting normative values.[146] However, Daniela Donno and Michael Neureiter assert that the efficacy and impact of conditioning aid on human rights is predicated on the degree of leverage held by one country over the other.[147] Debates around conditioning aid weighed the benefits of sending a powerful message to a host country, and directly impacting immediate improvements by host governments, against the possibility of a backlash against the community it aims to protect.[148] Thus, the negative consequences of conditioning aid also merit further discussion.

Cutting ties and adding requirements to foreign aid can also result in consequences, such as removing the support of projects funded by foreign aid, such as wells for clean water, maternal health services, food, and sometimes direct cash transfers. In lower-income countries, it is often the most economically marginalized people who receive benefits from international development aid. Conditioning aid places donor countries, such as the United States and Sweden, in a difficult political and moral position. Suspending health care–related aid has a clear correlation with hurting the local population. In this policy priority, vulnerable populations across Uganda would not receive foreign-funded vaccines for public health. Conditioning aid may backfire and hurt the intended marginalized community. Rachel Bergenfield and Alice Miller demonstrate how persons already facing punitive laws may then be blamed for the discontinuation of international aid that funds assistance for other populations in the country.[149] It may lead to increased popular support of local leaders perceived by their citizens as standing up to an outside foreign threat of their culture and thus hinder progress of LGBTI rights.[150] There remains a great debate among scholars and diplomats alike regarding the efficacy of making aid conditional on human rights improvements.[151]

While divergent perspectives remain regarding the issue of conditional aid, the majority of US advocates interviewed for *From Pariah to Priority* initially wanted a strong response from US foreign policy leaders. In diplomatic terms, this means incorporating the threat of ceasing foreign aid if a country does not reform or improve its human rights record. However, after consultations with local activists and the consideration of double victimization and other unintended consequences, many advcoates realized any action at all would have potential positive and negative repercussions, advising US diplomats to prioritize LGBTI rights in diplomatic dialogues instead.[152] On the one hand, many wanted the United States to flex its political power to the fullest extent in order to to pressure Ugandan lawmakers to change; on the other hand, they wanted to mitigate potential risk to the health and well-being of Ugandans, both within and outside the LGBTI Ugandan community. While policy makers took those recommendations into consideration, the ultimate decision was made by a handful of key leaders at the top of the State Department and reflected a hybrid approach. The United States did not cut all ties with Uganda, as some had initially proposed, nor did it maintain its existing aid to Uganda in the same manner. Instead, the State Department conditioned aspects of its aid. Honing in on government-to-government funding, US foreign assistance was cut from public security and health sectors. US funding was then redirected to work with local and regional civil society groups in these sectors. Along with these actions, US foreign policy leaders voiced strong public condemnation toward Ugandan leaders regarding the death penalty law. The tough language from the State Department, coupled with ceasing some military and security cooperation based on a country's LGBTI human rights record, was unprecedented for the State Department. This policy decision garnered great attention from international leaders that continues to influence contemporary foreign affairs.

Foreign attention to the AHA created political leverage for local LGBTI Ugandans. Nobel Peace Prize laureate Desmond Tutu of South Africa, an Ethiopian government minister, and other prominent African representatives condemned the AHA.[153] Richard Lusimbo, a representative of SMUG, "praised African and Western leaders who spoke out against the law and credited that criticism with the increased global attention to the plight of LGBTI Ugandans."[154] While local advocates decried the potential detrimental impacts of cutting foreign aid, they also recognized the political influence of foreign leaders condemning Uganda's domestic practices.

Rarely is there a direct outcome from diplomatic efforts; often a result will come years later, if at all. Funding civil society to document human rights abuses or conduct public awareness campaigns may only show measurable impact on a society years later. However, sometimes diplomatic efforts can produce the opposite impact of what they sought to achieve.[155] Vogelgesang echoes this concern, describing how both symbolic gestures and external pressures in pursuit of human rights can have such an unintended effect.[156] Yulius, Tang, and Offord analyze how the globalization of LGBTI identity has, in some regions of the world, both institutionalized new norms for sexual minorities while also creating counterreactions in local populations.[157] On the other end of the empirical debate, Dutta and Williamson exhibit how foreign assistance can aid journalists in authoritarian states.[158] Thereby, human rights conditions can impact and possibly improve domestic human rights practices. In another example in diplomatic history, the United States suspended all aid to the Indonesian military in 1999 because of severe human rights abuses occurring in East Timor and Aceh. As a result of this aid suspension, pressure from foreign governments, and the removal of President Suharto, some measures of democratic practices improved in the country.[159] At times, making aspects of comprehensive foreign assistance conditional to human rights reforms can effectively lead to measurable improvements in the recipient nation.

There were measurable, positive results on LGBTI rights in Uganda from the groundswell of international attention. After the collective tsunami of international response, the government did not pass the original death penalty version of the AHA. Instead, Ugandan lawmakers revised the proposed law to include life imprisonment for homosexual acts. While imprisonment is still a severe infringement on human rights, local advocates articulated this change in the law to be a modicum of improvement. Frank Mugisha, executive director of SMUG, stated that it gave him hope that the Ugandan court overturned the AHA, asserting, "It was a big step. And although we still have the penal code that criminalises some sex acts, at least my work is now legal. . . it is very good for the international communities to see that there is legal redress for minority groups in Uganda."[160] Tom

Malinowski, assistant secretary of state for Democracy, Human Rights and Labor, echoed Mugisha and stated, "These local efforts have often been successful, and we will continue to stand by those whose only crime is to demand the same human rights as everyone else.[161] Former Canadian foreign service officer Janoff Douglas describes how foreign diplomats manage to assert LGBTI rights in the face of opposition from unfriendly states, and that high-level engagement by foreign diplomats has, to an extent, a measurable impact on LGBTI persons at the grassroots level in collaboration with local civil society.[162] The immediate negative consequences of stopping aid delivery are measurable: health clinics are not built, maternal health programs lose funding. It is much harder to document the potential long-term effect of threatening to cease aid on authoritarian leaders. However, at times, cutting bilateral ties can lead to long-term systemic change. Cutting ties with South Africa risked vulnerable populations in the short term, but in the long term led to the institutional reform of ending apartheid. Foreign policy leaders often act in crisis but also think long-term; what is best for their own nation's long-term interest, and what will ultimately lead to policy reform in another country. How diplomats leverage financial and political pressure, and which tool they use from the diplomatic toolbox, needs a great deal more scrutiny from researchers and scholars.

Bilateral relations are constantly reassessed according to changing norms in international relations. One of the most poignant examples in modern foreign affairs of the impact of evolving human rights norms on foreign relations was in the 1990s, when the international community sanctioned apartheid South Africa. Prior to this time, many countries had a robust trade and security relationship with apartheid South Africa. However, because of the changing norm of racial equality, foreign governments transitioned to hold South African laws as no longer acceptable. Countries such as Australia, Canada, and Sweden ended trade with South Africa and risked their own security cooperation in the sub-Saharan African region.[163] In this case, the normative value of racial inequality within a country led to ostracism by international partners. Klotz examines this case of global cooperation against apartheid South Africa as a rare moment of collective action where norms trumped market interests for many nations.[164] Norms are diffused by the socialization of states and dissemination of new concepts of human rights across borders.[165] Identities of states are shaped by evolving norms over time to create political change.[166] Similarly, LGBTI rights abuses, once overlooked by foreign policy leaders, have risen to importance in diplomatic affairs and at times influence trade relations. Randy Berry, the State

Department's special envoy for the human rights of LGBTI persons, asserted that it is not acceptable that members of the LGBTI community should be discriminated against; should be arrested, detained, and subjected to torture and harassment; and should be executed in some countries; "Singling out sexual minorities in that way runs counter to the core American value that people should have the freedom to be who you are regardless of who you love or your identity."[167] In contemporary diplomatic dialogue, US leaders now articulate the changing norm of LGBTI rights, where violence and abuse in foreign countries is no longer acceptable in international relations.

Since WWII, and largely during and after the Carter administration in the 1970s, the US State Department occasionally decreased aid allocations to countries because of human rights violations. For example, in 1991, in reaction to grave human rights abuses in Yugoslavia, the United States cut parts of its economic aid to Yugoslavia.[168] In recent decades, US military assistance could be thwarted by human rights considerations in recipient countries.[169] Since the 1990s, "Leahy laws" mandate restrictions to the US Foreign Assistance Act and Department of Defense based on human rights considerations.[170] In 2012 alone, State Department officials vetted more than 160,000 individuals and units for human rights abuses before individuals would receive US military training or material.[171] Mertus's central thesis in her book analyzing modern human rights in US foreign policy is that "human rights matter for all the actors involved in the creation and promotion of US foreign policy, including the US military.[172] Human rights considerations in foreign relations have been legislated by Congress for decades. Irrespective of the political party in power, US embassy personnel are required to document and vet foreign counterparts before approving diplomatic and defense work. It is a common and widespread practice in US foreign policy to include incentives related to human rights in comprehensive diplomatic engagements. However, a large part of human rights diplomacy is conducted quietly and thus does not gain the attention of international media.[173] A great deal of this work is not public and thereby understudied by outside analysts.

When human rights abuses are egregious enough, they rise to the top of the American foreign policy agenda. Responses from top US foreign policy leaders in *From Pariah to Priority* demonstrate that the egregious nature of the Ugandan law grabbed the attention of even reticent US policy leaders. In Ambassador Power's book, she recollects how gruesome attacks globally on LGBTI people called for the US government's attention, and that its support was breaking new ground.[174] As Power emphasizes, the issuing of public statements from world leaders, including the US president, "was unheard of" before the 2000s.[175] In a statement of support for LGBTI rights, Assistant Secretary of State for Democracy, Human Rights and Labor Michael Posner stated, "Rather than stand in the sidelines, America has decided to get in."[176] After the law came into the international spotlight, internal opposition or hesitation to address LGBTI rights was largely muted inside the State Department. While officials in the DRL were convinced to take action, leaders throughout the department, especially in regional bureaus, previously had needed convincing. The Ugandan law was a turning point to gain enough support in the State Department for action.

Diplomatic responses to human rights abuses are largely predicated on the status of the bilateral relationship between countries.[177] For example, the same action from Iran—a country excluded from many international partnerships—will draw the ire of the international community, while countries often remain silent toward Saudi Arabia—a country with close economic ties to many foreign nations.[178] Saudi Arabia's strategic security relationship, as well as its economic power with oil exports, often trumps human rights concerns in foreign relations. Conversely, when a small, un-strategic country such as Brunei proposes draconian new human rights laws, more powerful nations in the international system can be quick to voice harsh condemnation.[179] Richard Nielsen finds that aid sanctions are more often applied to weaker nations that do not have close political ties to the donor nation.[180] Responses to global human rights abuses are not evenly applied to each country, nor are they always public.

Foreign affairs officials debate whether to raise LGBTI abuses in closed-door diplomatic meetings. Tehmina Mahmood defines "quiet diplomacy" as meetings and negotiations regarding "complex and sensitive issues without the fanfare of attendant publicity."[181] Similarly, closed-door diplomacy options are chosen at times to protect the bilateral relationship and to not shame or embarrass foreign officials. Special Envoy Randy Berry commented on his work of raising LGBTI human rights concerns through diplomatic methods with foreign officials:

> We have to proceed with great care and make sure that often-times that we are making sure that we are conducting our diplomacy with our counterparts in government and not necessarily through the press as an opening salvo. But I think that those conversations are entirely possible. I think they carry the capacity

of being fundamentally productive, as long as we engage in a careful and reasoned way.[182]

Rather than release a condemning public statement against the country, State Department officials may call a private meeting with foreign representatives behind closed doors to ask them to release a political prisoner, cease harassment of human rights activists, or allow public Pride events in their home country. Officials may determine that public shaming of another country could have the opposite to the intended impact, and that meeting behind closed doors may lead to a more positive outcome to improve human rights. Deputy Assistant Secretary of the Bureau of Democracy, Human Rights, and Labor Daniel Baer noted, "There are many cases where we might urgently reach out to the prime minister or the president or reach out to members of parliament and convey our concerns."[183] Meeting with officials from Oman, Jordan, Kuwait, Morocco and other strategic partner nations, and working with them in collegial diplomatic channels, is at times more effective. Incentives may be offered to a foreign country, sometimes on an unrelated matter, in exchange for a human rights action. One exchange example would be to offer expediting a trade negotiation if the country allows international observers for an election, showing how two seemingly unrelated issues could result in improved democratic practices in the country. If the foreign representatives agree, the connection between the two issues may never be known publicly. Valentina Carraro and Hortense Jongen recognize the important role of closed-door deliberations of diplomatic representatives while also cautioning against the negative consequences of a lack of public transparency in diplomatic actions.[184] The very nature of closed-door diplomacy is that it is not known openly. In reference to quiet diplomacy, Ambassador Power recounts in her book, "Leaders rarely get political credit for preventing harms or for attempting to improve the lives of vulnerable people."[185] Their actions are often done outside the public eye. Furthermore, it is difficult to measure a direct causality of improved protections or improving rule of law, human rights, and equality.[186] For example, if the president of Gambia changes an executive order, or the Gambian country mission changes a stance in the UN, rarely do leaders clearly state what influenced their change. They could be perceived as politically weak by their constituents or as bending to foreign powers. Furthermore, results may appear in a country years later. Programs to train young lawyers in new improved human rights laws for women, for example, may take years to show results in improved rule of law. Thus, definitively crediting diplomatic action to human rights improvements is challenging. Closed-door diplomacy can be effective, but often lacks impact assessment or public accolades.

Researchers, journalists, and outside observers cannot document what they do not see. By design, aspects of diplomatic efforts are kept classified and thereby unidentifiable to the public. Human rights advocates in Iran and Syria risk their lives to conduct their work; it is vital that their names, locations, and work with the US government remain classified. These human rights diplomatic engagements, therefore, likely are missing from scholarship on human rights diplomacy. Research methods often rely on content analysis or close examination of speeches, public announcements, published country reports, or data that are public. By nature of classified work, there is a dearth of research on diplomatic relations. Keeping within the parameters of unclassified material and data, *From Pariah to Priority* seeks to offer insights into foreign policy deliberations, recognizing that under the modern mechanisms of diplomatic practice, outside observers do not have access to the full scope of practice in human rights diplomacy.

US Evangelical Leaders' Impact on Anti-homosexuality Legislation in Uganda

While US diplomats and advocates deliberated over a policy response to AHA, faith-based US civil society groups and influential leaders were working to counter LGBTI rights in Uganda and other foreign countries. Although the United States hosts some of the strongest public and private organizational support of LGBTI rights worldwide, it is also home to some of the most vehement opposition to LGBTI equality. Pastor Lou Engle of Missouri addressed a crowd of approximately two hundred people in St. Louis, Missouri, in 2010, decrying: "if we're struggling with a homosexual, same-sex desire, let the bible kill you."[187] Warren has also made inflammatory comments, such as equating same-sex acts to punching someone or consuming arsenic.[188] Opposition toward LGBTI equality still manifests itself in the United States, as well as in foreign countries, including Uganda.

The activities of Western evangelical religious leaders have at times led to measurable regression in public attitudes regarding homosexuality in Uganda and other foreign nations. Deborah Kintu's research establishes that "U.S. evangelicals were the driving force behind General Museveni's adversity towards homosexuals."[189] US evangelical pastors, such as Scott Lively of Massachusetts, Lou Engle of Missouri, and Rick Warren of California, among others, independently traveled to Uganda numerous times leading up to the 2009 proposed law to speak before the country's leadership against homosexuality. These men founded organizations to support their missions and thus have been hosted by the Ugandan Parliament to preach against the "sins of homosexuality."[190] Scott Lively is known for comparing homosexuality with pedophilia, Nazism, and fascism.[191] He blamed the 1994 Rwandan genocide—a civil war where over 800,000 people died—on gay people; Lively preaches HIV/AIDS as "just punishment" for homosexuality.[192] These evangelical ministers gained audiences for their messages against homosexuality at the highest levels of government in Uganda.

Evangelical pastors were active in stoking anti-homosexuality rhetoric within the Ugandan population, while also having a direct impact specifically on the Ugandan Parliament to draft the initial death penalty proposal.[193] Ugandan LGBTI advocate and leader of SMUG Frank Mugisha attributed the AHA to Scott Lively's influence; in an interview with *Mother Jones*, Mugisha stated, "the bill is essentially his [Lively's] creation."[194] Kintu asserts that Lively and other pastors had "considerable influence in shaping the Ugandan government's agenda."[195] Respondents in this research and also in the *Economist* in 2014 noted that as support for LGBTI equality increases in the West, opposition advocates are increasingly looking overseas to captivate new audiences receptive to their anti-homosexuality beliefs.[196] LGBTI advocates in Kenya have found that "negative forces from Uganda and other countries hinder our own growth as a movement [in Kenya]."[197] As extreme anti-homosexual sentiment wanes in many liberal democracies, evangelical leaders find new audiences for their message in foreign countries.

The interaction between the Ugandan Parliament, LGBTI rights, and American evangelicals led to a new frontier in international human rights law. SMUG and the Center for Constitutional Rights sued Scott Lively under the US Alien Tort Statute for his presentations in the Ugandan Parliament.[198] The statute enables non-US citizens to sue Americans in US courts for violations of US laws, including hate crimes. By the time Lively was sued, the Alien Tort Statute had already been successful in pursuing cases of torture and genocide committed by US citizens on foreign soil. SMUG and US-based advocates made the claim that Lively's messaging constituted a hate crime, albeit against foreign audiences. The Lively v. Uganda case is the first time the Alien Tort Statute was applied to a case related to LGBTI rights in a foreign context, breaking new ground for an international human rights law.

The anti-homosexuality rhetoric of pastors Lively, Warren, and Engle contrasts with diplomats who promote LGBTI rights. In many countries, there is a distinct polarization of global messaging and public diplomacy for, and against, LGBTI rights to foreign audiences. On the one hand, foreign evangelical leaders spread intolerance and hinder efforts of LGBTI advocates. On the other hand, US and other foreign diplomats support tolerance and fund local civil society organizations with the goal of improving LGBTI rights in East Africa and globally. This contradictory public messaging is jarring for Ugandan and foreign audiences. Formal US foreign policy supports LGBTI civil society and includes raising LGBTI rights in high-level diplomatic dialogue. During the Trump administration, evangelical leaders expected "Trump's State Department to stop pressuring other countries into embracing gay rights norms and freedoms."[199] Kyle James Rohrich denotes a "World War LGBT" in the global battle for contested LGBTI rights.[200]

The contested nature of LGBTI rights among the US population leads some observers to call for the United States to cease LGBTI diplomacy. As Burack thoroughly demonstrates, LGBTI diplomacy is vehemently criticized by both the political right as well as the left wing, who would seemingly be natural political supporters of LGBTI equality.[201] Encarnación asserts that the United States is a "flawed global leader" with a troubled history on homosexuality.[202] The message from influential US-based religious leaders directly contradicts and undermines the message delivered by US diplomats. However, it is important to contextualize that conflicting norms within a population exist for many human rights issues.

The duplicity found in LGBTI diplomacy is not exceptional to LGBTI rights. Within the broader framework of human rights diplomacy, many issues are a part of foreign policy, yet remain contested domestically. Anti-Semitism abounds in the United States,[203] yet the State Department has a special envoy to monitor and combat anti-Semitism. For example, I traveled with the special envoy to monitor and combat anti-Semitism, Hannah Rosenthal, in 2010 to Tunisia. In her words, the purpose of the trip was to "Reinforce the importance of pluralism and the protection of the rights of all religious minorities."[204] Similarly, Islamophobia is widespread within the United States, while at the same time the State Department's special representative to Muslim communities' central message to foreign audiences is tolerance toward Muslims.[205] Likewise, the State Department's Secretary's Office of Global Women's Issues advocates for women's empowerment in places such as Afghanistan and the Democratic Republic of Congo, while gender-based violence remains a pervasive societal issue in the United States.[206] Discrimination against persons with disabilities, torture, gender-based violence, substandard prison conditions, and violence against ethnic minorities are all examples of domestic human rights problems, yet diplomats raise these issues with foreign dignitaries in diplomatic dialogue. The entire endeavor of human rights diplomacy can be charged with hypocrisy, yet it remains a cornerstone of modern foreign affairs to promote peace and stability in foreign countries.

Not unique to the United States, many countries grapple with their own domestic human rights record while simultaneously addressing human rights issues with foreign audiences. Sweden is a country with an international reputation of gender equality. Nevertheless, gender-based violence persists in Sweden.[207] Representatives from Qatar raise freedom of the press in their foreign policy agenda,[208] especially from the vantage point of the Doha-based international media outlet Al-Jazeera.[209] And yet, Qatar has significant human rights issues of forced labor, curbing civil liberties, and not allowing citizens to criticize the government.[210] To be certain, this chapter is not making a cultural relativist argument that all countries are hypocritical; it recognizes that some countries exhibit higher degrees of discrepancies between domestic and foreign policies and of severity of human rights abuses. The point here is to highlight that diplomats and foreign policy leaders seeking to improve human rights in foreign contexts work in an imperfect world.

Practitioners of human rights often start from the vantage point that working with foreign counterparts on a human rights issue does not imply their own country has somehow solved that issue.[211] Former American diplomat Daniel Mahanty asserted that the objective of human rights diplomacy "is always intended to be a collaborative and mutually involved process of dealing with human rights in international relations."[212] Some foreign affairs officers see it as a form of solidarity across borders to improve human rights domestically and internationally.[213] Deputy Assistant Secretary of State Daniel Baer, a central architect of the State Department's LGBTI human rights diplomacy, reflected on promoting human rights amid the United States' imperfect record:

> Obviously, we've seen a rash of killings of trans women of color in this country [the United States] in the last few months, too. So, there's plenty of work left to do. But there are also places around the world where the United States embassy flying that flag is a sign of our standing with people who are vulnerable, and I think we should always be willing to do that.[214]

Ambassador Baer recognizes that there is a great deal of work to do globally as well as domestically to improve LGBTI rights. As no human rights issue is likely to become "perfected" in any country, diplomats must engage on human rights in foreign countries, while public policy makers simultaneously work toward improvements within their country. Since WWII, the international community recognized the importance of including human rights in foreign engagements; what other countries do within their borders, and how leaders treat their own people, impacts regional and global security. While perceived hypocrisy is one aspect of human rights diplomacy, international relations devoid of human rights considerations is far more precarious for peace and global stability.

Conclusion

The Ugandan chapter analyzes the process by which foreign policy leaders formally conditioned aid based on a country's LGBTI human rights record for the first time in diplomatic history.[215] Alarmed by the AHA's extreme nature, leaders in Washington and Stockholm realized the grave importance of establishing LGBTI rights as a unique human rights pillar. Discursive institutional scholars have determined that a sensitizing event may provoke "serious societal and political concerns that can cause institutional renewal and shape the ideas and plans for future decision making."[216] Sensitizing events such as beheadings, stoning, or extreme violence can, at times, (re) shape public opinions and shift institutions' policy agendas. The AHA opened the political opportunity for foreign policy leaders to rethink and reorganize policy agendas around LGBTI rights, a topic previously unaddressed formally in diplomatic agenda. From the initial proposal of the death penalty within the AHA, Uganda subsequently received a groundswell of international political and media attention.[217] The law generated unprecedented response from foreigners in what Kristen Cheney refers to as "moral panic over issues of sexual diversity."[218] In response to the law, LGBTI advocates in Sweden and the United States cautioned against cutting foreign aid to Uganda, as doing so had the potential to have detrimental effects on already marginalized people who are dependent on foreign aid.[219] Thus, the United States, Swedish, and other foreign governments changed their donor aid strategies to Uganda. This led largely to bypassing funding to government ministries and instead increased funding to local NGOs and non-state agencies. These foreign governments thereby still provided funding to the Ugandan people, but also sent a strong diplomatic signal by cutting government-to-government funding. Uganda received "widespread international pressure," and later the AHA was determined invalid (on procedural grounds) and subsequently dropped by the Ugandan Parliament.[220] However, the fight for LGBTI rights in Uganda is far from over. In October 2019, members of the Ugandan government once again announced plans to introduce a bill imposing the death penalty for same-sex relations.[221] Due to the groundswell of international attention, coupled with the extreme nature of the AHA in Uganda, LGBTI rights became an institutionalized aspect of modern human rights foreign policy.

Transnational activism remains an important factor for the durability of LGBTI rights in Swedish and American foreign policy. Activists brought LGBTI rights concerns into the international spotlight and solidified their importance to the general public. Executive director of Outright Action International Jessica Stern brought awareness to the broader implications of the law for local LGBTI Ugandans: "If you're perceived to be LGBT, no one's going to rent to you, for fear of their own criminal responsibility. . . So if this law is enacted in its current form, it's basically a homelessness sentence for LGBT Ugandans."[222] Transnational advocacy networks were critical in bringing the severity of the law to the world's attention. They also motivated insider allied government leaders to create a formal policy response to LGBTI rights abuses. Coalitions of transnational networks and human rights groups influenced the initial LGBTI movement in Sweden and its sustainability in Swedish foreign policy and international business practices. LGBTI Ugandan activist Mugisha called for increased pressure from foreign governments, especially by incorporating human rights considerations into security concerns: "When security interests are on the line, it often takes significant pressure to get foreign governments to act on any human rights issue."[223] Allying with the global movement helped Swedish, American, Ugandan, and international advocates keep the issue a priority in foreign policy.

The AHA led to the formal institutionalization of LGBTI rights in US and Swedish foreign policy. Former Secretary of State Kerry, in 2015, recognized the importance of LGBTI rights diplomacy in stating, "The issue is a 'strategic necessity' because greater protections for human rights lead to greater stability and prosperity."[224] The broader implication of formally institutionalizing a new agenda in human rights diplomacy is that it leads to long-term impacts in foreign affairs. Institutionalizing a new agenda of foreign policy is difficult to accomplish; however, once achieved, it is bureaucratically hard to reverse and has lasting impact on foreign relations.[225] Establishing a new pillar of foreign policy requires many stakeholders to reach a consensus that the issue is important to national interest and of global significance. Formally changing a bureau in the executive branch necessitates that Congress legislate changes to the State Department's priorities and funding distributions. Rebecca Ingber denotes the power of congressional "process controls" to influence the internal workings of the executive branch and maintain influence over US foreign policy.[226] Similarly, in Sweden, and other countries with parliamentary systems, Parliament makes formal changes to the Swedish Foreign Ministry and assumes continued oversight over foreign ministries.

Even with more conservative-leaning governments in both Sweden and the United States, LGBTI right considerations became an institutionalized consideration in both foreign policy agendas. Many observers assumed the Trump administration would cease LGBTI diplomacy.[227] However, on February 19, 2019, the Trump administration surprised advocates and critics alike by continuing LGBTI diplomacy from the State Department.[228] The US ambassador to Germany launched the administration's renewed efforts in a global campaign to end the criminalization and violence toward LGBTI persons.[229] The difficulty of extracting an institutionalized policy in a bureaucracy partly explains the Trump administration's actions. A robust bureaucracy, actors inside the State Department, and stakeholders in multiple branches of government help to explain the seemingly incongruent policies coming from the Trump administration. Deputy Assistant Secretary of State Daniel Baer commented, "As you start to integrate a new policy, at the beginning, there's, big events, speeches, etc., but in order to make it happen day to day, you really need to institutionalize it. . . I think the most concrete achievements are the way that it's become part of the daily work of the State Department and USAID."[230] Integrating LGBTI rights with multifaceted national interests in the State Department, USAID, embassies, trade and labor affairs left a lasting impact on US bilateral and multilateral relations.

While LGBTI rights diplomacy continues, the application is not applied evenly across foreign countries. Some countries continue to behead LGBTI people, yet see no impact on trade and military partnerships with the United States or the EU. Foreign policy leaders do not consistently place values above economic or security interests. Mertus denotes a "bait and switch" quality of US foreign policy in relation to human rights, whereby the United States holds a double standard on its own human rights record, as well as uneven application of human rights across its foreign engagements.[231] The United States' bilateral relationship with a country, plays a pivotal role in how and when human rights abuses are addressed in diplomatic exchanges.[232] Countries with anti-homosexuality policies similar to Uganda's, such as Pakistan, do not receive the same level of criticism or attention from foreign government officials. As Johanne Saltnes argues, "human rights conditionality is not applied in an automated fashion in accordance with impartial rules and standards."[233] In an asymmetrical power dynamic of modern international relations, some nations are treated more harshly with punishments and sanctions for human rights practices. Diplomats are required to assess a myriad of national interests when engaging with foreign countries. They also have a complex assortment of policy options to use in human rights diplomacy. The Ugandan case marks a fundamental change in international relations: cutting ties based on LGBTI abuses. Similar policies have been formulated in the EU, whose leaders are working to develop a comprehensive foreign policy with LGBTI rights guiding collective external relations.[234] Cutting foreign aid to the Ugandan government was one of the most drastic policy options chosen available to modern diplomats, a choice that is often hard to measure.

It is exceedingly challenging to quantify causality of long-term effects of human rights diplomacy. Sanctions or cutting aid may have a chilling effect five years, ten years, or decades after the time of policy implementation. Kathryn Sikkink documents how authoritarian leaders may curb abusive behavior if they believe they may be punished at a later date, for example, by the International Criminal Court.[235] As an NGO worker from Pakistan commented, "financial or legal aid . . . to ensure crimes against transgender people and students are taken more seriously would be more useful . . . than making the leaders angry or resentful because of aid withdrawal from outside."[236] Frank Mugisha, executive director of SMUG, assessed that there will always be backlash against activism; however, Mugisha implores international donor agencies to continue diplomatic work to improve human rights in Uganda and in other countries where LGBTI people experience violence.[237] Many frontline human rights defenders depend on foreign aid to run their civil society organizations and appeal to government donors to continue the support. Mugisha challenges common analyses, stating that it is "homophobia, not funding, that is at fault."[238] One Russian advocate, emblematic of many besieged global activists, called for Western funders to "not abandon them."[239] Many global advocates seek outside powers to enforce political pressure on their own governments, as they lack the political power to so domestically and incorporate LGBTI rights concerns into broader diplomatic relations. Assessing the most effective diplomatic response and engagement on LGBTI rights in international affairs needs more analysis from broader international relations scholarship.

LGBTI rights diplomacy is now an institutionalized aspect of foreign relations. In 2015, Secretary of State Kerry stated, ""Defending and promoting the human rights of LGBT persons is at the core of our commitment to advancing human rights globally—the heart and conscience of our diplomacy."[240] The AHA catapulted LGBTI rights into the consciousness of the international community, leading foreign leaders to articulate LGBTI rights as a strategically important matter for peace and stability. How this diplomacy is applied, to which nations, and under what conditions warrants a great deal more analysis to aid practitioners in understanding best practices of human rights diplomacy.

Chapter 5

Theoretical Framework of LGBTI and Human Rights Diplomacy

Introduction

From Pariah to Priority seeks to explain the unexpected incorporation of LGBTI rights in foreign affairs. In doing so, the book presents original data from numerous primary sources within Swedish and US foreign policy institutions. This section provides a discussion of relevant scholarship and a theoretical framework to contextualize these data. Human rights theory, social movement theory, and international relations theory are the leading fields of scholarship that help explain why and how LGBTI human rights abuses became a central concern for foreign policy leaders. Human rights literature examines the premise of contemporary human rights, the various definitions of human rights, and how LGBTI rights evolved from being considered a crime to a core human right in some countries. Human rights scholars illustrate how normative values impact international affairs, illuminating the tipping point for when states change bilateral relations based on human rights. Additionally, social movement scholarship elucidates varying tactics and strategies of successful and failed movements from within and outside the state. Social movement scholars scrutinize how organizations strategically use sometimes limited human and financial resources to achieve their goals. Last, international relations theory explores the evolving nature of a state's national identity. Reputation and identity are critical factors in foreign policy decisions and can be of equal importance as material gain for a nation. National identity is often constructed by foreign policy leaders and changes over time. The national identity of a state, and leaders' perceived constructed national interests, are of critical importance to analyzing policy change.

LGBTI Rights Diplomacy: A New Field of Inquiry in International Relations

While LGBTI topics have drawn more attention in scholarly publishing in recent years, these concepts are still comparatively understudied in international relations literature. LGBTI rights began impacting bilateral relations from the early 2000s.[1] Since this time, diplomatic efforts have dramatically increased engagement on LGBTI rights in international relations in both bilateral and multilateral venues. A great deal of academic literature analyzes LGBTI policy reforms on domestic policies in liberal democracies.[2] The vast majority of LGBTI theoretical studies are largely from schools of thought from culture and identity studies, queer theory, women and gender studies, or comparative politics.[3] It is rare for studies to analyze LGBTI rights from a vantage point of international relations and diplomatic practices.

While approximately sixteen countries, as of 2021, formally incorporate LGBTI rights into their respective foreign policy, most of these nations are in North America and Europe.[4] Accordingly, a majority of the literature focuses on LGBTI diplomatic engagement from wealthy Global North countries directed toward the Global South, and the neocolonialism and legacy of imperialism imbedded in these relationships.[5] As anti-homosexuality was often codified into law by colonial powers, namely the British, French, and Dutch, the history of Global North countries engaged in foreign relations on homosexuality is complex and polarized. Over the span of a century, often the same countries that formalized anti-homosexuality statutes in their colonized nations later became the same countries to lead global efforts to improve LGBTI rights. Susan Haskins asserts that the contemporary surge of homophobia across Africa can be traced back to the Western import of homophobic laws.[6] In former British colonies, the legal code had the same law and number, Section 377, from Zambia to India, and in more than forty countries globally.[7] That Britain and the Netherlands becoming leading nations championing LGBTI rights in global affairs is a paradox in history. It also demonstrates how societies and concepts of human rights evolve over time. It is important to note that even though LGBTI diplomacy is conducted mainly from Northern nations, Brazil, Argentina, South Africa, and other countries in the Global South have measurably impacted the attitude of the United Nations (UN) toward LGBTI inclusion as well as had an impact on the societal norms of their neighboring countries.[8]

The limited scholarship of LGBTI diplomacy often focuses on external factors—such as NGOs' advocacy outside the state—and often lacks the vantage point of an insider governmental analysis that this book provides. Furthermore, scholarship of LGBTI rights in foreign affairs is often centrally concerned with the problematic actors in LGBTI diplomacy, such as the sometimes harmful impact of foreign normative ideals on African LGBT people,[9] or backlash on local populations from foreign leaders raising LGBTI rights in diplomatic affairs.[10] For example, Hakeem Onapajo and Christopher Isike demonstrate how leaders in Uganda and Nigeria have taken an unusually hard stance against punitive measures of some Western governments seeking to exert pressure for LGBTI rights reforms in their countries.[11] Queer theorists contextualize the vast diversity of human sexuality that does not necessarily fit into Western concepts of "LGBTI rights."[12] Cynthia Weber and Amy Lind focus their analysis on how the asymmetries in international power shape sexual norms and logics, replicating infringements on sovereignty and persistent heterosexual frames in international relations.[13] Observers criticize LGBTI diplomacy as a new form of colonialism imposing norms of sexuality and/or reinforcing structural discrimination.[14] More broadly, many researchers problematized the whole project of universal human rights, arguing that it is an inherently neocolonial manifestation spearheaded by Western/Northern nations that encourages a one-size-fits-all approach to changing others' cultural values.[15] Leading scholars, by and large, are skeptical of the motivation and intent of governments conducting LGBTI diplomacy, focusing on central themes of neocolonialism, percieved potential economic gain, and asymmetrical power relations between nations.[16] Many challenge whether governments should fund or support LGBTI rights in foreign policy at all.[17] Contemporary human rights scholarship also often points to the deep hypocrisy of the US government and other governments for promoting LGBTI rights.

On the other hand, practitioners of human rights demonstrate the measurable positive impact on global equality through diplomatic efforts. Studies validate the growth of LGBTI civil society from foreign funding and collaborative efforts of foreign officials working with local advocates to end violence against LGBTI populations.[18] Many foreign-based LGBTI civil society organizations exist solely due to international donor support, and individual human rights defenders operating under perilous conditions

receive emergency support.[19] Carnegie and Marinov evidence improved
human rights and democracy standards for some EU-based foreign aid
recipient nations.[20] This evidence validates the importance of LGBTI diplomacy centering on the critical need of foreign funds to support fledgling
LGBTI civil society groups that otherwise would not be able to function or
advocate for local human rights improvements. Burack demonstrates that a
pervasive argument among many academics is that government engagement
on human rights constitutes a form of neoimperialism, despite Ugandan,
Russian, and other global activists imploring the international community
for continued engagement and LGBTI foreign assistance funding.[21] There
tends to be a disconnect between critical theorists, contrasted with human
rights advocates and foreign policy implementers.

The divergent critiques from scholars and practitioners of human
rights demonstrates the need for further study on the efficacy of LGBTI
human rights diplomacy. Given the contestation of LGBTI rights diplomacy, the long-term durability of this new aspect of international relations
remains in question. This book presents findings with broader implications
for international relations theory and practice while providing a framework
to analyze LGBTI rights through a diplomatic lens.

Theorizing How LGBTI Rights Became a Human Right

Scholars have long been concerned with the definition of human rights and
its evolution over time.[22] The signing of the Universal Declaration of Human
Rights (UDHR) in 1948 marks the birth of the modern framework for international human rights.[23] As homosexuality was initially considered a mental
illness or crime by most of the signatory nations of the UDHR, LGBTI
equality was not included. More broadly than LGBTI rights, many theorists
contest the UDHR's assumed universal applicability.[24] Human rights are an
ever evolving group of concepts implemented differently according to region
and culture.[25] Swiebel asserts that defining LGBTI rights as a fundamental
human right meant that the very concept of universal human rights had to
change; thus, allies used "entrepreneurial tactics" and human rights framing
in multilateral forums to build international recognition.[26] Changing the
definition of what was considered a human right was critical for LGBTI
groups to gain traction in the international community.

Not all issues succeed in gaining international recognition as a human
right; some movements never gain traction in the international commu-

nity. Clifford Bob argues that there is a four-stage process for a grievance to become considered an international human right.[27] First, the aggrieved must frame their problem as a human rights violation. Second, they must convince gatekeeper NGOs to place their issue on the international agenda. Third, nations and international organizations under pressure from NGOs must accept the new norm. Last, national institutions need to implement the new right. In a constant state of evolution, human rights concepts change with modern society. Oliver Diggelmann and Maria Nicole Cleis demonstrate how varying issues in contemporary affairs, such as the right to privacy, have become considered a fundamental right. Advocates for the right to privacy apply the original concept of the "inviolability of the home and of correspondence," which is enshrined in the UDHR, to the internet and social media.[28] With new issues, human rights groups appropriate older concepts of human rights connected to the UDHR to legitimate their cause. It is critical that an organization frames its issue as a fundamental human right.

It was not inevitable that LGBTI rights would be accepted under the rubric of international human rights. There are numerous cases where human rights causes failed in being accepted by the international community as a human right. For example, the Dalit (untouchables) movement in India, children of wartime rape seeking international recognition from the Bosnian war, and universal health care in the United States are all considered failed human rights campaigns.[29] Gatekeeper organizations, such as Amnesty International or UNICEF, have not taken up the issue of children of wartime rape. R. Charli Carpenter assesses that the key impediment to this issue is the inability of stakeholders to address intersectional issues such as gender-based violence while also responding to the needs of the child as the human rights subject; sometimes advocacy networks cast doubt on the primacy of another cause.[30] Further, another example is that many—but not all—countries have abolished the death penalty as a human rights norm.[31] In the case of states abolishing the death penalty, Sangmin Bae argues that norms are the "intervening variable between material incentive and state behavior."[32] Moreover, indigenous people, and their related human rights abuses by their respective governments, are treated differently by the international community based on where the abuse occurs. China's critical economic relations as a powerful trade partner with most countries often surpass human rights concerns.[33] Many human rights movements, although moral and just, may fail to achieve their goal of changing policy. As Busby finds, there are numerous "moral movements" trying to impact foreign policy

that advocate reforms to institutions, yet gain no traction.[34] Busby synthe-
sizes the central factors identified for failed movements as groups lacking
a defined, coherent strategy, disagreement over the nature of the problem,
and no single organization hub emerging to tamp down on interorganiza-
tional rivalry.[35] By contrast, LGBTI national movements gained traction
by developing their goals for equality into a coherent targeted strategy of
direct advocacy to key stakeholders with the power to influence concepts
of human rights. While it may seem certain in retrospect that LGBTI
became considered a human right in many governments and international
institutions, the path for an issue to become accepted as a human right is
challenging, the outcome uncertain.

LGBTI social movements, specifically those across Europe, worked to
redefine human rights as part and parcel of "modern democracies."[36] Advocates, as well as foreign policy leaders in Sweden, Germany, the Netherlands,
and elsewhere, sought to frame European-ness as inclusive of democratic
principles of equality and tolerance for all minority groups, including sexual
minorities. LGBTI advocates have strategically framed the issue within the
broader ideals of fairness and equality being central to any democracy.[37]
David Paternotte and Phillip Ayoub establish how LGBTI rights coalesced
as a powerful symbol of Europe. They assert that especially in reaction
to homophobic actions of Russia and other governments outside Europe,
there is a value association between Europe and LGBT rights.[38] Thus, social
movements make claims to redefine broader concepts and societal ideals.
The incorporation of LGBTI rights into EU policies extended the very
concept of human rights, such that a modern society must include equal
rights and protections for all.

Connecting LGBTI equality with "European" identity created division
outside Europe's borders, and also at times with new EU member states.
Decried by Russian leaders as "LGBTI propaganda against traditional values,"[39] LGBTI rights discourse became a dividing line between the European continent and nations outside its borders. Agius and Edenborg thus
characterize a "gendered border," where LGBTI norms newly underwrite
relations between Sweden and Russia in both foreign and security policies.[40] In places such as Poland, scholars find that the "Europeanization of
nondiscrimination norms regarding sexual minorities" was a factor in an
anti-gay backlash movement and helped to solidify power of illiberal elites
perceived as standing up to foreign EU pressure.[41] Leaders across the EU
pushed for improved LGBTI rights as a precondition of membership into
the EU for new member states.[42] Consequently, some newer EU member
states have more stringent protections for LGBTI populations in labor and

housing, for example, than older member states. Croatia and Slovenia, for instance, reformed their domestic laws on LGBTI rights as required for EU member accession in the early 2000s.[43] Paradoxically, as these preconditions came later for new members, original members of the EU, such as Greece and Italy, have fewer national protections for LGBTI citizens than newer EU member states. LGBTI rights became a symbol of European national identity and thus institutionalized in EU policies.

Sensitizing Event: Theory to Explain how Uganda's Law Influenced Global Foreign Policy Institutions

While norms often take generations to change, sometimes societies can evolve rapidly on an issue. The Ugandan Anti-Homosexuality Act (AHA) catalyzed an urgent international discourse that catapulted LGBTI rights into an important and unique aspect of international human rights promotion. In this research, Swedish and US leaders attributed Uganda's AHA—dubbed "Kill the Gays"—as one of the critical factors that changed public opinion, reshaped foreign policy discourse, and ultimately institutionalized LGBTI diplomacy in foreign policy agencies. Scholars argue that a global sensitizing event can provide the opportunity to rethink and reorganize current events around an emergent issue.[44] Stassen, Smolders, and Leroy argue that "new, sudden events can change the public discourse, or reposition it into a new focus."[45] In this case, the new, extreme law in Uganda served to shock public audiences and spur government representatives to act. Keck and Sikkink document that human rights causes have the greatest and most rapid success in becoming accepted by the international community if their agenda appeals to protecting vulnerable and innocent individuals from bodily harm.[46] The severity and potential for bodily harm espoused in the Ugandan law triggered a need for an urgent response from foreign policy leaders. Rather than a glacial evolution of a human rights issue over years, a sensitizing event can lead to a rapid response from the international community and unexpected policy change.

Conditioning Foreign Aid: Empirical Debate

International sanctions, or conditioning aid, is a punitive measure from a government seeking rapid normative change in other governments. However, scholars fiercely debate the effectiveness of sanctions in changing state behavior and improving human rights.[47] From Myanmar to Iraq, international partners have used sanctions as a foreign policy tool to try to shape local leaders' behavior and decisions.[48] While pressure from the external leaders has influenced policy reform and changed international norms in the long run, in the short term, policies have been enacted at the expense of vulnerable populations. In Iraq, for example, sanctions translated into a lack of medicine arriving from abroad and a subsequent public health crisis and death of children and other vulnerable populations.[49] Inherent in sanctions is an asymmetry of power; these measures are meant to make a weaker country comply with demands of stronger, wealthy nations providing financial aid. Cutting relations with another state can lead to disruption in supply chains, public health crises, and economic hardship. Yitan Li and Drury Cooper contend that maintaining diplomatic ties with a nation is more beneficial to the population than cutting ties.[50]

Nevertheless, sanctions and threats to trade partnerships can be effective in changing local policies and pressure governments to cease harmful human rights practices. Therefore, conditioning international aid remains a key leveraging point for diplomats.[51] Governments in Indonesia, the former Yugoslavia, and Pakistan have curbed abusive behavior in the face of punitive measures from foreign governments.[52] In the case study in this book, Ugandan advocates both criticized Western pressure but, on the other hand, also attributed LGBTI diplomacy from foreign governments as the pressure that led Ugandan lawmakers to strike down the death penalty for homosexuality in their country.[53] Cutting ties with another country can be one of the sharpest methods to force new human rights norms in international affairs. Whether to continue to work with a country or sever relations to protect human rights is a sharply contested issue among scholars and foreign policy practitioners.

Social Movement Theory: Coalescing the Global LGBTI Movement

The Ugandan law sparked immense international attention that ignited foreign policy leaders to act. It also served to coalesce aspects of the international LGBTI social movement and identify shared priorities for LGBTI advocates. Laurel Weldon assesses organized social movements as a way for groups to achieve recognition, define their agenda, identify priorities, and advocate to authorities.[54] Social movements are inherently a struggle for recognition,[55] often forming in response to experiences of repression and domination.[56] As seen by Weldon and others, some scholars focus on how protests influence policy, in which more visible movements rally to contest state priorities. Movements often look across physical national borders and to international organizations for varying tactics and political opportunities.[57] For example, LGBTI groups assessed best practices from early tactics of the women's and civil rights movement. Advocates draw on best practices, tactics, and discursive strategies from other social movements and human rights groups.

Social movements garner strategies from other human rights movements. Scholars denote this process of cribbing tactics as a spillover effect, linkage, or the bridging of social movements.[58] Sweden was the first country to legislate against LGBTI discrimination in the workplace. Connecting LGBTI equality to a labor rights issue provided a guide for global advocates around the world to link equality issues to labor rights and codify equality into labor law standards.[59] Kollman documents how the tactic of linking LGBTI equality as a labor rights issue quickly spread to other European states.[60] A few decades later, labor networks in Europe and other countries in Asia advocate for equality measures in society through labor networks and unions.[61] Coalition building has also been an important factor for LGBTI groups to change foreign policy institutions. The concept of intersectional advocacy, or advocacy that spans multiple forms of societal injustice, helps explain how social movements apply advocacy tactics across sectors.[62] Social movement literature helps explain the process, strategies, and resource mobilization used by groups seeking to reform public policy over time.

Lang delineates NGOs as professionalized, institutionalized, and bureaucratized forms of social movements.[63] As such, NGO advocacy comes in many forms. Public protest, media campaigns, or closed-door meetings targeting institutional advocacy with influential leaders are tactics advocates employ to reform foreign policy. As influential as NGOs are in international politics, Lang and other scholars argue that the specific approaches allowing civil societies to contribute to the public sphere are underexamined.[64] The relationship between state and NGO actors is a key issue to help explain changes in human rights policy development. Pierson identifies phases of power between advocates and stakeholders. One set of actors must initially impose their preferences on another set of actors through open conflict.[65] Power dynamics shift over time as the anticipated reactions of stakeholders make open policy conflict unnecessary.[66] The LGBTI movement's ability to impact foreign policy was generated in part from contesting with US State

Department policies. The Mattachine Society, founded in the 1950s, was originally established to combat the government's policy of firing homosexuals serving as diplomats.[67] Similarly, a group of State Department employees founded Gays and Lesbians in Foreign Affairs Agencies (GLIFAA) in 1992 to organize against discrimination of gays and lesbians in the security clearance process.[68] Theorists help to explain that out of repression comes organized resistance.

While protest can be a catalyst for policy reform, the most effective tactics vary by country, and experts do not agree on a single best approach.[69] Social movement scholarship debates the most effective tactics for advocates given certain structures of political opportunity within the context of a specific country.[70] For example, advocates working within authoritarian regimes lack leverage to influence their own governments and thereby often employ tactics of allying with transnational advocacy networks. Conversely, in more democratic governments, advocates are allowed more influence within government decision-making bodies and thereby engage more institutional advocacy tactics.

Institutional advocacy was a critical tactic employed by advocates working to reform the LGBTI rights agenda. By using political opportunities, harnessing influential allies, and mobilizing the institutional structures of international bodies, advocates can reorient the debate toward their issue.[71] Joachim identifies key mechanisms for social movements changing and shifting policy agendas focusing on women's rights groups and their use of political opportunities and mobilization of institutional structures. Similar to LGBTI rights, insiders can be catalysts for change, even in large bureaucracies.

In Sweden, institutional advocacy is a form of deliberative democracy. Katzenstein and Micheletti assert that European political ideas of solidarity have encouraged collective activism that stresses cooperation, pragmatism, and compromise.[72] Micheletti finds that "the 'Swedish model' of civil society is hallmarked by deliberative democracy" and enables opposing political actors to meet and discuss their differences.[73] Advocacy organizations are able to shape institutional agendas through informal discussions, written statements, and regular visits to government ministries. Rydström documents Scandinavian LGBTI advocates working for decades to influence national parliaments to pass more incremental laws leading to contemporary progressive LGBTI laws in Scandinavia.[74] Because of the more open, transparent structure of government in Sweden, Swedish civil society had more political opportunity to voice their claims. They used access to institutions, influential allies, and changes in political alignments for sustained advocacy.

Debating Civil Society's Position Vis-à-Vis the State

The comparative analysis of these two case studies exemplifies the debate of how close civil society groups should become to government institutions. NGO advocacy in these two countries presents contrasting tactics toward influencing foreign affairs. The US case presents a movement with a central strategy of resistance from the state, fueled mainly by private funding. By contrast, Swedish activists largely work with public funding and are highly connected to government and state leadership. The Swedish movement is more deeply integrated within the state, whereas advocacy in the United States remains more autonomous. Even with the close relationship with the state, Swedish advocates are not hindered in their advocacy work, and when necessary continue with their vocal criticism of government policy, political parties, or political opposition in Parliament. Nevertheless, accepting funding from the government and maintaining a close relationship with government bodies is highly debated among human rights practitioners and theorists alike.

There is disagreement in the literature among social movement scholars as to whether a movement should work within the government toward full integration or remain autonomous from the state. Amy Elman demonstrates that states can hinder mobilizing potential and that activists risk co-optation and depoliticization.[75] Additionally, Laurel Weldon asserts that social movements should be cautious of becoming too closely integrated into political parties, warning that when movements are subsumed into a party, "their mobilizing potential decreases, their links to marginalized constituencies weaken, and substantive representation is decreased."[76] Some empirical data demonstrate that when some social movements seek full integration in either large political parties or the state, the state can potentially neutralize movement goals.[77] By becoming too close to the state or relying on public funding, there is a risk of state agencies taking control of social movement agendas and neutralizing the movement.[78] NGOs working closely with the government may risk increased oversight of their work, thus hindering their movement.

However, remaining politically and financially autonomous from the state presents difficulties as well. Banaszak suggests that social movements should be assessed on a continuum rather than on a dichotomy of radical versus conformist. Furthermore, social movement actors often are found both within and outside the state. Unless state structures expressly forbid officials working directly with outside advocates, actors can work both within and outside the state in different roles toward the same end goal.[79]

Given that the state funds most civil society groups in Sweden, Lars Trägårdh raises the question about whether Sweden truly has "non" governmental NGOs.[80] Even with a close relationship to the state, Swedish LGBTI groups have used public funds, vocally shamed antagonistic leaders, and integrated their work inside the state, achieving a broad range of policy adoption toward LGBTI equality.

There is general consensus in social movement literature that the location of the social movement actor is important.[81] Most social movement research focuses on players outside the state, where NGOs leaders generate movement agendas and bureaucrats receive them.[82] Pettinicchio challenges the insider/outsider dichotomy used by many social movement scholars, asserting that "institutional activists have access to resources and power—who proactively take up causes that overlap with those of grassroots challengers."[83] Sometimes insider bureaucrats are also outsider activists during their personal time.[84] Insider government allies have played key roles in gaining access to institutions and mobilizing resources toward a movement's goals.[85] In the case of the women's movement, feminist activists within a bureaucracy, or "femocrats," in Australia, Canada, and the United States influenced change from within government.[86] In the Australian case, Eisenstein documents a strategy of employing women in key agencies within the government to "ensure women-friendly policies can be produced."[87] Olsson and Hysing, Banaszak, and Pettinicchio assert the importance of insider allies, forwarding movement goals from within government and using their position of influence toward this end.[88] Like an external civil society group, stakeholders within the state can have enormous influence on a social movement's objectives. This study offers lessons to other social movements debating how closely to integrate their work and advocacy efforts within government agencies.

International Relations Theory and National Interest

Although there have been documented cases of homophobia for generations across countries, cultures, societies, and religions, it wasn't until the 2000s that homophobic violence became the subject of diplomatic relations.[89] International relations theory grounded in constructivism, small state theory, and national identity provides insight into how changing normative values influence state and multilateral relations, and what factors motivate policy reform.

For the better part of the twentieth century, human rights considerations were largely neglected in the field of international relations (IR).
Tim Dunne and Nicholas Wheeler attribute the neglect of human rights
in IR theory to the "suspicion by realists that morality in foreign policy
was potentially disruptive of international order."[90] Former US Secretary of
State Henry Kissinger, for example, argued that human rights had no place
in foreign relations.[91] He asserted that raising human rights in diplomatic
relations and attempting to shape foreign nations' domestic policies was
"dangerous" for the United States.[92] Kissinger is considered a leading practitioner of realism.[93] For instance, Kissinger ordered the US ambassador to
Chile to cease raising the issue of Chilean governments' practice of torture
of political opponents, maintaining instead that détente and security policy
over Russia took precedence. In Kissinger's perspective, shared by many
like-minded foreign policy officials at the time, raising controversial human
rights issues would only damage strategic partnerships with allies in international relations. Realist scholars and practitioners dominated the political
debate and populated foreign policy institutions after the Cold War.[94]

Over time, however, scholars argued that addressing human rights in
the international system is part of a realist theoretical model. In response
to the realist criticism that human rights in foreign policy was idealist or
unrealistic, international relations scholars began to make the case of human
rights in security terms. Mahanty argues, "When human-rights abuses could
degrade the legitimacy of a partner, rupture the stability of a country, or
threaten political processes, it becomes a U.S. prerogative to at least consider
how it might approach the issue of human rights."[95] Similarly, Müllerson
argues that it is in a state's calculated economic and security interest to
promote a stable world.[96] Empirical evidence from conflict demonstrates
that the violation of human rights is often a direct indicator of impending
instability.[97] Unstable countries, in turn, create poor trade and security partners, thus making human rights considerations an imperative component
of modern foreign policy. In response to the consequences for US long-
term interests in stifling human rights in Latin America, President Carter's
administration established human rights as a formal aspect of US foreign
policy and founded the Human Rights Bureau.[98] Secretary Cyrus Vance,
in explaining the Carter administration's human rights policy to the Senate
Committee on Foreign Relations, asserted, "The advancement of human
rights is more than an ideal. It, too, is an interest. Peaceful gains for freedom
and also steps toward stability abroad, and greater security for America."[99]
Thus, Secretary Vance started a diplomatic tradition in the State Department

of making the case for human rights based on security terms. Over the past decade especially, there is building evidence from the Council on Foreign Relations, Stockholm International Peace Research Institute, the United States Institute of Peace, and other research institutes that demonstrate the connection between improving human rights and democratic institutions for ensuring stable societies and economic growth.[100] Hudson and Leidl explain that the premise of the "Hillary Doctrine" in 2010 was the "proposition that the empowerment of women is a stabilizing force for domestic and international peace."[101] Ensuring equal education, employment, and opportunity for more than half of the population is imperative for a strong economy and stable society. Specifically related to LGBTI inclusion, research from the Williams Institute in 2019 shows a measurable GDP increase in countries that increase legal rights for LGBTI people.[102] There is mounting evidence that addressing human rights in foreign policy not only benefits the greater good, but also improves long-term security and trade partnerships.

Realism, however, is insufficient to fully explain human rights diplomacy, as human rights diplomatic engagements are not always motivated by measurable interests. Rather, foreign policy goals are sometimes driven by moral outrage on an issue, national identity of a country or leader, or shifting normative values in the international community. Jack Donnelly contends that realism is not a helpful theory to explain human rights diplomacy in that it "provides mostly negative insights into the difficulties of incorporating human rights concerns into foreign policy."[103] Therefore, constructivism is the most relevant theory to explain the importance of ideas and identity in shaping foreign political actions in international affairs.

Constructivism provides a useful theoretical framework for this study. Building on Wendt and other foundational constructivist scholars,[104] Trine Flockhart provides a working definition of constructivism in international relations relevant to this study: constructivism is a social construction of reality, where ideas and norms shape identity and are the motivation for political action.[105] Data in *From Pariah to Priority* establish a constructivist identity association between LGBTI equality and national identity as a key motivator for foreign policy leaders to commence LGBTI diplomacy.

Leaders' political and ideological convictions shape foreign policy and international development frames, thus having critical repercussions for international aid policy.[106] For example, in terms of Swedish foreign aid, "the basic values and core beliefs among decision-makers, and the images of reality they hold, are important ingredients in any theory trying to explain aid policy change."[107] The moral convictions of specific leaders in power can have a disproportionate impact on a social movement; a sympathetic leader can create substantial change, whereas an oppositional leader can similarly exert power to stymie an agenda. As Greene finds, the personal conviction of a leader determines their foreign policy decisions—at times to the detriment of their political career.[108] For international institutions and governments to be receptive to shifting their agendas, leaders must also be convinced that doing so is in their national interest. National interest and reputation drive aspects of foreign policy and thereby are central focuses of international relations theory.

Reputation can shape and contain state behavior. For many scholars, outside pressure is key to upholding human rights norms.[109] The state will lose credibility and power by not engaging in the international human rights movement.[110] Mercer's work on reputation in international affairs illustrates the importance of reputation as a driver of actors' behavior.[111] He holds that states act in relationship to allies' and adversaries' perceived reputation when calculating their own foreign policies. Foreign policy leaders in Sweden often referenced Sweden's reputation as a human rights leader as a motivating factor to continue their work in LGBTI diplomacy. National identity motivates great and small nations alike in shaping a country's global presence and politics.[112]

States pursue human rights in foreign policy to promote a positive image of their country globally. Stoum asserts that Scandinavians perceive themselves to be from tolerant, benevolent nations "whose citizens are sexually liberated and wish others to be as well."[113] Given their strong domestic record of upholding LGBTI rights, Stoum maintains that Scandinavians regard themselves as "legitimate promoters" of LGBTI rights.[114] Rydström demonstrates that promoting LGBTI equality is a source of shaping and evolving national identity. He asserts that "ever since laws on registered partnership in the Scandinavian countries were first introduced, they have been connected with national identity."[115] He further contends that critics of those laws were silenced because of fears that their country would be internationally shamed if they were not perceived as upholding human rights for all.[116] Additionally, Forsythe identifies self-image, public opinion, bureaucratic infighting, legislative independence, and political party platforms as the most critical factors impacting the crafting of modern human rights foreign policies.[117] He finds that US human rights foreign policy is closely associated with US nationalism and religious ideals. American leaders and organizations are largely motivated by Judeo-Christian values, both for and against LGBTI rights in their humanitarian work and moral ethical frames. By contrast, Brysk, Hyden, and Mukandala find that Scandinavian human rights foreign policies are largely associated with the welfare state and social democratic motivations.[118] Religion has not historically motivated Scandinavian humanitarian efforts abroad.[119]

Small states, which sometimes lack the political weight of large states, at times rely on reputation to create change in the international system. Small state theory illustrates how a small country could be deemed an international "superpower" of human rights diplomacy. *From Pariah to Priority* suggests that, rather than leading the issue, officials from large states such as the United States were willing to join smaller countries who proposed new policy ideas to promote LGBTI rights in the UN and other multilateral venues. Small states have a disproportionate amount of power and leverage to elevate human rights concerns.[120] Elgström contends, "for nations of their size, Scandinavia has enormous influence in the development arena and the power to direct the human rights agenda in recipient countries."[121] Scandinavian countries have fewer restraints from economic and military agreements than larger governments, leading some to argue that they are able to generate and raise human rights issues more freely.[122] Scandinavian nations have used their position of neutrality and relative diplomatic freedom to maneuver their goals more easily than large states with more constraints in international affairs.[123] Sweden's pioneering of norms and ideas, namely LGBTI rights, in the international arena has pushed other countries, such as the United States, to incorporate those norms as part of their own policies. Small states can have substantial leverage in defining international norms, including on global LGBTI rights.

Conclusion

In the relatively new field of LGBTI diplomacy, there are very few books that specially examine how LGBTI rights shape and change international relations. This book is guided by principles founded in human rights theory, social movement, and international relations theory. These fields provide the theoretical explanations for the unexpected institutionalization of LGBTI rights in modern diplomatic relations. As Ann Towns and Karin Aggestam demonstrate, diplomacy is gendered, both in representation and diplomatic norms, as well as the outcomes of negotiations.[124] In contemporary diplomatic affairs, LGBTI rights have become a fault line for determining a nation's reputation and the longevity of bilateral relations. The advocacy for LGBTI rights has changed the way that leaders in Uganda, and other countries such as Nigeria, have conducted affairs with Western nations.[125] The literature examined in this chapter helps explain how rights are constituted, as well as the process of why and how an issue of injustice may be taken up by civil society advocates, accepted by gatekeeper organizations, and socialized by states for acceptance into foreign affairs norms. Universal human rights evolve over time through social movement advocacy. Pressure to change human rights norms can come from small norm-entrepreneurial states and international institutions as well as transnational advocates. This book asserts that LGBTI rights were not an inevitable agenda issue of concern in foreign affairs. Using theoretical frameworks of constructivism developed by leading human rights and social movement scholars, this study helps explain the unexpected reformation of human rights diplomacy to include LGBTI rights considerations.

Chapter 6

Conclusion

LGBTI Diplomacy and Policy Recommendations

Discussion of Key Findings

Research related to LGBTI diplomacy, and how new normative values impact foreign affairs, is a new cutting-edge aspect of international relations theory. As of 2021, there are only a few academic studies regarding LGBTI rights in foreign policy. In light of the lack of a comprehensive definition of LGBTI diplomacy, this book provides an original definition: *global policies and programs with the long-term goal of promoting the social, political, and economic equal rights of LGBTI persons.* Furthermore, this analysis is distinctive because I leverage more than a decade of practitioner experience from my position in the State Department's Bureau of Democracy, Human Rights, and Labor. From this vantage point, this research provides evidence from an unusual degree of high-level access to key leaders, diplomats, special envoys, and ambassadors. This book is a culmination of analysis from professional practice in human rights diplomacy, dovetailed with scholarship from international relations theory.

This book explains how LGBTI rights were incorporated into US and Swedish foreign policy institutions. These two countries are prominent players in human rights and international humanitarian assistance. In actual numbers, the United States is the largest donor of international aid in the world, and Sweden ranks as one of the highest donors per capita.[1] Sweden and the United States have influence and sway in global cultural and political

production that is rare for most states. This book charts how these two countries have come to champion (with important limitations and problems) the
acceptance of LGBTI people in global politics. By illuminating the effects of
US and Swedish foreign policy decisions, this book demonstrated how new
agendas can become institutionalized into modern foreign policy.

Before the 2000s, LGBTI rights were not a part of diplomatic agendas.
At that time, considerations related to poverty and discrimination specific
to LGBTI populations were largely absent from foreign policy and international development agencies. Over the past few decades, shifts have occurred
across international institutions, such as the World Bank, to include within
donor aid packages incentives and pressure to end discrimination. According to Jim Yong Kim, the former World Bank president, with regard to
discrimination against all minorities, including LGBTI communities, stated,
"Eliminating discrimination is not only the right thing to do; it's also critical
to ensure that we have sustained, balanced and inclusive economic growth
in all societies."[2] A global norm shifted when leaders from Sweden, the
United States, and a host of other wealthy donor nations began to correlate
global development programs with discrimination and the need for equality
of LGBTI populations.

Modern human rights treaties, laws, and international norms remain
largely predicated on the Universal Declaration of Human Rights (UDHR).
However, the UDHR reflects an understanding of human rights norms
from 1948 that does not include LGBTI rights. While human rights significantly impact modern foreign relations, the collective understanding of
what is considered to be a universal human right is far from static. Far
from every country progressing toward acceptance, many regions of the
world are regressing on human rights. For example, research from the Williams Institute evidences a global polarization on LGBTI rights where "the
most accepting countries are becoming more accepting, the least accepting
countries are becoming less accepting."[3] As Susan Dicklitch-Nelson and
Indira Rahman demonstrate, in some parts of the world there is a "renewed
vigor in punitive state-sanctioned persecution" toward LGBTI populations.[4]
Graeme Reid, director of the LGBTI Program at Human Rights Watch,
asserts, "what seems distinct about this particular time in our history is the
way that LGBTI rights have become a lighting-rod for competing visions
of the world."[5] Amid these polarizing debates on human rights, diplomats
have the complex task of developing a foreign policy strategy in each country and determining which issues will rise to the top of bilateral agendas.

Conclusions from the US Case Study

Foreign policy goals generally reflect entrenched domestic social values. Yet, the United States, a historically conservative nation on homosexuality, elevated LGBTI rights abuses into one of its central foreign policy agendas in bilateral relations with Uganda and other countries after 2011. Some outside observers criticized the United States for being rather late to raise LGBTI rights abuses, especially compared to its European counterparts. However, this analysis argues that in some ways it was surprising that the State Department incorporated LGBTI rights into its agenda at all, given the contentious history within the society, as well as the discriminatory practices of US foreign affairs institutions. *From Pariah to Priority* evaluates how the US Department of State became a leading institution in funding global LGBTI civil society and raising issues of LGBTI abuse and discrimination in foreign countries in high-level diplomatic engagements. With the establishment of the special envoy of the human rights of LGBTI persons in 2015, the United States was one of the first governments to establish a high-level representative whose sole focus was to raise LGBTI rights in diplomatic US engagements. Similarly, the United States Agency for International Development (USAID) established a senior LGBTI coordinator and office to integrate considerations for LGBTI populations into USAID's programs. The United States thus allocated high-level diplomatic efforts, as well as high levels of funding, to support LGBTI civil society globally. Starting in 2011, the US State Department, similar to Sweden, delineated LGBTI persons as a distinct group, earmarking this community for global humanitarian aid, similar to other minority groups.[6] That delineation led to vast implications for international development policy. As the United States is one of the largest financial supporters of small local and large international LGBTI civil society organizations, this demarcation had an enormous impact on financial support for LGBTI human rights groups worldwide.

Along with financial support, the United States provides political clout to advocates seeking to change the agenda of international institutions. Jessica Stern, executive director of OutRight Action, noted, "U.S. leadership really changed the discourse."[7] Stern recounted in the United Nations (UN) that her advocacy organization was having trouble getting other governments to attend an event on global LGBTI rights abuses. When they were able to secure Secretary of State John Kerry as the keynote speaker, Stern recounted, "I wish I could tell you that the event would have happened had Secretary

Kerry had not been there; I wish I could tell you that all the other governments would have seen that this issue was right and just; but the truth is,
because Kerry was there, the event happened."[8] Leadership from the Obama
administration empowered global LGBTI advocacy groups and helped institutionalize LGBTI rights diplomacy into international institutions.

US foreign policy institutions incorporated LGBTI diplomacy because
of a confluence of factors: NGO advocacy, insider government leadership,
and foreign policy leaders' perception of the United States as a nation that
defends human rights. Decades of NGO advocacy laid the groundwork for
sustained domestic reform. Repressive laws often catalyzed powerful social
movements. Public protest was the hallmark of US-based NGO advocacy,
often in response to discriminatory federal practices. Historically, LGBTI
groups were often met with repression, societal exclusion, and structural
discrimination.[9] Individuals mobilized efforts within civil society to respond
to the federal government's neglect and antagonism. To this day, Amie
Bishop, a senior researcher with OutRight Action International, recognizes
the global trend of "a proliferation of organizations in the face of hostility
and danger."[10] Organizations worked for decades to combat repressive state
policies. These factors, coupled with global events in Uganda, led to the
institutionalization of LGBTI rights into US foreign affairs.

While direct, public protests are the most common form of advocacy
efforts in the United States, activists also employ other tactics to influence
foreign policy. The ability of advocates to garner support from gatekeeper
organizations such as Amnesty International (AI) and Human Rights Watch
(HRW) became critical to coalesce the international LGBTI movement.
Large, reputable human rights organizations were initially amenable to listening to small LGBTI groups, but required documentation of human rights
violations to justify the cause. However, while mob killings of LGBTI individuals in Honduras, Chechnya, and Pakistan occurred regularly, they were
rarely officially documented. Advocates needed credible documentation of
abuses to gain legitimacy with international institutions and foreign policy
leaders, but there was a near complete lack of global, professional, systematic documentation concerning LGBTI rights discrimination. Amie Bishop
asserted, "The more documentation there is, the more visible our issues
become."[11] Advocates in the 1980s and 1990s began the difficult and dangerous work of documenting abuses in places such as Russia, Brazil, and Turkey.
LGBTI advocacy groups and researchers tracked cases of police raids on gay
establishments, harassment of university students, public instances of beating
and torture, and arrest of activists.[12] Through systematic documentation

of human rights abuses, LGBTI activists were able to convince gatekeeper organizations of their cause. Fledgling LGBTI organizations partnered and built alliances with powerful, more established human rights organizations. Strategic coalitions enabled financial sustainability and political legitimacy of early LGBTI human rights advocacy in the United States.

Advocates began focusing their resources on assisting LGBTI asylum claims in the early 1990s. To this end, institutional advocacy was a critical avenue for resource mobilization of the LGBTI movement. LGBTI coalition leaders began institutional advocacy toward the US State Department, specifically the Bureau of Democracy, Human Rights, and Labor (DRL). DRL officers draft the annual Country Reports on Human Rights Practices.[13] Country reports often inform asylum case law. Thereby, LGBTI activists understood the strategic importance of lobbying the State Department to include LGBTI abuses within the human rights reports. After decades of advocacy, in 2009, DRL added a section to the reports called "Human Acts of Violence, Discrimination, and Other Abuses Based on Sexual Orientation and Gender Identity" to document abuses specific toward LGBTI communities.[14] Improving documentation led to increased evidence for LGBTI asylum cases. NGOs, such as the Council for Global Equality, continue to train editors of the annual State Department human rights report in terminology usage and evidence collection for LGBTI rights abuses in countries around the world.[15] Receptivity of government officials during the Obama administration led to openings for new advocacy methods and allowed NGOs to conduct targeted institutional advocacy more strategically.

At times, institutional advocacy may be more effective than large-scale public protests. Large street-level mass movements, such as the Women's March, Million Man March, or Pride marches, can be powerful.[16] However, these large public manifestations take enormous financial resources—as well as effort—to plan, organize, and manage. Public protests can garner media attention to an issue as well as influence shifts in public opinion. However, at times mass protests lack a specific policy goal. By contrast, targeted institutional advocacy may not gain wide media attention, but it aims messaging at specific agencies and individuals with decision-making power. Depending on the receptiveness of the political party in power, advocates can foster close relationships with target agencies and offices to further their work.

Successful social movements need strong leaders. Central actors such as Secretary Clinton, President Obama, and their leadership team, including Randy Berry, Samantha Power, Michael Posner, Susan Rice, Daniel Baer, Todd Larson, and countless other officers within the State Department, were crucial to changing foreign affairs' institutional agendas. Convincing and harnessing powerful allies within the halls of government was critical to changing US foreign policy. Assistant Secretary Michael Posner recounted that Secretary Clinton "was committed, absolutely, from day one to say, this is part of what we're going to do, and help me (Clinton) figure out how to do it."[17] A central finding in this research, from NGO and government leaders alike, was that without Secretary Clinton, the State Department would not have commenced LGBTI rights diplomacy in 2011. In an NGO advocates' own assessment, their lobbying efforts would not have been sufficient to change US foreign policy without powerful insider leadership. NGO advocates stressed that "without Clinton's and other top foreign policy leaders' support, US foreign policy would not have shifted to include LGBTI rights."[18] Similarly, Obama's leadership was critical. As America's first Black president, foreign policy leaders assessed that Obama came to understand LGBTI equality as a logical extension of the civil rights movement.[19] Once Obama became convinced of the justice of equality, he championed LGBTI rights in Senegal, Jamaica, and Kenya. Ambassador Samantha Power recounted working with pro-equality diplomats to improve global LGBTI rights in the UN, some of whom she perceived were closeted LGBTI individuals themselves. She recounted how many "relished being part of a historic process that could help people living in the shadows."[20] From the highest levels of diplomacy to the desk-officer civil servant, there were allies on every policy level within the State Department and across US foreign policy institutions.

U.S. foreign policy leaders were concerned about both global LGBTI abuses and about the United States' reputation in the world. In 2011, LGBTI diplomacy became a new framework for Obama administration leaders to make a clear departure from the previous Bush administration. Battered by policies during the Bush administration, including the occupation of Iraq and torture at the Guantanamo Bay detention camp, Obama's foreign policy team was anxious to establish a new reputation for the United States in the world. As late as 2008, Bush administration officials blocked LGBTI reforms in the UN. After 2009, leaders in the State Department prioritized human rights in the UN and other international forums. This policy shift was motivated, in part, to protect the human rights of LGBTI people, as well as for a new administration to construct a renewed national image for the United States within the international community. Similarly, the Biden foreign policy team articulates that including LGBTI rights in US foreign policy, as well as accepting asylum seekers based on LGBTI abuses, is part of our national "values."[21] Thus, the Biden administration pledged to "use the full range of our diplomatic tools and foreign assistance to protect and advance human rights and development, and actively combat violence and discrimination."[22] Similar to the Obama administration, Biden's foreign policy leaders align promoting LGBTI rights abroad with the United States' national values and image.

Under the Trump administration, advocates assumed a more defensive stance to protect progressive reforms. Advocacy groups turned to different tactics, such as working with allied leadership in other countries. LGBTI civil society organizations used the courts to contest hate speech, and continue with strategic framing of fundamental freedoms. Advocates launched legal battles, charging claims of hate speech, to block US evangelical Christians from supporting criminalization of homosexuality in places such as Uganda.[23] Diffusing political opposition to LGBTI rights is not new for US-based advocates. As seen in 2010, OutRight Action International garnered political support from other governments and non-state allies within the UN to combat Republican congressmen attempting to block their UN consultative status.[24] NGO actors countered political opposition, mainly by focusing diplomacy on the most egregious human rights abuses. Interest groups' strategic framing of saving lives and protecting "fundamental freedoms" rather than "rights" made the issue more palatable to conservative legislators.[25] Antagonism for LGBTI equality by federal leaders and institutional policies has been the rule, not the exception, over the decades. Thus, advocates developed creative and strategic tactics to diffuse opposition over the years.

Institutionalization of a new policy mandate is paramount to its sustainability. Before the 2016 US election, civil servants worked to imbed LGBTI rights within the bureaucracy of the State Department and USAID. Deputy Assistant Secretary Daniel Baer, an accomplished foreign policy leader responsible for helping to construct LGBTI diplomacy, surprisingly described his biggest achievement as institutionalizing LGBTI diplomacy in the State Department and the daily workings of US embassies worldwide:

> I think my biggest accomplishment is probably the least flashy . . . as you start to integrate a new policy at the beginning, there's you know, big events, speeches, etc., but in order to really make it happen, and to make it happen day to day, you really need to institutionalize it, and one of the things that we've succeeded in doing. . . We have in our colleagues around the world, at 250 posts around the world. . . To make sure that

this is not just something that happens in one speech from the Secretary, but something that becomes part of the day to day work of our foreign policy, of implementing our foreign policy, and I think one of the greatest successes is that there are hundreds of people around the world who work for the State Department, and USAID, who are diplomacy and development assistance professionals, for whom this is some part of their daily work.[26]

By integrating gender and LGBTI considerations in programmatic and funding mandates across global USAID and US embassies, Deputy Assistant Secretary Daniel Baer illuminates how foreign policy leaders worked for years to institutionalize LGBTI rights considerations in the comprehensive agenda of US foreign affairs. Even with opposition from the Trump administration, it became exceedingly difficult to dismantle an institutionalized policy within the State Department. As State Department official Wesley Reisser noted in a public briefing, "Once you put something in a U.S. government report; it is virtually impossible to ever take it away again."[27] Congress continues to mandate reporting on LGBTI abuses; every embassy in the world is required to document abuses as well as engage with LGBTI rights as part of their comprehensive human right strategy. Many career civil servants, whose work is not dependent on the political party in power, staff the State Department. In 2019, the Trump administration established a Commission on Unalienable Rights in an attempt to redefine human rights.[28] In a rebuke, former assistant secretaries of DRL under both Republican and Democratic presidents wrote a joint article in the *Hill*, stating, "The writings of many commissioners reveal a lack of concern for LGBTQI, gender and reproductive rights."[29] Ultimately, despite great media attention, the Commission recommended only small changes to the State Department's work. This Commission, and other fleeting actions of opponents, evidences how difficult it is to change a foreign policy mandate once it becomes institutionalized in foreign affairs agencies.

LGBTI rights programs and diplomatic dialogue remain on the foreign policy agenda, not as a separate boutique issue, but rather as part of the comprehensive human rights diplomacy strategy. The Biden foreign policy team articulates its intention to "permanently make upholding LGBTQ+ rights a priority of the foreign policy of the United States."[30] As evidence of this intention, just as this book was going to the press, on June 25, 2021, President Biden appointed former executive director of OutRight Action International, Jessica Stern, to serve as the second US Special Envoy for the Human Rights of LGBTI persons. The position was revived by Biden's

foreign policy team after remaining dormant under the Trump Administration.[31] LGBTI rights in US foreign policy survived the Trump administration, and following the transition to a Biden administration in January
2021, LGBTI diplomacy has become an enduring aspect of US diplomacy.

Many LGBTI civil society groups depend on foreign funding and
political support from foreign diplomats for their organizations to function.
US foreign policy leaders at times provide the political leverage for advocates to celebrate Pride events in their countries. Czeslaw Walek, chairman
of Prague Pride, stated that the US ambassador was the first foreign leader
to support their efforts to organize a Pride march in Prague in 2011. In
response, Walek further recounted:

> The President (of the Czech Republic Václav Klaus) publicly
> condemned on television that this was a disgrace for the U.S.
> to get involved, and that this was an internal matter. Regardless
> of the criticism, the U.S. Ambassador walked with us in the
> Pride parade. Since then, every year they support us. I can tell
> you, it is a great help, both psychologically and in other terms,
> to know there are embassies and officers supporting our cause.[32]

Global LGBTI civil society groups use the political leverage of the
United States and other foreign governments to further amplify their cause.
However, this alliance does not come without political risks to local advo-
cates. Kenya LGBTI activist Anthony Adero raised the complexity of US
LGBTI engagement in Kenya:

> I have a love/hate relationship when America gets involved;
> America has been a big ally in terms of resources and capacity,
> and everything, but sometimes the way Americans gets involved
> in world politics is problematic. . . . The United States is a very
> strategic partner when it comes to human rights because of the
> way of global power dynamics. I feel like America can sometimes
> give you power, and at other times, disempower you.[33]

It can be risky for local human rights groups to become associated
with the United States. US leaders can provide political support to advocates, while at the same time accepting funding or creating a close alliance
with US partners can lead to negative political repercussions for local civil
society groups in some countries. Advocates and diplomats alike in each
country context regularly assess the moral, strategic, and financial strategic

importance of promoting LGBTI rights. Given its deeply flawed history on human rights and support for LGBTI equality, there is great debate as to how much, if at all, the United States should engage on global LGBTI rights. There is, however, agreement in the literature and human rights practitioner community that whatever capacity in which the United States decides to engage diplomatically has far-reaching global impact.

Conclusions from the Sweden Case Study

While Sweden is a small state, it allocates a higher proportion of its gross national product (GNP) to foreign aid than most nations.[34] In actual numbers, Sweden is Europe's largest per-capita donor of foreign aid, making it one of the largest donors of international development aid in the world.[35] Swedish leaders promote human rights policies by prioritizing them on par with their government's other foreign policy goals. LGBTI diplomacy represents a progression of the core values of gender equality. It is a continuation of challenging gender norms and social hierarchies. In the early 2000s, the Swedish government began to document the relationship between discrimination based on sexual orientation and gender identity, and poverty and international development. In 2005, Sweden became the first government to institutionalize LGBTI rights diplomacy formally.

The Swedish government openly and vocally promotes human rights in foreign engagements, even at the expense of its bilateral relations. A key illustration of this prioritization of human rights over military agreements was seen in 2015, when Sweden's foreign minister, Margot Wallström, ended a long-standing military agreement with Saudi Arabia. Wallström made this decision in part to condemn Saudi Arabia's human rights abuses against women, LGBTI persons, and other marginalized groups. Another example was in 2012, when the Swedish government prioritized human rights in Belarus at the expense of its overall relations with Belarus. LGBTI rights and protecting democratic norms became a major foreign policy priority for Sweden's ambassador to Belarus in 2012, who was then deemed persona non grata and removed from Belarus for his actions.[36] LGBTI rights concerns are included in trade negotiations and EU accession talks. Sweden's EU Affairs Minister Birgitta Ohlsson warned new member states, such as Serbia, that EU negotiations are partly predicated on allowing domestic Pride events.[37] It is rare for a country's foreign policy leaders to be willing to stand up for human rights in diplomatic relations with other nations in the face of economic and political backlash.

Sweden has significant political influence in global gender equality norms. Observers have documented how, for decades, the country has significantly influenced multilateral agencies to prioritize gender equality. Anders Danielson and Lennart Wohlgemuth document the influence of Swedish policy on international institutions, finding that "other donors—including the World Bank—have adjusted their thinking to the Swedish philosophy."[38] Other foreign ministries, including the US Department of State, emulate aspects of Swedish international aid, both by way of Swedish funding streams and policy directives to support global LGBTI rights.

From Pariah to Priority's central findings in the Swedish case demonstrated that early adoption of LGBTI rights promotion in Sweden was dependent on broad social acceptance and a critical mass of public support. The legacy of solidarity with marginalized groups and equality for all people under the law enabled leadership to rapidly incorporate these rights. Bolstered by a strong human rights record at home, the Swedish government reformed its foreign policy to become the first country in history to take a human rights–based approach. The evolution of Sweden's policy to incorporate LGBTI rights into its foreign policy can be attributed to the following central factors: NGO advocacy, targeted institutional advocacy and public protest, the work of insider government allies, repressive laws that sensitize global events, and a national image of being a global leader on human rights.

The state, not the street, is the primary location for advocacy in Sweden. The lion's share of activists' time, focus, and resources remain directed toward targeted institutional advocacy. Swedish NGO leaders knew the specific offices within SIDA and the Ministry of Foreign Affairs relevant to their work. Similarly, advocates fostered close relationships with central decision makers in the government and Parliament. Swedish foreign policy leaders allowed civil society groups to be involved in the LGBTI policy discussion from the beginning, which contributed to early institutionalization of LGBTI rights in Swedish foreign policy. The largest and oldest organization, advocating for equality since 1950, is the Swedish Federation for Lesbian, Gay, Bisexual and Transgender Rights (RFSL).[39] RFSL representatives have been intermittently included in foreign policy deliberations in Parliament and the government for decades. Advocates brought individuals from war-torn countries, such as Sierra Leone, to the Swedish International Development Cooperation Agency (SIDA) to raise the issue of sexual orientation and gender-based violence during war. Advocates articulated the distinct needs of the LGBTI community in postwar reconciliation, which were theretofore unaddressed by SIDA's international development work. Allowing NGO advocates into the decision-making process enabled a conducive environment for them to present their claims within the government and help shape policy.

One of the most striking findings from the Swedish case study is the unprecedented integration and close relationship of civil society advocates with Swedish foreign affairs officers. In interviews for this book, Swedish activists often blurred the lines between civil society actors and government leaders, even at times pushing government officials to take the lead role in promoting LGBTI rights. In public seminars at Stockholm Pride, civil society leaders and advocates voiced that the state had the "responsibility to lead and fund the movement" and that the movement was well situated in the government.[40] These assertions are remarkable in that it is rare globally for human rights advocates to expect government leaders to fund and/or lead their social movement. From the government side, foreign policy officers across government agencies from SIDA, the Swedish Ministry of Foreign Affairs, and the Swedish Parliament exhibited a collegial attitude to using RFSL's expertise. Diplomats and members of Parliament regularly consulted with RFSL officers regarding developing LGBTI norms and evolving Swedish foreign policy mandates.

The close relationship between civil society and foreign policy leaders in Sweden is remarkable because in many other countries, by contrast, governments are closed to civil society groups. NGOs exert little to no influence over state agendas or foreign policy.[41] Government agencies across the Middle East, Africa, and Asia often heavily monitor and censor civil society groups.[42] Even in democratic countries, NGOs often lack influence over government agendas, cannot get meetings with foreign policy leaders, and struggle to influence foreign policy agendas.[43] Swedish foreign policy institutions presents an exception to this global norm. Swedish civil servants and representatives in Parliament consult with civil society leaders regarding new policy formation on LGBTI rights. Illustrative of this uniquely close relationship to civil society was the response to the Ugandan Parliament's proposition of the death penalty for homosexuality in 2009. Swedish government officers turned to RFSL and requested policy recommendations from its organization for how the Swedish government should respond to the law. In a historic diplomatic policy decision, the Swedish government followed RFSL's recommendations and funneled its international development aid away from Ugandan public ministries and instead directed Swedish funds to Ugandan civil society. Swedish civil society exhibits unprecedented influence over foreign policy agendas.

Advocacy efforts to change Swedish foreign policy came from civil society groups, but also from allied leaders within the government. There was not one dominant champion of foreign policy institutions reform, but rather a host of powerful voices within the Swedish government echoing the need for such reform. Prominent diplomats, members of Parliament, agency directors, and MFA diplomats and SIDA desk officers were responsible for agenda prioritization to focus on LGBTI rights abuses in Swedish foreign affairs. Efforts across agencies from a host of leaders influenced progressive reform for decades. In the 1990s, leaders from the Liberal Party (*Folkpartiet*) advocated for the Swedish Ministry of Foreign Affairs to include considerations of gay and bisexual populations in Swedish foreign policy.[44] Barbro Westerholm, the head of the Swedish National Board of Health and Welfare (*Socialstyrelsen*), repealed the classification of homosexuality as a mental illness in 1979, which led to sweeping changes in the Swedish health, military, and security sectors. Further, Swedish representatives Jan Nordlander, Hans Ytterberg, and Thomas Hammarberg were some of the first high-level foreign policy leaders to voice the need for antidiscrimination protections based on sexual orientation within the EU and UN. Mona Sahlin, the former deputy prime minister of Sweden in leadership positions from 1982 to 2011, used her political clout to push Sweden to stand strong against countries such as Russia and other powerful nations that violently oppressed LGBTI populations. In 2013, Birgitta Ohlsson, the former head of the Liberal party (*Folkpartiet*), used her diplomatic protection in Pride marches in Lithuania and across the Baltics to provide physical protection to local Pride marchers.[45] As exemplified in the aforementioned examples, members of Parliament and high-level representatives in government, as well as diplomats and civil servants, influenced Swedish institutions from their specific positions from within the government.

Stockholm Pride is the annual focal point of Swedish LGBTI public advocacy. As the single largest event in Scandinavia, Stockholm Pride has since become an annual hub of the international LGBTI movement. During Pride week, civil society groups, international advocates, diplomats, film directors, and political party leaders debate Sweden's role in the international LGBTI movement. In public seminars, advocates from Moldova and other countries seeking EU membership raised the importance of foreign support from the Swedish government when advocating for domestic change.[46] Public advocacy puts the spotlight on corporate practices and names and shames business practices in public venues. Scandinavia-based multinational corporations such as IKEA and Scandia are both praised for their progressive corporate social responsibility policies, as well as shamed at times for not upholding these standards consistently. While still working to combat discrimination domestically, advocates articulated Swedish solidarity with global activists and support for global LGBTI civil society groups. Stockholm Pride serves as an important annual public event for advocates to voice strengths of their movement, build international coalitions, and highlight reforms needed in government policy.

Like all countries, Sweden does not have a perfect domestic record on LGBTI rights, nor is it a country absent of political opposition to equality. Over the decades, advocates met resistance to addressing LGBTI rights in Swedish foreign policy. They countered resistance with tactics of "naming and shaming" of public officials, ultimately bringing down top foreign policy leaders in the country in a few key cases and bolstering their political capital. Through strategic framing and a focus on the most egregious human rights abuses of LGBTI people globally, conservative Swedish leaders, who once reviled LGBTI persons, incorporated equality as an intrinsic aspect of Swedish and European values. Advocates focused efforts on the Swedish asylum policy, providing evidence of how LGBTI people were jailed and killed worldwide. As such, the Christian Democratic Party (*Kristdemokraterna*, KD), a historically conservative party, came to accept LGBTI equality as part of its political platform. In 2019, the leader of the KD, Ebba Busch Thor, participated in Pride events expressing her support and defending LGBTI rights as part of Swedish values.[47] Over the decades, through strategic framing, naming, shaming, and making LGBTI rights a part of Swedish values, advocates were able to diffuse political opposition.

National identity was a critical motivating factor for establishing LGBTI diplomacy. Civil servants, advocates, and diplomats alike referenced Swedes' self-perception of their country as a protector of human rights. Swedish leaders and mainstream political parties articulate "Swedish values" and national identity as congruent with LGBTI equality.[48] Officers from SIDA and other government agencies conceptualized RFSL's work as part of their nation's expertise. In terms of political or economic benefit, the average Swedish citizen has little to gain by providing funding to a lesbian in Uganda or transgender rights group in Jamaica. Rather than economic or security justifications, Swedish leaders leverage their reputation as a country that will uniquely stand for human rights in international affairs.

Traditional realist claims are insufficient to explain human rights diplomacy fully, as these policies do not always lead to measurable economic benefit for the donor nation. Rather, constructivism theory better explains Swedish leaders' constructed national identity. Stoum denotes how this identity of a tolerant nation, coupled with a legacy of sexual liberation, creates sentiments of Scandinavians as "legitimate promoters" of LGBTI rights globally.[49] Leaders' political and ideological convictions shape foreign policy. Scandinavian leaders are acutely aware of, and take pride in, their international reputation for tolerance and human rights leadership.[50] Moral conviction and national identity of a country or leader at times drives foreign policy goals. Swedish foreign policy goals, and the high levels of international humanitarian aid, therefore are often justified by Sweden's national identity as a protector of global human rights.

Linking LGBTI equality with Swedish national identity became mainstream in Swedish progressive politics but also unexpectedly incorporated into right-wing party politics. The Swedish Democrats (SD) appropriated Swedish national identity as support for LGBTI equality, mainly with the motivation to exclude newcomers to the country. The SD grew in political popularity considerably in 2015. This surge came largely in response to the Swedish government accepting thousands of refugees, asylum seekers, and immigrants from Muslim nations.[51] Contemporary right-wing Swedish political leaders claim that Muslims and immigrants are a threat to LGBTI equality and Swedish values.[52] Reinforcing the stereotype that Muslims are monolithic, anti–LGBTI rights, and a threat to gender equality, these leaders call to end immigration into Sweden. Many LGBTI advocates work to combat this appropriation of the LGBTI equality movement by right-wing politicians. They contest political parties' use of supporting LGBTI rights as justification for the exclusion of others. The battle to define national identity to include tolerance and equality, or exclude foreigners, takes center stage in contemporary Swedish political debates.

Conclusions from the Uganda Chapter

The AHA became a critical sensitizing event that triggered the decision to institutionalize LGBTI rights in foreign policy. The Ugandan Anti-Homosexuality Act (AHA) initially proposed the death penalty for homosexual acts in 2009. The law received wide coverage in the international media and sparked debate about addressing global LGBTI rights by foreign audiences.[53] Transnational advocacy networks amplified the acute situation for the LGBTI community in Uganda as well as voiced the need for foreign governments to generate new responses.

When Ugandan lawmakers proposed the AHA, it was the first high-profile test case for Sweden's emerging LGBTI foreign policy. Swedish foreign ministry and SIDA officials turned to Sweden's lead advocacy organization, RFSL, to help formulate a response. RFSL leaders consulted with Ugandan LGBTI advocates to create policy recommendations. Local advocates raised the need to promote freedom of assembly and association, freedom from arbitrary arrest and detention, press freedom, and NGO registration. RFSL leaders thereby recommended to the Swedish government that their international donor aid bypass the Ugandan government and instead support the work of Ugandan civil society. The Swedish government's response was to condition its aid to Ugandan governmental recipients but maintain aid to Ugandan civil society.

Thus, this case illuminates a historic shift in diplomatic norms. This move made diplomatic history as the first time a donor government formally cut bilateral foreign assistance because of LGBTI rights abuses. Prior to this time, LGBTI rights abuses would not put bilateral relations in jeopardy. After the AHA, the Swedish government's approach to addressing criminalization of homosexuality in foreign countries changed the way that leaders in Uganda and other African countries conducted affairs with Western nations.[54] Swedish government officials articulated the AHA law in Uganda as severe enough that it threatened a long-standing bilateral relationship between the two countries. With the proposed law, Swedish government officials reevaluated their foreign investment strategy in the country and revamped their international aid. The Swedish government's response also solidified LGBTI rights as a sustained pillar of human rights diplomacy.

Similar to Swedish officials, top US foreign policy leaders, in interviews for this book, overwhelmingly highlighted the AHA as the critical event that changed their thinking on LGBTI rights. Advocates recognized that international attention to the AHA is what raised awareness in the US Congress and State Department regarding the severity of global LGBTI discrimination and abuse.[55] The AHA shifted perceptions of LGBTI rights abuses from a nebulous global problem into a specific target for leaders to combat. Across the Department of State, Department of Defense, and National Security Council, US foreign policy leaders constructed a targeted new policy response. The response included funding cuts to certain Ugandan government ministries, cancelled US/Ugandan military cooperation exercises, denial of visas for specific Ugandan leaders, and a general overhaul of US foreign assistance to Uganda. US leaders also revamped funding toward support of local civil society groups and conducted diplomatic dialogue with Ugandan leaders on LGBTI rights. For example, Special Envoy Randy Berry, Assistant Secretary Michael Posner, Deputy Assistant Secretary Daniel Baer, and many other leaders traveled to Uganda from 2009 to 2014 to meet with Ugandan civil society leaders. In concert with local actors, they helped amplify the voices of local advocacy groups as well as raise the issue of NGO registration and police harassment in the country.[56] The AHA is an illustration of what scholars theorize as a sensitizing event, or an event that can cause institutional renewal, fresh debate, and new approaches to an issue, ultimately leading to new policy outcomes.[57] The AHA opened the political opportunity for foreign policy leaders to rethink and reorganize policy agendas around previously unaddressed human rights abuses. It was a central catalyst to institutionalize LGBTI rights as part of the comprehensive human rights agenda in the State Department.

Uganda's law was at the center of debate in the State Department, but also actively debated among local and international leaders within Uganda. The country became ground zero for the global battle—both for and against—LGBTI rights. While official US foreign policy sought to combat the AHA, US evangelicals actively supported the law and preached discrimination from the pulpit. Indeed, some observers attributed the hate speech and messaging from foreign evangelical pastors as the central motivation for Ugandan lawmakers to propose the AHA in the first place.[58] Many faith-based international organizations set up local offices in Uganda, preaching messages against condoms and homosexuality.[59] The condemnation of LGBTI rights by US evangelical pastors was, and remains, in stark contrast to the public outreach from foreign diplomats promoting tolerance and equal rights. LGBTI rights remains contested within the United States; the domestic contested values are reflected in the contradictory messaging to foreign audiences.

Within the broader human rights context, seemingly contradictory messaging from public and private sources is not unique or specific to LGBTI rights. This analysis highlights how many human rights issues—anti-Semitism, Islamophobia, and violence against women—remain contested domestically, yet are part of comprehensive modern foreign policy agendas. In human rights dialogues, diplomats often start from the vantage point of working in concert with their foreign counterpart on an issue, many times overtly addressing how their country struggles as well.[60] As no human rights issue is likely to become "perfected" in any country, diplomats promote human rights in foreign countries while public policy makers simultaneously work toward improvements within their country. In meetings with foreign leaders, Deputy Assistant Secretary of State Daniel Baer raises universal standards that all countries aspire to recognize: "You don't have to be perfect to support them. Supporting them does mean engaging in good faith and putting hard effort into making your own government more perfect."[61] Human rights diplomacy is complex and perceived at times as hypocritical. However, human rights abuses left unchecked by the international community is dangerous to regional and global security.

The violation of human rights is often a direct indicator of instability and conflict.[62] Conflicts in many countries evidence that human rights abuses degraded the legitimacy of a government, upended the political stability of institutions, and threatened peaceful democratic practices.[63] Unstable countries make poor trade and security partners. Daniel Mahanty and other foreign policy leaders argue that the rights of individuals in countries should be of concern to government of other nations; especially after WWII, foreign policy leaders understood the correlation between the way a government treats its citizens and the potential for regional and global instability.[64] Furthermore, gender inequality, the subjugation of women, and discrimination against LGBTI populations, and thus more than half of a nation's population, hurts economic growth and is a threat to national security.[65] Hudson and Leidl's research explaining the underpinnings of the "Hillary Doctrine" demonstrates that empowering women in communities is a stabilizing force, both politically and economically, and thus is important for international peace.[66] Therefore, international relations devoid of human rights considerations is far more precarious for peace and global security. In the case of Uganda, severe discrimination against the LGBTI community in education, employment, housing, and opportunity negatively impacts the country's economic growth and overall stability of the nation.

The Uganda chapter also analyzes the complexity of conditioning foreign assistance to pressure foreign governments to make human rights reforms. Aid conditionality remains a contested topic in both foreign policy circles and academic literature.[67] Research shows that political conditionality does not always lead to the desired impact of improving rights.[68] LGBTI populations can become further marginalized in the aftermath of the suspension of aid.[69] Cutting aid to communities in low-income countries can lead to severe negative outcomes on rural communities in poverty, such as the cessation of basic health care services, education, and infrastructure programs previously funded through international donor assistance.[70] In diplomatic dialogue, aid conditioning is often seen as a last resort. Special Envoy Randy Berry asserted that his goal was largely to avoid draconian measures such as sanctions or conditioning aid:

> I believe that we have much greater possibility of seeing constructive, productive results from members of civil society when

we don't have to rely on those types of levers. So I would never rule out—I think we need to look at all of the tools in our toolkit when we really need to push for the rights of others in some of these contexts, but my great hope is that we don't get to that point in the first place.[71]

Uganda, and other neighboring countries, are heavily dependent on foreign aid; approximately 25 percent of Uganda's GDP comes from foreign development assistance.[72] Precisely because of this economic dependence, even the threat of revamping assistance gains the attention of the highest leadership in a donor recipient country.

While conditioning aid can lead to negative consequences, on the other side of the debate, empirical data demonstrate instances of human rights improvements after foreign governments condition their international aid. Allison Carnegie and Nikolay Marinov's research published in the *American Journal of Political Science* found that at times, "conditionality associated with an increased aid commitment is responsible for the positive effects in the domains of human rights and democracy.[73] Similarly, Han Dorussen's research demonstrates that economic incentives are effective instruments to transform conflict into cooperation.[74] Most small states are vulnerable to, and dependent on, trade. It is thereby untenable for them to choose to be ostracized by the international community. Dorussen and other researchers have also found that nations have changed specific policies as the result of the mere threat of sanctions. Evidence from programming in Morocco also exhibits that connecting human rights to foreign assistance can lead to long-term improvements in democratic institutions.[75] In this case, because of international pressure, Ugandan lawmakers removed the death penalty punishment aspect of their proposed law. Local LGBTI advocates expressed this change as a win for their community. Frank Mugisha expressed relief that they were no longer worried about losing their lives, but rather fighting a legal battle of a potential jail sentence.[76] While conditioning aid to human rights is often used as a last resort in diplomacy, even the threat of an overhaul of a foreign assistance can result in measurable human rights reform.

There is a critical need for further analytical scholarship regarding the effectiveness of both positive incentives in foreign aid, as well as the effects of negative pressure through conditioning aid. Because improvements to human rights and democracy in a country may take years or even decades, the effectiveness of these diplomatic strategies is exceedingly difficult to measure and study.[77] In nondemocratic nations, in particular, there is a lack of documentation and transparency. Policy deliberations often occur behind closed doors, between a handful of powerful people. It is thus challenging to assess the factors that changed state policy or a leader's perspective on an issue. Scholars overwhelmingly focus on the negative consequences of sanctions, with ample evidence of how vulnerable groups can be hurt by cutting foreign aid.[78] While it is possible to document the immediate negative consequences of stopping aid delivery, it is much harder to document the potential long-term effect on policy reform. Data from South Africa or Myanmar, for example, exhibit measurable changes in state behavior due to external pressure on human rights concerns.[79] The practice of putting human rights stipulations on foreign aid is part of many countries' foreign policy. Wealthy Asian nations, such as Japan, incorporate human rights considerations into foreign aid to Thailand and Indonesia, for example.[80] Qatar and other Gulf countries contribute to global humanitarian and charitable works.[81] Foreign policy leaders think in the long term about what is best for their own nations' interests and simultaneously evaluate what could lead to policy reform in another country. Evaluating the causality of cutting international aid to improve domestic human rights practices needs more scrutiny by both foreign policy leaders and scholars.

Policy Recommendations

This book seeks to explain the puzzle of how Sweden and the United States unexpectedly incorporated LGBTI rights into their respective foreign policy agendas. Lessons from these cases are applicable to other emerging human rights movements seeking to influence foreign affairs. After ignoring LGBTI violence for decades in diplomatic affairs, in the early 2000s, Sweden, the United States, and a handful of other countries began to revamp their bilateral relations with Uganda and other states that sanctioned violence against LGBTI minority groups. Similarly, other dormant normative issues may become the focal point of the international community in the future. Climate change, acceptance of refugees, ending capital punishment, and other issues may rise to increasing importance in international affairs. The following general policy recommendations derived from this study are applicable broadly to social movements that aim to reform foreign policy mandates:

1. Civil society groups need to understand and better use large bureaucracies.

2. Local advocates need to lead in local human rights advocacy strategies, international program development, and policy reformation.

3. Sensitizing events are important moments for advocates to capture the world's attention.

4. At times, closed-door diplomacy is the most effective action for change.

5. Conditioning aid remains a powerful tool for diplomats to influence domestic human rights practices.

6. A human rights issue does not have to be "perfected" domestically before it can become an issue of foreign affairs.

7. Sweden provides a blueprint for human rights diplomacy.

8. Researchers and scholars need to provide more evidence as to the interlinkage between global security, economic development, and LGBTI equality.

Civil society groups need to understand and better use large bureaucracies. Especially in the United States, regardless of the political party in power, civil society groups need to transition from conceptualizing "the government" as a handful of people at the top, or as a monolithic entity. In the US federal service, political appointments make up fewer than 1 percent of all positions.[82] In large bureaucracies, civil servants with expertise on an issue often remain in their jobs after the transition of power regardless of the political party. From US embassies in Burundi to Belize, diplomats report documented human rights violations to Congress as well as regularly meet with human rights groups. Individuals of influence from the city of Seattle to the UN in Geneva are at times located within large institutions. Officers across sectors in the State Department, USAID, embassies, and consulates worldwide allocate funding for human rights and democracy programs. In doing so, they often seek creative policy directive ideas from local groups. There is vast opportunity to liaise tactically with a variety of offices on the municipal, state, national, and international levels. NGO leaders can better situate themselves as strategic advisors, come into the halls of power, and provide specific policy recommendations. Targeted institutional advocacy may not make headlines, like a large street protest. However, rather than spending limited human and financial resources on mass protests, civil society organizations may benefit from building strategic coalitions with insider government leaders.

Local advocates need to lead in local human rights advocacy strategies, international program development, and policy reformation. As recognized by diplomats, advocates, and scholars alike, local NGOs need to be the central architects of human rights programming in their country. Hailing from their respective country and culture, locals residents have the best understanding of how to best articulate public diplomacy efforts and effectively address controversial human rights issues within their cultural context. Foreign actors need to listen to local advocates, and support and bolster the efforts that locals identify as priorities. Human rights advocacy is diverse and expansive: from curating an LGBTI film festival, to training lawyers in international law, to helping NGOs to register, to funding a shelter for homeless youth, diplomatic programs vary widely. Following the lead of local advocates allows them to curate programs that will have the most political salience in their community. Supporting the people on the front lines making change within their own communities is one of the most effective ways to create sustainable change from within a country. Tailoring country strategic plans in concert with local allies is critical for durable human rights outcomes.

Sensitizing events are important moments for advocates to capture the world's attention. While LGBTI advocates decried global state-sanctioned violence for decades, policy responses from foreign leaders languished. It took the extreme and sudden nature of Ugandan lawmakers proposing the death penalty in the Ugandan Anti-Homosexuality Act (AHA) to awaken the world's attention. A sensitizing event can catalyze new discourse in institutions. The AHA opened new political opportunity for foreign policy leaders to deliberate and rethink policy agendas around a previously unaddressed human rights concern. Rather than tackling a nebulous global problem, the AHA gave foreign leaders a specific problem to target. Civil society groups need to be ready to take the spotlight and provide policy recommendations to the highest levels of government working to construct a new policy response.

At times, closed-door diplomacy is the most effective action for change. Sometimes public shaming of a foreign leader or the open condemnation of a nation's human rights abuses can be effective; however, at times, public diplomatic responses can backfire. If seen as losing face, leaders can become recalcitrant or even double down abusive practices to gain political clout from their conservative supporters. By contrast, closed-door diplomacy can be the most effective diplomatic tool for tangible human rights reforms in a country. Ambassadors in-country or assistant secretaries from Washington or Stockholm, for example, can directly access a foreign country's president, foreign minister or highest levels of leadership within the foreign country. They can hold a private meeting to express condemnation on an issue behind closed doors. Foreign leaders may agree to improve a specific human rights issue in private meetings in exchange for an unrelated foreign investment incentive, for example. They may discreetly release political prisoners without public comments or stop harassing an NGO. Incentives may be offered to a foreign country, sometimes on an unrelated matter, in exchange for a human rights reform. In some cases, this is the most effective method for change, especially with partner and strategically allied nations. Closed-door diplomacy can be effective but receives little public accolades. The impact of closed-door diplomacy is exceedingly difficult to measure. Outsiders try, often in vain, to measure the effectiveness of human rights diplomacy. Scholars and human rights activists may not perceive the connection between a trade negotiation and improvements in local human rights practices. Thus, this book helps shed light on the full scope of human rights diplomatic practice that is often missing from research of outside observers.

Conditioning aid remains a powerful tool for diplomats to influence human rights practices. While cutting bilateral foreign aid wholesale is rarely done in diplomatic practice, placing preconditions on foreign assistance to improve human rights practices or political reform is common. All foreign aid is conditional in some regard, and donor countries are not required to give international humanitarian aid. Some countries, such as China, hardly engage in human rights diplomacy at all, despite China's vast foreign investment. The purpose of conditioning aid can be used to apply pressure on foreign governments to change repressive laws and discriminatory practices. Whether seeking to address grave human rights abuses in the former Yugoslavia, Indonesia, or Sri Lanka, political pressure from foreign governments at times is the biggest influencer for domestic change. While this kind of action represents the most severe diplomatic lever, sometimes this high-level external pressure is the only leverage powerful enough to pressure change, especially in authoritarian regimes. Cutting or revamping aid must be done with the utmost caution and in consultation with local advocates. It needs to be strategically directed and short-lived, targeting a specific law or policy. The immediate negative consequences of stopping aid delivery are measurable. It is much harder to document the long-term effects of threatening to cease aid in authoritarian regimes. However, at times, cutting bilateral ties can lead to long-term systemic change, potentially leading to positive improvements in human rights practices and laws.

A human rights issue does not have to be "perfected" domestically before it can become an issue of foreign affairs. No country has a perfect record on any human rights issue. Thus diplomats conduct human rights diplomacy with foreign audiences with the understanding that their country struggles with human rights issues as well. For instance, one domestic violence murder in northern Sweden, does not negate Sweden's feminist foreign policy. Similarly, evangelical opposition to LGBTI rights does not negate diplomatic work to promote universal standards of equal rights for all people, including LGBTI populations. LGBTI diplomacy is relatively new. Decrying hypocrisy is not helpful to embassy officials observing stoning and mob killings in their host countries. Rather, the diplomatic corps would welcome thorough culturally appropriate policy recommendations and programmatic ideas from outside experts for more strategic implementation of this new aspect of foreign affairs.

Diplomats and advocates work across borders, aspiring to universal standards of human rights together. Topics of climate change and care for refugees, for example, will increasingly rise on the diplomatic agenda; however, leaders will address these issues despite less-than-perfect domestic environmental or refugee policies. Furthermore, for every human rights issue, one can always find domestic opposition, no matter how fringe. Many governments engage in diplomatic dialogue to combat anti-Semitism or Islamophobia, for example, notwithstanding some domestic political parties supporting these beliefs. Nonpractitioner academics tend to focus intensely on the hypocritical nature of human rights diplomacy. And yet no country will ever have complete moral legitimacy to promote an issue internationally. International relations devoid of human rights diplomacy is dangerous for peace and global security. Dictators left unchecked by the international community can destabilize their country and create regional conflict. Despite potential domestic inconsistency, diplomats need to engage on human rights issues, even while an issue evolves within their own country. It would therefore be more pragmatic for scholars to apply astute methodological skills to recommend how to better conduct human rights diplomacy.

Sweden provides a blueprint for human rights diplomacy. What happens in Scandinavia matters globally. Other governments replicate human rights norms and gender policies generated in Scandinavia. Sweden was first to enact policies on freedom of expression, divorce and family law, feminist foreign policy, and LGBTI diplomacy. Half the world away, in 2015, lawmakers in Seattle, Washington, reformed state law on prostitution based upon Sweden's law as blueprint to criminalize the buyer, not the sex worker.[83] Sweden was the first country to legislate anti-LGBTI discrimination in the workplace. Connecting LGBTI equality to a labor rights issue provided a guide to global advocates to link LGBTI equality to labor rights.[84] Similarly, it was the first country to link poverty and international development programmatic needs specifically to LGBTI populations. Transnational activists and foreign policy advisors later used this framework across Europe and North America. The EU and UN at times employ Swedish laws as a blueprint for their emerging external and internal policies. Scandinavia is thereby an important region to study and follow in the development of human rights in order to understand potential future trends. The Swedish case study provides implications for other nascent LGBTI movements around the world. It serves as an example to LGBTI organizations in how to gain power through consistent and persistent advocacy within government institutions. It behooves civil society organizations to closely watch the tactics and broader strategies of human rights groups in Scandinavia for best practices, but also to observe future human rights trends.

Researchers and scholars need to provide more evidence as to the interlinkage between security, economic development, and LGBTI equality. Hawkish foreign policy leaders often need to be convinced of the importance of human rights in foreign policy, not based on the morality or justice or a cause, but rather on measurable national interests. Moral outrage about a gay man stoned to death in Iran, or corrective rape of a lesbian in South Africa, for example, tends to be fleeting. Advocates need to think in terms of long-term national security interests.

More traditional security and economic policy frameworks resonate with foreign policy leaders. LGBTI diplomacy is relatively new in diplomatic history; therefore, there is a lack of comprehensive research about the correlation of LGBTI rights and national security. However, there is building evidence from the Council on Foreign Relations, Stockholm International Peace Research Institute, the United States Institute of Peace, and other research institutes that demonstrates the connection between improving human rights for ensuring stable societies and economic growth.[85] Researchers can help sustain LGBTI diplomacy in foreign policy institutions by providing increased empirical evidence that demonstrates how equality for all, including LGBTI minority groups, improves economic and political stability.

Conclusions of LGBTI Diplomacy

This study has analyzed the policy development of LGBTI rights in US and Swedish foreign policy that marks an institutional shift from ostracization and pariah status to promotion of LGBTI rights in foreign relations. Human rights concepts and foreign policy agendas change over time, in part from more diversity within foreign ministries. Susan Harris Rimmer asserts that new representation of women and LGBTI persons in the practice of diplomacy changes both the content and focus of foreign policy.[86] Elise Stephenson's research demonstrates how lesbians, once barred from serving in foreign ministries for being both married and lesbian, challenge traditional gender norms in diplomatic practice, where diplomatic women with wives perform the "dual roles" of formal and informal diplomacy, albeit still overcoming deep exclusion.[87] Foreign policy leaders closely watch, copy, and influence other governments. As of 2021, approximately sixteen countries have incorporated LGBTI rights as a formal aspect of their respective foreign policy agendas.[88] Brazil, the Netherlands, Spain, and Norway, among other countries, have been vocal champions in the UN to spread global LGBTI equality norms.[89] Many other foreign ministries, especially new EU member states, deliberate on whether to coalesce with that small group of nations and incorporate LGBTI diplomacy in their bilateral relations. However, LGBTI equality remains challenged in many international venues and societies.

While much progress as has been made internationally on LGBTI rights, global backlash is gaining ground. Governments in the United States, Brazil, Hungary, Poland, and elsewhere elected conservative governments in the last decade and began to repeal gender and LGBTI equality policies.[90] In light of backlash, LGBTI advocacy leader Amie Bishop commented that "Progress often triggers backlash. Change usually means that someone is losing power and position. Backlash comes in the form of homophobia, xenophobia, racism, and curtailing civil society."[91] Observers denote LGBTI rights as a harbinger for other democratic values, such as general freedom of assembly and expression.[92] Along with LGBTI rights, many liberal democracies are also repealing policies related to freedom of association, expression, and election standards.[93] In places such as Uganda, LGBTI people are a scapegoat for the COVID-19 pandemic: "Security forces raided homeless shelters for LGBTI youth and denied legal access to detainees on grounds of the COVID-19 pandemic."[94] Ugandan researcher and LGBTI activist Stella Nyanzi asserted, "The fight is fundamentally about power, about how the powerful can use even sexuality as a proxy for angry nationalism, as fuel for social division and as a means to deflect attention from what's really going on."[95] Nationalist rhetoric across borders attempts to delegitimize LGBTI equality. It is clear there is no linear progression of LGBTI rights gaining increased acceptance globally.

Despite fierce global contestation, LGBTI diplomacy remains an institutionalized pillar of foreign policy for some liberal democracies. Severe persecution and violence also persist globally, and thereby diplomats continue to engage in LGBTI diplomacy. When countries such as Brunei implemented death by stoning for gay men in April 2019, there was an international outcry and swift diplomatic response.[96] LGBTI diplomacy has become an aspect of the comprehensive human rights strategy of both Sweden and the United States despite more conservative opposition. This sustained policy is due in part to the work of advocates and diplomats who worked to integrate and imbed the policy across foreign affairs institutions.

This book project began in the early years of the Obama administration with Secretary of State Hillary Clinton's leadership in 2009 and ends just as Biden assumed the presidency in 2021. Despite four years of the Trump administration attempting widespread repeal of LGBTI equality policies, LGBTI diplomacy remained in place in the State Department and USAID. Having survived the most anti-LGBTI leadership in modern US history, Biden's leadership team is poised to bolster LGBTI rights in the US foreign policy agenda and increase funds to global LGBTI civil society organizations. While at times marginalized, LGBTI diplomacy is a sustained aspect of comprehensive human rights foreign policy engagement.

Appendix 1

Interviews

All interviews were conducted either in person, over Skype, or by phone between April 2015 and August 2019. All interviews were made anonymous for two central reasons: 1) LGBTI advocacy work can be dangerous, and advocates' identities needs to be protected; 2) Because of the politically sensitive nature of this work, diplomats and high-level foreign policy leaders remain unidentified by their specific names. Individuals are identified at times in the text only when the reference comes from a public source. However, the sectoral position, nationality, number of interviews, and location are noted in the table below.

Sectoral Position	Definition or Clarification	Number of Interviews (National/ Supranational)
Activists	Representative of an organization	US—10 Sweden—10 EU—4 Afghan—1 Armenian—1 Belarusian—1 Dutch—1 Hong Kong—1 Iranian—3 Jamaican—2

continued on next page

Sectoral Position	Definition or Clarification	Number of Interviews (National/ Supranational)
Activists	Representative of an organization	Kenyan—3 Kurdish—1 Moldovan—1 Nigerian—3 Portuguese—1 Russian—1 Taiwan—1 Ugandan—3 Total = 48
Ambassador, special envoy, member of Parliament, assistant secretary, and high-level foreign policy maker	Government official in administrative or executive leadership position with direct influence in foreign policy formation	US—10 Sweden—7 EU—2 British—1 Canadian—1 Total = 21
Foreign policy officer, career diplomat, civil servant, private sector representative	A staff member, officer, or advisor serving in a support or advisory role	US—8 Sweden—8 EU—1 Australian—1 Indonesian—1 Romanian—1 Total = 20
		Total Interviews = 89

Appendix 2

Participant Observation

Stockholm Pride Observations: Representative List	
July 27, 2015	"In Lube in Uganda." Presentation at Stockholm Pride, Stockholm, Sweden, July 27, 2015.
	"Stop Violence in Iran." Presentation of Iranian activists at Stockholm Pride, Stockholm, Sweden, July 27, 2015.
July 28, 2015	Amnesty International Swedish representative. "Abolish LGBT discrimination laws!" (Gör slut med diskriminerande lagar!). Presentation at Stockholm Pride, Stockholm, Sweden, July 28, 2015.
	"Sveriges Moderaterna." Presentation by Sweden's Moderate Party at Stockholm Pride," Stockholm, Sweden, July 28, 2015.
	"Swedish Immigration Board (*Migrationverket*)." Presentation at Stockholm Pride, Stockholm, Sweden, July 28, 2015.
	Tupilak; Nordic Rainbow Cultural Workers. "Swedish Rainbow Co-op in East Europe." Presentation at Stockholm Pride, Stockholm, Sweden, July 28, 2015.
July 29, 2015	"Eastern Coalition for LGBT Equality." Presentation from Sida at Stockholm Pride, Stockholm, Sweden, July 29, 2015.

continued on next page

July 30, 2015	Scandia, Human Resources Specialist. "Swedish International Companies in a Homo-phobic World." Presentation at Stockholm Pride, Stockholm, Sweden, July 30, 2015.
July 31, 2015	Johansson, Morgan. Presentation of the Minister of Justice and Immigration Morgan Johansson at Stockholm Pride, Stockholm, Sweden, July 31, 2015. Gustav Fridolin. Presentation of Swedish Ministry of Education Gustav Fridolin at Stockholm Pride, Stockholm, Sweden, July 31, 2015. Lövin, Isabella. Presentation of the Minister for International Development Cooperation Isabella Lövin at Stockholm Pride, Stockholm, Sweden, July 31, 2015.
July 31, 2017– August 6, 2017	Seminars include LGBTI Rights and Swedish International Foreign Aid; Swedish and Global LGBTI Advocacy; Swedish Government Funding of Civil Society; Swedish Government Representatives Discussing Sweden's Role in International LGBTI Rights
August 2, 2017	Officer from the Left Political Party (Vänsterpartiet). "LGBTI Rights in 20 Years" (HBTQ Frågar om 20 År). Stockholm, Sweden, August 2, 2017.
July 29, 2019	"Trans Newcomers: Rights, Challenges, Experiences." Panel presentation at Stockholm Pride, Stockholm, Sweden, July 29, 2019.
July 30, 2019	"Understanding BDSM in Indonesia." Presentation at Stockholm Pride, Stockholm, Sweden, July 30, 2019. "Conversation with Cynthia Sobraty." Presentation at Stockholm Pride, Stockholm, Sweden, July 30, 2019. "Rainbow Gospel." Presentation at Stockholm Pride, Stockholm, Sweden, July 30, 2019. "Where Are We Going Now?" Panel presentation at Stockholm Pride, Stockholm, Sweden, July 30, 2019. "Xenophobia and LGBTI rights in Sweden." Presentation at Stockholm Pride, Stockholm, Sweden, July 30, 2019.

July 31, 2019	"Can I Be More Than a Transperson?" Presentation at Stockholm Pride, Stockholm, Sweden, July 31, 2019. "LGBTQIA+ in Higher Education." Presentation at Stockholm Pride, Stockholm, Sweden, July 31, 2019. "LGBTQIA Health." Presentation at Stockholm Pride, Stockholm, Sweden, July 31, 2019. "Our Rights Are Under Attack." Presentation at Stockholm Pride, Stockholm, Sweden, July 31, 2019. "The Struggle Is Real." Presentation at Stockholm Pride, Stockholm, Sweden, July 31, 2019.
August 1, 2019	"Art and Culture to Raise Awareness." Presentation at Stockholm Pride, Stockholm, Sweden, August 1, 2019. "Dancing for My Life: Trans in Afghanistan." Presentation at Stockholm Pride, Stockholm, Sweden, August 1, 2019. "Employees: A Strong Force for LGBTQ Inclusive Workplaces." Presentation at Stockholm Pride, Stockholm, Sweden, August 1, 2019. "Harm Reduction Approach to Sex Work." Presentation at Stockholm Pride, Stockholm, Sweden, August 1, 2019. "My Story, My Life: Trans Newcomers." Presentation at Stockholm Pride, Stockholm, Sweden, August 1, 2019. "Sverige och Homonationalism." Presentation at Stockholm Pride, Stockholm, Sweden, August 1, 2019. "We Are Needed." Presentation at Stockholm Pride, Stockholm, Sweden, August 1, 2019.
August 2, 2019	"Community Healing and Resistance." Presentation at Stockholm Pride, Stockholm, Sweden, August 2, 2019. "Our Spaces, Our Rights: Eastern Europe." Panel presentation at Stockholm Pride, Stockholm, Sweden, August 2, 2019.

continued on next page

August 2, 2019 (continued)	"Rainbow Riots India." Presentation at Stockholm Pride, Stockholm, Sweden, August 2, 2019.
	"Vision about Equal Industry." Presentation at Stockholm Pride, Stockholm, Sweden, August 2, 2019.
	"What Is Discrimination?" Presentation at Stockholm Pride, Stockholm, Sweden, August 2, 2019.

OutRight Action International Conferences Observations: Representative List	"Rights & Resistance: Lessons from the Frontlines of the Global LGBTIQ Movement." Presentation at OutRight Action International Event, Seattle, WA, April 25, 2017.
	"Rise Up in an Age of Backlash." Presentation at OutRight Action International Event, Seattle, WA, May 8, 2018.
	"OutRising: An Evening for Global LGBTIQ Equality." Presentation at OutRight Action International Event, Seattle, WA, February 7, 2019.
	"Human Rights Diplomacy." Presentation from Outright Action International for course at University of Washington, Seattle, WA, April 25, 2019.

Other US Conferences Observations	"On the Human Rights Frontier; the Global Struggle for LGBT Equality." Panel discussion with international LGBT activists at University of Washington, Seattle, WA, May 13, 2015.
	"Time to Thrive." Human Rights Campaign Annual Conference, Portland, Oregon, February 13–14, 2015.

Notes

Preface

1. Hillary Clinton, "Human Rights in the Twenty-First Century," Georgetown University, Washington, DC, December 14, 2009, https://anthonyclarkarend.com/video-and-transcript-hillary-clintons-georgetown-human-rights-address-560ff7e5f924.

2. International Lesbian, Gay, Bisexual, Trans, and Intersex Association, "Maps—Sexual Orientation Laws," ILGA World, accessed May 20, 2020, https://ilga.org/maps-sexual-orientation-laws.

3. For examples of societal violence in Jordan and Pakistan: John Alan Cohan, "Honor Killings and the Cultural Defense," *California Western International Law Journal* 40, no. 2 (2010): 178–249.

4. For more on foreign policy legislation from Congress, see Walter J. Oleszek et al., *Congressional Procedures and the Policy Process* (Thousand Oaks, CA: CQ Press, 1978).

5. All human rights activists in this text remain anonymous for sources' safety.

6. See, for example, Bureau of Democracy, Human Rights, and Labor, "Country Reports on Human Rights Practices," US Department of State, accessed March 13, 2019, https://www.state.gov/reports/2018-country-reports-on-human-rights-practices/.

7. Tom Malinowski, "Restoring Moral Authority: Ending Torture, Secret Detention, and the Prison at Guantanamo Bay," *Annals of the American Academy of Political and Social Science* 618, no. 1 (2008): 148–59, doi: 10.1177/0002716208217118.

8. Debra Liang-Fenton, ed., *Implementing US Human Rights Policy: Agendas, Policies, and Practices* (Washington, DC: US Institute of Peace Press, 2004).

9. Clinton, "Human Rights in the Twenty-First Century," 2009.

10. On corrective rape, see Roderick Brown, "Corrective Rape in South Africa: A Continuing Plight Despite an International Human Rights Response," *Annual Survey of International & Comparative Law* 18, no. 1 (2012): 45–66. On mob

killings in Nigeria, see Participant Observation #89, Stockholm Pride, Stockholm, Sweden, July 30, 2019.

11. See, for example: Robbie Corey-Boulet, *Love Falls on Us: A Story of American Ideas and African LGBT Lives* (London: Zed Books, 2019); S. M. Rodriguez, *The Economies of Queer Inclusion: Transnational Organizing for LGBTI Rights in Uganda* (London: Lexington Books, 2018).

12. Helene Coley Nicholson, "After the Visits. . . ," *Jamaica Observer*, December 30, 2015, http://m.jamaicaobserver.com/columns/After-the-visits_47377.

13. Gallup Poll, "Gay and Lesbian Rights," accessed May 19, 2020, https://news.gallup.com/poll/1651/gay-lesbian-rights.aspx.

14. Andrea L. Wirtz, Tonia C. Poteat, Mannat Malik, and Nancy Glass, "Gender-Based Violence against Transgender People in the United States: A Call for Research And Programming," *Trauma, Violence, & Abuse* 21, no. 2 (2020): 227–41.

15. Omar G. Encarnación, "The Troubled Rise of Gay Rights Diplomacy," *Current History* 115, no. 777 (January 2016).

16. Human Rights Campaign, "Violence Against the Transgender Community in 2020," accessed May 19, 2020, https://www.hrc.org/resources/violence-against-the-trans-and-gender-non-conforming-community-in-2020.

17. David K. Johnson, *The Lavender Scare: The Cold War Persecution of Gays and Lesbians in the Federal Government* (Chicago, IL: University of Chicago Press, 2006).

18. Samantha Power, *A Problem from Hell: America and the Age of Genocide* (New York City: Basic Books, 2012).

19. Elise Carlson-Rainer, "Sweden Is a World Leader in Peace, Security and Human Rights," *World Affairs Journal* 180, no. 4 (2018): 79–85, doi: 10.1177/0043820018759714.

20. Daniela Alaattinoğlu and Ruth Rubio-Marín, "Redress for Involuntarily Sterilised Trans People in Sweden against Evolving Human Rights Standards: A Critical Appraisal," *Human Rights Law Review* 19, no. 4 (January 2019): 705–32, https://doi.org/10.1093/hrlr/ngz026.

21. Tyra Jean, "Black Lives Matter: Police Brutality in the Era of COVID-19," Syracuse University Lerner Center for Public Health Promotion, Issue Brief no. 31, June 16, 2020.

22. See Kelly-Kate S. Pease, *Human Rights and Humanitarian Diplomacy: Negotiating for Human Rights Protection and Humanitarian Access* (Oxford: Oxford University Press, 2016).

23. See, for example: Bureau of Democracy, Human Rights and Labor, "Human Rights and Democracy Fund," US Department of State, accessed April 15, 2019, https://www.state.gov/j/drl/p/.

24. Bureau of Democracy, "Human Rights and Labor Country Reports on Human Rights Practices," US Department of State, 2015, http://www.state.gov/j/drl/rls/hrrpt/humanrightsreport/index.htm#wrapper.

Chapter 1

1. Participant observation #83, Stockholm Pride, Stockholm, Sweden, July 29, 2019.

2. Participant observation #90, Stockholm Pride, Stockholm, Sweden, July 29, 2019.

3. International Lesbian, Gay, Trans and Intersex Association, 2015, http://old.ilga.org/Statehomophobia/ILGA_State_Sponsored_Homophobia_2015.pdf.

4. Elizabeth Landau, Zain Verjee, and Antonia Mortensen, "Uganda President: Homosexuals Are 'Disgusting,'" *CNN World*, February 25, 2014, http://www.cnn.com/2014/02/24/world/africa/uganda-homosexuality-interview/.

5. Note: Ugandan lawmakers have proposed many iterations of a death penalty bill against homosexuality, specifically in 2009, 2014, and 2019. See Amnesty International, "Uganda: Parliament Must Reject Bill Imposing Death Penalty for Gay Sex," October 11, 2019, https://www.amnesty.org/en/latest/news/2019/10/uganda-parliament-must-reject-bill-imposing-death-penalty-for-gay-sex/. See also "Uganda Kill the Gays Bill," *Huffington Post*, 2009–2016, http://www.huffingtonpost.com/news/uganda-kill-the-gays-bill/.

6. This analysis uses the acronym "LGBTI" for lesbian, gay, bisexual, transgender, and intersex. This is the acronym used by the US and Swedish governments, as well as Amnesty International and Human Rights Watch as of 2019.

7. Lydia Malmedie, "Contested Issue and Incremental Change: The Example of LGBTI in EU Foreign Policy," *Der moderne Staat* (2016): 35–50, https://doi.org/10.3224/dms.v9i1.23639.

8. David Forsythe, *Human Rights in International Relations* (Cambridge: Cambridge University Press, 2000): 159.

9. While persecution may have existed for centuries in many places globally, historical documentation of LGBTI persecution in some countries has only existed since approximately the 1950s and 1960s.

10. This international debate in the UN in 2010 is analyzed more in-depth later in this book.

11. Office of the High Commissioner, "Annual Reports," United Nations Human Rights, http://www.ohchr.org/EN/Issues/Executions/Pages/AnnualReports.aspx.

12. Note: Sweden ranks eight of ten on the Organization for Economic Cooperation and Development's scale that measures acceptance of homosexuality. Sweden's score is three points higher than the average country. Source: Organization for Economic Co-Operation and Development, "How Does Sweden Compare?," in *Society at a Glance: OECD Social Indicators: A Spotlight on LGBT People* (Paris, France: OECD Publishing, 2019).

13. Note: This measurement is predicated on a formal incorporation of LGBTI rights in the foreign policy of these nations. It does not include countries that raise

the issue ad hoc in the UN, for example. This small number of nations have LGBTI rights as a formal pillar of their human rights portfolio and fund global LGBTI civil society. As such, this number is measured by formal partners and funders to the largest global multinational fund called the "Global Equality Fund": Bureau of Democracy, Human Rights, and Labor, "Global Equality Fund," US Department of State, accessed April 9, 2020, https://www.state.gov/global-equality-fund/.

14. Robert J. Palladino, "Implementation of Phases Two and Three of Brunei's Sharia Penal Code," Office of the Spokesperson, US Department of State, April 2, 2019, https://www.state.gov/r/pa/prs/ps/2019/04/290840.htm.

15. "Egypt: Stop Anti-LGBT Crackdown, Intimidation. 'Rainbow Flag' Arrests Violate Privacy, Freedom of Expression," Human Rights Watch, September 30, 2017, https://www.hrw.org/news/2017/09/30/egypt-stop-anti-lgbt-crackdown-intimidation.

16. Heather Nauert, "Department Press Briefing," US Department of State, August 23, 2017, https://www.state.gov/briefings/department-press-briefing-august-23-2017/#EGYPT.

See also "LGBT Community Under Attack in Egypt," Human Rights First, November 2017, https://www.humanrightsfirst.org/sites/default/files/Egypt-LGBT-Factsheet.pdf.

17. US case interview #47, San Francisco, February 10, 2016.

18. Bureau of Democracy, Human Rights and Labor, "Country Reports on Human Rights Practices," US Department of State, http://www.state.gov/j/drl/rls/hrrpt/humanrightsreport/index.htm#wrapper.

19. *Trafficking in Persons Report*, US Department of State, June 2019, https://www.state.gov/trafficking-in-persons-report-2019/. *Report on International Religious Freedom,* US Department of State, 2018, https://www.state.gov/reports/2018-report-on-international-religious-freedom/.

20. UN General Assembly, "University Declaration of Human Rights," 217 (III) A. Paris, 1948, accessed October 7, 2020, https://www.un.org/en/universal-declaration-human-rights/.

21. Alison Brysk, *Global Good Samaritans: Human Rights as Foreign Policy* (Oxford: Oxford University Press, 2009), 4.

22. Mark Goodale and Sally Engel Merry, *The Practice of Human Rights: Tracking Law between The Global and The Local* (Cambridge: Cambridge University Press, 2007), 7.

23. For an extensive discussion on modern human rights foreign policy practice, see Ann Marie Clark, *Diplomacy of Conscience: Amnesty International and Changing Human Rights Norms* (Princeton, NJ: Princeton University Press, 2001).

24. Kelly-Kate S. Pease, *Human Rights and Humanitarian Diplomacy: Negotiating for Human Rights Protection and Humanitarian Access* (Manchester: Manchester University Press, 2020).

25. Katrin Kinzelbach, *The EU's Human Rights Dialogue with China: Quiet Diplomacy and Its Limits* (London: Routledge, 2016).

26. See Angelina S. Godoy, *Of Medicines and Markets: Intellectual Property and Human Rights in the Free Trade Era* (Stanford, CA: Stanford University Press, 2013), 18; Balakrishnan Rajagopal, *International Law from Below: Development, Social Movements and Third World Resistance* (Cambridge: Cambridge University Press, 2004): 186.

27. Cynthia Burack, *Because We Are Human: Contesting U.S. Support for Gender and Sexuality Human Rights Abroad* (Albany, NY: State University of New York Press, 2018), 29.

28. See, for example, Omar G. Encarnación, "The Troubled Rise of Gay Rights Diplomacy," *Current History* 115, no. 777 (January 2016), 17; S. M. Rodriguez, *The Economies of Queer Inclusion: Transnational Organizing for LGBTI Rights in Uganda* (London: Lexington Books, 2018).

29. Annika Nilsson, Klara Lundholm, and Erik Vagberg, "Study on SIDA's Work on Human Rights of Lesbian, Gay, Bisexual, Transgender and Intersex Persons," Swedish International Development Agency, November 2013, http://www.sida.se/contentassets/e68f76aa89ca48cab8a17788fe9afe36/study-on-sida8217s-work-on-human-rights-of-lesbian-gay-bisexual-transgender-and-intersex-persons_3728.pdf.

30. Joe Myers, "Foreign Aid: These Countries Are the Most Generous," World Economic Forum, August 19, 2016, https://www.weforum.org/agenda/2016/08/foreign-aid-these-countries-are-the-most-generous/.

31. Annie O'Connell, "Why Sweden Is a Leader in Foreign Aid," The Borgen Project, August 20, 2019, https://borgenproject.org/sweden-is-a-leader-in-foreign-aid/.

32. "Sweden and Human Rights," Swedish government, October 2, 2018, https://sweden.se/society/sweden-and-human-rights/.

33. *Congressional Budget Justification,* US Department of State, Washington, DC, Fiscal Year 2020, https://www.usaid.gov/sites/default/files/documents/1868/FY_2020_CBJ.pdf.

34. On Spain's influential role, see Elisabeth Jay Friedman, "Constructing 'the Same Rights with the Same Names': The Impact of Spanish Norm Diffusion on Marriage Equality in Argentina," *Latin American Politics and Society* 54, no. 4 (2012): 29–59, https://doi.org/10.1111/j.1548-2456.2012.00171.x.

35. Maria B. B. Noguiera, "The Promotion of LGBT Rights as International Human Rights Norms: Explaining Brazil's Diplomatic Leadership," *Global Governance* 23, no. 4 (October 2017): 545–63, https://doi.org/10.1163/19426720-02304003.

36. Jim Yong Kim, "World Bank Group President Jim Yong Kim: Discrimination by Law Carries a High Price," *World Bank News,* February 28, 2014, http://www.worldbank.org/en/news/opinion/2014/02/28/world-bank-group-president-jim-yong-kim-discrimination-law-price.

37. Susie Jolly, *Poverty and Sexuality: What Are the Connections?,* Stockholm: Swedish International Development Agency, 2010, http://www.globalequality.org/storage/documents/pdf/sida%20study%20of%20poverty%20and%20sexuality.pdf.

38. Stoum, Tina Maria Sæteraas. "Sexually (Dis) Orientated?: Conceptualizing the Norwegian Ministry of Foreign Affairs' Promotion of LGBT Rights." Master's thesis, Norges teknisk-naturvitenskapelige universitet, Det humanistiske fakultet, Institutt for tverrfaglige kulturstudier, 2012: 58.

39. Hakeem Onapajo and Christopher Isike, "The Global Politics of Gay Rights: The Straining Relations between the West and Africa," *Journal of Global Analysis* 6, no. 1 (January 2013): 21–45, https://therestjournal.com/wp-content/uploads/2019/03/JGA_Vol.6_No.1_A_2.pdf.

40. See Carol Lancaster, *Foreign Aid: Diplomacy, Development, Domestic Politics* (Chicago, IL: University of Chicago Press, 2008); Ilan Kapoor, "Foreign Aid as G(r)ift," in *The Postcolonial Politics of Development* (Routledge, 2008): 76–94; and Shamima Ahmed and David Potter, *NGOs in International Politics* (Boulder, CO: Kumarian Press, 2013).

41. Kelly Kollman, *The Same-Sex Unions Revolution in Western Democracies: International Norms and Domestic Policy Change* (Manchester: Manchester University Press, 2013).

42. Phillip M. Ayoub, "Tensions in Rights: Navigating Emerging Contradictions in the LGBT Rights Revolution," *Contesting Human Rights*, January 2019, 43–58, https://doi.org/10.4337/9781788972864.00011.

43. See ILGA's map for current laws on homosexuality globally: International Lesbian, Gay, Bisexual, Trans and Intersex Association: (ILGA), "Map: Sexual Orientation Laws in the World, 2019," ILGA, March 20, 2019, https://ilga.org/ilga-map-sexual-orientation-laws-2019.

44. Claire Felter and Danielle Renwick, "Same-Sex Marriage: Global Comparisons," Council on Foreign Relations, October 29, 2019, https://www.cfr.org/backgrounder/same-sex-marriage-global-comparisons.

45. Julie Dorf as quoted in Felter and Renwick, October 29, 2019.

46. ILGA, "Map," 2020.

47. Daniela Vazquez Loriga, "LGBT Rights in Russia: The 'Gay Propaganda' Law and Its Consequences in Chechnya," *Bellarmine Law Society Review* 11, no. 1 (2020): 1–14.

48. Thomas Hanley, "Homophobia in Poland and Hungary: Assessing Its Political Motives and Influences," in *Body Politics: What's the State Got to Do With It?*, ed. Jordan A. Pino and Konstantinos Karamanakis (Boston, MA: Boston College, 2017).

49. Frank Mugisha, "India and the Global Fight for LGBT Rights," *Foreign Policy*, January 22, 2019, https://foreignpolicy.com/gt-essay/india-and-the-global-fight-for-lgbt-rights/.

50. Ashley Currier, *Out in Africa: LGBT Organizing in Namibia and South Africa* (Minneapolis: University of Minnesota Press, 2012).

51. Maria Beatriz Bonna Nogueira, "The Promotion of LGBT Rights as International Human Rights Norms," *Global Governance*, 2017.

52. Ben Westcott, "Brunei to Punish Gay Sex and Adultery with Death by Stoning," CNN, March 30, 2019, https://www.cnn.com/2019/03/27/asia/brunei-anti-lgbt-stoning-law-intl/index.html.

53. Anne-Claire Stapleton, "Brunei's New Anti-Gay Law Goes Into Effect This Week. Here's How the World Is Reacting," CNN, March 31, 2019, https://www.cnn.com/2019/03/30/asia/brunei-lgbt-death-penalty-intl/index.html.

54. Elise Carlson-Rainer, "Khashoggi Prompts Trump to Reconsider Human Rights in Foreign Policy," *The Hill*, October 18, 2018, https://thehill.com/opinion/international/412058-khashoggi-prompts-trump-to-reconsider-human-rights-in-foreign-policy.

55. Josh Lederman, "Trump Administration Launches Global Effort to End Criminalization of Homosexuality," *NBC News*, February 19, 2019, https://www.nbcnews.com/politics/national-security/trump-administration-launches-global-effort-end-criminalization-homosexuality-n973081.

56. Valerie Hudson and Patricia Leidl, *The Hillary Doctrine: Sex and American Foreign Policy* (New York: Columbia University Press, 2015).

57. "Disparate Trends in Permissiveness: Homosexuality and Prostitution," World Values Survey, accessed May 18, 2016, http://www.worldvaluessurvey.org/WVSDocumentationWV5.jsp.

58. "Disparate Trends in Permissiveness: Homosexuality and Prostitution," World Values Survey, accessed May 18, 2016, http://www.worldvaluessurvey.org/WVSDocumentationWV5.jsp.

59. "Briefing by Special Envoy for the Human Rights of LGBTI Persons Randy Berry," Special Briefing, Office of the Spokesperson, Washington, DC, April 20, 2016, https://2009-2017.state.gov/r/pa/prs/ps/2016/04/256425.htm.

60. United Nations, "The Universal Declaration of Human Rights," 1948, http://www.un.org/en/documents/udhr/.

61. United Nations, "Human Rights," accessed September 6, 2019, https://www.un.org/en/sections/issues-depth/human-rights/.

62. Francine D'Amico, "LGBT and (Dis) United Nations," in *Sexualities in World Politics: How LGBTQ Claims Shape International Relations*, ed. Manuela Lavinas Picq and Markus Thiel (Abingdon, UK: Routledge, 2015), 54–74. See also Maria Beatriz Bonna Nogueira, "The Promotion of LGBT Rights as International Human Rights Norms," *Global Governance* 23, no. 4 (2017): 545–63, https://doi.org/10.1163/19426720-02304003.

63. International Commission of Jurists, "The Yogyakarta Principles: Principles on the Application of International Human Rights Law in Relation to Sexual Orientation and Gender Identity," 2006, http://www.yogyakartaprinciples.org/.

64. Brysk, *Global Good Samaritans*, 2009: 5.

65. See: Cynthia Weber, *Queer International Relations: Sovereignty, Sexuality and the Will to Knowledge* (Oxford: Oxford University Press, 2016); Encarnación, "The Troubled Rise of Gay Rights Diplomacy," 2016: 17.

66. Karin Aggestam and Ann Towns, "The Gender Turn in Diplomacy: A New Research Agenda," *International Feminist Journal of Politics* 21, no. 1 (June 2018): 9–28, https://doi.org/10.1080/14616742.2018.1483206.

67. Ann Towns and Birgitta Niklasson, "Gender, International Status, and Ambassador Appointments," *Foreign Policy Analysis* 13, no. 3 (2016): 521–40.

68. On Turkey, see Bahar Rumelili and Rahime Suleymanoglu-Kurum, "Women and Gender in Turkish Diplomacy: Historical Legacies and Current Patterns," in *Gendering Diplomacy and International Negotiation* (Cham: Palgrave Macmillan, 2018), 87–106. On the Netherlands, see Susanna Erlandsson, "Off the Record: Margaret van Kleffens and the Gendered History of Dutch World War II Diplomacy," *International Feminist Journal of Politics* 21, no. 1 (2019): 29–46. On France, see Harry J. Mace, "Emancipating Marianne: Gendering French Diplomacy and the Quai d'Orsay in European Context, 1944–1950" (PhD diss., University of Kent, 2017). On India, see Khushi Singh Rathore, "Where Are the Women in Indian Diplomacy?," *The Diplomat*, November 12, 2020, https://the-diplomat.com/2020/11/where-are-the-women-in-indian-diplomacy/. See also Birgitta Niklasson, "The Gendered Networking of Diplomats," *The Hague Journal of Diplomacy* 15, no. 1–2 (2020): 13–42, https://doi.org/10.1163/1871191X-BJA1 0005.

69. Ann Towns and Birgitta Niklasson, "Gender, International Status, and Ambassador Appointments," *Foreign Policy Analysis* 13, no. 3 (2017): 521–40.

70. These are hypothetical examples of LGBTI rights diplomacy. However, the example of intersectionality of programs comes from programs funded by the Global Equality Fund, as well as US case interviews #40 and 43 in this book.

71. Nilsson, Lundholm, and Vagberg, "Study on SIDA's Work," 2013.

72. Stephan Roth, Director, Alturi, *Human Rights Speakers Series—LGBT Rights Abroad*, June 7, 2016, https://www.youtube.com/watch?v=flrAPcZx0Gc.

73. Burack, *Because We Are Human*, 2018: 29.

74. Burack, *Because We Are Human*, 2018.

75. For example, see Encarnación, "The Troubled Rise of Gay Rights Diplomacy," 2016.

76. "Meet Randy Berry, The First U.S. Diplomat For LGBT Rights," *Huffington Post*: Queer Voices, April 29, 2015, https://www.huffpost.com/entry/randy-berry-lgbt-rights-diplomat_n_7173328.

77. Michael K. Lavers, "USAID-Supported Gay Training to Take Place in Colombia," *Washington Blade*, May 29, 2013, https://www.washingtonblade.com/2013/05/29/usaid-supported-gay-training-to-take-place-in-colombia/.

78. US Department of State, "Global Equality Fund."

79. US Department of State, "Global Equality Fund."

80. US Department of State, "Global Equality Fund."

81. Niall McCarthy, "Global Humanitarian Assistance: Who Are the Biggest Contributors?," *Forbes*, July 21, 2015, http://www.forbes.com/sites/niallmccarthy/

2015/07/21/global-humanitarian-assistance-who-are-the-biggest-contributors-info
graphic/#7f1b6a6769af.

82. Angelia R. Wilson, *Why Europe Is Lesbian and Gay Friendly (and Why America Never Will Be)* (Albany, NY: State University of New York Press, 2014).

83. Burack, *Because We Are Human,* 2018: 27.

84. The White House, "Presidential Memorandum—International Initiatives to Advance the Human Rights of Lesbian, Gay, Bisexual, and Transgender Persons," Office of the Press Secretary, December 6, 2011, https://obamawhitehouse.archives.gov/the-press-office/2011/12/06/presidential-memorandum-international-initiatives-advance-human-rights-l.

85. US Department of State, "Global Equality Fund."

86. Lederman, "Trump Administration Launches Global Effort to End Criminalization of Homosexuality," 2019.

87. David Forsythe, *Human Rights and Comparative Foreign Policy* (Tokyo, Japan: United Nations University Press, 2000), 8.

88. Cynthia Burack, "Sexual Orientation and Gender Identity (SOGI) Human Rights Assistance in the Time of Trump," *Politics & Gender* 14, no. 4 (2018): 561–80, https://doi.org/10.1017/s1743923x1800065x.

89. Angelia R. Wilson, *Why Europe Is Lesbian and Gay Friendly (and Why America Never Will Be)* (Albany, NY: State University of New York Press, 2014).

90. Pew Research Center, "Global Views on Morality," Global Attitudes Project, June 1, 2015, http://www.pewglobal.org/2014/04/15/global-morality/country/united-states/.

91. This research recognizes that LGBTI laws and social norms are changing rapidly in the United States. Over the course of this research, same-sex marriage became legal nationwide with the Supreme Court ruling on June 26, 2015. The laws listed above may change in the near future as well. Surveys from independent organizations such as Pew Research indicate that there is an upward trajectory of acceptance for LGBTI equality in the United States, especially among younger Americans.

92. "Growing Up LGBT in America: View and Share Statistics," Human Rights Campaign, accessed October 4, 2018, https://www.hrc.org/youth-report/view-and-share-statistics.

93. Eduard Jordaan, "South Africa and Sexual Orientation Rights at the United Nations: Batting for Both Sides," *Politikon* 44, no. 2 (2017): 205–30, https://doi.org/10.1080/02589346.2017.1284469.

94. Forsythe, *Human Rights in International Relations,* 2000: 2.

95. Bureau of Democracy, Human Rights, and Labor, "Report on International Prison Conditions," US Department of State, Washington, DC, March 22, 2013, https://2009-2017.state.gov/j/drl/rls/209944.htm.

96. World Prison Brief, "Prison Population Total," Institute for Crime & Justice Policy Research, Birkbeck, University of London, November 2018, https://www.prison-studies.org/highest-to-lowest/prison-population-total?field_region_taxonomy_tid=All.

97. "Preventing and Responding to Gender-Based Violence," US Agency for International Development, May 7, 2019, accessed October 12, 2019, https://www.usaid.gov/gbv.

98. *2016 Biennial Report*, US Department of Justice Office on Violence Against Women, Washington, DC, 2016, https://www.justice.gov/ovw/page/file/933886/download.

99. President Dwight Eisenhower Signs Executive Order 10450. Source: "Milestones in the American Gay Rights Movement," *The American Experience*, PBS, accessed November 25, 2019, http://www.pbs.org/wgbh/americanexperience/features/stonewall-milestones-american-gay-rights-movemet/.

100. David K. Johnson, *The Lavender Scare: The Cold War Persecution of Gays and Lesbians in the Federal Government* (Chicago, IL: University of Chicago Press, 2006).

101. Johnson, *The Lavender Scare,* 2006: 9.

102. "Milestones in the American Gay Rights Movement," PBS, accessed 2019.

103. "Milestones in the American Gay Rights Movement," PBS, accessed 2019.

104. "History," GLIFAA, February 7, 2014, https://glifaa.org/archive/history-long/.

105. John Kerry, "Apology for Past Discrimination toward Employees and Applicants Based on Sexual Orientation," US Department of State, Washington, DC, January 9, 2017, https://2009-2017.state.gov/secretary/remarks/2017/01/266711.htm.

106. Kerry, "Apology," 2017.

107. Kerry, "Apology," 2017.

108. Jeff Sharlet, "Letter from Kampala: Straight Man's Burden," *Harper's Magazine*, September 2010, https://harpers.org/archive/2010/09/straight-mans-burden/.

109. "The Anti-Homosexuality Act," Ugandan government, 2014, https://www.refworld.org/pdfid/530c4bc64.pdf?fbclid=IwAR0r_ZCq2az0HsiSbQmm9wyJMc3Vj33bZZ22y_cWtlaN_U8GirNeCoa6sw8,%201-11%20(2014).

110. "Uganda Kill the Gays Bill," *Huffington Post*, 2009–2016.

111. See, for example, Barbara Bompani, "'For God and for My Country': Pentecostal-Charismatic Churches and the Framing of a New Political Discourse in Uganda," in *Public Religion and the Politics of Homosexuality in Africa* (Routledge, 2016), 19–34. Or Amar Wahab, "'Homosexuality/Homophobia Is Un-African'?: Un-Mapping Transnational Discourses in the Context of Uganda's Anti-Homosexuality Bill/Act," *Journal of Homosexuality* 63, no. 5 (2016): 685–718, https://doi.org/10.1080/00918369.2015.1111105.

112. Kristien Stassen, Roel Smolders, and Pieter Leroy, "Sensitizing Events as Trigger for Discursive Renewal and Institutional Change in Flanders' Environmental Health Approach, 1970s–1990s," *Environmental Health* 12, no. 46 (June 2013), https://doi.org10.1186/1476-069X-12-46.

113. Martin Heidenreich, "The Renewal of Regional Capabilities: Experimental Regionalism in Germany," *Research Policy* 34, no. 5 (June 2005): 739–57, https://doi.org/10.1016/j.respol.2005.04.004.

114. "Sweden Reconsidering Aid to Uganda," Sveriges Radio, February 24, 2014, https://sverigesradio.se/artikel/5793295.

115. "Statement by NSC Spokesperson Caitlin Hayden on the Response to Uganda's Enactment of the Anti-Homosexuality Act," Office of the Press Secretary, The White House, June 19, 2014, https://obamawhitehouse.archives.gov/the-press-office/2014/06/19/statement-nsc-spokesperson-cailin-hayden-response-uganda-s-enactment-an.

116. Omar G. Encarnación, "Trump and Gay Rights," *Foreign Affairs*, March 31, 2017, https://www.foreignaffairs.com/chapters/2017-02-13/trump-and-gay-rights.

117. Lederman, "Trump Administration Launches Global Effort to End Criminalization of Homosexuality," 2019.

118. Rex Tillerson, "Transgender Day of Remembrance," US Department of State, Washington, DC, November 20, 2017, https://uy.usembassy.gov/rex-w-tillerson-statement-transgender-day-remembrance/.

119. Trudy Ring, "Secretary of State Rex Tillerson Recognizes Transgender Day of Remembrance," *Advocate*, November 20, 2017, https://www.advocate.com/transgender/2017/11/20/secretary-state-rex-tillerson-recognizes-transgender-day-remembrance.

120. John Hudson, "Trump Keeps Obama's Top Gay Rights Envoy at State Department," *Foreign Policy*, February 13, 2017, http://foreignpolicy.com/2017/02/13/trump-keeps-obamas-top-gay-rights-envoy-at-state-department/.

121. Christine Ingebritsen, *Scandinavia in World Politics* (Lanham, MD: Rowman and Littlefield Publishers, 2006).

122. Brysk, *Global Good Samaritans,* 2009.

123. Note: This analysis examines governments that have formally incorporated LGBTI rights in their diplomatic pillars. Other nations such as South Africa, Brazil, and the Netherlands raised LGBTI abuses in the UN early on, but did not have LGBTI rights as a part of their formal policy, programmatic, and funding streams within their foreign policy institutions.

124. The Dutch Ministry of Foreign Affairs formally commenced international work in LGBTI rights in 2007. Source: Dutch Government, "Simply Gay: Dutch Government's LGBT Policy Document 2008–2011," The Hague, Netherlands, November 9, 2007, http://www.globalequality.org/storage/documents/pdf/simply%20gay_%20dutch%20lgbt%20policy.pdf.

125. "Human Rights Based Approach at SIDA: Rights of LGBTI Persons," Swedish International Development Agency (SIDA), September 2015, https://www.sida.se/English/partners/resources-for-all-partners/methodological-materials/human-rights-based-approach-at-sida/rights-of-lgbti-persons/.

126. "Feminist Foreign Policy," Swedish Ministry for Foreign Affairs, accessed May 14, 2019, https://www.government.se/government-policy/feminist-foreign-policy/. See also Karin Aggestam and Annika Bergman-Rosamond, "Swedish Feminist Foreign Policy in the Making: Ethics, Politics, and Gender," *Ethics & International Affairs* 30, no. 3 (2016): 323–34.

127. Jenny Nordberg, "Who's Afraid of a Feminist Foreign Policy?" *New Yorker*, April 15, 2015, http://www.newyorker.com/news/news-desk/swedens-feminist-foreign-minister.

128. Adam Tailor, "Sweden Stood Up for Human Rights in Saudi Arabia. This Is How Saudi Arabia Is Punishing Sweden," *Washington Post*, March 20, 2015, https://www.washingtonpost.com/news/worldviews/wp/2015/03/20/sweden-stood-up-for-human-rights-in-saudi-arabia-this-is-how-saudi-arabia-is-punishing-sweden/.

129. Swedish Ministry of Foreign Affairs, "Sweden Is Taking a Proactive Role in International LGBT Efforts," 2013.

130. Kyoung-Hee Moon, Kyung-Ock Chun, Mi-Sung Kim, and Eun-Kyung Kim, "A Comparative Study of Electoral Gender Quotas in Sweden, Germany, and South Korea," *Asian Women* 28, no. 1 (2008): 75–100, https://doi.org/10.14431/aw.2008.03.24.1.75.

131. "Sweden and Gender Equality," Swedish government, April 10, 2019, https://sweden.se/society/gender-equality-in-sweden/.

132. Sue Duke, "The Key to Closing the Gender Gap? Putting More Women in Charge," World Economic Forum, November 2, 2017, https://www.weforum.org/agenda/2017/11/women-leaders-key-to-workplace-equality/.

133. Susan Dicklitch-Nelson, Scottie Thompson Buckland, Berwood Yost, and Daniel Draguljić, "From Persecutors to Protectors: Human Rights and the F&M Global Barometer of Gay Rights TM(GBGR)," *Journal of Human Rights* 18, no. 1 (2019): 1–18, https://doi.org/10.1080.14754835.2018.1563863.

134. "Working for a Gay-Friendly Sweden," Swedish Ministry for Foreign Affairs, accessed May 19, 2016, https://sweden.se/society/working-for-a-gay-and-equal-sweden/.

135. Jeff Hearn, Sofia Strid, Lisa Husu, and Mieke Verloo, "Interrogating Violence against Women and State Violence Policy: Gendered Intersectionalities and the Quality of Policy in the Netherlands, Sweden and the UK," *Current Sociology* 64, no. 4 (November 2016): 551–67.

136. Tom Smith, Jaesok Son, and Jibum Kim, "Public Attitudes towards Homosexuality and Gay Rights across Time and Countries," The Williams Institute: UCLA School of Law, November 2014, https://williamsinstitute.law.ucla.edu/research/international/public-attitudes-nov-2014/.

137. "Sweden and Human Rights," Swedish government, accessed 2018, https://sweden.se/society/sweden-and-human-rights/.

138. Joke Swiebel, "Lesbian, Gay, Bisexual, and Transgender Human Rights: The Search for an International Strategy," *Contemporary Politics* 15, no. 1 (2009): 26.

139. Brysk, *Global Good Samaritans,* 2009: 42.

140. Ingebritsen, *Scandinavia in World Politics,* 2006: 2.

141. Ingebritsen, *Scandinavia in World Politics,* 2006: 2.

142. Kati Mustola and Jens Rydström, *Criminally Queer: Homosexuality and Criminal Law in Scandinavia, 1842–1999* (Amsterdam, Netherlands: Aksant, 2007).

143. Brysk, *Global Good Samaritans,* 2009: 4.

144. Myrdal, Gunnar (1945) as cited by Brysk, *Global Good Samaritans,* 2009: 61.

145. Brysk, *Global Good Samaritans,* 2009: 59.

146. Brysk, *Global Good Samaritans,* 2009: 42.

147. Brysk, *Global Good Samaritans,* 2009: 4.

148. The acronym comes from the Swedish name Riksförbundet för homosexuellas, bisexuellas och transpersoners rättigheter (RFSL).

149. See Kathryn Sikkink, "Patterns of Dynamic Multilevel Governance and the Insider-Outsider Coalition," in *Transnational Protest and Global Activism* (Oxford: Rowman and Littlefield Publishers, 2004), 151–73; and Rebecca Neaera Abers and Luciana Tatagiba, "Institutional Activism: Mobilizing for Women's Health from Inside the Brazilian Bureaucracy," in *Social Movement Dynamics* (New York: Routledge, 2016), 72–101.

150. Swedish case interview #5, Stockholm, Sweden, August 13, 2015.

151. Swedish case interview #4, Stockholm, Sweden, July 31, 2015.

152. Alfred de Zayas, "UN Independent Expert Reports on World Bank and IMF Human Rights Performance," Brettonwoods Project, September 27, 2017, https://www.brettonwoodsproject.org/2017/09/un-independent-expert-reports-world-bank-imf-human-rights-performance/.

153. The American-based Millennium Challenge Corporation doles out foreign aid when countries meet certain democracy and human rights standards. Source: "Reducing Poverty through Growth," Millennium Challenge Corporation, accessed December 19, 2019, https://www.mcc.gov/.

154. See "Working for the Rights of Lesbian, Gay, Bisexual, Trans and Intersex People in the European Parliament," European Parliament's LGBTI Intergroup, accessed December 19, 2019, lgbti-ep.eu.

155. Annika Nilsson and Jessica Rothman, "Evaluation of the Sida Supported RFSL Projects 'LGBT Voices' and 'Rainbow Leaders,'" SIDA, Stockholm, Sweden, 2017, https://www.sida.se/contentassets/a09863bdac41467ea541a12e2160caf5/22051.pdf.

156. For examples, see Barbara Hobson, *Recognition Struggles and Social Movements* (Cambridge: Cambridge University Press, 2003). Or Amy Elman, *Sexual Subordination and the State: Comparing Sweden and the United States* (New York: Berghahn Publishers, 1996).

157. Elman, *Sexual Subordination and the State,* 1996.

158. Amnesty International currently does not accept government funding, stating, "Amnesty International is funded by dedicated individual supporters and foundations to safeguard our objectivity and ensure that our research is not funded by governments and corporations." Source: "Who We Are," Amnesty International, accessed April 5, 2016, http://www.amnestyusa.org/about-us/who-we-are.

159. Laurel Weldon, *When Protest Makes Policy: How Social Movements Represent Disadvantaged Groups* (Ann Arbor: University of Michigan Press, 2012).

160. "Growing Up LGBT in America," Human Rights Campaign, accessed 2018, https://www.hrc.org/resources/lgbtq-youth-report/view-and-share-statistics?ftag=MSF 0951a18.

161. "The American-Western European Values Gap: American Exceptionalism Subsides," Global Attitudes Project, Pew Research Center, February 29, 2012, http://www.pewglobal.org/2011/11/17/the-american-western-european-values-gap/#homosexuality.

162. Karin Aggestam and Annika Bergman-Rosamond, "Swedish Feminist Foreign Policy in the Making: Ethics, Politics, and Gender," *Ethics & International Affairs* 30, no. 3 (2016): 323–34.

163. Elżbieta Drążkiewicz-Grodzicka, " 'State Bureaucrats' and 'Those NGO People': Promoting the Idea of Civil Society, Hindering the State," *Critique of Anthropology* 36, no. 4 (2016): 341–62.

164. Kati Mustola and Jens Rydström, "Criminally Queer: Homosexuality and Criminal Law in Scandinavia, 1842–1999" (Amsterdam, Netherlands: Aksant, 2007), 23. And David Johnson, *The Lavender Scare: The Cold War Persecution of Gays and Lesbians in the Federal Government* (Chicago, IL: University of Chicago Press, 2006).

165. Note: South Africa, Sweden, Norway, Brazil, and other nations raised LGBTI abuses starting around the 1990s mainly related to the HIV/AIDS crisis in global venues. The distinction here in 2011 is that Sweden and the United States formally incorporated LGBTI rights into their foreign policy mandates. Accordingly, this was the first time Sweden cut aid in formal bilateral relations based on the praxis of LGBTI rights abuses.

166. Kristen Cheney, "Locating Neocolonialism, 'Tradition,' and Human Rights in Uganda's 'Gay Death Penalty,' " *African Studies Review* 55, no. 2 (2012): 77–95.

167. Stassen et al., 2013.

168. See, for example, Themal Ellawala, "Legitimating Violences: The 'Gay Rights' NGO and the Disciplining of the Sri Lankan Queer Figure," *Journal of South Asian Development* 14, no. 1 (2019): 83–107. Or Matthew Waites, "LGBT and Queer Politics in the Commonwealth," in *Oxford Research Encyclopedia of Politics*, 2019.

169. Havard Bergo, "Has Foreign Aid Led to Economic Growth in Uganda?," *Global Risk Insights*, May 18, 2015, https://globalriskinsights.com/2015/05/has-foreign-aid-led-to-economic-growth-in-uganda/.

170. Deborah Kintu, "The Ugandan Morality Crusade: The Brutal Campaign against Homosexuality and Pornography under Yoweri Museveni" (McFarland, 2017).

171. Rachel Bergenfield and Alice Miller, March 2014; Currier 2012.

172. See Omar G. Encarnación, "The Troubled Rise of Gay Rights Diplomacy," *Current History* 115, no. 777 (January 2016): 17.

173. Chris Johnson, "Dan Baer: Time for U.S. to Change Its Relationship with Saudi Arabia," *Washington Blade*, July 9, 2019, https://www.washingtonblade.com/2019/07/09/dan-baer-time-for-u-s-to-change-its-relationship-with-saudi-arabia/.

174. Tim Dunne and Nicholas J. Wheeler, "Great Illusions or Great Transformations? Human Rights and International Relations a Hundred Years On," *International Relations* 33, no. 2 (2019): 338–56.

175. Rein Müllerson, *Human Rights Diplomacy* (New York: Routledge, 2014).

176. Rein Müllerson, 1997: 5; Daniel Mahanty, "Realists, Too, Can Stand for Human Rights," *National Interest*, 2013, http://nationalinterest.org/commentary/realists-too-can-stand-human-rights-9208. See the State Department's Bureau of Democracy, Human Rights and Labor: https://www.state.gov/j/drl/.

177. Bureau of Democracy, Human Rights and Labor, "Country Reports on Human Rights Practices," US Department of State, https://www.state.gov/reports/2018-country-reports-on-human-rights-practices/.

178. ILGA Europe headquarters is in Brussels, Belgium. Source: "LGBTI Equality and Human Rights in Europe and Central Asia," ILGA Europe, accessed December 19, 2019, http://www.ilga-europe.org/.

Chapter 2

1. Hillary Clinton, "Hillary Clinton's Address in Geneva on International Human Rights Day," US Department of State Global Public Affairs, December 6, 2011, http://translations.state.gov/st/english/texttrans/2011/12/20111206180616su0.4842885.html#ixzz3KP317fJN.

2. See, for example, Jonathan Symons and Dennis Altman, "International Norm Polarization: Sexuality as a Subject of Human Rights Protection," *International Theory* 7 (2015): 61–95; Anthony J. Langlois, "Queer Rights?," *Australian Journal of International Affairs*, 71, no. 3 (2017): 241–46.

3. See "Reports on Human Rights Practices," US Department of State Bureau of Democracy, Human Rights and Labor Country, accessed February 16, 2016, http://www.state.gov/j/drl/rls/hrrpt/humanrightsreport/index.htm#wrapper.

4. "Global Equality Fund," US Department of State Bureau of Democracy, Human Rights and Labor, accessed April 26, 2021, http://www.state.gov/globalequality/about/index.htm.

5. Barack Obama, "Presidential Memorandum: International Initiatives to Advance the Human Rights of Lesbian, Gay, Bisexual, and Transgender Persons," Office of the Press Secretary, December 6, 2011, https://obamawhitehouse.archives.gov/the-press-office/2011/12/06/presidential-memorandum-international-initiatives-advance-human-rights-l.

6. Bureau of Democracy, Human Rights and Labor, US Department of State, accessed February 16, 2016, http://www.state.gov/j/drl/.

7. For further context on internal State Department LGBTI policies, see Elise Carlson-Rainer, "Trump's New LGBTI Policy Contradicts U.S. Human Rights Diplomacy," *Washington Diplomat*, October 31, 2018, https://washdiplomat.com/op-ed-trumps-new-lgbti-policy-contradicts-us-human-rights-diplomacy/.

8. Omar G. Encarnación, "Clinton's Legacy on Gay Rights: From Skeptic to Supporter," *Foreign Affairs*, June 16, 2016, https://www.foreignaffairs.com/articles/2016-06-16/clintons-legacy-gay-rights/.

9. Associated Press in Warsaw, "Obama Uses Embassies to Push for LGBT Rights Abroad," *The Guardian*, June 28, 2014, https://www.theguardian.com/world/2014/jun/28/obama-gay-rights-abroad-embassies-activism.

10. "Remarks by John Kerry Announcing the Appointment of Special Envoy for the Human Rights of LGBT Persons, Randy Berry," US Department of State, February 23, 2015, http://www.state.gov/secretary/remarks/2015/02/237772.htm.

11. Michael K. Lavers, "Advancing Obama's LGBT Rights Agenda Abroad," *Washington Blade*, July 23, 2014, https://www.washingtonblade.com/2014/07/23/retired-u-n-official-leads-usaid-lgbt-initiatives/.

12. David K. Johnson, *The Lavender Scare: The Cold War Persecution of Gays and Lesbians in the Federal Government* (Chicago, IL: University of Chicago Press, 2004), 3.

13. See, for example, Peter Stanley Federman and Nicole M. Rishel Elias, "Beyond the Lavender Scare: LGBT and Heterosexual Employees in the Federal Workplace," *Public Integrity* 19, no. 1 (2017): 22–40.

14. Johnson 2004: 9.

15. Johnson 2004: 56.

16. US case study interview #69, Washington, DC, November 28, 2016; #70, Seattle, Washington, March 6, 2017.

17. Colin Dueck, "The Future of Conservative Foreign Policy," *Texas National Security Review* 2, no. 1 (2018): 171–76, https://tnsr.org/roundtable/the-future-of-conservative-foreign-policy/.

18. Lederman, 2019.

19. Linda Grimm, "President Trump Announces Transgender Military Ban," *Historic Documents of 2017*, ed. Heather Kerrigan (Thousand Oaks, CA: CQ Press, 2018), 398–404.

20. For example, in North Carolina, see Avianne Tan, "North Carolina's Controversial 'Anti-LGBT' Bill Explained," *ABC News*, March 24, 2016, http://abcnews.go.com/US/north-carolinas-controversial-anti-lgbt-bill-explained/story?id=37898153.

21. "Growing Up LGBT in America," Human Rights Campaign, accessed February 8, 2019, https://www.hrc.org/youth-report/view-and-share-statistics.

22. "Views on Gay Rights by Political Affiliation in the U.S.," Gallup Statista 2015, accessed February 8, 2019, http://www.statista.com/statistics/226165/views-on-gay-rights-by-political-affiliation-in-the-us/.

23. "Americans' Moral Stance towards Gay or Lesbian Relations in 2019," Statista Research Department, September 8, 2020, https://www.statista.com/statistics/225968/americans-moral-stance-towards-gay-or-lesbian-relations/.

24. These numbers and figures are changing rapidly; they are not stagnant. The presentation here focuses on recent studies from the Pew Research Center, World Values Survey, and Gallup in 2011–2012, the year the State Department formally incorporated LGBTI diplomacy in foreign affairs.

25. "The American-Western European Values Gap: American Exceptionalism Subsides," Pew Research Center, Global Attitudes and Trends, November 17, 2011, updated February 29, 2012, http://www.pewglobal.org/2011/11/17/the-american-western-european-values-gap/#homosexuality.

26. Graph is shown in the introduction chapter. Source: World Values Survey, accessed September 24, 2014, http://www.worldvaluessurvey.org/WVSContents.jsp.

27. "Global Views on Morality," Pew Research Center's Global Attitudes Project, April 2014, http://www.pewglobal.org/2014/04/15/global-morality/country/united-states/.

28. Angelia R. Wilson, "Why Europe Is Lesbian and Gay Friendly (and Why America Never Will Be)," in *Queer Politics and Cultures* (Albany, NY: State University of New York Press, 2013), 1–18.

29. Phillip Ayoub, "Tensions in Rights: Navigating Emerging Contradictions in the LGBT Rights Revolution," in *Contesting Human Rights* (Cheltenham, UK: Edward Elgar Publishing, 2019).

30. US interview #41, Seattle, Washington, January 19, 2016; #43, Washington, DC, January 15, 2016.

31. Samantha Power, *The Education of an Idealist* (New York: HarperCollins Books, 2019): 276.

32. "Fiscal Year 2019: An American Budget, Budget of the U.S. Government," Office of Management and Budget (Washington, DC, 2019): 79–84.

33. "Congressional Budget Justification: Department of State, Foreign Operations, and Related Programs Fiscal Year 2019," Office of the Secretary of State (Washington, DC, 2019): 1–3.

34. Participant observation #65, Seattle, Washington, January 27, 2016.

35. David Forsythe, *Human Rights in International Relations*, 3rd ed. (Cambridge: Cambridge University Press, 2012).

36. Rein Müllerson, *Human Rights Diplomacy* (London: Routledge, 1997), 71.

37. Müllerson 1997: 71.

38. See, for example, Ilan Kapoor, "Foreign Aid as G(r)ift," *The Postcolonial Politics of Development* (London: Routledge, 2008), 76–94.

39. US case interview #41, Seattle, Washington, January 19, 2016; US case interview #65, Seattle, Washington, January 27, 2016.

40. "Bureau of Democracy, Human Rights, and Labor—United States Department of State," US Department of State, 2019, https://www.state.gov/bureaus-offices/under-secretary-for-civilian-security-democracy-and-human-rights/bureau-of-democracy-human-rights-and-labor/.

41. David F. Schmitz and Vanessa Walker, "Jimmy Carter and the Foreign Policy of Human Rights: The Development of a Post-Cold War Foreign Policy," *Diplomatic History* 28, no. 1 (2004): 113–43.

42. Jimmy Carter, Speech on Humane Purposes in Foreign Policy Carter Humane Foreign Policy, 1977, accessed November 2, 2014, http://www.third-worldtraveler.com/Human%20Rights%20Documents/Carter_HumaneFP.html.

43. Note: These reports are discussed further at length in the "Targeted Institutional Advocacy" section.

"2018 Country Reports on Human Rights Practices," US Department of State, March 13, 2019, https://www.state.gov/reports/2018-country-reports-on-human-rights-practices/; "2019 Trafficking in Persons Report," US Department of State, June 20, 2019, https://www.state.gov/trafficking-in-persons-report-2019/; "2018 Report on International Religious Freedom," US Department of State, June 21, 2019, https://www.state.gov/reports/2018-report-on-international-religious-freedom/; "International Child Labor & Forced Labor Reports," US Department of Labor Bureau of International Labor Affairs, 2019, https://www.dol.gov/agencies/ilab/resources/reports/child-labor.

44. Judith Innes de Neufville, "Human Rights Reporting as a Policy Tool: An Examination of the State Department Country Reports," *Human Rights Quarterly* 8 (1986): 681.

45. Moon Charania, "Outing The Pakistani Queer: Pride, Paranoia and Politics in U.S. Visual Culture," *Sexualities* 20, no. 1–2 (2017): 41–64.

46. Associated Press in Warsaw, "Obama Uses Embassies to Push for LGBT Rights Abroad," *The Guardian*, June 28, 2014, https://www.theguardian.com/world/2014/jun/28/obama-gay-rights-abroad-embassies-activism.

47. Adam Nossiter, "Senegal Cheers Its President for Standing Up to Obama on Same-Sex Marriage," *New York Times,* June 28, 2013, https://www.nytimes.com/2013/06/29/world/africa/senegal-cheers-its-president-for-standing-up-to-obama-on-same-sex-marriage.html.

48. See, for example, Ilan Kapoor, "Foreign Aid as G(r)ift," in *The Postcolonial Politics of Development* (New York: Routledge, 2008), 76–94. Or A. Van Klinken, "Sexual Orientation, (Anti-) Discrimination and Human Rights in a 'Christian Nation': The Politicization of Homosexuality in Zambia," *Critical African Studies* 9, no. 1 (2017): 9–31.

49. Anthony Weber Chase, "Human Rights Contestations: Sexual Orientation and Gender Identity," *The International Journal of Human Rights* 20, no. 6 (2016): 703–23. See also A. J. Langlois, "International Relations Theory and Global Sexuality Politics," *Politics* 36, no. 4 (2016): 385–99.

50. Picq and Thiel, 2015; Rahman, 2014: 75.

51. See Arvind Narrain, Adrian Jjuuko, Monica Tabengwa, Gary Kinsman, Amar Wahab, Pere DeRoy, Namela Baynes Henry, et al., "Envisioning Global LGBT Human Rights: (Neo) Colonialism, Neoliberalism, Resistance and Hope," Human Rights Consortium, School of Advanced Study, University of London, 2018. Or Kristen Cheney, "Locating Neocolonialism, 'Tradition,' and Human Rights in Uganda's 'Gay Death Penalty,'" *African Studies Review* 55, no. 2 (2012): 77–95.

52. US case participant observation #65, Seattle, Washington, January 27, 2016.

53. US case study interview #53, New York, January 13, 2016; and #59, New York, January 29, 2016.

54. For an overview of realpolitik, see John Bew, *Realpolitik: A History* (Oxford: Oxford University Press, 2016).

55. Henry Kissinger, 1973. As cited by Roberta Cohen, "Integrating Human Rights in U.S. Foreign Policy: The History, the Challenges, and the Criteria for an Effective Policy," Speech at Brookings Foreign Service Institute, Brookings Institution, Washington, DC, 2008: 2. http://www.brookings.edu/~/media/research/files/speeches/2008/4/human-rights-cohen/04_human_rights_cohen.pdf.

56. Alison Brysk, *Global Good Samaritans: Human Rights as Foreign Policy* (Oxford: Oxford University Press, 2009); Christine Ingebritsen, Iver Neumann, Siegline Gstohl, and Jessica Beyer, *Small States in International Relations* (Seattle: University of Washington Press, 2006); Audie Klotz, *Norms in International Relations* (Ithaca, NY: Cornell University Press, 1999.

57. Trine Flockhart, "Constructivism and Foreign Policy," in *Foreign Policy: Theories, Actors, Cases*, ed. Steve Smith, Amelia Hadfield, and Timothy Dunne (Oxford: Oxford University Press, 2016), 84.

58. Klotz, 1999: 15.

59. Brysk, 2009: 4.

60. Cohen, 2008: 2.

61. Steven G. Calabresi, "A Shining City on a Hill: American Exceptionalism and the Supreme Court's Practice of Relying on Foreign Law," *Boston University Law Review* 86 (2006): 1335–1416.

62. Joshua W. Busby, *Moral Movements and Foreign Policy* (Cambridge: Cambridge University Press, 2010).

63. "International Principles Relating to Sexual Orientation and Gender Identity," The Yogyakarta Principles, 2006, http://www.yogyakartaprinciples.org/.

64. "Reflections on the Obama Administration's Human Rights Policies and the Way Forward," Council on Foreign Relations, March 4, 2013, https://www.cfr.org/event/reflections-obama-administrations-human-rights-policies-and-way-forward.

65. Corneliu Bjola and Markus Kornprobst, *Understanding International Diplomacy: Theory, Practice and Ethics* (New York: Routledge, 2018).

66. David C. Mulford, US Ambassador to India, "Issue of Gujarat Chief Minister Narendra Modi's Visa Status," US Embassy New Delhi, March 21, 2005, https://2001-2009.state.gov/p/sca/rls/rm/2005/43701.htm.

67. See, for example, Ekrem Yaşar Akçay and Selim Kanat, "Carrot and Stick Approach in International Relations: An Evaluation Throughout Turkey's Accession Negotiations with the European Union," *Süleyman Demirel Üniversitesi Sosyal Bilimler Enstitüsü Dergisi* 31 (2017): 1–22. Or Thomas Conzelmann, "Beyond the Carrot and the Stick: State Reporting Procedures in the World Trade Organization and

the Organization for Economic Cooperation and Development," in *International Organizations and Implementation* (New York: Routledge, 2007), 57–69.

68. "Global Equality Fund," US Department of State Bureau of Democracy, Human Rights and Labor, accessed April 10, 2019, http://www.state.gov/global equality/about/index.htm.

69. "Global Equality Fund—"Dignity for All": LGBTI Emergency Assistance Program," US Department of State Bureau of Democracy, Human Rights and Labor, accessed October 8, 2019, http://www.state.gov/globalequality/about/index.htm.

70. Julie Moreau and Ashley Currier, "Queer Dilemmas: LGBT Activism and International Funding," in *Routledge Handbook of Queer Development Studies*, ed. Corinne L. Mason (New York: Routledge, 2018): 223–38.

71. Burack, 2018: 27.

72. "Advancing LGBTI-Inclusive Development," USAID, 2018, accessed January 21, 2020, https://www.usaid.gov/LGBTI.

73. USAID, 2018.

74. "LGBTI Programs: The LGBTI Global Development Partnership," USAID, accessed April 23, 2021, https://www.usaid.gov/what-we-do/democracy-human-rights-and-governance/protecting-human-rights/lgbti-programs.

75. "LGBTI Programs: The LGBTI Global Development Partnership," USAID, accessed October 8, 2019, https://www.usaid.gov/what-we-do/democracy-human-rights-and-governance/protecting-human-rights/lgbti-programs.

76. M. Tremblay, D. Paternotte, and C. Johnson, *The Lesbian and Gay Movement and the State: Comparative Insights into a Transformed Relationship* (Burlington, VT: Ashgate Publishing Company, 2011).

77. "Human Rights: The Gay Divide," *Economist*, October 11, 2014, http://www.economist.com/news/leaders/21623668-victories-gay-rights-some-parts-world-have-provoked-backlash-elsewhere-gay.

78. Johnson, 2004: 214.

79. "The American Experience: Milestones in the American Gay Rights Movement," PBS, 2011, http://www.pbs.org/wgbh/americanexperience/features/timeline/stonewall/.

80. "The American Experience: Milestones in the American Gay Rights Movement," PBS, 2011, http://www.pbs.org/wgbh/americanexperience/features/timeline/stonewall/.

81. Note: All interviews in this research have been made anonymous. US case interview #65, Seattle, Washington, January 27, 2016.

82. Laurel Weldon, *When Protest Makes Policy: How Social Movements Represent Disadvantaged Groups* (Ann Arbor: University of Michigan Press, 2012), 6.

83. Weldon, 2012.

84. Charles Tilly and Lesley Wood, *Social Movements 1768–2012*, 3rd ed. (Boulder, CO: Paradigm, 2013), 4.

85. Hobson, 2003: 3; Weldon, 2012; Doug McAdam, Sidney Tarrow, and Charles Tilly, *Dynamics of Contention* (Cambridge: Cambridge University Press, 2001).

86. See, for example, Jacob Richards, "From One to Windsor: Sixty Years of the Movement for LGBT Rights," *GPSolo* 31 (2014): 35. Or Marc Stein, "Theoretical Politics, Local Communities: The Making of US LGBT Historiography," *GLQ: A Journal of Lesbian and Gay Studies* 11, no. 4 (2005): 605–25.

87. Johnson 2004: 211.

88. Johnson 2004: 123. As cited, President Dwight Eisenhower signs Executive Order 10450.

89. Heather Hines, "The LGBT Community Responds: The Lavender Scare and the Creation of Midwestern Gay and Lesbian Publications" (PhD diss., Bowling Green State University, 2017).

90. For a succinct synopsis of the timeline of the US domestic policy changes, see "American Experience: Milestones in the American Gay Rights Movement," PBS, 2011, http://www.pbs.org/wgbh/americanexperience/features/timeline/stonewall/.

91. US interview #47, San Francisco, California, February 10, 2016.

92. US interview #43, Washington, DC, February 5, 2016.

93. US case #42, Seattle, Washington, May 13, 2015; #43, Washington, DC, February 5, 2016; #45, Seattle, Washington, March 6, 2015.

94. US case interview #47, San Francisco, California, February 10, 2016.

95. France, 2012.

96. Joachim, 2007; Weldon, 2012; Hobson, 2003.

97. For example, see Bretton A. Varga, Terence A. Beck, and Stephen J. Thornton, "Celebrating Stonewall at 50: A Culturally Geographic Approach to Introducing LGBT Themes," *The Social Studies* (2019): 1–10.

98. US interview #43, Washington, DC, February 5, 2016.

99. "UN: General Assembly Statement Affirms Rights for All: 66 States Condemn Violations Based on Sexual Orientation and Gender Identity," Human Rights Watch, December 18, 2008, https://www.hrw.org/news/2008/12/18/un-general-assembly-statement-affirms-rights-all.

100. US interview #51, Portland, Oregon, February 14, 2015; and #43, Washington, DC, February 5, 2016.

101. US interview #43, Washington, DC, February 5, 2016.

102. US interview #43, Washington, DC, February 5, 2016.

103. Amy Elman, *Sexual Subordination and the State; Comparing Sweden and the United States* (New York: Berghahn Publishers, 1996).

104. US case interview #67, San Francisco, California, February 12, 2016.

105. US case interview #42, Seattle, Washington, May 13, 2015.

106. Margaret E. Keck and Kathryn Sikkink, *Activists beyond Borders: Advocacy Networks in International Politics* (Ithaca, NY: Cornell University Press, 1998): 19.

107. Amie Bishop and Anthony Adero, "Global LGBTQI Movements, Human Rights, and Health: Notes from the Frontlines," Western Washington University Fairhaven College of Interdisciplinary Studies, World Issues Forum, May 10, 2016, https://cedar.wwu.edu/fairhaven_wif/2016-2017/2016-2017/2/.

108. Bob 2009: 52; Busby 2010: 34.

109. Bob 2009: 53.

110. Bob, 2009: 4; Joachim, 2007: 6.

111. US case interview #41, Seattle, Washington, January 19, 2016; #45, Seattle, Washington, March 6, 2015; #47, San Francisco, California, February 10, 2016; #61, Seattle, Washington, December 3, 2014.

112. Becker, 2013: 218.

113. Keck and Sikkink, 1998: 27.

114. See, for example, Charlotte Knight and Kath Wilson, "International Perspectives on the Rights and Criminalization of LGBT People," in *Lesbian, Gay, Bisexual and Trans People (LGBT) and the Criminal Justice System* (London: Palgrave Macmillan, 2016): 207–31.

115. US case interview #47, San Francisco, California, February 10, 2016.

116. US case interview #47, San Francisco, California, February 10, 2016.

117. Johnson, 2004: 6.

118. Jessica Toops, "The Lavender Scare: Persecution of Lesbianism during the Cold War," *Western Illinois Historical Review* 5 (2013): 91–107.

119. Zehra F. Arat, Kabasakal, and Caryl Nuñez, "Advancing LGBT Rights in Turkey: Tolerance or Protection?," *Human Rights Review* 18, no. 1 (2017): 1–19.

120. US case interview #47, San Francisco, California, February 10, 2016; and #41, Seattle, Washington, January 19, 2016.

121. Note: "gender identity" came later in time.

122. "LGBT Rights Framework," Human Rights Watch, accessed April 22, 2021, https://www.hrw.org/topic/lgbt-rights; "Gender, Sexuality, & Identity Framework," Amnesty International, accessed April 27, 2021, https://www.amnestyusa.org/issues/gender-sexuality-identity/.

123. US case interview #67, San Francisco, California, February 12, 2016.

124. US case interview #41, Seattle, Washington, January 19, 2016.

125. US case interview #40, Washington, DC, January 15, 2016.

126. Bob, 2009: 61.

127. This rubric is largely predicated on the UN Declaration of Human Rights.

128. US interview #40, Washington, DC, January 15, 2016.

129. Edwin Amenta, Kenneth T. Andrews, and Neal Caren, "The Political Institutions, Processes, and Outcomes Movements Seek to Influence," in *The Wiley Blackwell Companion to Social Movements* (Oxford: Wiley Blackwell, 2018), 447–65.

130. Sabine Lang, *NGOs, Civil Society, and the Public Sphere* (Cambridge: Cambridge University Press, 2013), 22.

131. Lang, 2013: 22–23.

132. For an overview of asylum claims in the US based on sexual orientation, see Kimberly D. Topel, "So, What Should I Ask Him to Prove That He's Gay: How Sincerity, and Not Stereotype, Should Dictate the Outcome of an LGB Asylum Claim in the United States," *Iowa Law Review* 102 (2017): 2357–84.

133. Matter of Toboso-Alfonso 20 I&N Dec. 819 (BIA 1994); discussed in Hollis V. Pfitsch, "Homosexuality in Asylum and Constitutional Law: Rhetoric of Acts and Identity," in *Law & Sexuality: A Review of Lesbian, Gay, Bisexual, and Transgender Legal Issues* 15 (2006): 59–90.

134. For US State Department annual human rights reports, see http://www.state.gov/j/drl/rls/hrrpt/.

135. "Report: Brazil Human Rights Practices, 1993," US Department of State, January 31, 1994, http://dosfan.lib.uic.edu/ERC/democracy/1993_hrp_report/93hrp_report_ara/Brazil.html.

136. "Reports on Human Rights Practices," US Department of State Bureau of Democracy, Human Rights and Labor, accessed February 16, 2016, http://www.state.gov/j/drl/rls/hrrpt/humanrightsreport/index.htm#wrapper.

137. Rebecca Cordell, K. Chad Clay, Christopher J. Fariss, Reed M. Wood, and Thorin M. Wright, "Changing Standards or Political Whim? Evaluating Changes in the Content of the US State Department Human Rights Reports," *Journal of Human Rights* 19, no. 1 (2020): 3–18.

138. US interview #63, Washington, DC, October 15, 2015.

139. Mark Bromley, "Building a Strategy for an LGBT-Inclusive U.S. Foreign Policy," The Council for Global Equality, November 2007, http://www.globalequality.org/storage/documents/pdf/lgbt_foreign_policy_project-discussion_paper.pdf.

140. US case interview #66, Washington, DC, October 15, 2015.

141. Participant observation #63, Washington, DC, October 15, 2015.

142. The Council for Global Equality, November 2020, "Centering the Rights of LGBTI Individuals in U.S. Foreign Policy: A Pathway to Effective Global Leadership" http://www.globalequality.org/storage/documents/CGE_Transition_Paper.pdf.

143. The Council for Global Equality, November 2020, "Centering the Rights of LGBTI Individuals in U.S. Foreign Policy: A Pathway to Effective Global Leadership," http://www.globalequality.org/storage/documents/CGE_Transition_Paper.pdf.

144. US case interview #43, Washington, DC, January 15, 2016.

145. Lang, 2013: 61.

146. Ryan R. Thoreson, *Transnational LGBT Activism Working for Sexual Rights Worldwide* (Minneapolis: University of Minnesota Press, 2014).

147. Joachim, 2007: 7.

148. Pierson, 2005: 44.

149. Jennifer Hadden and Lorien Jasny, "The Power of Peers: How Transnational Advocacy Networks Shape NGO Strategies on Climate Change," *British Journal of Political Science* 49, no. 2 (2019): 637–59.

150. See, for example, Kimberly H. Conger, "The Christian Right in US Politics," in *Oxford Research Encyclopedia of Politics*, 2019. Or Ethan Stokes and Rebecca Schewe, "Framing from the Pulpit: A Content Analysis of American Conservative Evangelical Protestant Sermon Rhetoric Discussing LGBT Couples and Marriage," *Journal of Communication & Religion* 39, no. 3 (2016): 59–75.

151. As one example: "Homosexuality, Theology, and the Church," Focus on the Family, accessed June 10, 2019, http://www.focusonthefamily.com/socialissues/sexuality/homosexuality-theology-and-the-church/homosexuality-theology-and-the-church. For broader analysis of a host of organizations, see Jojanneke van der Toorn, John T. Jost, Dominic J. Packer, Sharareh Noorbaloochi, and Jay J. Van Bavel, "In Defense of Tradition: Religiosity, Conservatism, and Opposition to Same-Sex Marriage in North America," *Personality and Social Psychology Bulletin* 43, no. 10 (2017): 1455–68.

152. Clyde Wilcox, *Onward Christian Soldiers? The Religious Right in American Politics* (New York: Routledge, 2018).

153. "Attitudes on Same-Sex Marriage" Pew Research Center, May 14, 2019, https://www.pewforum.org/fact-sheet/changing-attitudes-on-gay-marriage/.

154. See Marjorie Randon Hershey, *Party Politics in America* (New York: Routledge, 2017). Or Caroline Beer and Victor D. Cruz-Aceves, "Extending Rights to Marginalized Minorities: Same-Sex Relationship Recognition in Mexico and the United States," *State Politics & Policy Quarterly* 18, no. 1 (2018): 3–26.

155. Ilona Klímová-Alexander, *The Romani Voice in World Politics: The United Nations and Non-State Actors* (New York: Routledge, 2017).

156. Marika Gereke and Tanja Brühl, "Unpacking the Unequal Representation of Northern and Southern NGOs in International Climate Change Politics," *Third World Quarterly* (2019): 1–19.

157. Note: Outright Action International was formerly called the International Gay and Lesbian Human Rights Committee (IGLHRC). See also United Nations Economic and Social Council (ECOSOC), United Nations, accessed October 2, 2020, https://www.un.org/ecosoc/en/home.

158. "UN and Regional Mechanisms," OutRight Action International, accessed June 10, 2019, https://www.outrightinternational.org/region/un-and-regional-mechanisms.

159. Christopher H. Smith, "Letter to the Secretary General of the United Nations," Congress of the United States, House of Representatives, July 9, 2010.

160. Colum Lynch, "Republicans Join Forces with Islamic Governments against America," *Foreign Policy*, July 15, 2010, http://foreignpolicy.com/2010/07/15/republicans-join-forces-with-islamic-governments-against-america/.

161. US case interview #55, New York, January 20, 2016; #67, San Francisco, California, February 12, 2016.

162. Lynch, July 15, 2010.

163. Johnson, 2006; Weldon, 2012.

164. Conor O'Dwyer, "The Benefits of Backlash: EU Accession and the Organization of LGBT Activism in Post-Communist Poland and the Czech Republic," *East European Politics and Societies* 32, no. 4 (2018): 892–923.

165. "UN and Regional Mechanisms," OutRight Action International, accessed June 10, 2019, https://www.outrightinternational.org/region/un-and-regional-mechanisms.

166. Joachim, 2007: 6.

167. Elizabeth Anderson, *Freedom and Equality* (Oxford: Oxford University Press, 2016).

168. Christina Kiel and Jamie Campbell, "Intergovernmental Organizations and LGBT Issues," in *Oxford Research Encyclopedia of Politics*, 2019, https://doi.org/10.1093/acrefore/9780190228637.013.1270.

169. US case interview #43, Washington, DC, January 15, 2016.

170. US case interview #43, Washington, DC, January 15, 2016.

171. US case interview #43, Washington, DC, January 15, 2016.

172. Paul Snell, "Equality in the House: The Congressional LGBT Equality Caucus and the Substantive," *LGBTQ Politics: A Critical Reader* (2017): 309.

173. As cited by Paul Snell, "Equality in the House: The Congressional LGBT Equality Caucus and the Substantive," *LGBTQ Politics: A Critical Reader* (2017): 309.

174. US case interview #41, Seattle, Washington, January 19, 2016; #43, Washington, DC, January 15, 2016.

175. Phillip Ayoub, "Protean Power in Movement: Navigating Uncertainty in the LGBT Rights Revolution," *Protean Power* 146 (2018): 79.

176. Samuel Moyn, *Not Enough: Human Rights in an Unequal World* (Cambridge, MA: Harvard University Press, 2018).

177. Jane K. Cowan and Julie Billaud, "Between Learning and Schooling: The Politics of Human Rights Monitoring at the Universal Periodic Review," *Third World Quarterly* 36, no. 6 (2015): 1175–90.

178. Elise Carlson-Rainer, "Khashoggi Prompts Trump to Reconsider Human Rights in Foreign Policy," *The Hill,* October 18, 2018.

179. Kathryn Sikkink, *Mixed Signals: US Human Rights Policy and Latin America* (Ithaca, NY: Cornell University Press, 2018), 198.

180. Tom Malinowski, "Human Rights in the New Approach to U.S.-Cuba Policy," as Prepared Remarks for the Senate Committee on Foreign Relations, Washington, DC, US Department of State Bureau of Democracy, Human Rights, and Labor, February 3, 2015, https://2009-2017.state.gov/j/drl/rls/rm/2015/237120.htm.

181. Josh Lederman, "Trump Administration Launches Global Effort to End Criminalization of Homosexuality," *NBC News*, February 19, 2019, https://www.nbcnews.com/politics/national-security/trump-administration-launches-global-effort-end-criminalization-homosexuality-n973081.

182. Burack, 2018: 27.

183. Erik Hysing and Jan Olsson, "The Political Nature of Inside Activism," in *Green Inside Activism for Sustainable Development* (Cham: Palgrave Macmillan, 2018), 47–71.

184. Lee Ann Banaszak, 2010: 2. Note: "Main State" is the colloquial term used by civil servants for the central State Department headquarters in Foggy Bottom, Washington, DC.

185. As discussed in the Uganda section of this book, policy discussions amplified in the State Department in 2009 when Uganda proposed a bill for the death penalty for homosexual acts.

186. This work is summarized for public audiences here: "The Department of State's Accomplishments Promoting the Human Rights of Lesbian, Gay, Bisexual and Transgender People," US Department of State Office of the Spokesperson, Washington, DC, December 6, 2011, https://2009-2017.state.gov/r/pa/prs/ps/2011/12/178341.htm.

187. Chris Johnson, "Dan Baer: Time for U.S. to Change Its Relationship with Saudi Arabia," *Washington Blade,* July 9, 2019, https://www.washingtonblade.com/2019/07/09/dan-baer-time-for-u-s-to-change-its-relationship-with-saudi-arabia/.

188. For an example of a "Mission Strategic Plan," see "FY 2014–2017 Department of State and USAID Strategic Plan," US Department of State, accessed February 14, 2014, http://www.state.gov/s/d/rm/rls/dosstrat/2014/.

189. US case interview #40, Washington, DC, January 15, 2016.

190. Interview #40, Washington, DC, January 15, 2016; and #53, New York, January 13, 2016.

191. Michael K. Lavers, "Advancing Obama's LGBT Rights Agenda Abroad," *Washington Blade*, July 23, 2014, https://www.washingtonblade.com/2014/07/23/retired-u-n-official-leads-usaid-lgbt-initiatives/.

192. Freya Johnson Ross, "Professional Feminists: Challenging Local Government Inside Out," *Gender, Work & Organization* 26, no. 4 (2019): 520–40.

193. "History," Gays and Lesbians in Foreign Affairs Agencies (GLIFAA), accessed October 2, 2020, https://glifaa.org/archive/history-long/. Note: GLIFAA's mandate has broadened to support the rights of all LGBTI people. Robyn McCutcheon, the first transgender Foreign Service officer to come out on the job in 2011, served as GLIFAA president.

194. Note: "Sexual misconduct" is still a category of assessment for a federal security clearance, but not specific to sexual orientation: "Security Clearance Frequently Asked Questions," Clearance Jobs, accessed 20 October 2020, https://www.clearancejobs.com/security-clearance-faqs.

195. "Human Rights for LGBT Persons: A Q&A with Special Envoy Randy Berry," *The Foreign Service Journal* 92, no. 5 (June 2015): 20–24, https://www.afsa.org/sites/default/files/fsj-2015-06-june.pdf.

196. "Human Rights for LGBT Persons: A Q&A with Special Envoy Randy Berry," *The Foreign Service Journal* 92, no. 5 (June 2015): 20–24, https://www.afsa.org/sites/default/files/fsj-2015-06-june.pdf.

197. US case interview #40, Washington, DC, January 15, 2016.

198. Samantha Power, *The Education of an Idealist* (New York: HarperCollins Books, 2019), 278.

199. Power, 2019: 422.

200. US case interview #40, Washington, DC, January 15, 2016.

201. US case interview #40, Washington, DC, January 15, 2016.

202. US case interview #40, Washington, DC, January 15, 2016; and #58, Washington, DC, September 1, 2015.

203. Burack, 2018: 161.

204. US case interview #52, Washington, DC, September 15, 2015.

205. Power, 2019: 276.

206. Alexander Beresford, "A Responsibility to Protect Africa from the West? South Africa and the NATO Intervention in Libya," *International Politics* 52, no. 3 (2015): 288–304.

207. Douglas Janoff, "Homophobia, Human Rights and Diplomacy," in *The Social Practice of Human Rights: Charting Frontiers of Research and Advocacy, 2017,* November 10, 2017, https://ecommons.udayton.edu/cgi/viewcontent.cgi?article=1268&context=human_rights.

208. Power, 2019: 78.

209. US case interview #44, Washington, DC, September 24, 2015.

210. US case interview #43, follow-up, Washington, DC, February 5, 2016.

211. US case interview #40, Washington, DC, January 15, 2016.

212. US case interview #43, follow-up, Washington, DC, February 5, 2016.

213. US case interview #53, follow-up, New York, January 29, 2016.

214. Power, 2019: 280.

215. Power, 2019: 280.

216. Power, 2019: 280.

217. Holly J. McCammon, and Amanda J. Brockman, "Feminist Institutional Activists: Venue Shifting, Strategic Adaptation, and Winning the Pregnancy Discrimination Act," *Sociological Forum* 34, no. 1 (2019): 5–26.

218. "Global Equality Fund," US Department of State Bureau of Democracy, Human Rights and Labor, accessed September 4, 2020, http://www.state.gov/globalequality/about/index.htm.

219. Elise Carlson-Rainer, "Bureaucrats and Resistance: Social Movement Actors inside the State," Albany, NY: *NPR Academic Minute*, WAMC Northeast Public Radio (ed. David Hopper II, Producer), April 9, 2018, http://wamc.org/programs/academic-minute.

220. "Remarks by John Kerry Announcing the Appointment of Special Envoy for the Human Rights of LGBT Persons, Randy Berry," US Department of State, February 23, 2015, http://www.state.gov/secretary/remarks/2015/02/237772.htm.

221. Steve Smith, Amelia Hadfield, and Timothy Dunne, eds., *Foreign Policy: Theories, Actors, Cases* (Oxford: Oxford University Press, 2016).

222. "A Survey of LGBT Americans: Attitudes, Experiences and Values in Changing Times," Pew Research Center, June 13, 2013, http://www.pewsocialtrends.org/2013/06/13/a-survey-of-lgbt-americans/.

223. Power, 2019: 278.

224. US interview #53, New York, January 13, 2016.

225. Banaszak, 2010: 6.

226. US interview #53, New York, January 13, 2016.

227. Family Liaison Office, US Department of State, 2009.

228. US case interview #81, Washington, DC, February 14, 2016; and #52, Washington, DC, September 15, 2015.

229. For more specifics on the internal changes, see "State Department Issues Guidance on How to Implement New Rules for Foreign Service Officers with Same-Sex Partners," Family Equality, January 11, 2010, https://www.familyequality.org/2010/01/11/state-department-issues-guidance-on-how-to-implement-new-rules-for-foreign-service-officers-with-same-sex-partners/.

230. US case interview #52, Washington, DC, September 15, 2015.

231. US case interview #52, Washington, DC, September 15, 2015.

232. Jackie Kucinich, "New Hillary Clinton Emails Detail Her State Department Battle for Gay Rights," *The Daily Beast*, July 2, 2015, http://www.thedailybeast.com/articles/2015/07/02/new-hillary-clinton-emails-detail-her-state-department-battle-for-gay-rights.html.

233. As reported in the *Daily Beast*: Jackie Kucinich, "New Hillary Clinton Emails Detail Her State Department Battle for Gay Rights," *The Daily Beast*, July 2, 2015, http://www.thedailybeast.com/articles/2015/07/02/new-hillary-clinton-emails-detail-her-state-department-battle-for-gay-rights.html.

234. US interview #40, Washington, DC, January 15, 2016.

235. "A Survey of LGBT Americans: Attitudes, Experiences and Values in Changing Times," Pew Research Center, June 13, 2013, http://www.pewsocialtrends.org/2013/06/13/a-survey-of-lgbt-americans/.

236. US interview #55, New York, January 20, 2016.

237. See, for example, Peter Hays Gries, *The Politics of American Foreign Policy: How Ideology Divides Liberals and Conservatives Over Foreign Affairs* (Stanford, CA: Stanford University Press, 2014).

238. Omar G. Encarnación, "The Troubled Rise of Gay Rights Diplomacy," *Current History* 115, no. 777 (2016).

239. Klapeer, Christine M. "Dangerous Liaisons?: (Homo) Developmentalism, Sexual Modernization and LGBTIQ Rights in Europe." In *Routledge Handbook of Queer Development Studies*, 102–18. London: Routledge, 2018.

240. See, for example, Sook Jong Lee and Kyoung Sun Lee, "The Complex Relationship between Government and NGOs in International Development Cooperation: South Korea as an Emerging Donor Country," *International Review of Public Administration* 21, no. 4 (2016): 275–91. Or Jennifer N. Brass, *Allies or Adversaries: NGOS and the State in Africa* (Cambridge: Cambridge University Press, 2016).

241. US interview #41, Seattle, Washington, January 19, 2016.

242. US interview #41, Seattle, Washington, January 19, 2016.

243. Andrew Sullivan, "The First Gay President," *Newsweek*, May 21, 2012, http://www.newsweek.com/andrew-sullivan-barack-obamas-gay-marriage-evolution-65067.

244. White House, December 6, 2011.

245. US case interviews: #43, Washington, DC, January 15, 2016.

246. US case interviews: #43, Washington, DC, January 15, 2016; #62, Portland, Oregon, February 14, 2015; #64, Seattle, Washington, May 13, 2015, #40, Washington, DC, January 15, 2016.

247. Note: In 2013, the US Supreme Court overturned the Defense of Marriage Act (DOMA). Since 1996, DOMA defined marriage as a union between a man and a woman and prevented the federal government from recognizing any marriages between gay or lesbian couples, even if those couples are considered legally married by their home state. See also Federika A. Cariati, "How Eric Holder's Role as Attorney General Impacted the Obama Presidency," *Inquiries Journal* 7, no. 2 (2015).

248. White House Press Office, *Remarks from President Obama and President Sall of Senegal Joint Press Conference*, June 27, 2013, https://www.whitehouse.gov/the-press-office/2013/06/27/remarks-president-obama-and-president-sall-republic-senegal-joint-press-.

249. "President Obama Joins President Kenyatta of Kenya in a Joint Press Conference," White House Office of the Press Secretary, July 25, 2015, https://www.whitehouse.gov/the-press-office/2015/07/25/remarks-president-obama-and-president-kenyatta-kenya-press-conference.

250. "How the United States Can Help Counter Violent Extremism and Support Civil Society in Kenya: Blueprint for U.S. Government Policy," Human Rights First, July 2015, accessed February 14, 2019, http://www.humanrightsfirst.org/sites/default/files/HRF-Kenya-Blueprint-Final.pdf.

251. "How the United States Can Help Counter Violent Extremism and Support Civil Society in Kenya: Blueprint for U.S. Government Policy," Human Rights First, July 2015, accessed on February 14, 2019, http://www.humanrightsfirst.org/sites/default/files/HRF-Kenya-Blueprint-Final.pdf.

252. Lucy Westcott, "Kenyan Leaders Respond to Obama's Support for LGBT Rights," *Newsweek*, July 25, 2015, http://www.newsweek.com/kenyan-leaders-respond-obamas-support-lgbt-rights-357563.

253. Christopher Williams, "Assessing South Africa's Ambivalent SOGI Diplomacy in Africa," *South African Journal of International Affairs* 24, no. 3 (2017): 375–94; Ashley Currier, *Out in Africa; LGBT Organizing in Namibia and South Africa* (Minneapolis: University of Minnesota Press, 2012).

254. Phillip M. Ayoub, "With Arms Wide Shut: Threat Perception, Norm Reception, and Mobilized Resistance to LGBT Rights," *Journal of Human Rights* 13, no. 3 (March 2014): 337–62.

255. US case interview #79, Seattle, Washington, April 25, 2019.

256. Power, 2019: 281.

257. Robbie Corey-Boulet, "The Trump Effect: Elections at Home and Abroad Dampen Liberia's Gay-Rights Revival," *World Policy Journal* 34, no. 3 (2017): 83–89.

258. Corey-Boulet, 2017.

259. Robert L Tsai, "Obama's Conversion on Same-Sex Marriage: The Social Foundations of Individual Rights," *Connecticut Law Review* 50 (2018): 1.

260. US case interview #52, New York, January 13, 2016.

261. "Timeline: Iraq War," *BBC News*, July 5, 2016, https://www.bbc.com/news/magazine-36702957.

262. "Has the U.S Been Committing Torture in Guantanamo?," in *Report On Torture and Cruel, Inhuman, and Degrading Treatment of Prisoners at Guantanamo Bay* (New York: Center for Constitutional Rights, 2006), 36–39.

263. Seymour M. Hersh, "Torture in Abu Ghraib," *New Yorker*, May 10, 2004, https://www.newyorker.com/magazine/2004/05/10/torture-at-abu-ghraib.

264. "The Bush Global Gag Rule: Endangering Women's Health, Free Speech and Democracy," Center for Reproductive Rights, July 1, 2003, https://reproductiverights.org/document/the-bush-global-gag-rule-endangering-womens-health-free-speech-and-democracy.

265. Ilan Peleg, *The Legacy of George W. Bush's Foreign Policy: Moving beyond Neo-conservatism* (New York: Routledge, 2018).

266. Cohen, 2008: 2.

267. Adam Jacobson, " 'The True Ugly Face of America': Al Qaeda's Propaganda Use of Guantanamo Bay and Implications for US Counterterrorism," SSRN 2614056 (2015), http://dx.doi.org/10.2139/ssrn.2614056.

268. McClintock, 2016. Note: Because of legal complications and international law related to non-refoulement, the center remains open as of November 2019.

269. US case interview #40, Washington, DC, January 15, 2016; and #59, New York, January 29, 2016.

270. Power, 2019: 276.

271. Brian Padden, "US Foreign Policy on Gay Rights Sparks Debate," Voice of America, July 16, 2011, accessed October 10, 2014, http://www.voanews.com/content/us-foreign-policy-gay-rights-sparks-debate/1703238.html.

272. Daniel Baer, "LiveAtState: Human Rights of Lesbian, Gay, Bisexual, and Transgender People," US Department of State, International Media Engagement, June 20, 2013, https://2009-2017.state.gov/r/pa/ime/211005.htm.

273. Jasbir K. Puar, *Terrorist Assemblages: Homonationalism In Queer Times* (Durham: Duke University Press, 2007).

274. Puar, 2018.

275. Miriam Smith, "Homonationalism and the Comparative Politics of LGBTQ Rights," in *LGBTQ Politics: A Critical Reader*, ed. Marla Brettschneider, Susan Burgess, and Christine Keating (New York: New York University Press, 2017), 458–76.

276. US case interview #40, Washington, DC, January 15, 2016.

277. Michael Posner, interview by Jacob Weisberg, "Reflections on the Obama Administration's Human Rights Policies and the Way Forward," Council on Foreign Relations, March 4, 2013, https://www.cfr.org/event/reflections-obama-administrations-human-rights-policies-and-way-forward.

278. These foreign ministers remain anonymous, as it was in the context of quiet diplomacy.

279. US case interview #59, New York, January 29, 2016.

280. US case interview #59, New York, January 29, 2016.

281. Phillip Ayoub, "Protean Power in Movement: Navigating Uncertainty in the LGBT Rights Revolution," *Protean Power* 146 (2018): 79.

282. Elise Carlson-Rainer, "Bureaucrats and Resistance: Social Movement Actors inside the State," National Public Radio's (NPR) Academic Minute, Albany, NY, April 9, 2018, http://wamc.org/programs/academic-minute.

283. Charles Tilly and Lesley Wood, *Social Movements 1768–2012*, 3rd ed. (Boulder, CO: Paradigm, 2013).

284. See Kelly Kollman, "Same-Sex Unions: The Globalisation of an Idea," in *The Same-Sex Unions Revolution In Western Democracies* (Manchester: Manchester University Press, 2016), 329–57. Or Julie Moreau, "Political Science and the Study of LGBT Social Movements in the Global South," in *LGBTQ Politics: A Critical Reader*, ed. Marla Brettschneider, Susan Burgess, and Christine Keating (New York: New York University Press, 2017), 439–57.

Chapter 3

1. "Andrei Fighting for LGBT Rights Despite Death Threats," SIDA LGBTI Human Rights Work, Example of Result October 10, 2018, accessed February 26, 2019, https://www.sida.se/English/where-we-work/Europe/Moldova-/examples-of-results/andrei-fighting-for-lgbt-rights-despite-death-threats/.

2. Susan Dicklitch-Nelson, Scottie Thompson Buckland, Berwood Yost, and Daniel Draguljić, "From Persecutors to Protectors: Human Rights and the F&M Global Barometer of Gay Rights TM(GBGR)," *Journal of Human Rights* 18, no. 1 (2019): 1–18, https://doi.org/10.1080.14754835.2018.1563863.

3. See Lotta Samelius and Erik Wågberg, "Sexual Orientation and Gender Identity Issues in Development," SIDA Department for Democracy and Social Development, November 2005, accessed April 5, 2020, https://tandis.odihr.pl/bitstream/20.500.12389/19549/1/02220.pdf.

4. Annika Nilsson and Jessica Rothman, "Evaluation of the Sida Supported RFSL Projects "LGBT Voices" and "Rainbow Leaders": Final Report," Sida, 2017, accessed April 29, 2021, https://www.sida.se/contentassets/a09863bdac41467ea541a12e2160caf5/22051.pdf.

5. "Sweden Population: Live," Worldometer, February 20, 2020, https://www.worldometers.info/world-population/sweden-population/.

6. "The Anti-Homosexuality Act," Ugandan government, 2014, https://www.refworld.org/pdfid/530c4bc64.pdf?fbclid=IwAR0r_ZCq2az0HsiSbQmm9wyJMc3Vj33bZZ22y_cWtlaN_U8GirNeCoa6sw8,%201-11%20(2014).

7. "Uganda Kill the Gays Bill," *Huffington Post*, 2009–2016.

8. This acronym comes from the Swedish name: Riksförbundet för homosexuellas, bisexuellas och transpersoners rättigheter (RFSL) and will be used in this study.

9. Lisa M. Dellmuth and Elizabeth A. Bloodgood, "Advocacy Group Effects in Global Governance: Populations, Strategies, and Political Opportunity Structures," *Interest Groups & Advocacy* 8, no. 3 (2019): 255–69.

10. Kristien Stassen, Roel Smolders, and Pieter Leroy, "Sensitizing Events as Trigger for Discursive Renewal and Institutional Change in Flanders' Environmental Health Approach, 1970s–1990s," *Environmental Health* 12, no. 46 (June 2013), https://doi.org10.1186/1476-069X-12-46.

11. Note, this analysis is a limited scope focusing on Sweden and the United States. The Ugandan AHA also sparked changed in other countries' foreign policy agendas, as well as international institutions such as the World Bank to address LGBTI rights abuses in international development policies.

12. Anna-Maria Sörberg, "Homonationalism," translated from Swedish by the author (Stockholm: Leopard förlag, 2017): 13.

13. "Setting Examples in Human Rights," Sweden and Human Rights, accessed January 5, 2016, https://sweden.se/society/sweden-and-human-rights/.

14. Kati Mustola and Jens Rydström, *Criminally Queer: Homosexuality and Criminal Law in Scandinavia, 1842–1999* (Amsterdam, Netherlands: Aksant, 2007): 17.

15. Annica Kronsell, 2002.

16. Sofia Murray, "Framing a Climate Crisis: A Descriptive Framing Analysis of How Greta Thunberg Inspired the Masses to Take to the Streets" (2020).

17. "Working for a Gay-friendly Sweden," Swedish Ministry for Foreign Affairs, accessed May 19, 2016, https://sweden.se/society/working-for-a-gay-and-equal-sweden/.

18. Daniela Alaattinoğlu and Ruth Rubio-Marín, "Redress for Involuntarily Sterilised Trans People in Sweden against Evolving Human Rights Standards: A Critical Appraisal," *Human Rights Law Review* (2020). Note: While innovative at the time, this law also required applicants to be sterilized, a law that was replicated by other nations. The "Swedish Compensation Act in 2018" overturned the requirement for sterilization and provided reparations to persons who were forced to be sterilized. See Mikael Landén and Sune Innala, 2000.

19. "Development Aid Drops in 2018, Especially to Neediest Countries," *Organisation for Economic Co-operation and Development (OECD)*, accessed February 20, 2020, http://www.oecd.org/development/development-aid-drops-in-2018-especially-to-neediest-countries.htm.

20. Karin Aggestam and Annika Bergman-Rosamond, "Swedish Feminist Foreign Policy in the Making: Ethics, Politics, and Gender," *Ethics & International Affairs* 30, no. 3 (2016): 323–34.

21. Ingebritsen 2006: 2. See also Annika Björkdahl, "Swedish Norm Entrepreneurship in the UN," *International Peacekeeping* 14, no. 4 (2007): 538–52.

22. Bengt Held, "Utrikesminister Margot Wallström (s) om HBTQ-Palestiniers Situation (Foreign Minister Margot Wallström (s) on the Situation of LGBTQ Palestinians)," Helds HBT-nyheter (Held's LGBT News), May 3, 2015, http://bengtheld.blogspot.com/2015/05/utrikesminister-margot-wallstrom-s-om.html.

23. Rydström, 2011: 28.

24. Stoum, 2014: 35-43. Note: Stoum provides an in-depth discussion of postcolonial theoretical claims of representation of LGBTI within Norwegian foreign policy, where the problem of LGBTI rights abuses is percieved as a foreign issue, and violations of human rights are not tolerated based on cultural claims.

25. Brysk, 2009: 4.

26. Note: Europe generally is documented as the birthplace of the movement, Germany housing the first movement in the 1800s,with strong networks across Europe. These advocates passed on the torch to postwar groups that laid the groundwork in states like Sweden and the Netherlands. See, for example, Phillip M. Ayoub, "Cooperative Transnationalism in Contemporary Europe: Europeanization and Political Opportunities for LGBT Mobilization in the European Union," *European Political Science Review: EPSR* 5, no. 2 (2013): 279; Andrew Stewart, "A Journal for Manly Culture: An Exploration of the World's First Gay Periodical," *Papers of the Bibliographical Society of Canada/Cahiers de la Société bibliographique du Canada* 57 (2019): 85–105.

27. B. Rexed, "Sweden and the World Health Organization over 40 Years (Sverige och WHO i 40 år)," Socialdepartementet, Socialstyreslen & Allmänna Förlaget: Stockholm, 1988.

28. Swedish Ambassador for Human Rights: Department for International Law, Human Rights and Treaty Law Ministry for Foreign Affairs, Sweden, Jan Nordlander, Participation in OSCE Conference on Activities and Expanding the Role of NGOs, October 2009, http://www.osce.org/odihr/38684?download=true.

29. Galit Andersson, "Quality of Life and Sexual Health among Transgender People and People Living with HIV in Sweden" (PhD diss., Karolinska Institutet, 2019).

30. Rachel Irwin, "Sweden's Engagement in Global Health: A Historical Review," *Globalization and Health* 15, no. 1 (2019): 79.

31. Margareta Edling, "New Ombudsman Fights Discrimination on Grounds of Sexual Orientation," Eurofound, December 27, 1999, http://www.eurofound.europa.eu/observatories/eurwork/articles/new-ombudsman-fights-discrimination-on-grounds-of-sexual-orientation.

32. Thomas Hammarberg, "Human Rights and Gender Identity," Council of Europe Commissioner for Human Rights Strasbourg, 29 July 2009, CommDH/IssuePaper (2009): 2.

33. Swedish case study interview #5, Stockholm, Sweden, August 13, 2015.

34. Participant observation #27, Stockholm, Sweden, July 29, 2015.

35. Abby Peterson, Mattias Wahlström, and Magnus Wennerhag, "The Histories of Pride," in *Pride Parades and LGBT Movements* (London: Routledge, 2018), 18–70.

36. Swedish case interview #7, Stockholm, Sweden, August 25, 2015.

37. Swedish case interview #7, Stockholm, Sweden, August 25, 2015; and #3, Stockholm, Sweden, August 26, 2015.

38. "Swedish Christian Democrat Leader Attends Pride for First Time," *Sveriges-Radio*, August 1, 2016, https://sverigesradio.se/sida/artikel.aspx?artikel=6485455.

39. Fia Sundevall and Alma Persson, "LGBT in the Military: Policy Development in Sweden 1944–2014," *Sexuality Research and Social Policy* 13, no. 2 (2016): 119–29.

40. Oscar Örum, "The Swedish Democrats Are Expelled from the Pride Festival," *Dagens Opinion,* July 18, 2014, http://dagensopinion.se/artikel/sverigedemokraterna-portas-fran-pridefestivalen/; Solveig Rundquist, "Stockholm Pride Bars Sweden Democrats," *The Local Sweden*, July 29, 2014, https://www.thelocal.se/20140729/sweden-democrats-barred-from-stockholm-pride.

41. "Gay Sweden Democrat Backs Party's Pride Flag Decision," *The Local Sweden,* September 15, 2019, https://www.thelocal.se/20190915/gay-sweden-democrat-backs-council-vote-to-stop-flying-pride-flah.

42. Swedish case study participant observation: #10, Stockholm, Sweden, July 28, 2015; #11, Stockholm, Sweden, July 29, 2015; #12, Stockholm, Sweden, July 28, 2015; #18, Stockholm, Sweden, July 27, 2015; #21, Stockholm, Sweden, July 28, 2015; and #23, Stockholm, Sweden, July 31, 2015.

43. For consistency between both Swedish and English languages, this study uses the Swedish language acronyms for Swedish government autories and Swedish-based organizations, i.e., MV for *Migrationsverket*, or the Swedish Migration Agency.

44. Aggestam and Bergman-Rosamond, 2016: 323–34.

45. Johan Karlsson Schaffer, "How Democracy Promotion Became a Key Aim of Sweden's Development Aid Policy," in *Do-gooders at the End of Aid,* ed. Kristian Bjørkdahl and Antoine de Bengy Puyvallé (Cambridge: Cambridge University Press, 2019).

46. Suisheng Zhao, *Chinese Foreign Policy: Pragmatism and Strategic Behavior:* (London: Routledge, 2016).

47. Mahanty, 2013. On realist scholarship, see, for example, Goldstein and Keohane, 1993; Kagan, 2003; and Mearsheimer, 2001.

48. Chandra Lekha Sriram, Olga Martin-Ortega, and Johanna Herman, *War, Conflict and Human Rights: Theory and Practice* (London: Routledge, 2017). See also

Matthias Basedau, Jonathan Fox, Jan H. Pierskalla, Georg Strüver, and Johannes Vüllers, "Does Discrimination Breed Grievances—and Do Grievances Breed Violence? New Evidence from an Analysis of Religious Minorities in Developing Countries," *Conflict Management and Peace Science* 34, no. 3 (2017): 217–39.

49. Isabella Lövin, Presentation hosted by RFSL with the Minister for International Development Cooperation, Isabella Lövin, Stockholm Pride, translated from Swedish, July 31, 2015.

50. Gunnar Myrdal, 1945, as cited by Malmborg, 2001: 158 in Brysk, 2010: 61.

51. Brysk 2010: 59.

52. On China's fluctuating position on human rights in the UN, see, for example, Ted Piccone, "China's Long Game on Human Rights at the United Nations," *Foreign Policy at Brookings*, the Brookings Institution (2018).

53. Swedish Foreign Ministry "Feminist Foreign Policy," accessed May 14, 2019, https://www.government.se/government-policy/feminist-foreign-policy/.

54. Karin Aggestam and Annika Bergman-Rosamond, "Swedish Feminist Foreign Policy in the Making: Ethics, Politics, And Gender," *Ethics & International Affairs* 30, no. 3 (2016): 323–34.

55. Jenny Nordberg, "Who's Afraid of a Feminist Foreign Policy?" *New Yorker*, April 15, 2015, http://www.newyorker.com/news/news-desk/swedens-feminist-foreign-minister.

56. Karin Aggestam and Annika Bergman Rosamond, "Feminist Foreign Policy 3.0: Advancing Ethics and Gender Equality in Global Politics," *SAIS Review of International Affairs* 39, no. 1 (2019): 37–48.

57. Adam Tailor, "Sweden Stood Up for Human Rights In Saudi Arabia. This Is How Saudi Arabia Is Punishing Sweden," *Washington Post*, March 20, 2015, https://www.washingtonpost.com/news/worldviews/wp/2015/03/20/sweden-stood-up-for-human-rights-in-saudi-arabia-this-is-how-saudi-arabia-is-punishing-sweden/.

58. On Saudi Arabia's human rights record, see "Freedom in the World 2021—Saudi Arabia," Freedom House, 2021, https://freedomhouse.org/country/saudi-arabia/freedom-world/2021.

59. Elise Carlson-Rainer, "Khashoggi Prompts Trump to Reconsider Human Rights in Foreign Policy," *The Hill*, October 18, 2018, https://thehill.com/opinion/international/412058-khashoggi-prompts-trump-to-reconsider-human-rights-in-foreign-policy.

60. Tailor, "Sweden Stood Up for Human Rights in Saudi Arabia."

61. Abdul Karim Bangura, *Sweden vs Apartheid: Putting Morality Ahead of Profit* (London: Routledge, 2017).

62. Maysam Behravesh, "Gender Clash: Why Is Saudi Arabia so Angry at Sweden?," *Your Middle East* (2015): 5–26.

63. "Sweden's Trustworthiness as a Trade Partner Is at Stake (in Swedish: Sveriges trovärdighet som handelspartner står på spel)," Dagens Nyheter DN Debate

Editorial of 31 Swedish Business Leaders, March 6, 2015, http://www.dn.se/debatt/sveriges-trovardighet-som-handelspartner-star-pa-spel/.

64. Note: New protests erupted in Belarus in August 2020, protesting the Lukashendo regime and human rights abuses. See "Belarus: Amid Vicious Crackdown on Peaceful Protests, Businesses Bear Responsibility to Respect Human Rights," Amnesty International, August 21, 2020, https://www.amnesty.org/en/latest/news/2020/08/belarus-amid-vicious-crackdown-on-peaceful-protests-businesses-bear-responsibility-to-respect-human-rights/. See also Mikkel Sejersen, "Democratic Sanctions Meet Black Knight Support: Revisiting the Belarusian Case," *Democratization* 26, no. 3 (2019): 502–20.

65. Swedish Government Press Release, Embassy of Sweden, Warsaw, August 6, 2012, http://www.swedenabroad.com/Pages/StandardPage.aspx?id=38854&epslanguage=en-GB.

66. Presentation with Mona Sahlin, Birgitta Ohlsson, and Barbro Westerholm, Stockholm Pride, Stockholm, Sweden, August 1, 2015, translated from Swedish.

67. Isabella Lövin, Presentation hosted by RFSL with the Minister for International Development Cooperation, Isabella Lövin, Stockholm Pride, Stockholm Sweden, July 31, 2015, translated from Swedish.

68. Isabella Lövin, Stockholm Pride, Stockholm, Sweden, July 31, 2015, translated from Swedish.

69. Isabella Lövin, Stockholm Pride, Stockholm Sweden, July 31, 2015, translated from Swedish.

70. Government bill 2002/03:122, "Shared Responsibility: Sweden's Policy for Global Development," Ministry for Foreign Affairs, May 15, 2003, https://www.government.se/legal-documents/2003/05/200203122/.

71. A. Runeborg, *Sexuality: A Missing Dimension in Development. Department of Democracy and Social Development* (Stockholm: SIDA, 2008).

72. "Study on SIDA's Work on Human Rights of Lesbian, Gay, Bisexual, Transgender and Intersex Persons," Swedish International Development Agency (SIDA), November 2013, https://publikationer.sida.se/contentassets/d7abd0467e4742068d8650796e615d4d/15389.pdf.

73. SIDA, November 2013.

74. Naomi Hossain and Nalini Khurana, "Donor Responses and Tools for Responding to Shrinking Space for Civil Society: A Desk Study," Swiss Agency for Development and Cooperation (SDC), 2019.

75. SIDA, November 2013.

76. SIDA, November 2013.

77. For more info on SIDA's work on specific current programs, see http://www.sida.se/English/partners/resources-for-all-partners/methodological-materials/human-rights-based-approach-at-sida/rights-of-lgbti-persons/.

78. "Rainbow Academy," RFSL, November 15, 2016, accessed April 20, 2020, https://www.rfsl.se/en/organisation/international/rainbow-academy/.

79. SIDA program with RFSL, the Eastern Coalition for LGBT Equality International, SIDA, accessed November 10, 2018, http://www.rfsl.se/en/organisation/international/eastern-coalition/.

80. "Andrei Fighting for LGBTI Rights Despite Death Threats," SIDA, October 10, 2018, https://www.sida.se/English/where-we-work/Europe/Moldova-/examples-of-results/andrei-fighting-for-lgbt-rights-despite-death-threats/.

81. SIDA LGBTI Human Rights Work, accessed April 30, 2021, https://www.sida.se/English/where-we-work.

82. Naomi Hossain and Nalini Khurana, "Donor Responses and Tools for Responding to Shrinking Space for Civil Society: A Desk Study," Swiss Agency for Development and Cooperation (SDC), 2019.

83. SIDA, November 2013.

84. "The Government's Statement of Foreign Policy," Swedish Foreign Ministry, accessed February 1, 2019, https://www.government.se/.

85. SIDA, November 2013.

86. Isabella Lövin, Presentation hosted by RFSL with the Minister for International Development Cooperation, Isabella Lövin. Stockholm Pride, Stockholm Sweden, July 31, 2015, translated from Swedish.

87. Martin Scheinin, "Impact of Post-9/11 Counter-Terrorism Measures on All Human Rights," in *Using Human Rights to Counter Terrorism* (Cheltenham, UK: Edward Elgar Publishing, 2018).

88. Aliens Act (2005:716), Swedish government, September 29, 2005, https://www.government.se/contentassets/784b3d7be3a54a0185f284bbb2683055/aliens-act-2005_716.pdf.

89. Joseph Mayton, "LGBT Asylum Seekers: A Silent Revolution," Qantara, February 6, 2014, https://en.qantara.de/content/lgbt-asylum-seekers-a-silent-revolution. See also Nicole Laviolette, "Independent Human Rights Documentation and Sexual Minorities: An Ongoing Challenge for the Canadian Refugee Determination Process," *International Journal of Human Rights* 13, no. 2–3 (2009): 437–76.

90. "The Swedish Migration Board Policy for LGBT People Who Seek Protection in Sweden," Migration Sverket, accessed March 1, 2019, http://www.migrationsverket.se/Privatpersoner/Skydd-och-asyl-i-Sverige/For-hbtq-personer.html.

91. Participant observation #89, Stockholm Pride, Stockholm, Sweden, July 30, 2019.

92. Jihan Najjar, "The Experiences of Iranian Sexual Minority Refugees and Asylum Seekers: A Phenomenological Study" (PhD diss., The University of Nebraska-Lincoln, 2020).

93. Georgios Zekos, "Asylum: The Vehicle for Channeling Economic Immigrants into Countries for 'Politico-Economic' Reasons," available at SSRN 3386059 (2019).

94. Edward Mogire, "Refugees and the Terrorist Threat," in *Victims as Security Threats*, (London: Routledge, 2016), 147–62.

95. Markus Rheindorf and Ruth Wodak, "Borders, Fences, and Limits—Protecting Austria from Refugees: Metadiscursive Negotiation of Meaning in the Current Refugee Crisis," *Journal of Immigrant & Refugee Studies* 16, no. 1–2 (2018): 15–38.

96. James C. Simeon, Patricia Tuitt, Julia Kienast, Barbara Kőhalmi, Anita Rozália Nagy-Nádasdi, and Selina March, "Terrorism and Asylum (RLI Working Paper Series Mini-Volume)," 2019.

97. Migrationverket, accessed March 1, 2019.

98. Participant observation #89, Stockholm Pride, Stockholm, Sweden, July 30, 2019.

99. Participant observation #89, Stockholm Pride, Stockholm, Sweden, July 30, 2019.

100. Giorgia Matheson, "The Rights and Experiences of LGBTI Refugees in Europe: A Comparative Study of Procedures and Practices in Italy and Sweden," Uppsala University, Disciplinary Domain of Humanities and Social Sciences, Faculty of Theology, Department of Theology, 2019.

101. Nathalie Rothschild, "Lawyers Open First Office Focused on Assisting LGBT Asylum Seekers," Sveriges Radio, November 10, 2017, accessed April 5, 2020, https://sverigesradio.se/sida/artikel.aspx?programid=2054&artikel=6819364.

102. Participant observation #89, Stockholm Pride, Stockholm, Sweden, July 30, 2019.

103. Jon Binnie and Christian Klesse, " 'Like a Bomb in the Gasoline Station': East–West Migration and Transnational Activism Around Lesbian, Gay, Bisexual, Transgender and Queer Politics in Poland," *Journal of Ethnic and Migration Studies* 39, no. 7 (2013): 1107–24.

104. Swedish case interview #1, Falun, Sweden, August 21, 2015.

105. Swedish case interview #5, Stockholm, Sweden, August 13, 2015.

106. Acronym comes from the Swedish name Riksförbundet för homosexuellas, bisexuellas och transpersoners rättigheter (RFSL) and is used in this study. Note: Other groups such as the *Lesbian Front* (Lesbisk Front) and *Homosexual Socialists* (Homosexuella Socialister) have actively organized to challenge male dominance and work toward a more radical left political agenda. See Abby Peterson, Mattias Wahlström, and Magnus Wennerhag, "The Histories of Pride," in *Pride Parades and LGBT Movements* (London: Routledge, 2018), 18–70.

107. Lang, 2013: 22.

108. Swedish case interview #1, Falun, Sweden, August 21, 2015.

109. Swedish case interview #3, Stockholm, Sweden, August 26, 2015.

110. Pia Laskar, "The Illiberal Turn," *lambda nordica* 19, no. 1 (2014): 87–100.

111. Jo Becker, *Campaigning for Justice: Human Rights Advocacy in Practice* (Stanford, CA: Stanford University Press, 2013), 247.

112. Swedish case interview #3, Stockholm, Sweden, August 26, 2015.

113. Swedish case interview #3, Stockholm, Sweden, August 26, 2015.

114. Participant observation #27, Stockholm Pride, Stockholm, Sweden, July 29, 2015; Participant observation #30, Stockholm Pride, Stockholm, Sweden, July 28, 2015.

115. Swedish case interview #3, Stockholm, Sweden, August 26, 2015; "Poverty and Sexuality: What Are the Connections?," SIDA, September 2010.

116. SIDA, September 2010 Report.

117. EU interview #36, Brussels, Belgium, April 27, 2015; EU interview #37, Brussels, Belgium, April 14, 2015; US case interview #43, Washington, DC, January 15, 2016.

118. EU interview #36, Brussels, Belgium, April 27, 2015; EU interview #37, Brussels, Belgium, April 14, 2015; US case interview #43, Washington, DC, January 15, 2016.

119. See M. V. Lee Badgett, Kees Waaldijk, Yana Van Der Meulen Rodgers, "The Relationship between LGBT Inclusion and Economic Development: Macro-Level Evidence," *World Development* 120, The Williams Institute 2019. See also M. V. Lee Badgett, Sheila Nezhad, Kees Waaldijk, and Yana van der Meulen Rodgers, "The Relationship between LGBT Inclusion and Economic Development: An Analysis of Emerging Economies," The Williams Institute, November 2014, http://williamsinstitute.law.ucla.edu/research/international/lgbt-incl-econ-devel-nov-2014/.

120. Steffen Jensena, Tobias Kelly, Morten Koch Andersen, Catrine Christiansen, and Jeevan Raj Sharma, "Torture and Ill-Treatment Under Perceived: Human Rights Documentation and the Poor," *Human Rights Quarterly* 39, no. 2 (2017): 393–415.

121. Swedish case interview #3, Stockholm, Sweden, August 26, 2015.

122. Swedish case interview #3, Stockholm, Sweden, August 26, 2015.

123. Swedish case interview #5, Stockholm, Sweden, August 13, 2015.

124. Swedish case interview #5, Stockholm, Sweden, August 13, 2015.

125. Morgan Johansson, Minister of Justice and Immigration, Presentation hosted by RFSL, Stockholm Pride, Stockholm, Sweden, August 2015, translated from Swedish; "Festivals 2020," Stockholm Pride, accessed April 20, 2020, https://www.stockholmpride.org/.

126. Swedish case interview #3, Stockholm, Sweden, August 26, 2015.

127. Swedish case interview #3, Stockholm, Sweden, August 26, 2015.

128. Elżbieta Drążkiewicz-Grodzicka, " 'State Bureaucrats' and 'Those NGO People': Promoting the Idea of Civil Society, Hindering the State," *Critique of Anthropology* 36, no. 4 (2016): 341–62.

129. David Lewis, "Civil Society and the Authoritarian State: Cooperation, Contestation and Discourse," *Journal of Civil Society* 9, no. 3 (2013): 325–40.

130. See, for example, J. Burt, *Political Violence and the Authoritarian State in Peru: Silencing Civil Society* (New York: Springer, 2016). And see Jessica C. Teets,

Civil Society under Authoritarianism: The China Model (Cambridge: Cambridge University Press, 2014).

131. Keck and Sikkink, 1998: 37.

132. Tiffany Jones, "Researching and Working for Transgender Youth: Contexts, Problems and Solutions," *Social Sciences* 5, no. 3 (2016): 10.

133. Swedish case interview #2, 5, 9.

134. Kati Mustola and Jens Rydström, *Criminally Queer: Homosexuality and Criminal Law in Scandinavia, 1842–1999* (Amsterdam: Aksant, 2007), 18.

135. "Festivals 2020," Stockholm Pride, accessed April 20, 2020, https://www.stockholmpride.org/.

136. "The Europride Parade Stockholm Broke All Records," EuroPride, August 5, 2018, http://europride2018.com/2018/08/05/pride-parade-broke-all-records/.

137. Participant observation, Stockholm Pride, Stockholm, Sweden, 2015–2019.

138. Participant observation, Stockholm Pride, Stockholm, Sweden, July 29–August 3, 2019.

139. Lang, 2013: 23.

140. Participant observation #97, Stockholm Pride, Stockholm, Sweden, August 2, 2019.

141. Participant observation #98, Stockholm Pride, Stockholm, Sweden, August 2, 2019.

142. Abby Peterson, Mattias Wahlström, and Magnus Wennerhag, " 'Normalized' Pride? Pride Parade Participants in Six European Countries," *Sexualities* 21, no. 7 (2018): 1146–69.

143. Keck and Sikkink, 1998: 12.

144. Participant observation #14, Stockholm Pride, Stockholm, Sweden, July 28, 2015.

145. Kath Browne, "A Party with Politics? (Re)making LGBTQ Pride Spaces in Dublin and Brighton," *Social and Cultural Geography* 8, no. 1 (2007): 63–77.

146. Peter Tatchell, "Has LGBT Pride Lost Its Way?," Peter Tatchell Foundation, July 6, 2017, www.petertatchellfoundation.org/has-lgbt-pride-lost-its-way/.

147. US participant observation #51, Portland, Oregon, February 14, 2015.

148. US participant observation #54, Portland, Oregon, February 14, 2015.

149. Swedish case interview #7, Stockholm, Sweden, August 25, 2015.

150. Participant observation #13, Stockholm Pride, Stockholm, Sweden, July 28, 2015.

151. Participant observation #12, Stockholm Pride, Stockholm, Sweden, July 28, 2015.

152. Safia Swimelar, "Nationalism and Europeanization in LGBT Rights and Politics: A Comparative Study of Croatia and Serbia," *East European Politics and Societies* 33, no. 3 (2019): 603–30.

153. Swimelar, 2019: 603–30.

154. EU interview #36, Brussels, Belgium, April 27, 2015.

155. Julie Dorf, as cited in Claire Felter and Danielle Renwick, "Same-Sex Marriage: Global Comparisons: International Norms, Democracy, and LGBT Rights," Council on Foreign Relations, March 8, 2019, https://www.cfr.org/backgrounder/same-sex-marriage-global-comparisons.

156. Participant observation #12, Stockholm Pride, Stockholm, Sweden, July 28, 2015.

157. Participant observation #13, Stockholm Pride, Stockholm, Sweden, July 28, 2015.

158. Participant observation #12, Stockholm Pride, Stockholm, Sweden, July 28, 2015.

159. Participant observation #97, Stockholm Pride, Stockholm, Sweden, August 2, 2019.

160. Valeriya V. Gelunenko, Marina V. Markhgeym, Azamat M. Shadzhe, Lyudmila A. Tkhabisimova, and Elnur E. Veliev, "Freedom of Speech in Constitutional Binds of Eastern European Countries," *Amazonia Investiga* 8, no. 19 (2019): 403–7.

161. Keck and Sikkink, 1998: 16; Ayoub, 2014(b): 355. See also Alicia Ely Yamin, Neil Datta, and Ximena Andion, "Behind the Drama: The Roles of Transnational Actors in Legal Mobilization over Sexual and Reproductive Rights," *Georgetown Journal of Gender and the Law* 19 (2017): 533.

162. Jan-Benedict Steenkamp, "Corporate Social Responsibility," in *Global Brand Strategy* (London: Palgrave Macmillan, 2017), 209–38.

163. Participant observation #26, Stockholm Pride, Stockholm, Sweden, July 30, 2015.

164. Scandia representative, "Swedish International Companies in a Homo-Phobic World," Presentation at Stockholm Pride, Stockholm, Sweden, July 30, 2015.

165. Rick Noack, "Polish Towns Advocate 'LGBT-Free' Zones while the Ruling Party Cheers Them On," *Washington Post*, July 21, 2019, https://www.washingtonpost.com/world/europe/polands-right-wing-ruling-party-has-found-a-new-targetlgbt-ideology/2019/07/19/775f25c6-a4ad-11e9-a767-d7ab84aef3e9_story.html.

166. Scandia representative, "Swedish International Companies in a Homo-Phobic World," Presentation at Stockholm Pride, Stockholm, Sweden, July 30, 2015.

167. "IKEA's Human Resource Policy," IKEA, accessed March 28, 2016, https://seeacareerwithus.com/about-us/recognition/.

168. J. Lester Feder, "LGBT Activists Stage Kiss-In at Brooklyn IKEA to Protest Store's Lesbian Scandal in Russia," *Buzzfeed News*, November 25, 2013,

https://www.buzzfeednews.com/article/lesterfeder/activists-stage-kiss-in-in-brooklyn-ikea-to-protest-removal.

169. Cavan Sieczkowski, "Ikea Pulls Lesbian Couple Feature from Russian Magazine," *Huffington Post*, November 21, 2013, http://www.huffingtonpost.com/2013/11/21/ikea-pulls-lesbian-couple_n_4316669.html.

170. Cavan Sieczkowski, *The Huffington Post*, November 21, 2013.

171. Daniel Avery, "IKEA Sued by Worker Fired for Posting Anti-Gay Bible Quotes, Attacking 'Promotion of Homosexuality," *Newsweek*, July 8, 2019, https://www.newsweek.com/ikea-poland-lgbt-lawsuit-1447954.

172. "Swedish International Companies in a Homo-Phobic World," Public forum at Stockholm Pride 2015, July 30, 2015.

173. Participant observation #26, Stockholm Pride, Stockholm, Sweden, July 30, 2015.

174. Carlos A. Ball, *The Queering of Corporate America: How Big Business Went from LGBT Adversary to Ally* (Boston: Beacon Press, 2019).

175. Sarah Alhouti, Catherine M. Johnson, and Betsy Bugg Holloway, "Corporate Social Responsibility Authenticity: Investigating Its Antecedents and Outcomes," *Journal of Business Research* 69, no. 3 (2016): 1242–49.

176. See, for example, Amy Lubitow and Mia Davis, "Pastel Injustice: The Corporate Use of Pinkwashing for Profit," *Environmental Justice* 4, no. 2 (2011): 139–44. Also Jason Ritchie, "Pinkwashing, Homonationalism, and Israel–Palestine: The Conceits of Queer Theory and the Politics of the Ordinary," *Antipode* 47, no. 3 (2015): 616–34.

177. Corinne E. Blackmer, "Pinkwashing," *Israel Studies* 24, no. 2 (2019): 171–81.

178. Abby Peterson, Mattias Wahlström, and Magnus Wennerhag, " 'Normalized' Pride? Pride Parade Participants in Six European Countries," *Sexualities* 21, no. 7 (2018): 1146–69.

179. Hans Rosling, O. Rosling, and A. R. Rönnlund, "Factfulness: Ten Reasons We're Wrong About the World–And Why Things Are Better Than You Think," Sceptre, 2018.

180. Participant observations #91 and #92, Stockholm Pride, Stockholm, Sweden, July 31, 2019.

181. Participant observation #92, Stockholm Pride, Stockholm, Sweden, July 31, 2019.

182. Jenny Persson Tholin and Linus Broström, "Transgender and Gender Diverse People's Experience of Non-Transition-Related Health Care in Sweden," *International Journal of Transgenderism* 19, no. 4 (2018): 424–35.

183. Davut Han Aslan and Deniz Doğanay, "Measuring Gender Equality. A Comparative Analysis of Sweden And Turkey," *Kwartalnik Naukowy Uczelni Vistula* 2, no. 60 (2019): 43–64. See also Jeff Hearn, Sofia Strid, Lisa Husu, and Mieke Verloo, "Interrogating Violence against Women and State Violence Policy: Gendered

Intersectionalities and the Quality of Policy in the Netherlands, Sweden and the UK," *Current Sociology* 64, no. 4 (2016): 551–67.

184. For a modern depiction of the impact of HIV/AIDS in Stockholm in the early 1980s and LGBTI discrimination in Sweden, see Simon Kaijser da Silva (Director), "Don't Ever Wipe Tears Without Gloves" (Swedish: Torka aldrig tårar utan handskar), written by Jonas Gardell, Swedish TV Series produced by SVT1, 2012.

185. Galit Andersson, "Quality of Life and Sexual Health among Transgender People and People Living with HIV in Sweden" (PhD diss., Karolinska Institutet, 2019).

186. A 2009 online field experiment study of LGBTI discrimination in the housing market indicated statistically significant lower rates of call-backs or invitations to showings of apartments or homes. See Ali M. Ahmed and Mats Hammarstedt, "Detecting Discrimination against Homosexuals: Evidence from a Field Experiment on the Internet," *Economica* 76, no. 303 (2009): 588–97. See also Mats Hammarstedt, Ali M. Ahmed, and Lina Andersson, "Sexual Prejudice and Labor Market Outcomes for Gays and Lesbians: Evidence from Sweden," *Feminist Economics* 21, no. 1 (2015): 90–109.

187. Swedish case interview #6, Stockholm, Sweden, December 14, 2015.

188. Mariecke van den Berg, "Rings for the Rainbow Family: Religious Opposition to the Introduction of Same-Sex Marriage in Sweden," *Theology and Sexuality* 23, no. 3 (2017): 229–44.

189. Mariecke van den Berg, "Rings for the Rainbow Family: Religious Opposition to the Introduction of Same-Sex Marriage in Sweden," *Theology and Sexuality* 23, no. 3 (2017): 229–44.

190. Swedish case interview #3, Stockholm, Sweden, August 26, 2015.

191. Swedish case interview #3, Stockholm, Sweden, August 26, 2015.

192. Aliens Act (2005:716), Swedish government, September 29, 2005, https://www.government.se/contentassets/784b3d7be3a54a0185f284bbb2683055/aliens-act-2005_716.pdf.

193. Translated by the author from the Swedish: "Nu får det väl vara slut på alla bögfrågor!"

194. Swedish case interview #1, Falun, Sweden, August 21, 2015.

195. "Now these gay questions need to come to an end" (Translated from Swedish: Nu får det väl vara slut på alla bögfrågor') Expressen, September 24, 2003, http://www.expressen.se/nyheter/nu-far-det-val-vara-slut-pa-alla-bogfragor/.

196. Swedish case interview #1, Falun, Sweden, August 21, 2015.

197. Swedish case interview #5, Stockholm, Sweden, August 13, 2015.

198. Swedish case interview #5, Stockholm, Sweden, August 13, 2015.

199. Swedish case interview #5, Stockholm, Sweden, August 13, 2015; Swedish case interview #7, Stockholm, Sweden, August 25, 2015.

200. Swedish Migration Agency, "About the Swedish Migration Agency," accessed April 26, 2019, https://www.migrationsverket.se/English/About-the-Migration-Agency/Statistics.html.

201. "Sweden Democrats Tap into Immigration Fears," *BBC News,* September 25, 2018, accessed April 26, 2019, https://www.bbc.com/news/world-europe-29202793.

202. Katharina Kehl, "In Sweden, Girls Are Allowed to Kiss Girls, and Boys Are Allowed to Kiss Boys': Pride Järva and the Inclusion of the 'LGBT Other' in Swedish Nationalist Discourses," *Sexualities* 21, no. 4 (2018): 674–91.

203. See Ann-Cathrine Jungar, "The Sweden Democrats," in *Understanding Populist Party Organisation* (London: Palgrave Macmillan, 2016): 189–219.

204. Tobias Hübinette and Catrin Lundström, "Sweden after the Recent Election: The Double-Binding Power of Swedish Whiteness through the Mourning of the Loss of 'Old Sweden' and the Passing of 'Good Sweden,'" *NORA—Nordic Journal of Feminist and Gender Research* 19, no. 1 (2011): 42–52.

205. Emma Bowman, "Sweden Election: Ruling Party Scrapes A Win As Far-Right Gains Support." *NPR News*, September 9, 2018, https://www.npr.org/2018/09/09/646116493/sweden-election-ruling-party-scrapes-a-win-as-far-right-gains-support.

206. Peter Stubley, "Sweden Democrats: Anti-immigration Party with Neo-Nazi roots on Course to Become Second Biggest in General Election," *Independent*, September 5, 2018, https://www.independent.co.uk/news/world/europe/sweden-democrats-election-poll-results-nationalist-populist-party-immigration-a8524181.html.

207. Jens Rydgren, *From Tax Populism to Ethnic Nationalism:Radical Right-Wing Populism in Sweden* (New York: Berghahn Books, 2006).

208. Anna-Maria Sörberg, *Homonationalism* (Stockholm, Sweden: Leopard förlag, 2017).

209. Sörberg, 2017: 50.

210. Swedish Democrats, "HBT," translated from Swedish by the author, August 27, 2018, https://sd.se/our-politics/hbt/.

211. Kehl, 2018: 674–91.

212. Jasbir K. Puar, *Terrorist Assemblages: Homonationalism in Queer Times* (Durham: Duke University Press, 2007).

213. Sörberg, 2017: 58.

214. Francesca Romana Ammaturo, "The 'Pink Agenda': Questioning and Challenging European Homonationalist Sexual Citizenship," *Sociology* 49, no. 6 (2015): 1151–66.

215. Ov Cristian Norocel, ""Give Us Back Sweden!" A Feminist Reading of the (Re) Interpretations of the Folkhem Conceptual Metaphor in Swedish Radical Right Populist Discourse," *NORA-Nordic Journal of Feminist and Gender Research* 21, no. 1 (2013): 4–20.

216. Participant Observation #93, Stockholm Pride, Stockholm, Sweden, August 1, 2019.

217. RFSL statement, "Hbtq-Personers Rättigheter Omsätts I Praktisk Politik," November 11, 2018, translated from Swedish by the author, accessed March 7,

2019, https://www.rfsl.se/aktuellt/debatt-sds-motstand-mot-hbtq-personers-rattigheter-omsatts-i-praktisk-politik/.

218. Participant observation #93, Stockholm Pride, Stockholm, Sweden, August 1, 2019; Participant observation #99, Stockholm Pride, Stockholm, Sweden, August 1, 2019; Participant observation #100, Stockholm Pride, Stockholm, Sweden, August 1, 2019.

219. Swedish case interview #94, Stockholm Pride, Stockholm, Sweden, August 1, 2019.

220. US case interview #95, Seattle, Washington, March 28, 2019.

221. Roman Kuhar and David Paternotte, *Anti-Gender Campaigns in Europe: Mobilizing against Equality* (Lanham, MD: Rowman and Littlefield International, 2017).

222. Participant observation #101, Stockholm Pride, Stockholm, Sweden, August 1, 2019.

223. Participant observation #101, Stockholm Pride, Stockholm, Sweden, August 1, 2019.

224. Participant observation #101, Stockholm Pride, Stockholm, Sweden, August 1, 2019.

225. "RFSL Support Service," RFSL Areas of Work, April 8, 2020, accessed May 15, 2020, https://www.rfsl.se/en/organisation/rfsl-stodmottagning/.

226. Banaszak, 2010: 12.

227. Lee Ann Banaszak, 2010: Banaszak's theory is explained and expanded in the theoretical chapter.

228. The *Liberal Party* In Swedish: (Liberalerna or *Folkpartiet; L*).

229. Pia Laskar, "The Illiberal Turn," *lambda nordica* 19, no. 1 (2014): 90.

230. Banaszak, 2010: 6.

231. Barbro Westerholm, member of Parliament, Stockholm, Sweden, December 2015.

232. "The Occupation of the National Board of Health and Welfare (SocialStyrelson), Swedish Radio P3 Documentary, broadcasted (in Swedish) on March 22, 2009, https://sverigesradio.se/sida/avsnitt/83613?programid=2519.

233. Barbro Westerholm, member of Parliament, Stockholm, Sweden, December 2015.

234. Banaszak, 2010: 17.

235. Fia Sundevall and Alma Persson, "LGBT in the Military: Policy Development in Sweden 1944–2014," *Sexuality Research And Social Policy* 13, no. 2 (2016): 119–29.

236. See, for example, D. Kulick, "Introduktion (Introduction)," in *Queersverige (Queer Sweden)*, ed. D Kulick (Stockholm, Sweden: Natur och kultur, 2005). Also Max Waltman, "Prohibiting Sex Purchasing and Ending Trafficking: The Swedish Prostitution Law," *Michigan Journal of International Law* 33 (2011): 133.

237. Mona Sahlin, Social Democrats, Stockholm Pride, Stockholm, Sweden, July 31, 2015, translated from Swedish.

238. Presentation with Mona Sahlin, Birgitta Ohlsson, and Barbro Westerholm, Stockholm Pride, Stockholm, Sweden, August 2015, translated from Swedish.

239. Mona Sahlin, Social Democrats, Stockholm Pride, Stockholm, Sweden, July 31, 2015, translated from Swedish.

240. Christine Agius and Emil Edenborg, "Gendered Bordering Practices in Swedish and Russian Foreign and Security Policy," *Political Geography* 71 (2019): 56–66.

241. Swedish case interview #2, Linköping, Sweden, August 10, 2015; Swedish case interview #5, Stockholm, Sweden, August 13, 2015; Swedish case interview #6, Stockholm, Sweden, December 14, 2015; Participant observation #30, Stockholm Pride, Stockholm, Sweden, July 28, 2015; EU interview #37, Brussels, Belgium, April 14, 2015.

242. Corinne Pinfold, "28 Arrested after Protesters Throw Eggs at Baltic Pride," *Pink News*, July 27, 2013, http://www.pinknews.co.uk/2013/07/27/28-arrested-after-protesters-throw-eggs-at-baltic-pride/.

243. Vytautas Valentinavicius, "Protesters Try to Disrupt Lithuania Gay Pride," *Omaha World-Herald*, July 27, 2013, https://www.omaha.com/news/protesters-try-to-disrupt-lithuania-gay-pride/article_25531d13-c436-520a-be88-55cc9144cb23.html.

244. Participant observation #30, Stockholm Pride, Stockholm, Sweden, July 28, 2015.

245. Nerijus Adomaitis, "Lithuania Holds First Gay March Amid Protests," *Reuters World News*, May 8, 2010, https://www.reuters.com/article/us-lithuania-gay/lithuania-holds-first-gay-march-amid-protests-idUSTRE64723Y20100508.

246. Katja Kahlina, "Local Histories, European LGBT Designs: Sexual Citizenship, Nationalism, and 'Europeanisation' in Post-Yugoslav Croatia and Serbia," in *Women's Studies International Forum*, Pergamon 49 (2015): 73–83.

247. Kahlina, 2015: 73–83.

248. Kevin Moss, "Split Europe: Homonationalism and Homophobia in Croatia," in *LGBT Activism and the Making of Europe* (London: Palgrave Macmillan, 2014), 212–32.

249. On carrots and sticks in international relations, see Ekrem Yaşar Akçay and Selim Kanat, "Carrot and Stick Approach in International Relations: An Evaluation throughout Turkey's Accession Negotiations with the European Union," *Süleyman Demirel Üniversitesi Sosyal Bilimler Enstitüsü Dergisi* 31 (2017): 1–22.

250. Government Offices of Sweden, Prime Minister's Office, Press Release, October 3, 2012, accessed August 29, 2017, www.swedenabroad.com/RSS/News/News-8166-en-GB.xml. As cited in Abby Peterson and Mattias Wahlström, "Between Politics and Party," in *Pride Parades and LGBT Movements* (London: Routledge, 2018), 223.

251. Swedish case interview #3, Stockholm, Sweden, August 26, 2015.

252. Swedish case interview #3, Stockholm, Sweden, August 26, 2015.

253. Swedish case interview #5, Stockholm, Sweden, August 13, 2015.

254. Nordlander fulfilled various diplomatic roles throughout his time in Swedish government, namely as Sweden's ambassador for Human Rights and alternate head of the Swedish delegation to the UN Human Rights Council in Geneva between 2006 and 2010 after years of championing human rights. See *Who is it* (National Encyclopedia, 2007).

255. "Recommendation 1117 (1989) on the Condition of transsexuals," European Parliament Resolution, September 12, 1989.

256. Lydia Malmedie, "Contested Issue and Incremental Change. The Example of LGBTI in EU Foreign Policy," *Der moderne Staat* (2016): 35–50, https://doi.org/10.3224/dms.v9i1.23639.

257. In Swedish: *Ombudsmannen mot diskriminering på grund av sexuell läggning.*

258. Brysk, 2009.

259. Anna-Maria Sörberg, *Homonationalism*, translated from Swedish (Stockholm, Sweden: Leopard förlag, 2017).

260. Ebba Busch Thor as documented in Sörberg, 2017: 14.

261. David Forsythe, "Human Rights and Comparative Foreign Policy," Foundation of Peace Series (Tokyo, Japan: United Nations University Press, 2000[a]): 8.

262. Clara Sandelind, "Constructions of Identity, Belonging and Exclusion in the Democratic Welfare State," *National Identities* 20, no. 2 (2018): 197–218.

263. SIDA report, June 8, 2004; as cited by Brysk, 2010: 42.

264. Niall McCarthy, "Global Humanitarian Assistance: Who Are the Biggest Contributors?" *Forbes*, July 21, 2015, http://www.forbes.com/sites/niall-mccarthy/2015/07/21/global-humanitarian-assistance-who-are-the-biggest-contributors-infographic/#7f1b6a6769af.

265. Mercer, 1996: 4.

266. Katarzyna Jezierska and Ann Towns, "Taming Feminism? The Place of Gender Equality in the 'Progressive Sweden' Brand," *Place Branding and Public Diplomacy* 14, no. 1 (2018): 55–63.

267. See, for example, "Policy Issue: Democracy and Human Rights," US Department of State, accessed May 22, 2019, https://www.state.gov/policy-issues/human-rights-and-democracy/.

268. See Brysk, 2009; Ingebritsen, 2006; Nordberg, 2015.

269. Brysk, 2009: 221.

270. David Ekbladh, *The Great American Mission: Modernization and the Construction of an American World Order* (Princeton, NJ: Princeton University Press, 2011); David Forsythe, *Human Rights and Comparative Foreign Policy,* Foundation of Peace Series (Tokyo, Japan: United Nations University Press, 2000[a]); Mercer, 2006.

271. Isabella Lövin, Presentation hosted by RFSL with the Minister for International Development Cooperation, Isabella Lövin, translated from Swedish, Stockholm Pride, Stockholm, Sweden, July 31, 2015.

272. "Human Rights Homepage," Swedish Foreign Ministry, accessed December 15, 2015, http://manskligarattigheter.dynamaster.se/en/human-rights-in-the-world/human-rights-in-swedish-foreign-policy.

273. Ayoub, 2013: 283.

274. Dace Dzenovska, *School of Europeanness: Tolerance and Other Lessons in Political Liberalism in Latvia* (Ithaca, NY: Cornell University Press, 2018).

275. Tova Andersson, "Live and Let Love: En kritisk studie av svensk homonationalism i en politisk manifestation i samband med de olympiska spelen i Sotji 2014" (Bachelor's thesis, Södertörn University, 2016).

276. Swedish case interview #2, Linköping, Sweden, August 10, 2015; Swedish case interview #3, Stockholm, Sweden, August 26, 2015.

277. Ayoub, 2013: 286.

278. Danielle McCartney, "Monitoring the World Society: LGBT Human Rights in Russia and Sweden," *Advances in Gender Research* 24 (2017): 309–32.

279. Participant observation #18, Stockholm Pride, Stockholm, Sweden, July 27, 2015; Participant observation #22, Stockholm Pride, Stockholm, Sweden, July 29, 2015; Participant observation #26, Stockholm Pride, Stockholm, Sweden, July 30, 2015.

280. Swedish case interview #7, Stockholm, Sweden, August 25, 2015; Participant observation #26, Stockholm Pride, Stockholm, Sweden, July 30, 2015.

281. Participant observation #18, Stockholm Pride, Stockholm, Sweden, July 27, 2015; Participant observation #22, Stockholm Pride, Stockholm, Sweden, July 29, 2015: Participant observation #26, Stockholm Pride, Stockholm, Sweden, July 30, 2015.

282. Participant observation #26, Stockholm Pride, Stockholm, Sweden, July 30, 2015.

283. Sörberg, 2017: 94.

284. See, for example, Karin Book and Lena Eskilsson, "Coming Out in Copenhagen: Homo Sports Events in City Marketing," *Sport In Society* 13, no. 2 (2010): 314–28.

285. Sanna Strand and Katharina Kehl, ""A Country to Fall in Love with/in": Gender and Sexuality in Swedish Armed Forces' Marketing Campaigns," *International Feminist Journal of Politics* 21, no. 2 (2019): 295–314.

286. Julia Lagerman, "Queering Space in a Place within a Place?: Geographical Imaginations of Swedish Pride Festivals" (Master's thesis, Uppsala University, 2018).

287. Swedish case interview #3, Stockholm, Sweden, August 26, 2015.

288. Swedish case interview #3, Stockholm, Sweden, August 26, 2015.

289. Ayoub, 2014(b): 338.

290. Swedish case interview #3, Stockholm, Sweden, August 26, 2015.

291. Swedish case interview #3, Stockholm, Sweden, August 26, 2015.

292. See, for example, in the Netherlands: Niels Spierings, "Homonationalism and Voting for the Populist Radical Right: Addressing Unanswered Questions by Zooming in on the Dutch Case," *International Journal of Public Opinion Research* (2020): edaa005, https://doi.org/10.1093/ijpor/edaa005.

293. Niels Spierings, Marcel Lubbers, and Andrej Zaslove, " 'Sexually Modern Nativist Voters': Do They Exist and Do They Vote for the Populist Radical Right?," *Gender and Education* 29, no. 2 (2017): 216–37.

294. Jens Rydgren, "Immigration Sceptics, Xenophobes or Racists? Radical Right-Wing Voting in Six West European Countries," *European Journal Of Political Research* 47, no. 6 (2008): 737–65.

295. Danielle Lee Tomson, "The Rise of Sweden Democrats: Islam, Populism and the End of Swedish Exceptionalism," The Brookings Institution, March 25, 2020, https://www.brookings.edu/research/the-rise-of-sweden-democrats-and-the-end-of-swedish-exceptionalism/.

296. Danielle Lee Tomson, The Brookings Institution, March 25, 2020.

297. See, for example, "Gay Sweden Democrat Backs Party's Pride Flag Decision," *The Local Sweden*, September 15, 2019, https://www.thelocal.se/20190915/gay-sweden-democrat-backs-council-vote-to-stop-flying-pride-flah.

298. Niels Spierings, Marcel Lubbers, and Andrej Zaslove, " 'Sexually Modern Nativist Voters': Do They Exist and Do They Vote for the Populist Radical Right?," *Gender and Education* 29, no. 2 (2017): 216–37.

299. Danielle Lee Tomson, The Brookings Institution, March 25, 2020.

300. Tomson, 2020.

301. See, for example, Russell F. Farnen, ed., *Nationalism, Ethnicity, and Identity: Cross National and Comparative Perspectives* (London: Routledge, 2017).

302. Michele Micheletti, *Civil Society and State Relations in Sweden* (London: Routledge, 2019).

303. Francesca Romana Ammaturo, "Gender, Sexuality and Human Rights: A European Perspective," in *European Sexual Citizenship* (Cham: Palgrave Macmillan, 2017), 7–30.

304. Note: Unfortunately, Sweden's influential presence in world politics sometimes comes with negative consequences, as seen with sterilization practices of transgender people across Europe. This case is beyond the scope of this foreign policy analysis; for more information on the practice, see Daniela Alaattinoğlu and Ruth Rubio-Marín, "Redress for Involuntarily Sterilised Trans People in Sweden against Evolving Human Rights Standards: A Critical Appraisal," *Human Rights Law Review* (2020).

305. Timo Fleckenstein and Soohyun Christine Lee, "The Politics of Postindustrial Social Policy: Family Policy Reforms in Britain, Germany, South Korea, and

Sweden," *Comparative Political Studies* 47, no. 2 (2014): 601–30; Finn Diderichsen, "Market Reforms in Health Care and Sustainability of the Welfare State: Lessons from Sweden," *Health Policy* 32 (1995): 141–53.

306. Fia Sundevall and Alma Persson, "LGBT in the Military: Policy Development in Sweden 1944–2014," *Sexuality Research and Social Policy* 13, no. 2 (2016): 119–29.

307. For a discussion on Sweden's status in global politics in 2020, see Richard Milne, "Sweden: Why the 'Moral Superpower' Dissented Over COVID-19," *Los Angeles Times*, October 16, 2020, https://www.latimes.com/world-nation/story/2020-10-16/sweden-why-the-moral-superpower-dissented-over-covid-19.

Chapter 4

1. Elizabeth Landau, Zain Verjee, and Antonia Mortensen, "Uganda President: Homosexuals Are 'Disgusting,' " *CNN World*, February 25, 2014, http://www.cnn.com/2014/02/24/world/africa/uganda-homosexuality-interview/.

2. Landau, Verjee, and Mortenson, 2014. See also "Uganda Kill the Gays Bill," *Huffington Post*, 2009–2016, http://www.huffingtonpost.com/news/uganda-kill-the-gays-bill//.

3. Note: The Ugandan law has undergone many revisions. The 2011 iteration removed the death penalty but added the crime of "attempted homosexuality." "Attempted homosexuality" is defined under the Ugandan law as an attempt to engage any form of sexual behavior with someone of the same sex. Ultimately, the Ugandan Parliament passed the AHA in December 2013, and President Yoweri Museveni signed it into law in February 2014. Later, the AHA was invalidated by the Uganda's Constitutional Court on procedural grounds; however, in October 2019, members of the Ugandan government once again announced plans to introduce a bill imposing the death penalty for same-sex relations. See "Uganda Anti-Gay Timeline," Gay & Lesbian Advocates and Defenders, May 6, 2014, https://www.glad.org/wp-content/uploads/2014/05/uganda-timeline.pdf.

4. US case interview #40, Washington, DC, January 15, 2016; #44, Washington, DC, September 24, 2015.

5. US case interview #40, Washington, DC, January 15, 2016; #44, Washington, DC, September 24, 2015.

6. See Bureau of Democracy, Human Rights, and Labor, Human Rights Practices Report 2009, US Department of State, March 11, 2010, https://2009-2017.state.gov/j/drl/rls/hrrpt/2009/frontmatter/135936.htm. See also "Homophobia Is Defeated but Not Yet Deterred: Next Steps in the Struggle for Equality in Uganda and Beyond," *Global Equality Today*, May 14, 2010, https://globalequality.wordpress.com/tag/bi-sexual/.

7. Kristien Stassen, Roel Smolders, and Pieter Leroy, "Sensitizing Events as Trigger for Discursive Renewal and Institutional Change in Flanders' Environmental

Health Approach, 1970s–1990s," *Environmental Health* 12, no. 46 (June 2013), https://doi.org10.1186/1476-069X-12-46.

8. Wiering and Arts, 2006, as cited in Stassen et al., 2. See also Stassen, Smolders, and Leroy, "Sensitizing Events," 2013: 12.

9. See, for example, Martin B. Carstensen and Vivien A. Schmidt, "Power through, over and in Ideas: Conceptualizing Ideational Power in Discursive Institutionalism," *Journal of European Public Policy* 23, no. 3 (2015): 318–37, https://doi.org/10.1080/13501763.2015.1115534; or Frank Fischer and Herbert Gottweis, *The Argumentative Turn Revisited: Public Policy as Communicative Practice* (Durham: Duke University Press, 2012).

10. Stassen, Smolders, and Leroy, 2013.

11. Global Barometer of Gay Rights (GBGR) and Global Barometer of Transgender Rights (GBTR)," Franklin & Marshall College, accessed May 5, 2021, https://www.fandmglobalbarometers.org/. See also Susan Dicklitch, Berwood Yost, and Bryan M. Dougan, "Building a Barometer of Gay Rights (GBGR): A Case Study of Uganda and the Persecution of Homosexuals," *Human Rights Quarterly* 34, no. 2 (2012): 448–71, https://doi.org/10.1353/hrq.2012.0033.

12. Hristos Doucouliagos and Martin Paldam, "Conditional Aid Effectiveness: A Meta-Study," *Journal of International Development* 22, no. 4 (April 3, 2009), https://doi.org/10.1002/jid.1582.

13. Hilde Selbervik, "Aid and Conditionality," The Organisation for Economic Co-operation and Development, July 1999, https://www.oecd.org/countries/tanzania/35178610.pdf.

14. Kintu, *The Ugandan Morality Crusade*, 2018.

15. Havard Bergo, "Has Foreign Aid Led to Economic Growth in Uganda?," Global Risk Insights, May 18, 2015, https://globalriskinsights.com/2015/05/has-foreign-aid-led-to-economic-growth-in-uganda/.

16. See Carol Lancaster, *Foreign Aid: Diplomacy, Development, Domestic Politics* (Chicago, IL: University of Chicago Press, 2008); Ilan Kapoor, "Foreign Aid as G(r)ift," in *The Postcolonial Politics of Development* (Routledge, 2008), 76–94; Shamima Ahmed and David Potter, *NGOs in International Politics* (Boulder, CO: Kumarian Press, 2013); Markus Thiel, "Theorizing the EU's International Promotion of LGBTI Rights Policies in the Global South," *EU Development Policies*, 2019, 35–53, https://doi.org/10.1007/978-3-030-01307-3_3.

17. See Hristos Doucouliagos and Martin Paldam, "Conditional Aid Effectiveness: A Meta-Study," *Journal of International Development* 22, no. 4 (April 3, 2009), https://doi.org/10.1002/jid.1582).

18. Simone Dietrich, "Bypass or Engage? Explaining Donor Delivery Tactics in Foreign Aid Allocation," *International Studies Quarterly* 57, no. 4 (2013): 698–712, https://doi.org/10.1111/isqu.12041.

19. "Swedish Minister Meets Ugandan Gay Activists," *The Local Sweden*, February 25, 2014, https://www.thelocal.se/20140225/swedish-minister-meets-ugandan-gay-activists-anders-borg-lgbt-homosexuality.

20. See, for example, "Issue of Gujarat Chief Minister Narendra Modi's Visa Status: Statement by David C. Mulford, U.S. Ambassador to India," US Department of State, March 21, 2005, https://2001-2009.state.gov/p/sca/rls/rm/2005/43701.htm.

21. Piotr Lis, "The Impact of Armed Conflict and Terrorism on Foreign Aid: A Sector-Level Analysis," *World Development* 110 (2018): 283–94.

22. Deborah Kintu, *The Ugandan Morality Crusade: The Brutal Campaign against Homosexuality and Pornography under Yoweri Museveni* (Jefferson, NC: McFarland & Company, Inc., Publishers, 2018).

23. Cecilia Strand, "The Rise and Fall of a Contentious Social Policy Option—Narratives around the Ugandan Anti-Homosexuality Bill in the Domestic Press," *Journal of African Media Studies* 5, no. 3 (January 2013): 275–94, https://doi.org/10.1386/jams.5.3.275_1.

24. Kintu, *The Ugandan Morality Crusade*, 2018.

25. Robbie Corey-Boulet, "The Trump Effect," *World Policy Journal* 34, no. 3 (2017): 83–89, https://doi.org/10.1215/07402775-4280064.

26. Samantha Power, *Education of an Idealist* (New York: HarperCollins Books, 2019), 282.

27. Margaret E. Keck and Kathryn Sikkink, *Activists beyond Borders: Advocacy Networks in International Politics* (Ithaca, NY: Cornell University Press, 1998): 79.

28. Daniel Chong, *Debating Human Rights* (Boulder, CO: Rienner, 2014), 25. See also David Forsythe, *Human Rights in International Relations* (Cambridge: Cambridge University Press, 2000), 159.

29. For context, see Oren Dorell, "Exclusive: First Diplomat for LGBT Rights Speaks Out," *USA Today*, April 26, 2015, https://www.usatoday.com/story/news/world/2015/04/26/us-diplomat-champion-for-lgbt-people/26314885/.

30. Helene Coley Nicholson, "After the Visits. . . ," *Jamaica Observer*, December 30, 2015, http://m.jamaicaobserver.com/columns/After-the-visits_47377.

31. Michael K. Lavers, "Gay U.S. Officials Travel to Jamaica," *Washington Blade*, May 30, 2015, https://www.washingtonblade.com/2015/05/30/gay-u-s-officials-travel-to-jamaica/.

32. Angeline Jackson, "On the Human Rights Frontier," The Global Struggle for LGBT Equality: Panel Discussion, University of Washington, Seattle, Washington, May 13, 2015.

33. Lavers, 2015.

34. Kyle James Rohrich, "Human Rights Diplomacy amidst "World War LGBT": Re-examining Western Promotion of LGBT Rights in Light of the "Traditional Values" Discourse," in *Transatlantic Perspectives on Diplomacy and Diversity*, ed. Anthony Chase (New York: Humanity in Action Press, 2015), 69–96.

35. Michael K. Lavers, "Gay U.S. Officials Travel to Jamaica," *Washington Blade*, May 30, 2015, https://www.washingtonblade.com/2015/05/30/gay-u-s-officials-travel-to-jamaica/.

36. Valerie Hudson and Patricia Leidl, *The Hillary Doctrine: Sex and American Foreign Policy* (New York: Columbia University Press, 2015).

37. For a global perspective of LGBTI rights, see Susan Dicklitch-Nelson, Scottie Thompson Buckland, Berwood Yost, and Danel Draguljić, "From Persecutors to Protectors: Human Rights and the Franklin and Marshall Global Barometer of Gay Rights TM (GBGR)," *Journal of Human Rights* 18, no. 1 (2019): 1–18.

38. Tim Fitzsimons, "Amid 'Kill the Gays' Bill Uproar, Ugandan LGBTQ Activist Is Killed," *NBC News*, October 16, 2019, https://www.nbcnews.com/feature/nbc-out/amid-kill-gays-bill-uproar-ugandan-lgbtq-activist-killed-n1067336. See also Neela Ghoshal and Maria Burnett, "Is It Now Legal to Be Gay in Uganda?," Human Rights Watch, September 12, 2014, https://www.hrw.org/news/2014/08/07/it-now-legal-be-gay-uganda#.

39. Katherine Fairfax Wright and Malika Zouhali-Worrall, *Call Me Kuchu* (Los Angeles, CA: Cinedigm Entertainment Group, 2012), film.

40. Fitzsimons, "Amid 'Kill the Gays' Bill Uproar," 2019.

41. Ibid.

42. Kristen Cheney, "Locating Neocolonialism, 'Tradition,' and Human Rights in Ugandas 'Gay Death Penalty,'" *African Studies Review* 55, no. 2 (2012): 77–95, https://doi.org/10.1353/arw.2012.0031.

43. James Kassaga Arinaitwe, "How US Evangelicals Are Shaping Development in Uganda," *Al Jazeera*, July 25, 2014, https://www.aljazeera.com/indepth/opinion/2014/07/us-evangelicals-uganda-2014724135920268137.html.

44. Josh Kron, "In Uganda, Push to Curb Gays Draws U.S. Guest," *New York Times*, May 3, 2010, https://www.nytimes.com/2010/05/03/world/africa/03uganda.html.

45. Wright and Zouhali-Worrall, *Call Me Kuchu*, 2012.

46. Robbie Corey-Boulet, *Love Falls on Us: a Story of American Ideas and African LGBT Lives* (London: Zed Books, 2019).

47. Cynthia Burack, "Getting What 'We' Deserve: Terrorism, Tolerance, Sexuality, and the Christian Right," *New Political Science* 25, no. 3 (2003): 329–49, https://doi.org/https://doi.org/10.1080/07393140307180.

48. "Human Rights: The Gay Divide," *Economist*, October 9, 2014, https://www.economist.com/leaders/2014/10/09/the-gay-divide).

49. Alison Brysk, *The Future of Human Rights* (Cambridge: Polity Press, 2018).

50. Brysk, 2018.

51. African Studies Center, "Uganda History," in *East Africa Living Encyclopedia* (University of Pennsylvania), accessed April 11, 2020, http://www.africa.upenn.edu/NEH/uhistory.htm.

52. Joseph O'Mahoney, "How Britain's Colonial Legacy Still Affects LGBT Politics around the World," *The Conversation*, April 16, 2019, https://theconversation.com/how-britains-colonial-legacy-still-affects-lgbt-politics-around-the-world-95799.

53. Kay Lalor and Adrian Jjuuko, "International Solidarity and Its Role in the Fight against Uganda's Anti-Homosexuality Bill," in *Sexuality, Gender and Social Justice: What's Law Got to Do with It?* (Institute of Development Studies, 2016), 126.

54. "Briefing: Punitive Aid Cuts Disrupt Healthcare in Uganda," *The New Humanitarian*, April 2, 2014, https://www.thenewhumanitarian.org/analysis/2014/04/02/briefing-punitive-aid-cuts-disrupt-healthcare-uganda.

55. Pia Laskar, "The Illiberal Turn: Aid Conditionalis and the Queering of Sexual Citizenship," *Lambda Nordica* 1 (2014): 86–100.

56. Laskar, 2014: 86–100.

57. "IGLHRC Demands Investigation into Killing of Ugandan LGBT Rights Defender," Outright Action International, January 27, 2010, https://outrightinternational.org/content/iglhrc-demands-investigation-killing-ugandan-lgbt-rights-defender.

58. Keck and Sikkink, *Activists beyond Borders,* 1998: 3.

59. US case interviews #55, New York, NY, January 20, 2016; #41, Seattle, Washington, January 19, 2016.

60. Phillip M. Ayoub, "With Arms Wide Shut: Threat Perception, Norm Reception, and Mobilized Resistance to LGBT Rights," *Journal of Human Rights* 13, no. 3 (March 2014): 337–62, https://doi.org/10.1080/14754835.2014.919213.

61. Swedish case interview #6, Stockholm, Sweden, December 14, 2015.

62. Katarina Jungar and Salla Peltonen, "Acts of Homonationalism: Mapping Africa in the Swedish Media," *Sexualities* 20, no. 5–6 (2016): 715–37, https://doi.org/10.1177/1363460716645806.

63. Swedish case interview #5, Stockholm, Sweden, August 13, 2015.

64. "Swedish Minister Meets Ugandan Gay Activists," *The Local Sweden*, February 25, 2014, https://www.thelocal.se/20140225/swedish-minister-meets-ugandan-gay-activists-anders-borg-lgbt-homosexuality.

65. Here again I make the distinction between formal policy mandates and ad hoc public statements. For example, South African leaders at times support LGBT rights in international institutions, yet it is not a formal institutionalized mandate in the country. See Abadir M. Ibrahim, "LGBT Rights in Africa and the Discursive Role of International Human Rights Law," *African Human Rights Law Journal* 15, no. 2 (2015): 263–81.

66. US case interviews #39, Seattle, Washington, May 13, 2015; #41, Seattle, Washington, January 19, 2016; #61, Seattle, Washington, December 3, 2015.

67. Saurav Jung Thapa, "LGBT Uganda Today: Continuing Danger Despite Nullification of Anti-Homosexuality Act," Human Rights Campaign Foundation, September 25, 2015, https://assets2.hrc.org/files/assets/resources/Global_Spotlight_Uganda__designed_version__September_25__2015.pdf.

68. Clifford Bob, *The International Struggle for New Human Rights* (Philadelphia: University of Pennsylvania Press, 2010), 61.

69. See, for example, Mario Hugo Ramirez, "The Fate of Many, the Brutality of Others: Human Rights Documentation and the Margins of Subjectivity in El Salvador" (PhD diss., UCLA, 2017).

70. Nicole Laviolette, "Independent Human Rights Documentation and Sexual Minorities: an Ongoing Challenge for the Canadian Refugee Determination Process," *International Journal of Human Rights* 13, no. 2–3 (2009): 437–76, https://doi.org/10.1080/13642980902758234.

71. Strand, 2013.

72. Participant observation #83, Stockholm Pride, Stockholm, Sweden, July 29, 2019.

73. For example: "Understanding BDSM in Indonesia," Presentation at Stockholm Pride, Stockholm, Sweden, July 30, 2019; or "Art and Culture to Raise Awareness," Presentation at Stockholm Pride, Stockholm Sweden, August 1, 2019.

74. Tiffany Jones, "Researching and Working for Transgender Youth: Contexts, Problems and Solutions," *Social Sciences* 5, no. 3 (2016): 43, https://doi.org/10.3390/socsci5030043.

75. Jones, 2016: 12.

76. Frederik Nilsson as quoted in Jones, 2016: 10.

77. Frederik Nilsson as quoted in Jones, 2016: 11.

78. Christine M. Klapeer, "Dangerous Liaisons?: (Homo) Developmentalism, Sexual Modernization and LGBTIQ Rights in Europe," in *Routledge Handbook of Queer Development Studies* (London: Routledge, 2018): 102–18.

79. Therese Brolin, "Framing the Results Agenda in Swedish Development Co-operation," *Development Policy Review* 35 (May 2017), https://doi.org/10.1111/dpr.12298.

80. "Swedish Minister Meets Ugandan Gay Activists," *The Local Sweden*, February 25, 2014, https://www.thelocal.se/20140225/swedish-minister-meets-ugandan-gay-activists-anders-borg-lgbt-homosexuality.

81. Swedish case interview #8, Stockholm, Sweden, August 26, 2015.

82. Swedish case interview #8, Stockholm, Sweden, August 26, 2015.

83. Amanda Terkel, "Sweden Cutting Aid to Uganda over 'Appalling' Anti-Homosexuality Bill," ThinkProgress, December 3, 2009, https://archive.thinkprogress.org/sweden-cutting-aid-to-uganda-over-appalling-anti-homosexuality-bill-7c99e3fbbf89/.

84. Swedish case interview #2, Linköping, Sweden, August 10, 2015.

85. Swedish case interview #8, Stockholm, Sweden, August 26, 2015.

86. Sveriges Radio, "Sweden Reconsidering Aid to Uganda," February 24, 2014, https://sverigesradio.se/artikel/5793295.

87. It is important to note that many news outlets incorrectly reported that Sweden cut its aid to Uganda across the board, missing the important distinction that Sweden in fact cut aid to the Ugandan government, but maintained it to Ugandan civil society and nongovernmental entities. This is still considered making aid conditional, but not necessarily cutting it.

88. Pia Laskar, "The Illiberal Turn: Aid Conditionalis and the Queering of Sexual Citizenship," *Lambda Nordica* 19, no. 1 (2014): 87–100.

89. Joe Morgan, "Gay Uganda's Plea: 'Don't Cut Aid, You'll Make It Worse," *Gay Star News*, February 26, 2014, https://www.gaystarnews.com/article/gay-ugandas-plea-dont-cut-aid-youll-make-it-worse260214/.

90. Joe Morgan, "Gay Uganda's Plea: 'Don't Cut Aid, You'll Make It Worse," *Gay Star News*, February 26, 2014, https://www.gaystarnews.com/article/gay-ugandas-plea-dont-cut-aid-youll-make-it-worse260214/.

91. "Speech by the Minister for Foreign Affairs Margot Wallström at the Seminar about #femdefenders, Arranged by Women to Women International (Kvinna till Kvinna)," Sweden Ministry for Foreign Affairs, November 28, 2014, https://www.government.se/speeches/2014/11/speech-by-the-minister-for-foreign-affairs-margot-wallstrom-at-the-seminar-about-femdefenders-arranged-by-kvinna-till-kvinna/.

92. Dietrich, "Bypass or Engage?," 2013.

93. Simone Dietrich and Amanda M. Murdie, "Human Rights Shaming through INGOs and Foreign Aid Delivery," *SSRN Electronic Journal*, 2015, https://doi.org/10.2139/ssrn.2641766.

94. Joseph Wright, "How Foreign Aid Can Foster Democratization in Authoritarian Regimes," *American Journal of Political Science* 53, no. 3 (2009): 552–71, https://doi.org/10.1111/j.1540-5907.2009.00386.x.

95. Participant observation #21, Stockholm, Sweden, July 28, 2015.

96. In Lube in Uganda, accessed September 13, 2015, http://www.oliver-ocheva.se/i-lube-uganda/.

97. "How Can I Protect My Partners," Centers for Disease Control and Prevention, accessed May 7, 2021, https://www.cdc.gov/hiv/basics/livingwithhiv/protecting-others.html.

98. In Lube in Uganda, accessed March 16, 2020.

99. In Lube in Uganda, accessed March 16, 2020.

100. "The Anti-Homosexuality Act," Ugandan government, 2014, https://www.refworld.org/pdfid/530c4bc64.pdf?fbclid=IwAR0r_ZCq2az0HsiSbQmm 9wyJMc3Vj33bZZ22y_cWtlaN_U8GirNeCoa6sw8,%201-11%20.

101. The Anti-Homosexuality Act," 2014.

102. Daisy Carrington, "On Homosexuality: Uganda's Religious Leaders," CNN, October 16, 2014, https://www.cnn.com/2014/10/16/world/africa/on-homosexuality-ugandas-religious-leaders.

103. Participant observation #10, Stockholm, Sweden, July 28, 2015.

104. Participant observation #10, Stockholm, Sweden, July 28, 2015.

105. See, for example, Betty Reardon and Asha Hans, *The Gender Imperative: Human Security vs State Security* (Milton Park, Abingdon, Oxon: Routledge, 2019).

106. Participant observation #10, Stockholm, Sweden, July 28, 2015.

107. "RAFD: 1992-10-20: Tobias Wikström to Margaretha af Ugglas," RFSL Archives, quoted in Laskar, "The Illiberal Turn," 2014: 89.

108. RFSL Archives, 1992.

109. David Forsythe, *Human Rights and Comparative Foreign Policy* (Tokyo, Japan: United Nations University Press, 2000).

110. US case interview #40, Washington, DC, January 15, 2016.

111. US case interview #53, New York, NY, January 13, 2016.

112. US case interview #59, New York, NY, January 29, 2016.

113. US Department of State, "Country Reports on Human Rights Practices: Kyrgyz Republic," 2011, https://2009-2017.state.gov/j/drl/rls/hrrpt/2011humanrights-report/index.htm#wrapper.

114. Jo Becker, *Campaigning for Justice: Human Rights Advocacy in Practice* (Stanford, CA: Stanford University Press, 2013).

115. US case interview #40, Washington, DC, January 15, 2016.

116. "Homophobia Is Defeated but Not Yet Deterred: Next Steps in the Struggle for Equality in Uganda and Beyond," *Global Equality Today*, May 14, 2010, https://globalequality.wordpress.com/tag/bi-sexual/.

117. See "Freedom in the World," Freedom House 2021, accessed May 7, 2021, https://freedomhouse.org/report/freedom-world.

118. "LiveAtState: Assistant Secretary of State Michael Posner on the 2011 Human Rights Report," US Department of State, June 28, 2012, https://2009-2017.state.gov/r/pa/ime/194287.htm.

119. Example of mission strategic plans: "FY 2014–2017 Department of State and USAID Strategic Plan," US Department of State, accessed April 15, 2019, http://www.state.gov/s/d/rm/rls/dosstrat/2014/.

120. "Integrated Country Strategy: Uganda," US Department of State, August 3, 2018, https://www.state.gov/wp-content/uploads/2019/01/ICS-Uganda_UNCLASS_508.pdf.

121. For a discussion on the modern human rights diplomatic toolbox, see Veronika Haász, Jakub Jaraczewski, and Karolina Podstawa, "The FRAME Toolbox for the EU Fundamental and Human Rights Policies," FRAME, 2017, http://www.fp7-frame.eu/frame-reps-14-3/.

122. "Thematic Programming Priorities," US Department of State Bureau of Democracy, Human Rights, and Labor, accessed April 3, 2020, https://www.state.gov/key-topics-bureau-of-democracy-human-rights-and-labor/programs/thematic-programming-priorities/.

123. See, for example, "Office of the Spokesperson," US Department of State Bureau of Global Public Affairs, https://www.state.gov/bureaus-offices/under-secretary-for-public-diplomacy-and-public-affairs/bureau-of-global-public-affairs/office-of-the-spokesperson/.

124. "Human Rights and Democracy Fund," US Department of State Bureau of Democracy, Human Rights and Labor, accessed April 15, 2019, https://www.state.gov/j/drl/p/.

125. "Thematic Program Priorities," US Department of State DRL, 2021, accessed May 7, 2021, https://www.state.gov/key-topics-bureau-of-democracy-human-rights-and-labor/programs/thematic-programming-priorities/.

126. "Assistant Secretary of State for Democracy, Tom Malinowski and Ugandan Activist Frank Mugisha Respond to *New York Times* Article 'U.S. Support

of Gay Rights in Africa May Have Done More Harm Than Good,'" *Global Equality Today*, January 4, 2016, https://globalequality.wordpress.com/2016/01/04/assistant-secretary-of-state-for-democracy-tom-malinowski-and-ugandan-activist-frank-mugisha-respond-to-new-york-times-article-u-s-support-of-gay-rights-in-africa-may-have-done-more-harm-th/.

127. "Reflections on the Obama Administration's Human Rights Policies and the Way Forward," Council on Foreign Relations, March 4, 2013, https://www.cfr.org/event/reflections-obama-administrations-human-rights-policies-and-way-forward.

128. Michael K. Lavers, "LGBT Envoy Travels to Uganda," *Washington Blade*, July 21, 2015, https://www.washingtonblade.com/2015/07/21/lgbt-envoy-travels-to-uganda/.

129. "Statement by Assistant Secretary of State Michael H. Posner on His Visit to Uganda," US Department of State Press Releases, September 6, 2012, https://2009-2017.state.gov/j/drl/rls/prsrl/2012/197591.htm.

130. "Human Rights for LGBT Persons: A Q&A with Special Envoy Randy Berry," *The Foreign Service Journal* 92, no. 5 (June 2015): 20–24, https://www.afsa.org/sites/default/files/fsj-2015-06-june.pdf.

131. Wright and Zouhali-Worrall, *Call Me Kuchu*, 2012.

132. See Audie Klotz, *Norms in International Relations: The Struggle against Apartheid* (Ithaca, NY: Cornell University Press, 1999).

133. US case interview #55, New York, NY, January 20, 2016.

134. Colin Stewart, "N.Y. Times under Continued Attack for Anti-LGBTI Article," *76 Crimes*, December 29, 2015, https://76crimes.com/2015/12/29/n-y-times-under-continued-attack-for-anti-lgbti-article/.

135. Cynthia Burack, *Because We Are Human: Contesting U.S. Support for Gender and Sexuality Human Rights Abroad* (Albany, NY: State University of New York Press, 2018): 202.

136. "Our Model For LGBTIQ Human Rights Change," Outright Action International, accessed April 15, 2019, https://www.outrightinternational.org/how-we-work.

137. US case #61, Seattle, Washington, December 3, 2015; #53, New York, NY, January 13, 2016; #59, New York, NY, January 29, 2016; #55, New York, NY, January 20, 2016.

138. "Statement by NSC Spokesperson Caitlin Hayden on the Response to Uganda's Enactment of the Anti-Homosexuality Act," The White House Office of the Press Secretary, June 19, 2014, https://www.whitehouse.gov/the-press-office/2014/06/19/statement-nsc-spokesperson-caitlin-hayden-response-uganda-s-enactment-an.

139. "Statement by NSC Spokesperson Caitlin Hayden on the Response to Uganda's Enactment of the Anti-Homosexuality Act."

140. Thapa, 2015.

141. Laskar, 2014: 87.

142. Jim Yong Kim, "World Bank Group President Jim Yong Kim: Discrimination by Law Carries a High Price," *World Bank News*, February 28, 2014.

143. See Rhonda L. Callaway and Elizabeth G. Matthews, *Strategic US Foreign Assistance: The Battle between Human Rights and National Security* (New York: Routledge, 2008); Timothy M. Peterson, Amanda Murdie, and Victor Asal, "Human Rights, NGO Shaming and the Exports of Abusive States," *British Journal of Political Science* 48, no. 3 (January 2016): 767–86, https://doi.org/10.1017/s0007123416000065; Gordon Crawford and Simonida Kacarska, "Aid Sanctions and Political Conditionality: Continuity and Change," *Journal of International Relations and Development* 22, no. 1 (August 2017): 184–214, https://doi.org/10.1057/s41268-017-0099-8; David C. Mowery and Carol Lancaster, "Aid's Purposes: A Brief History," in *Foreign Aid: Diplomacy, Development, Domestic Politics* (Chicago, IL: University of Chicago Press, 2006): 25–61.

144. Allison Carnegie and Nikolay Marinov, "Foreign Aid, Human Rights, and Democracy Promotion: Evidence from a Natural Experiment," *American Journal of Political Science* 61, no. 3 (2017): 671–83, https://doi.org/10.1111/ajps.12289.

145. Swedish case participant observation #18, Stockholm Pride, Stockholm, Sweden, July 27, 2015.

146. Gabriella R. Montinola, "When Does Aid Conditionality Work?," *Studies in Comparative International Development* 45, no. 3 (2010): 358–82.

147. See Daniela Donno and Michael Neureiter, "Can Human Rights Conditionality Reduce Repression? Examining The European Union's Economic Agreements," *Review of International Organizations* 13, no. 3 (2018): 335–57; Wayne Sandholtz, "United States Military Assistance and Human Rights," *Human Rights Quarterly* 38, no. 4 (2016): 1070–1101, https://doi.org/10.1353/hrq.2016.0057.

148. US interviews #39, Seattle, Washington, May 13, 2015; and #48, Seattle, Washington, May 13, 2015.

149. Rachel Bergenfield and Alice M. Miller, "Queering International Development? An Examination of New LGBT Rights Rhetoric, Policy, and Programming among International Development Agencies," *LGBTQ Policy Journal* (2014), https://doi.org/10.2139/ssrn.2507515;

150. On political trends of leaders using themes of LGBTI rights as an outside foreign threat, see Phillip M. Ayoub, "With Arms Wide Shut: Threat Perception, Norm Reception, and Mobilized Resistance to LGBT Rights," *Journal of Human Rights* 13, no. 3 (March 2014b): 337–62. https://doi.org/10.1080/14754835.2014.919213.

151. Fernando Nuñez-Mietz Lucrecia García Iommi, "Can Transnational Norm Advocacy Undermine Internalization? Explaining Immunization against LGBT Rights in Uganda," *International Studies Quarterly* 61, no. 1 (2017): 196–209. https://doi.org/10.1093/isq/sqx011.

152. US case interviews #39, Seattle, Washington, May 13, 2015; #41, Seattle, Washington, January 19, 2016; #48, Seattle, Washington, May 13, 2015.

153. Thapa, 2015.

154. Thapa, 2015.

155. Jan Eckel and Rachel Ward, *The Ambivalence of Good: Human Rights in International Politics since the 1940s* (Oxford: Oxford University Press, 2019).

156. Sandy Vogelgesang, "Diplomacy of Human Rights," *International Studies Quarterly* 23, no. 2 (1979): 216–45, https://doi.org/10.2307/2600243.

157. Hendri Yulius, Shawna Tang, and Baden Offord, "The Globalization of LGBT Identity and Same-Sex Marriage as a Catalyst of Neo-Institutional Values: Singapore and Indonesia in Focus," *Global Perspectives on Same-Sex Marriage* (October 2017): 171–96, https://doi.org/10.1007/978-3-319-62764-9_9.

158. Nabamita Dutta and Claudia R. Williamson, "Can Foreign Aid Free the Press?," *Journal of Institutional Economics* 12, no. 3 (February 2016): 603–21, https://doi.org/10.1017/s1744137415000557.

159. Alexis Kedo and Colby Goodman, "Defense Experts Highlight Effectiveness of Human Rights Conditioning," Security Assistance Monitor, Center for International Policy, December 10, 2015, https://www.securityassistance.org/blog/defense-experts-highlight-effectiveness-human-rights-conditioning.

160. Oscar Quine, "Frank Mugisha: Uganda's Most Outspoken Gay Rights Activist on Changing People's Attitudes, Coming Out, and the Threat of Being Attacked," *Independent*, August 22, 2014, https://www.independent.co.uk/news/people/profiles/frank-mugisha-uganda-s-most-outspoken-gay-rights-activist-changing-people-s-attitudes-coming-out-and-threat-being-attacked-9681476.html.

161. "Assistant Secretary of State for Democracy, Tom Malinowski and Ugandan Activist Frank Mugisha Respond to *New York Times* Article 'U.S. Support of Gay Rights in Africa May Have Done More Harm Than Good,'" *Global Equality Today*, January 4, 2016, https://globalequality.wordpress.com/2016/01/04/assistant-secretary-of-state-for-democracy-tom-malinowski-and-ugandan-activist-frank-mugisha-respond-to-new-york-times-article-u-s-support-of-gay-rights-in-africa-may-have-done-more-harm-th/.

162. Janoff Douglas, "Homophobia, Human Rights and Diplomacy," University of Dayton Human Rights Center, 2017, https://ecommons.udayton.edu/cgi/viewcontent.cgi?article=1268&context=human_rights.

163. David R. Black, "Addressing Apartheid: Lessons from Australian, Canadian and Swedish Policies in Southern Africa," in *Niche Diplomacy* (London: Palgrave Macmillan, 1997), 100–28.

164. Audie Klotz, *Norms in International Relations: The Struggle against Apartheid* (Ithaca, NY: Cornell University Press, 1999), 172.

165. See Conny Roggeband and Anna van der Vleuten, *Gender Equality Norms in Regional Governance: Transnational Dynamics in Europe, South America and Southern Africa* (London: Palgrave Macmillan, 2014), 43; Martha Finnemore, *National Interests in International Society* (Ithaca, NY: Cornell University Press, 1996).

166. Martha Finnemore and Kathryn Sikkink, "International Norm Dynamics and Political Change," *International Organization* 52, no. 4 (1998): 887–917, https://doi.org/10.1162/002081898550789.

167. Michael K. Lavers, "Gay U.S. Officials Travel to Jamaica," *Washington Blade*, May 30, 2015, https://www.washingtonblade.com/2015/05/30/gay-u-s-officials-travel-to-jamaica/.

168. Evan W. Sandlin, "Competing Concerns: Balancing Human Rights and National Security in US Economic Aid Allocation," *Human Rights Review* 17, no. 4 (2016): 439–62, https://doi.org/10.1007/s12142-016-0426-2.

169. Aaron P. Hansen, "US Military Assistance and Human Rights: An Examination of the Top 30 Recipients of US Military Aid between 1992–2011," The University of Nebraska-Lincoln, 2018.

170. June S. Beittel, Lauren Ploch Blanchard, and Liana Rosen, " 'Leahy Law' Human Rights Provisions and Security Assistance: Issue Overview," Congressional Research Service, January 29, 2014, https://fas.org/sgp/crs/row/R43361.pdf.

171. This vetting is known as "Leahy vetting"; for more context on human rights provisions for security assistance, see Beittel, Blanchard, and Rosen, 2014.

172. Julie A. Mertus, *Bait and Switch: Human Rights and US Foreign Policy* (New York: Routledge, 2008).

173. On quiet diplomacy, see, for example, Kuseni Dlamini, "Is Quiet Diplomacy an Effective Conflict Resolution Strategy?," *South African Yearbook of International Affairs* 3 (2002): 171–78.

174. Power, 2019: 276.

175. Power, 2019: 277.

176. Daniel Baer, "LiveAtState: Human Rights of Lesbian, Gay, Bisexual, and Transgender People," US Department of State, June 20, 2013, https://2009-2017.state.gov/r/pa/ime/211005.htm.

177. Elise Carlson-Rainer, "Chasing Rainbows: Some Country's LGBTI Fight Not Just for Equality, but Survival," *The Globe Post*, May 10, 2019, https://theglobepost.com/2019/05/10/lgbti-rights/.

178. Elise Carlson-Rainer, "Khashoggi Prompts Trump to Reconsider Human Rights in Foreign Policy," *The Hill*, October 22, 2018, https://thehill.com/opinion/international/412058-khashoggi-prompts-trump-to-reconsider-human-rights-in-foreign-policy.

179. Ben Westcott, "Brunei to Punish Gay Sex and Adultery with Death by Stoning," CNN, March 30, 2019, https://www.cnn.com/2019/03/27/asia/brunei-anti-lgbt-stoning-law-intl/index.html.

180. Richard A. Nielsen, "Rewarding Human Rights? Selective Aid Sanctions against Repressive States," *International Studies Quarterly* 57, no. 4 (2013): 791–803, https://doi.org/10.1111/isqu.12049.

181. Tehmina Mahmood, "Quiet Diplomacy," *Pakistan Horizon* 50, no. 4 (October 1997): 93–107, https://www.jstor.org/stable/41394635?seq=1.

182. "Briefing by Special Envoy for the Human Rights of LGBT Persons Randy Berry," US Department of State Office of the Spokesperson, April 20, 2016, https://2009-2017.state.gov/r/pa/prs/ps/2016/04/256425.htm.

183. Daniel Baer, "LiveAtState: Human Rights of Lesbian, Gay, Bisexual, and Transgender People," US Department of State, June 20, 2013, https://2009-2017.state.gov/r/pa/ime/211005.htm.

184. Valentina Carraro and Hortense Jongen, "Leaving the Doors Open or Keeping Them Closed? The Impact of Transparency on the Authority of Peer Reviews in International Organizations," *Global Governance* 24, no. 4 (October 2018): 615–35, https://doi.org/10.1163/19426720-02404008.

185. Power, 2019: 282.

186. While measuring the impact of human rights diplomatic efforts is challenging, the State Department has a comprehensive monitoring and evaluation strategy for international human rights programs. See "DRL Guide to Program Monitoring and Evaluation," US Department of State Bureau of Democracy, Human Rights, and Labor, accessed September 24, 2020, https://www.state.gov/wp-content/uploads/2019/01/DRL-Guide-to-Program-Monitoring-and-Evaluation.pdf.

187. Wayne Basen, "Inside Lou Engle' Anti-Gay Revival," Truth Wins Out, June 30, 2010, https://truthwinsout.org/pressrelease/2010/06/9500/.

188. See Zack Ford, "Rick Warren: Being Gay Is Like 'Punching a Guy in the Nose' or Consuming Arsenic," ThinkProgress, November 28, 2012, https://thinkprogress.org/rick-warren-being-gay-is-like-punching-a-guy-in-the-nose-or-consuming-arsenic-156846278109/.

189. Kintu, *The Ugandan Morality Crusade*, 2018. See also Marcia Oliver, "Transnational Sex Politics, Conservative Christianity, and Antigay Activism in Uganda," *Studies in Social Justice* 7, no. 1 (2012): 83–105, https://doi.org/10.26522/ssj.v7i1.1056.

190. Ford, 2012.

191. Renee Gadoua, "Scott Lively Could Face Fine for Anti-Gay Efforts," *Huffington Post*, October 1, 2015, https://www.huffpost.com/entry/scott-lively-anti-gay-uganda_n_560d85e6e4b0af3706dfef9c.

192. Gadoua, 2015.

193. Jeffrey Gettleman, "Americans' Role Seen in Uganda Anti-Gay Push," *New York Times*, January 3, 2010, https://www.nytimes.com/2010/01/04/world/africa/04uganda.html?_r=0.

194. Mariah Blake, "Meet the American Pastor behind Uganda's Anti-Gay Crackdown," *Mother Jones*, July 31, 2019, https://www.motherjones.com/politics/2014/03/scott-lively-anti-gay-law-uganda/2/.

195. Kintu, 2018: 74.

196. US case interview #49, Washington, DC, March 25, 2015; "Human Rights: The Gay Divide," *Economist*, October 9, 2014, https://www.economist.com/leaders/2014/10/09/the-gay-divide.

197. US case interview #79, Seattle, Washington, April 25, 2019.

198. "Court Cases: SMUG vs. Scott Lively," Sexual Minorities Uganda, accessed November 9, 2020, https://sexualminoritiesuganda.com/publications/court-cases/.

199. Omar G. Encarnación, "The Troubled Rise of Gay Rights Diplomacy," *Current History* 115, no. 777 (January 2016): 17.

200. See Kyle James Rohrich, "Human Rights Diplomacy amidst "World War LGBT": Re-examining Western Promotion of LGBT Rights in Light of the

"Traditional Values" Discourse," in *Transatlantic Perspectives on Diplomacy and Diversity*, ed. Anthony Chase (New York: Humanity in Action Press, 2015), 69–96.

201. Burack, *Because We Are Human*, 2018.

202. Encarnación, "The Troubled Rise of Gay Rights Diplomacy," 2016: 17.

203. Carey McWilliams, *Mask for Privilege: Anti-Semitism in America* (London: Routledge, 2018).

204. Hannah Rosenthal, special envoy to monitor and combat anti-Semitism, "Combating Anti-Semitism: Protecting Human Rights," US Department of State, April 14, 2010, https://2009-2017.state.gov/j/drl/rls/rm/2010/140284. htm. See also "Office of the Special Envoy to Monitor and Combat Anti-Semitism," US Department of State, Secretary for Civilian Security, Democracy, and Human Rights, accessed September 28, 2020, https://www.state.gov/bureaus-offices/under-secretary-for-civilian-security-democracy-and-human-rights/office-of-the-special-envoy-to-monitor-and-combat-anti-semitism/.

205. Farah Anwar Pandith, "Conversations with America: U.S. Engagement with Muslim Communities," US Department of State, July 9, 2010, https://2009-2017.state.gov/s/srmc/144398.htm.

206. "Office of Global Women's Issues," US Department of State, Bureaus and Offices Reporting Directly to the Secretary, https://www.state.gov/bureaus-offices/bureaus-and-offices-reporting-directly-to-the-secretary/office-of-global-womens-issues.

207. Enrique Gracia and Juan Merlo, "Intimate Partner Violence against Women and the Nordic Paradox," *Social Science & Medicine* 157 (2016): 27–30, https://doi.org/10.1016/j.socscimed.2016.03.040.

208. Sultan Barakat, "Priorities and Challenges of Qatar's Humanitarian Diplomacy," *CMI Brief*, no. 7 (2019), https://www.cmi.no/publications/6906-priorities-and-challenges-of-qatars-humanitarian-diplomacy.

209. Mohamed Zayani, *The Al Jazeera Phenomenon: Critical Perspectives on New Arab Media* (New York: Routledge, 2005).

210. "2020 Country Reports on Human Rights Practices: Qatar," US Department of State Bureau of Democracy, Human Rights, and Labor, March 30, 2021, https://www.state.gov/reports/2020-country-reports-on-human-rights-practices/qatar/.

211. US case interview #52, Washington, DC, September 15, 2015.

212. Elise Carlson-Rainer and Dan Mahanty, "The Importance of Human Rights Considerations in Foreign Policy," in *Homeland Security*, April 8, 2019, https://inhomelandsecurity.com/human-rights-foreign-policy/.

213. Swedish case interview #5, Stockholm, Sweden, August 13, 2015.

214. Chris Johnson, "Dan Baer: Time for U.S. to Change Its Relationship with Saudi Arabia," *Washington Blade*, July 9, 2019, https://www.washingtonblade.com/2019/07/09/dan-baer-time-for-u-s-to-change-its-relationship-with-saudi-arabia/.

215. Note: South Africa, the Netherlands, Norway, Brazil, and other nations raised LGBTI abuses starting around the 1990s mainly related to the HIV/AIDS

crisis in global venues. The distinction here in 2011 is that Sweden and the United States formally incorporated LGBTI rights into their foreign policy mandates. Accordingly, this was the first time Sweden cut aid in formal bilateral relations based on LGBTI rights abuses.

216. Wiering and Arts, 2006, as cited by Stassen et al., 2013: 2.

217. See, for example, Roger Ross Williams, *God Loves Uganda* (New York: First-Run Features, October 11, 2013).

218. Cheney, "Locating Neocolonialism, 'Tradition,' and Human Rights," 2012.

219. Swedish case interviews #8, Stockholm, Sweden, August 26, 2015; #9, Stockholm, Sweden, July 31, 2015; US case interviews #41, Seattle, Washington, January 19, 2016; #43, Washington, DC, January 15, 2016; #55, New York, NY, January 20, 2016.

220. Susan Dicklitch-Nelson, "Are LGBTQ Human Rights in Uganda a Lost Cause?," *Georgetown Journal of International Affairs*, February 27, 2020, https://gjia.georgetown.edu/2020/02/27/are-lgbtq-human-rights-in-uganda-a-lost-cause/.

221. "Uganda Threatens to Re-introduce 'Anti-Homosexuality Act,' " OutRight Action International, October 10, 2019, https://outrightinternational.org/content/uganda-plans-re-introduce-anti-homosexuality-act.

222. Gregory Warner, "Uganda Passes Anti-Gay Bill That Includes Life in Prison," NPR, December 20, 2013, https://www.npr.org/sections/parallels/2013/12/20/255825383/uganda-passes-anti-gay-bill-that-includes-life-in-prison.

223. Assistant Secretary of State for Democracy, Tom Malinowski and Ugandan Activist Frank Mugisha Respond to *New York Times* Article "U.S. Support of Gay Rights in Africa May Have Done More Harm Than Good," *Global Equality Today*, January 4, 2016, https://globalequality.wordpress.com/2016/01/04/assistant-secretary-of-state-for-democracy-tom-malinowski-and-ugandan-activist-frank-mugisha-respond-to-new-york-times-article-u-s-support-of-gay-rights-in-africa-may-have-done-more-harm-th/.

224. "Meet Randy Berry, The First U.S. Diplomat for LGBT Rights," *Huffington Post: Queer Voices*, April 29, 2015, https://www.huffpost.com/entry/randy-berry-lgbt-rights-diplomat_n_7173328.

225. Elise Carlson-Rainer, "Will Sexual Minority Rights Be Trumped? Assessing the Policy Sustainability of LGBTI Rights Diplomacy in American Foreign Policy," *Diplomacy & Statecraft* 30, no. 1 (February 2019): 147–63, https://doi.org/10.108 0/09592296.2019.1557422.

226. Rebecca Ingber, "Congressional Administration of Foreign Affairs," *SSRN Electronic Journal*, 2019, https://doi.org/10.2139/ssrn.3361299).

227. Omar G. Encarnación, "Trump and Gay Rights," *Foreign Affairs*, March 31, 2017, https://www.foreignaffairs.com/chapters/2017-02-13/trump-and-gay-rights.

228. Josh Lederman, "Trump Administration Launches Global Effort to End Criminalization of Homosexuality," *NBC News*, February 19, 2019, https://www.

nbcnews.com/politics/national-security/trump-administration-launches-global-effort-end-criminalization-homosexuality-n973081.

229. Lederman, February 19, 2019.

230. Daniel Baer, "LiveAtState: Human Rights of Lesbian, Gay, Bisexual, and Transgender People," US Department of State, June 20, 2013, https://2009-2017.state.gov/r/pa/ime/211005.htm.

231. Mertus, *Bait and Switch*, 2008.

232. Elise Carlson-Rainer, "Khashoggi Prompts Trump," 2018.

233. Johanne Saltnes, "To Sanction or Not to Sanction? Normative Dilemmas in the Promotion of LGBTI Human Rights," *SSRN Electronic Journal*, February 2020, https://doi.org/10.2139/ssrn.3536908.

234. See, for example, "European Parliament Condemns Crackdown on LGBTI Rights in Turkey," The European Parliament's LGBTI Intergroup, February 8, 2018, http://www.lgbt-ep.eu/press-releases/european-parliament-condemns-crackdown-on-lgbti-rights-in-turkey/.

235. Kathryn Sikkink, *The Justice Cascade: How Human Rights Prosecutions Are Changing World Politics* (New York: W.W. Norton Publishers, 2011).

236. Jones, "Researching and Working For Transgender Youth," 2016: 11.

237. See Fitzsimons, "Amid 'Kill the Gays' Bill Uproar," 2019. See also Burack, *Because We Are Human*, 2018: 199.

238. "Assistant Secretary of State for Democracy, Tom Malinowski and Ugandan Activist Frank Mugisha Respond to *New York Times* Article "U.S. Support of Gay Rights in Africa May Have Done More Harm Than Good," *Global Equality Today*, January 4, 2016, https://globalequality.wordpress.com/2016/01/04/assistant-secretary-of-state-for-democracy-tom-malinowski-and-ugandan-activist-frank-mugisha-respond-to-new-york-times-article-u-s-support-of-gay-rights-in-africa-may-have-done-more-harm-th/.

239. Ludmilla Alexeeva, "In Russia, Human Rights Groups Need Western Aid More Than Ever," *Washington Post*, February 24, 2016, https://www.washingtonpost.com/opinions/in-russia-human-rights-groups-need-western-aid-more-than-ever/2016/02/24/b8e934d2-d1c0-11e5-b2bc-988409ee911b_story.html.

240. "Meet Randy Berry, The First U.S. Diplomat for LGBT Rights," *Huffington Post: Queer Voices*, April 29, 2015, https://www.huffpost.com/entry/randy-berry-lgbt-rights-diplomat_n_7173328.

Chapter 5

1. Lydia Malmedie, "Contested Issue and Incremental Change. The Example of LGBTI in EU Foreign Policy," *Der moderne Staat* (2016): 35–50, https://doi.org/10.3224/dms.v9i1.23639. For a broad discussion on gender and diplomacy, see

Ann E. Towns and Karin Aggestam, eds., *Gendering Diplomacy and International Negotiation* (London: Palgrave Macmillan, 2018).

2. See: David K. Johnson, *The Lavender Scare: The Cold War Persecution of Gays and Lesbians in the Federal Government* (Chicago: University of Chicago Press, 2006); Kelly Kollman, *The Same-Sex Unions Revolution in Western Democracies: International Norms and Domestic Policy Change* (Manchester: Manchester University Press, 2013); Manon Tremblay, David Paternotte, and Carol Johnson, *The Lesbian and Gay Movement and the State: Comparative Insights into a Transformed Relationship* (London: Routledge, 2011).

3. See, for example, Roman Kuhar and David Paternotte, *Anti-Gender Campaigns in Europe: Mobilizing against Equality* (Lanham, MD: Rowman and Littlefield International, 2017); Peter Aggleton, Paul Boyce, Henrietta Moore, and Richard G. Parker, *Understanding Global Sexualities: New Frontiers* (London: Routledge, 2016).

4. Note: This measurement is predicated on a formal incorporation of LGBTI rights in the foreign policy of these nations. It does not include countries that raise LGBTI rights on an ad hoc basis in the UN, for example. This small number of nations have LGBTI rights as a formal pillar of their human rights portfolio and fund global LGBTI civil society. As such, this number is measured by formal partners and funders to the largest global multinational fund called the "Global Equality Fund." For a full list of countries, see "Global Equality Fund," US Department of State Bureau of Democracy, Human Rights, and Labor, accessed September 30, 2020, https://www.state.gov/global-equality-fund/.

5. Notably, in 2020, Mexico became the first Global South country to implement a formal "feminist foreign policy." See Lyric Thompson, "Mexican Diplomacy Has Gone Feminist," *Foreign Policy*, January 14, 2020, https://foreignpolicy.com/2020/01/14/mexican-diplomacy-feminist-foreign-policy/.

6. Susan Haskins, "The Influence of Roman Laws Regarding Same-Sex Acts on Homophobia in Africa," *African Human Rights Law Journal* 14, no. 2 (2014): 393–411, http://www.saflii.org/za/journals/AHRLJ/2014/21.html.

7. Enze Han and Joseph O'Mahoney, *British Colonialism and the Criminalization of Homosexuality: Queens, Crime and Empire* (London: Routledge, 2018).

8. On Brazil, see Maria B. B. Noguiera, "The Promotion of LGBT Rights as International Human Rights Norms: Explaining Brazil's Diplomatic Leadership," *Global Governance* 23, no. 4 (October 2017): 545–63, https://doi.org/10.1163/19426720-02304003. On South Africa, see Eduard Jordaan, "South Africa and Sexual Orientation Rights at the United Nations: Batting for Both Sides," *Politikon* 44, no. 2 (2017): 205–30, https://doi.org/10.1080/02589346.2017.1284469.

9. Robbie Corey-Boulet, *Love Falls on Us: A Story of American Ideas and African LGBT Lives* (London: Zed Books, 2019).

10. See, for example, Omar G. Encarnación, "The Troubled Rise of Gay Rights Diplomacy," *Current History* 115, no. 777 (January 2016): 17; Hakan Seckinelgin, "Same-Sex Lives between the Language of International LGBT Rights, International

Aid, and Anti-Homosexuality," *Global Social Policy* 18, no. 3 (May 2018): 284–303, https://doi.org/10.1177/1468018118795989.

11. Onapajo and Isike, 2013: 21–45.

12. Cynthia Weber, *Queer International Relations: Sovereignty, Sexuality and the Will to Knowledge* (Oxford: Oxford University Press, 2016).

13. Weber, *Queer International Relations.* See also Melanie Richter-Montpetit, "Everything You Always Wanted to Know About Sex (in IR) But Were Afraid to Ask: The 'Queer Turn' in International Relations," *Millennium* 46, no. 2 (2018): 220–40; Amy Lind, "'Out' in International Relations: Why Queer Visibility Matters," *International Studies Review* 16, no. 4 (2014): 601–4. doi:10.1111/misr.12184.

14. Dennis Altman and Jonathan Symons, *Queer Wars* (Hoboken, NJ: John Wiley & Sons, 2016).

15. On challenges to the universal quality of human rights, see discussions in Mark Goodale and Sally Engel Merry, eds., *The Practice of Human Rights: Tracking Law between the Global and the Local* (Cambridge: Cambridge University Press, 2007).

16. S. M. Rodriguez, *The Economies of Queer Inclusion: Transnational Organizing for LGBTI Rights in Uganda* (London: Lexington Books, 2018).

17. Hakan Seckinelgin, "Same-Sex Lives between the Language of International LGBT Rights, International Aid, and Anti-Homosexuality," *Global Social Policy* 18, no. 3 (May 2018): 284–303, https://doi.org/10.1177/1468018118795989.

18. Lewis Brooks and Felicity Daly, "A Commonwealth Toolkit for Policy Progress on LGBT Rights," The Royal Commonwealth Society, April 2016, http://menengage.org/wp-content/uploads/2016/04/Commonwealth-Toolkit-for-Policy-Progress-on-LGBT-Rights.pdf.

19. See for example "Andrei Fighting for LGBT Rights Despite Death Threats," Swedish International Development Cooperation Agency (SIDA), accessed February 26, 2019, https://www.sida.se/English/where-we-work/Europe/Moldova-/examples-of-results/andrei-fighting-for-lgbt-rights-despite-death-threats/; "'Dignity for All': LGBTI Emergency Assistance Program," US Department of State, Bureau of Democracy, Human Rights and Labor, accessed May 12, 2021, http://www.state.gov/globalequality/about/index.htm.

20. Allison Carnegie and Nikolay Marinov, "Foreign Aid, Human Rights, and Democracy Promotion: Evidence from a Natural Experiment," *American Journal of Political Science* 61, no. 3 (2017): 671–83, https://doi.org/10.1111/ajps.12289.

21. Cynthia Burack, *Because We Are Human: Contesting U.S. Support for Gender and Sexuality Human Rights Abroad* (Albany, NY: State University of New York Press, 2018), 199.

22. Goodale and Merry, 2007.

23. Johannes Morsink, *The Universal Declaration of Human Rights and the Holocaust: An Endangered Connection* (Washington, DC: Georgetown University Press, 2019).

24. Birgit Shippers, ed., *Critical Perspectives on Human Rights* (Lanham, MD: Rowman & Littlefield International, 2018). See also Balakrishnan Rajagopal, *International Law from Below: Development, Social Movements and Third World Resistance* (Cambridge: Cambridge University Press, 2004); Linda Hogan, *Keeping Faith with Human Rights* (Washington, DC: Georgetown University Press, 2015); Upendra Baxi, "Voices of Suffering, Fragmented Universality, and the Future of Human Rights," in *Human Rights*, ed. Robert McCorquodale (London: Routledge, 2017), 159–214.

25. Goodale and Merry, 2007: 119.

26. Joke Swiebel, "Lesbian, Gay, Bisexual, and Transgender Human Rights: The Search for an International Strategy," *Contemporary Politics* 15, no. 1 (2009).

27. Clifford Bob, *The International Struggle for New Human Rights* (Philadelphia: University of Pennsylvania Press, 2010).

28. Oliver Diggelmann and Maria Nicole Cleis, "How the Right to Privacy Became a Human Right," *Human Rights Law Review* 14, no. 3 (July 2014): 441–58, https://doi.org/10.1093/hrlr/ngu014.

29. See: Bob, 2010:30.; Jo Becker, *Campaigning for Justice: Human Rights Advocacy in Practice* (Stanford, CA: Stanford University Press, 2013); Joshua W. Busby, *Moral Movements and Foreign Policy* (Cambridge: Cambridge University Press, 2010).

30. Bob, 2010: 26.

31. Sangmin Bae, *When the State No Longer Kills: International Human Rights Norms and Abolition of Capital Punishment* (Albany: State University of New York Press, 2007).

32. Ibid.

33. See for example Scott Simon, "All Our Relations: Indigenous Rights Movements in Contemporary Taiwan," in *Taiwan's Social Movements under Ma Ying-jeou*, ed. Dafydd Fell (London: Routledge, 2017), 236–57.

34. Busby, 2010: 264.

35. Ibid.

36. Phillip Ayoub, "Cooperative Transnationalism in Contemporary Europe: Europeanization and Political Opportunities for LGBT Mobilization in the European Union," *European Political Science Review* 5, no. 2 (January 2013): 279–310, https://doi.org/10.1017/s1755773912000161.

37. Ayoub, 2013: 299.

38. Phillip M. Ayoub and David Paternotte, *LGBT Activism and the Making of Europe a Rainbow Europe?* (Oxford: Oxford Public International Law, 2014).

39. Nataliya S. Semenova et al., "Traditional Values and Human Rights of LGBT under the Contemporary International Law," *Mediterranean Journal of Social Sciences* 6, no. 5 (January 2015): 305, https://doi.org/10.5901/mjss.2015.v6n5p305.

40. Christine Agius and Emil Edenborg, "Gendered Bordering Practices in Swedish and Russian Foreign and Security Policy," *Political Geography* 71 (2019): 56–66, https://doi.org/10.1016/j.polgeo.2019.02.012.

41. Conor O'Dwyer and Katrina Z. S. Schwartz, "Minority Rights after EU Enlargement: A Comparison of Antigay Politics in Poland and Latvia," *Comparative European Politics* 8, no. 2 (2010): 220–43, https://doi.org/10.1057/cep.2008.31.

42. George Vasilev, "LGBT Recognition in EU Accession States: How Identification with Europe Enhances the Transformative Power of Discourse," *Review of International Studies* 42, no. 4 (2016): 748–72, https://doi.org/10.1017/s0260210515000522.

43. Roman Kuhar, "Resisting Change: Same-Sex Partnership Policy Debates in Croatia and Slovenia," *Südosteuropa. Zeitschrift Für Politik Und Gesellschaft* 1 (2011): 25–49.

44. Kristien Stassen, Roel Smolders, and Pieter Leroy, "Sensitizing Events as Trigger for Discursive Renewal and Institutional Change in Flanders' Environmental Health Approach, 1970s–1990s," *Environmental Health* 12, no. 46 (June 2013), https://doi.org10.1186/1476-069X-12-46.

45. Stassen, Smolders, and Leroy, 2013.

46. Margaret E. Keck and Kathryn Sikkink, *Activists beyond Borders: Advocacy Networks in International Politics* (Ithaca: Cornell University Press, 1998).

47. See, for example, David Barnhizer, *Effective Strategies for Protecting Human Rights Economic Sanctions, Use of National Courts and International Fora and Coercive Power* (London: Routledge, 2017); Emilie M. Hafner-Burton, "Trading Human Rights: How Preferential Trade Agreements Influence Government Repression," *International Organization* 59, no. 3 (2005): 593–629, https://doi.org/10.1017/s0020818305050216.

48. Thomas G. Weiss, "Sanctions as a Foreign Policy Tool: Weighing Humanitarian Impulses," *Journal of Peace Research* 36, no. 5 (1999): 499–509, https://doi.org/10.1177/0022343399036005001.

49. Scott Harding and Kathryn Libal, "War and the Public Health Disaster in Iraq," in *War and Health: The Medical Consequences of the Wars in Iraq and Afghanistan*, ed. Catherine Lutz and Andrea Mazzarino (New York: New York University Press, 2019), 111–36.

50. Yitan Li and A. Cooper Drury, "Threatening Sanctions When Engagement Would Be More Effective: Attaining Better Human Rights in China," *International Studies Perspectives* 5, no. 4 (2004): 378–94, https://doi.org/10.1111/j.1528-3577.2004.00185.x.

51. Seung-Whan Choi and Patrick James, "Are US Foreign Policy Tools Effective in Improving Human Rights Conditions?," *The Chinese Journal of International Politics* 10, no. 3 (2017): 331–56, https://doi.org/10.1093/cjip/pox010.

52. See, for example, Alexis Kedo and Colby Goodman, "Defense Experts Highlight Effectiveness of Human Rights Conditioning," Security Assistance Monitor, Center for International Policy, December 10, 2015, https://www.securityassistance.org/blog/defense-experts-highlight-effectiveness-human-rights-conditioning. Or Evan

W. Sandlin, "Competing Concerns: Balancing Human Rights and National Security in US Economic Aid Allocation," *Human Rights Review* 17, no. 4 (2016): 439–62, https://doi.org/10.1007/s12142-016-0426-2.

53. See, for example, Oscar Quine, "Frank Mugisha: Uganda's Most Outspoken Gay Rights Activist on Changing People's Attitudes, Coming Out, and the Threat of Being Attacked," *Independent*, August 22, 2014, https://www.independent.co.uk/news/people/profiles/frank-mugisha-uganda-s-most-outspoken-gay-rights-activist-changing-people-s-attitudes-coming-out-and-threat-being-attacked-9681476.html.

54. Laurel Weldon, *When Protest Makes Policy How Social Movements Represent Disadvantaged Groups* (Ann Arbor: University of Michigan Press, 2012).

55. Barbara Hobson, *Recognition Struggles and Social Movements* (Cambridge: Cambridge University Press, 2003),14.

56. See, for example, Iris Marion Young, "Five Faces of Oppression," in *The Community Development Reader*, ed. Susan Saegert and James DeFilippis (New York: Routledge, 2012), 346–55; Hobson, 2003: 3; Weldon, 2012.

57. See, for example, Donatella Della Porta and Mario Diani, *Social Movements: An Introduction* (Hoboken, NJ: John Wiley & Sons, 2020).

58. On spillover effect, see Weldon, *When Protest Makes Policy,* 2012: 27. On linkage, see Bob, *The International Struggle* (2010): 61. On bridging, see Swiebel, "Lesbian, Gay, Bisexual, and Transgender Human Rights" (2009): 30.

59. Swedish Ministry for Foreign Affairs, "Working for A Gay-friendly Sweden," accessed May 19, 2016, https://sweden.se/society/working-for-a-gay-and-equal-sweden/.

60. Kollman, 2013: 6.

61. Sabrina Zajak, Niklas Egels-Zandén, and Nicola Piper, "Networks of Labour Activism: Collective Action across Asia and Beyond. An Introduction to the Debate," *Development and Change* 48, no. 5 (2017): 899–921, https://doi.org/10.1111/dech.12336.

62. Phillip Ayoub, "Intersectional and Transnational Coalitions during Times of Crisis: The European LGBTI Movement," *Social Politics: International Studies in Gender, State & Society* 26, no. 1 (2018): 1–29, https://doi.org/10.1093/sp/jxy007.

63. Sabine Lang, *NGOs, Civil Society, and the Public Sphere* (Cambridge: Cambridge University Press, 2014).

64. Ibid.

65. Paul Pierson, "The Study of Policy Development," *Journal of Policy History* 17, no. 1 (2005): 34–51, https://doi.org/10.1353/jph.2005.0006.

66. Ibid., 46.

67. Johnson (2004): 123. As cited, President Dwight Eisenhower signs Executive Order 10450.

68. Sean Lyngaas, "LGBT Rights Becomes Pillar of U.S. Foreign Policy," *Washington Diplomat*, May 29, 2015, https://washdiplomat.com/gay-rights-becomes-pillar-of-us-foreign-policy/.

69. Weldon, *When Protest Makes Policy* (2012).

70. Ibid.

71. Jutta Joachim, *Agenda Setting, the UN, and NGOs: Gender Violence and Reproductive Rights* (Washington, DC: Georgetown University Press, 2007), 6; Jutta Joachim and Birgit Locher, *Transnational Activism in the UN and the EU: A Comparative Study* (London: Routledge, 2008).

72. Peter J. Katzenstein, *Small States in World Markets* (Ithaca, NY: Cornell University Press, 1985).

73. Michele Micheletti, *Civil Society and State Relations in Sweden* (London: Routledge, 2019).

74. Rydström Jens, *Odd Couples: A History of Gay Marriage in Scandinavia* (Amsterdam: Aksant, 2011), 7.

75. Amy Elman, *Sexual Subordination and the State: Comparing Sweden and the United States* (New York: Berghahn Publishers, 1996).

76. Weldon, 2012: 10.

77. Hobson, 2003.

78. Hobson, 2003: 31.

79. Lee Ann Banaszak, *The Women's Movement inside and outside the State* (Cambridge: Cambridge University Press, 2010): 3.

80. Trägårdh Lars, *State and Civil Society in Northern Europe: The Swedish Model Reconsidered* (New York: Berghahn Books, 2007).

81. Banaszak, 2010: 3; Joachim, 2007: 163.

82. Vleuten, 2014.

83. David Pettinicchio, "Institutional Activism: Reconsidering the Insider/Outsider Dichotomy," *Sociology Compass* 6, no. 6 (2012): 499–510, https://doi.org/10.1111/j.1751-9020.2012.00465.x.

84. Jan Olsson and Erik Hysing, "Theorizing inside Activism: Understanding Policymaking and Policy Change from Below," *Planning Theory & Practice* 13, no. 2 (2012): 257–73, https://doi.org/10.1080/14649357.2012.677123.

85. Banaszak, 2010: 22.

86. Hester Eisenstein, "The Australian Femocratic Experiment: A Feminist Case for Bureaucracy," in *Feminist Organizations: Harvest of the New Women's Movement,* ed. Myra Marx Ferree (Philadelphia: Temple University Press, 1995), 69–83.

87. Ibid., 72.

88. Olsson and Hysing, "Theorizing Inside Activism" (2012); Banaszak, *The Women's Movement* (2010); Pettinicchio, "Institutional Activism" (2012).

89. For further context of religion and homophobia, see, on Theravada Buddhism: Rita James Simon and Alison Brooks, *Gay and Lesbian Communities The World Over* (Lanham, MD: Rowman & Littlefield, 2009); on Christianity: Robert Kuloba Wabyanga, "The Destruction of Sodom and Gomorrah Revisited: Military and Political Reflections," *Old Testament Essays* 28, no. 3 (2015): 847–73; on Islam: Sin How Lim, Shan-Estelle Brown, Stacey A. Shaw, Adeeba Kamarulzaman, Frederick L. Altice, and Chris Beyrer, " 'You Have to Keep Yourself Hidden': Perspectives from Malaysian Malay-Muslim Men Who Have Sex with Men on Policy, Network,

Community, and Individual Influences on HIV Risk," *Journal Of Homosexuality* 67, no. 1 (2020): 104–26.

90. Tim Dunne and Nicholas J. Wheeler, "Great Illusions or Great Transformations? Human Rights and International Relations a Hundred Years On," *International Relations* 33, no. 2 (2016): 338–56, https://doi.org/10.1177/0047117819851256.

91. Joe Renouard, *Human Rights in American Foreign Policy: from the 1960s to the Soviet Collapse* (Philadelphia: University of Pennsylvania Press, 2016).

92. Henry Kissinger, 1973, as cited by Roberta Cohen, "Integrating Human Rights in U.S. Foreign Policy: The History, the Challenges, and the Criteria for an Effective Policy," Speech, Brookings Foreign Service Institute, Washington, DC, 2008, http://www.brookings.edu/~/media/research/files/speeches/2008/4/human-rights-cohen/04_human_rights_cohen.pdf.

93. On realist approaches to foreign policy formation, see David Forsythe, *Human Rights in International Relations* (Cambridge: Cambridge University Press, 2012); Judith Goldstein and Robert Keohane, *Ideas and Foreign Policy: Beliefs, Institutions, and Political Change* (Ithaca, NY: Cornell University Press, 1993); Robert Kagan, *Of Paradise and Power: America and Europe in the New World Order* (New York: Random House, 2003); and J. J. Mearsheimer, *The Tragedy of Great Power Politics* (New York: W.W. Norton & Company, 2001).

94. Robert O. Keohane, "Institutional Theory and the Realist Challenge after the Cold War," *Neorealism and Neoliberalism: The Contemporary Debate* 269 (1993): 271.

95. Daniel Mahanty, "Realists, Too, Can Stand for Human Rights," *National Interest*, 2013, http://nationalinterest.org/commentary/realists-too-can-stand-human-rights-9208.

96. Rein Müllerson, *Human Rights Diplomacy* (London: Routledge, 1997).

97. Ibid., 71.

98. Later this bureau became known as the Bureau of Democracy, Human Rights, and Labor: US Department of State, Bureau of Democracy, Human Rights and Labor, https://www.state.gov/j/drl/.

99. Secretary of State Cyrus R. Vance, "U.S. Foreign Policy Objectives: Hearing before the Committee on Foreign Relations, United States Senate, Ninety-sixth Congress, Second Session, on a Comprehensive Statement of U.S. Foreign Policy Objectives," US Government Printing Office, March 27, 1980.

100. "What We Do," United States Institution for Peace, accessed September 24, 2020, https://www.usip.org/; "Peace and Development," Stockholm International Peace Research Institute, accessed September 24, 2020, https://www.sipri.org/research/peace-and-development; "Human Rights," Council on Foreign Relations, accessed September 24, 2020, https://www.cfr.org/human-rights.

101. Valerie Hudson and Patricia Leidl, *The Hillary Doctrine: Sex and American Foreign Policy* (New York: Columbia University Press, 2015).

102. M. V. Lee Badgett, Kees Waaldijk, and Yana Van Der Meulen-Rodgers, "The Relationship between LGBT Inclusion and Economic Development: Macro-Level Evidence," *World Development* 120 (2019): 1–14, https://doi.org/10.1016/j.worlddev.2019.03.011.

103. Jack Donnelly, *Realism and International Relations* (Cambridge: Cambridge University Press, 2014).

104. Stefano Guzzini and Anna Leander, *Constructivism and International Relations: Alexander Wendt and His Critics* (London: Routledge, 2011).

105. Trine Flockhart, "Constructivism and Foreign Policy," in *Foreign Policy: Theories, Actors, Cases*, ed. Steve Smith, Amelia Hadfield, and Timothy Dunne (Oxford: Oxford University Press, 2016), 84.

106. Göran Hyden and Rwekaza Mukandala, *Agencies in Foreign Aid: Comparing China, Sweden and the United States in Tanzania* (London: Palgrave Macmillan, 1999).

107. Hyden and Mukandala, 1999: 122.

108. Toby Greene, "When Conviction Trumps Domestic Politics: Tony Blair and the Second Lebanon War," *Foreign Policy Analysis* (2019): 43–64, https://doi.org/10.1093/fpa/orx004.

109. Judith G. Kelley, *Scorecard Diplomacy: Grading States to Influence Their Reputation and Behavior* (London: Cambridge University Press, 2017).

110. Jamie Mayerfeld, "The Democratic Legacy of the International Criminal Court," *Fletcher Forum of World Affairs* 28, no. 2 (2004): 147–56; Müllerson, 2014.

111. Jonathan Mercer, *Reputation and International Politics* (Ithaca, NY: Cornell University Press, 1996).

112. Hoo Tiang Boon, *China's Global Identity: Considering the Responsibility of Great Power* (Washington, DC: Georgetown University Press, 2018).

113. Tina Maria Sæteraas Stoum, "Sexually (Dis)orientated?: Conceptualizing the Norwegian Ministry of Foreign Affairs' Promotion of LGBT Rights" (Master's thesis, Norges teknisk-naturvitenskapelige universitet, Det humanistiske fakultet, Institutt for tverrfaglige kulturstudier, 2012), 43.

114. Ibid., 35.

115. Rydström, 2011: 8.

116. Rydström, 2011: 13.

117. Forsythe, 2012.

118. Brysk, 2009: 221; Hyden and Mukandala, 1999.

119. Phil Zuckerman, *Society without God: What the Least Religious Nations Can Tell Us about Contentment* (New York: New York University Press, 2008).

120. On small state theory, see Katzenstein, *Small States in World Markets* (1985); Jessica Beyer, Christine Ingebritsen, Iver B. Neumann, and Sieglinde Gstohl, *Small States in International Relations* (Seattle: University of Washington Press, 2006).

121. Elgström, as cited in Hyden and Mukandala, *Agencies in Foreign Aid* (1999).

122. Christine Ingebritsen, *Scandinavia in World Politics* (Lanham, MD: Rowman and Littlefield Publishers, 2006); Louis W. Pauly and Bruce W. Jentleson, *Power in a Complex Global System* (London: Routledge, 2014).

123. Ingebritsen, 2006; Brysk, 2009.

124. Ann E. Towns and Karin Aggestam, eds., *Gendering Diplomacy and International Negotiation* (London: Palgrave Macmillan, 2018). See also Ann E. Towns, " 'Diplomacy Is a Feminine Art': Feminised Figurations of the Diplomat," *Review of International Studies* (2020): 1–21.

125. Hakeem Onapajo and Christopher Isike, "The Global Politics of Gay Rights: The Straining Relations between the West and Africa," *Journal of Global Analysis* 6, no. 1 (January 2013): 21–45, https://therestjournal.com/wp-content/uploads/2019/03/JGA_Vol.6_No.1_A_2.pdf.

Chapter 6

1. "Development Aid Drops in 2018, Especially to Neediest Countries," Organization for Economic Cooperation and Development, October 4, 2019, http://www.oecd.org/development/development-aid-drops-in-2018-especially-to-neediest-countries.htm.

2. Jim Yong Kim, "World Bank Group President Jim Yong Kim: Discrimination by Law Carries a High Price," *World Bank News*, February 28, 2014, http://www.worldbank.org/en/news/opinion/2014/02/28/world-bank-group-president-jim-yong-kim-discrimination-law-price.

3. M. V. Lee Badgett, Kees Waaldijk, and Yana Van Der Meulen Rodgers, "The Relationship between LGBT Inclusion and Economic Development: Macro-Level Evidence," *World Development* 120 (2019): 1–14, https://doi.org/10.1016/j.worlddev.2019.03.011.

4. Susan Dicklitch-Nelson and Indira Rahman, "Joint Responsibility: LGBT Rights in a Polarized World," *The Globe Post*, April 18, 2019, https://theglobepost.com/2019/04/18/lgbt-rights/.

5. Reid Graeme, 2015, as cited in Richard Sandell, *Museums, Moralities and Human Rights* (London: Routledge, 2017), 142.

6. "Global Equality Fund," US Department of State Bureau of Democracy, Human Rights and Labor, accessed September 15, 2015, http://www.state.gov/globalequality/about/index.htm.

7. Jessica Stern, "Human Rights Speakers Series—LGBT Rights Abroad," OutRight Action International, June 7, 2016, https://www.youtube.com/watch?v=flrAPcZx0Gc.

8. Jessica Stern, "Human Rights Speakers Series—LGBT Rights Abroad," OutRight Action International, June 7, 2016, https://www.youtube.com/watch?v=flrAPcZx0Gc.

9. Johnson, *The Lavender Scare,* 2006.

10. Amie Bishop and Anthony Adero, "Global LGBTQI Movements, Human Rights, and Health: Notes from the Frontlines," Western Washington University Fairhaven College of Interdisciplinary Studies, Bellingham, Washington, World Issues Forum, May 10, 2016, https://cedar.wwu.edu/fairhaven_wif/2016-2017/2016-2017/2/.

11. Amie Bishop and Anthony Adero, "Global LGBTQI Movements, Human Rights, and Health: Notes from the Frontlines," Western Washington University Fairhaven College of Interdisciplinary Studies, Bellingham, Washington, World Issues Forum, May 10, 2016, https://cedar.wwu.edu/fairhaven_wif/2016-2017/2016-2017/2/.

12. US case interview #47, San Francisco, February 10, 2016; and #41, Seattle, Washington, January 19, 2016.

13. "Country Reports on Human Rights Practices," US Department of State Bureau of Democracy, Human Rights and Labor, http://www.state.gov/j/drl/rls/hrrpt/humanrightsreport/index.htm#wrapper.

14. See, for example, "2009 Country Reports on Human Rights Practices: Uganda," US Department of State Bureau of Democracy, Human Rights, and Labor, March 11, 2010, https://2009-2017.state.gov/j/drl/rls/hrrpt/2009/af/135982.htm.

15. "Briefing by Special Envoy for the Human Rights of LGBTI Persons Randy Berry," Special Briefing, Office of the Spokesperson, Washington, DC, April 20, 2016, https://2009-2017.state.gov/r/pa/prs/ps/2016/04/256425.htm.

16. See Sierra Brewer and Lauren Dundes, "Concerned, Meet Terrified: Intersectional Feminism and the Women's March," *Women's Studies International Forum* 69 (2018): 49–55, https://doi.org/10.1016/j.wsif.2018.04.008; Carlos Morrison and Jacqueline Trimble, "Still Work to Be Done: The Million Man March and the 50th Anniversary Commemoration Selma to Montgomery March as Mythoform and Visual Rhetoric," *Howard Journal of Communications* 28, no. 2 (2017): 132–43.

17. "Reflections on the Obama Administration's Human Rights Policies and the Way Forward," Council on Foreign Relations, March 4, 2013, https://www.cfr.org/event/reflections-obama-administrations-human-rights-policies-and-way-forward.

18. US interview #41, Seattle, Washington, January 19, 2016.

19. US interview #43, Washington DC, January 15, 2016; Participant observation #62, February 13, 2016; #64, Seattle, Washington, May 13, 2015.

20. Samantha Power, *The Education of an Idealist* (New York: HarperCollins Books, 2019), 278.

21. "The Biden Plan to Advance LGBTQ+ Equality in America and around the World," Biden for President Campaign, accessed November 9, 2020, https://joebiden.com/lgbtq-policy/.

22. "The Biden Plan to Advance LGBTQ+ Equality in America and around the World," Biden for President Campaign, accessed November 9, 2020, https://joebiden.com/lgbtq-policy/.

23. See "Court Cases SMUG vs. Scott Lively," Sexual Minorities Uganda, accessed November 9, 2020, https://sexualminoritiesuganda.com/publications/court-cases/.

24. Colum Lynch, "Republicans Join Forces with Islamic Governments against America," *Foreign Policy,* July 15, 2010, http://foreignpolicy.com/2010/07/15/republicans-join-forces-with-islamic-governments-against-america/.

25. US case interview #43, Washington, DC, January 15, 2016.

26. Daniel Baer, "LiveAtState: Human Rights of Lesbian, Gay, Bisexual, and Transgender People," US Department of State, International Media Engagement, June 20, 2013, https://2009-2017.state.gov/r/pa/ime/211005.htm.

27. Wesley Reisser, "Human Rights Speakers Series—LGBT Rights Abroad," OutRight Action International, June 7, 2016, https://www.youtube.com/watch?v=flrAPcZx0Gc.

28. "Report of the Commission on Unalienable Rights," US Department Commission on Unalienable Rights, August 26, 2020, https://www.state.gov/report-of-the-commission-on-unalienable-rights/.

29. John Shattuck, Harold Hongju Koh, David J. Kramer, Michael Posner, and Tom Malinowski, "The Pandemic and Human Rights: State Department CUR Is Not the Cure," *The Hill*, May 14, 2020, https://thehill.com/opinion/civil-rights/497309-the-pandemic-and-human-rights-state-departments-cur-is-not-the-cure.

30. "The Biden Plan to Advance LGBTQ+ Equality in America and around the World," Biden for President Campaign, accessed November 9, 2020, https://joebiden.com/lgbtq-policy/.

31. White House Press Statement, "President Biden Announces U.S. Special Envoy to Advance the Human Rights of LGBTQI+ Persons," June 25, 2021, https://www.whitehouse.gov/briefing-room/statements-releases/2021/06/25/president-biden-announces-u-s-special-envoy-to-advance-the-human-rights-of-lgbtqi-persons/.

32. Czeslaw Walek, chairman, Prague Pride and Board member for Alturi, "Human Rights Speakers Series—LGBT Rights Abroad," OutRight Action International, June 7, 2016, https://www.youtube.com/watch?v=flrAPcZx0Gc.

33. Amie Bishop and Anthony Adero, "Global LGBTQI Movements, Human Rights, and Health: Notes from the Frontlines," Western Washington University Fairhaven College of Interdisciplinary Studies, World Issues Forum, May 10, 2016, https://cedar.wwu.edu/fairhaven_wif/2016-2017/2016-2017/2/.

34. Joe Myers, "Foreign Aid: These Countries Are the Most Generous," World Economic Forum, August 19, 2016, https://www.weforum.org/agenda/2016/08/foreign-aid-these-countries-are-the-most-generous/.

35. Karin Aggestam and Annika Bergman-Rosamond, "Swedish Feminist Foreign Policy in the Making: Ethics Politics, and Gender," *Ethics & International Affairs* 30, no. 3 (2016): 323–34.

36. Mikkel Sejersen, "Democratic Sanctions Meet Black Knight Support: Revisiting the Belarusian Case," *Democratization* 26, no. 3 (2019): 502–20.

37. Katja Kahlina, "Local Histories, European LGBT Designs: Sexual Citizenship, Nationalism, and 'Europeanisation' in Post-Yugoslav Croatia and Serbia," *Women's Studies International Forum, Pergamon* 49 (2015): 73–83.

38. Anders Danielson and Lennart Wohlgemuth, "Swedish Development Co-operation in Perspective," Lund University, Department of Economics, July 3–7, 2002, https://pdfs.semanticscholar.org/a77d/e32a3c24c1e2137a74d4d9a37934aec5134d.pdf.

39. This acronym comes from the Swedish name: Riksförbundet för homosexuellas, bisexuellas och transpersoners rättigheter (RFSL) and is used in this study.

40. Officer presentation, "LGBTI Rights in 20 Years" (HBTQ Frågar om 20 År), The Left Political Party (Vänsterpartiet), Stockholm, Sweden, August 2, 2017.

41. See, for example, Gianluca Antonucci, "The Relationships between Government and Civil Society in Performing Public Service Hybrid Organisations: Some Insights from a Comparative Study," in *Cross-Sectoral Relations in the Delivery of Public Services* (Bingley, UK: Emerald Publishing Limited, 2018), 195–213.

42. See, for example, Marlies Glasius, Jelmer Schalk, and Meta De Lange, "Illiberal Norm Diffusion: How Do Governments Learn to Restrict Nongovernmental Organizations?," *International Studies Quarterly* 64, no. 2 (2020): 453–68.

43. See, for example, Reini Schrama and Asya Zhelyazkova, "'You Can't Have One without the Other': The Differential Impact of Civil Society Strength on the Implementation of EU Policy," *Journal of European Public Policy* 25, no. 7 (2018): 1029–48.

44. Pia Laskar, "The Illiberal Turn: Aid Conditionalis and the Queering of Sexual Citizenship," *Lambda Nordica* 1 (2014): 90.

45. Corinne Pinfold, "28 Arrested after Protesters Throw Eggs at Baltic Pride," *Pink News*, July 27, 2013, http://www.pinknews.co.uk/2013/07/27/28-arrested-after-protesters-throw-eggs-at-baltic-pride/.

46. Participant observation #13, Stockholm Pride, Stockholm, Sweden, July 28, 2015.

47. Anna-Maria Sörberg, *Homonationalism* (Stockholm: Leopard förlag, 2017), 14, translated from Swedish.

48. Sörberg, *Homonationalism*, 2017: 13.

49. Stoum, 2014: 35.

50. Swedish case study interview #5, Stockholm, Sweden, August 13, 2015.

51. Swedish Migration Agency, "About the Swedish Migration Agency," accessed May 10, 2021, https://www.migrationsverket.se/English/About-the-Migration-Agency/Statistics.html.

52. Jens Rydgren, "Immigration Sceptics, Xenophobes or Racists? Radical Right-Wing Voting in Six West European Countries," *European Journal of Political Research* 47, no. 6 (2008): 737–65.

53. Katarina Jungar and Salla Peltonen, "Acts of Homonationalism: Mapping Africa in the Swedish Media," *Sexualities* 20, no. 5–6 (2016): 715–37, https://doi.org/10.1177/1363460716645806.

54. Hakeem Onapajo and Christopher Isike, "The Global Politics of Gay Rights: The Straining Relations between the West and Africa," *Journal of Global Analysis* 6, no. 1 (January 2013): 21–45, https://therestjournal.com/wp-content/uploads/2019/03/JGA_Vol.6_No.1_A_2.pdf.

55. "Homophobia Is Defeated but Not Yet Deterred: Next Steps in the Struggle for Equality in Uganda and Beyond," *Global Equality Today*, May 14, 2010, https://globalequality.wordpress.com/tag/bi-sexual/.

56. "Statement by Assistant Secretary of State Michael H. Posner on His Visit to Uganda," US Department of State Press Releases, September 6, 2012, https://2009-2017.state.gov/j/drl/rls/prsrl/2012/197591.htm.

57. Kristien Stassen, Roel Smolders, and Pieter Leroy, "Sensitizing Events as Trigger for Discursive Renewal and Institutional Change in Flanders' Environmental Health Approach, 1970s–1990s," *Environmental Health* 12, no. 46 (June 2013), https://doi.org10.1186/1476-069X-12-46.

58. Mariah Blake, "Meet the American Pastor behind Uganda's Anti-Gay Crackdown," *Mother Jones*, July 31, 2019, https://www.motherjones.com/politics/2014/03/scott-lively-anti-gay-law-uganda/2/.

59. James Kassaga Arinaitwe, "How US Evangelicals Are Shaping Development in Uganda," *Al Jazeera*, July 25, 2014, https://www.aljazeera.com/indepth/opinion/2014/07/us-evangelicals-uganda-2014724135920268137.html.

60. US case interview #52, Washington, DC, September 15, 2015.

61. Chris Johnson, "Dan Baer: Time for U.S. to Change Its Relationship with Saudi Arabia," *Washington Blade*, July 9, 2019, https://www.washingtonblade.com/2019/07/09/dan-baer-time-for-u-s-to-change-its-relationship-with-saudi-arabia/.

62. Rein Müllerson, *Human Rights Diplomacy*, 2nd ed. (London: Routledge, 2014).

63. Daniel Mahanty, "Realists, Too, Can Stand for Human Rights," *National Interest*, October 9, 2013, http://nationalinterest.org/commentary/realists-too-can-stand-human-rights-9208.

64. Dan Mahanty and Elise Carlson-Rainer, "The Importance of Human Rights Considerations in Foreign Policy," in Homeland Security, April 8, 2019, https://inhomelandsecurity.com/human-rights-foreign-policy/.

65. On the economic impact of LGBTI discrimination, see M. V. Lee Badgett, Kees Waaldijk, and Yana Van Der Meulen-Rodgers, "The Relationship between LGBT Inclusion and Economic Development: Macro-Level Evidence," *World Development* 120 (2019): 1–14, https://doi.org/10.1016/j.worlddev.2019.03.011. On the national security link to gender equality, see "UN Resolution 1325: Landmark Resolution on Women, Peace and Security," UN Office of the Special Adviser on Gender Issues and Advancement of Women, October 31, 2000, https://www.un.org/womenwatch/osagi/wps/.

66. See Valerie Hudson and Patricia Leidl, *The Hillary Doctrine: Sex and American Foreign Policy* (New York: Columbia University Press, 2015).

67. David Barnhizer, *Effective Strategies for Protecting Human Rights: Economic Sanctions, Use of National Courts, and International Fora and Coercive Power* (London: Routledge, 2017).

68. Gordon Crawford and Simonida Kacarska, "Aid Sanctions and Political Conditionality: Continuity and Change," *Journal of International Relations and Development* 22, no. 1 (August 2017): 184–214.

69. Robbie Corey-Boulet, "The Trump Effect," *World Policy Journal* 34, no. 3 (2017): 83–89, https://doi.org/10.1215/07402775-4280064.

70. Seifudein Adem, "China in Ethiopia: Diplomacy and Economics of Sino-Optimism," *African Studies Review* 55, no. 1 (2012): 143–60.

71. "Briefing by Special Envoy for the Human Rights of LGBTI Persons Randy Berry," Special Briefing, Office of the Spokesperson, Washington, DC, April 20, 2016, https://2009-2017.state.gov/r/pa/prs/ps/2016/04/256425.htm.

72. Havard Bergo, "Has Foreign Aid Led to Economic Growth in Uganda?," Global Risk Insights, May 18, 2015, https://globalriskinsights.com/2015/05/has-foreign-aid-led-to-economic-growth-in-uganda/.

73. Allison Carnegie and Nikolay Marinov, "Foreign Aid, Human Rights, and Democracy Promotion: Evidence from a Natural Experiment," *American Journal of Political Science* 61, no. 3 (2017): 671–83, https://doi.org/10.1111/ajps.12289.

74. Han Dorussen, "Mixing Carrots with Sticks: Evaluating the Effectiveness of Positive Incentives," *Journal of Peace Research* 38, no. 2 (2001): 251–62.

75. Erin A. Snider, "US Democracy Aid and the Authoritarian State: Evidence from Egypt and Morocco," *International Studies Quarterly* 62, no. 4 (2018): 795–808.

76. Oscar Quine, "Frank Mugisha: Uganda's Most Outspoken Gay Rights Activist on Changing People's Attitudes, Coming Out, and the Threat of Being Attacked," *Independent*, August 22, 2014, https://www.independent.co.uk/news/people/profiles/frank-mugisha-uganda-s-most-outspoken-gay-rights-activist-changing-people-s-attitudes-coming-out-and-threat-being-attacked-9681476.html.

77. For a discussion on the difficulties of measuring foreign aid on rights and democracy, see Allison Carnegie and Nikolay Marinov, "Foreign Aid, Human Rights, and Democracy Promotion: Evidence from a Natural Experiment," *American Journal of Political Science* 61, no. 3 (2017): 671–83, https://doi.org/10.1111/ajps.12289.

78. Thomas G. Weiss, "Sanctions as a Foreign Policy Tool: Weighing Humanitarian Impulses," *Journal of Peace Research* 36, no. 5 (1999): 499–509.

79. Elise Carlson-Rainer and Anish Goel, "Myanmar's Military Is Only Hurting Itself," *Foreign Policy*, November 8, 2019, https://foreignpolicy.com/2019/11/08/myanmar-military-rohingya/.

80. Fumitaka Furuoka, "Japan's Positive and Negative Aid Sanctions Policy toward Asian Countries: Case Studies of Thailand and Indonesia," *MPRA Paper No. 6218* (December 2007), https://mpra.ub.uni-muenchen.de/6218/1/MPRA_paper_6218.pdf.

81. Sultan Barakat, "Priorities and Challenges of Qatar's Humanitarian Diplomacy," *CMI Brief*, no. 2019:07 (2019).

82. See "Categories of Federal Civil Service Employment: A Snapshot," Congressional Research Service, March 26, 2019, https://fas.org/sgp/crs/misc/R45635.pdf.

83. See Ane Mathieson, Easton Branam, and Anya Noble, "Prostitution Policy: Legalization, Decriminalization and the Nordic Model," *Seattle Journal for Social Justice* 14, no. 2 (2015): 367–428, https://digitalcommons.law.seattleu.edu/cgi/viewcontent.cgi?article=1814&context=sjsj.

84. "Working for a Gay-Friendly Sweden," Swedish Ministry for Foreign Affairs, accessed May 19, 2016, https://sweden.se/society/working-for-a-gay-and-equal-sweden/.

85. See "Human Rights," Council on Foreign Relations, accessed September 24, 2020, https://www.cfr.org/human-rights; "Peace and Development," Stockholm International Peace Research Institute, accessed September 24, 2020, https://www.sipri.org/research/peace-and-development; "Human Rights," United States Institute of Peace, accessed May 11, 2021, https://www.usip.org/issue-areas/human-rights.

86. Susan Harris Rimmer, "Women as Maker of International Law: Towards Feminist Diplomacy," in *Research Handbook on Feminist Engagement with International Law*, ed. Susan Harris Rimmer and Kate Ogg (Cheltenham: Edward Elgar, 2019), 26–43.

87. Elise Stephenson, "Invisible while Visible: An Australian Perspective on Queer Women Leaders in International Affairs," *European Journal of Politics and Gender* 3, no. 3 (2020): 427–43, https://doi.org/10.1332/251510820X15880614774555. See also Elise Stephenson, "Domestic Challenges and International Leadership: A Case Study of Women in Australian International Affairs," *Australian Journal of International Affairs* 73, no. 3 (2019): 234–53, https://doi.org/10.1080/10357718.2019.1588224.

88. As measured by the partners of the multilateral Global Equality Fund: "Global Equality Fund," US Department of State Bureau of Democracy, Human Rights, and Labor, accessed April 14, 2019, https://www.state.gov/global-equality-fund/.

89. On Spain's influence, see Elisabeth Jay Friedman, "Constructing 'the Same Rights with the Same Names': The Impact of Spanish Norm Diffusion on Marriage Equality in Argentina," *Latin American Politics and Society* 54, no. 4 (2012): 29–59, https://doi.org/10.1111/j.1548-2456.2012.00171.x. On Brazil's influence, see Maria B. B. Nogueira, "The Promotion of LGBT Rights as International Human Rights Norms: Explaining Brazil's Diplomatic Leadership," *Global Governance* 23, no. 4 (2017): 545–63, https://doi.org/10.1163/19426720-02304003.

90. Elise Rainer, "When Fundamentalists Come to Power, Women Lose," *Modern Diplomacy*, October 17, 2020, https://moderndiplomacy.eu/2020/10/17/when-fundamentalists-come-to-power-women-lose/.

91. Amie Bishop and Anthony Adero, "Global LGBTQI Movements, Human Rights, and Health: Notes from the Frontlines," Western Washington University Fairhaven College of Interdisciplinary Studies, World Issues Forum, May 10, 2016, https://cedar.wwu.edu/fairhaven_wif/2016-2017/2016-2017/2/.

92. Claire Felter and Danielle Renwick, "Same-Sex Marriage: Global Comparisons," Council on Foreign Relations, October 29, 2019, https://www.cfr.org/backgrounder/same-sex-marriage-global-comparisons.

93 See, for example, Conor O'Dwyer and Katrina Z. S. Schwartz, "Minority Rights after EU Enlargement: A Comparison of Antigay Politics in Poland and Latvia," *Comparative European Politics* 8, no. 2 (2010): 220–43, https://doi.org/10.1057/cep.2008.31.

94. John Shattuck, Harold Hongju Koh, David J. Kramer, Michael Posner, and Tom Malinowski, "The Pandemic and Human Rights: State Department CUR Is Not the Cure," *The Hill*, May 14, 2020, https://thehill.com/opinion/civil-rights/497309-the-pandemic-and-human-rights-state-departments-cur-is-not-the-cure.

95. Cooper Inveen, "Dr. Stella Nyanzi Kicks Off 11th Annual WRIHC with Powerful Keynote Address," University of Washington Department of Global Health, August 20, 2014, https://globalhealth.washington.edu/news/2014/08/20/dr-stella-nyanzi-kicks-11th-annual-wrihc-powerful-keynote-address. See also "Dr. Stella Nyanzi," Front Line Defenders, accessed October 18, 2020, https://www.frontlinedefenders.org/en/profile/dr-stella-nyanzi.

96. Ben Westcott, "Brunei to Punish Gay Sex and Adultery with Death by Stoning," CNN, March 30, 2019, https://www.cnn.com/2019/03/27/asia/brunei-anti-lgbt-stoning-law-intl/index.html; note: Lesbian homosexual acts receive a different punishment: forty strokes of the cane and/or a maximum of ten years in jail.

.

References

Abers, Rebecca Neaera, and Luciana Tatagiba. "Institutional Activism: Mobilizing for Women's Health from inside the Brazilian Bureaucracy." In *Social Movement Dynamics*, 72–101. London: Routledge, 2016.

Adem, Seifudein, ed. *China's Diplomacy in Eastern and Africa.* New York: Routledge, 2016.

Adomaitis, Nerijus. "Lithuania Holds First Gay March amid Protests." *Reuters World News.* May 8, 2010. https://www.reuters.com/article/us-lithuania-gay/lithuania-holds-first-gay-march-amid-protests-idUSTRE64723Y20100508.

"Advancing LGBTI Human Rights Development." USAID. 2016. Last updated February 2, 2017. https://www.usaid.gov/what-we-do/democracy-human-rights-and-governance/protecting-human-rights/advancing-lgbti-human-rights.

"Uganda History." In *East Africa Living Encyclopedia.* University of Pennsylvania African Studies Center. Accessed April 11, 2020. http://www.africa.upenn.edu/NEH/uhistory.htm.

"A Guide to the Foreign Service: For Those New to the Foreign Service." US Department of State Family Liaison Office 2009. Accessed October 10, 2014. http://www.state.gov/documents/organization/101170.pdf.

Aggestam, Karin, and Ann Towns. "The Gender Turn in Diplomacy: A New Research Agenda." *International Feminist Journal of Politics* 21, no. 1 (June 2018): 9–28. https://doi.org/10.1080/14616742.2018.1483206.

Aggestam, Karin, and Annika Bergman-Rosamond. "Feminist Foreign Policy 3.0: Advancing Ethics and Gender Equality in Global Politics." *SAIS Review of International Affairs* 39, no. 1 (2019): 37–48.

Aggestam, Karin, and Annika Bergman-Rosamond. "Swedish Feminist Foreign Policy in the Making: Ethics, Politics, and Gender." *Ethics & International Affairs* 30, no. 3 (2016): 323–34.

Aggleton, Peter, Paul Boyce, Henrietta L. Moore, and Richard Parker, eds. *Understanding Global Sexualities: New Frontiers.* London: Routledge, 2016.

Agius, Christine, and Emil Edenborg. "Gendered Bordering Practices in Swedish and Russian Foreign and Security Policy." *Political Geography* 71 (2019): 56–66. https://doi.org/10.1016/j.polgeo.2019.02.012.

Ahmed, Ali M., and Mats Hammarstedt. "Detecting Discrimination against Homosexuals: Evidence from a Field Experiment on the Internet." *Economica* 76, no. 303 (2009): 588–97.

Ahmed, Shamima, and David Potter. *NGOs in International Politics*. Boulder, CO: Kumarian Press, 2013.

Akçay, Ekrem Yaşar, and Selim Kanat. "Carrot and Stick Approach in International Relations: An Evaluation throughout Turkey's Accession Negotiations with the European Union." *Süleyman Demirel Üniversitesi Sosyal Bilimler Enstitüsü Dergisi* 31 (2017): 1–22.

Alaattinoğlu, Daniela, and Ruth Rubio-Marín. "Redress for Involuntarily Sterilised Trans People in Sweden against Evolving Human Rights Standards: A Critical Appraisal." *Human Rights Law Review* 19, no. 4 (2019): 705–32. https://doi.org/10.1093/hrlr/ngz026.

Alhouti, Sarah, Catherine M. Johnson, and Betsy Bugg Holloway. "Corporate Social Responsibility Authenticity: Investigating Its Antecedents and Outcomes." *Journal of Business Research* 69, no. 3 (2016): 1242–49.

Aliens Act (2005:716). Swedish government. September 29, 2005. https://www.government.se/contentassets/784b3d7be3a54a0185f284bbb2683055/aliens-act-2005_716.pdf.

Alimi, Adebisi. "Why I Oppose the United States' Special Envoy for LGBT Human Rights." *The Daily Beast*. March 10, 2015. http://www.thedailybeast.com/contributors/adebisi-alimi.html.

Allendoerfer, Michelle Giacobbe. "Who Cares About Human Rights? Public Opinion About Human Rights Foreign Policy." *Journal of Human Rights* 16, no. 4 (2017): 428–51.

Alm, Erika, and Lena Martinsson. "The Rainbow Flag As Friction: Transnational Imagined Communities of Belonging among Pakistani LGBTQ Activists." *Culture Unbound: Journal of Current Cultural Research* 8, no. 3 (2017): 218–39.

Altman, Dennis, and Jonathan Symons. *Queer Wars*. Cambridge, UK: Polity Press, 2016.

"Americans' Moral Stance towards Gay or Lesbian Relations in 2019." Statista Research Department. September 8, 2020. https://www.statista.com/statistics/225968/americans-moral-stance-towards-gay-or-lesbian-relations/.

Ammaturo, Francesca Romana. "Gender, Sexuality and Human Rights: A European Perspective." In *European Sexual Citizenship*, 7–30. Cham: Palgrave Macmillan, 2017.

Ammaturo, Francesca Romana. "The 'Pink Agenda': Questioning and Challenging European Homonationalist Sexual Citizenship." *Sociology* 49, no. 6 (2015): 1151–66.

Anderson, Elizabeth. *Freedom and Equality*. Oxford: Oxford University Press, 2016.

Andersson, Galit. "Quality of Life and Sexual Health among Transgender People and People Living with HIV in Sweden." PhD diss., Karolinska Institutet, 2019.

Andersson, Tova. "Live and Let Love: En kritisk studie av svensk homonationalism i en politisk manifestation i samband med de olympiska spelen i Sotji 2014." Bachelor's thesis, Södertörn University, 2016.

"Andrei Fighting for LGBT Rights Despite Death Threats." Swedish International Development Cooperation Agency (SIDA). Accessed February 26, 2019. https://www.sida.se/English/where-we-work/Europe/Moldova-/examples-of-results/andrei-fighting-for-lgbt-rights-despite-death-threats/.

"Annual Report." Human Rights Campaign. 2012. Accessed November 3, 2014. http://hrc-assets.s3-website-us-east-1.amazonaws.com//files/assets/resources/HRC-AnnualReport2012-web.pdf.

"Annual Reports." United Nations Office of the High Commissioner. Accessed November 5, 2014. http://www.ohchr.org/EN/Issues/Executions/Pages/AnnualReports.aspx.

Antonucci, Gianluca. "The Relationships between Government and Civil Society in Performing Public Service Hybrid Organisations: Some Insights from a Comparative Study." In *Cross-Sectoral Relations in the Delivery of Public Services*, 195–213. Bingley, UK: Emerald Publishing Limited, 2018.

Apodaca, Clair. "Foreign Aid as Foreign Policy Tool." In *Oxford Research Encyclopedia of Politics*. Oxford: Oxford University Press, 2017.

Apodaca, Clair. "Emerging Contradictions in US Human Rights Policy: The Trump Agenda." In *Contesting Human Rights: Norms, Institutions and Practice*, edited by Allison Brysk and Michael Stohl, 198–218. Cheltenham, UK: Edward Edgar Publishing, 2019.

Arat, Zehra F. Kabasakal, and Caryl Nuñez." Advancing LGBT Rights in Turkey: Tolerance or Protection?" *Human Rights Review* 18, no. 1 (2017): 1–19.

Arinaitwe, James Kassaga. "How US Evangelicals Are Shaping Development in Uganda." *Al Jazeera*. July 25, 2014. https://www.aljazeera.com/indepth/opinion/2014/07/us-evangelicals-uganda-2014724135920268137.html.

Aslan, Davut Han, and Deniz Doğanay. "Measuring Gender Equality. A Comparative Analysis of Sweden and Turkey." *Kwartalnik Naukowy Uczelni Vistula* 2, no. 60 (2019): 43–64.

"Assistant Secretary of State for Democracy, Tom Malinowski and Ugandan Activist Frank Mugisha Respond to *New York Times* Article 'U.S. Support of Gay Rights in Africa May Have Done More Harm Than Good.'" *Global Equality Today*. January 4, 2016. https://globalequality.wordpress.com/2016/01/04/assistant-secretary-of-state-for-democracy-tom-malinowski-and-ugandan-activist-frank-mugisha-respond-to-new-york-times-article-u-s-support-of-gay-rights-in-africa-may-have-done-more-harm-th/.

"A Survey of LGBT Americans: Attitudes, Experiences and Values in Changing Times." *Pew Research Center.* June 13, 2013. http://www.pewsocialtrends. org/2013/06/13/a-survey-of-lgbt-americans/.

Associated Press in Warsaw. "Obama Uses Embassies to Push for LGBT Rights Abroad." *The Guardian.* June 28, 2014. https://www.theguardian.com/world/ 2014/jun/28/obama-gay-rights-abroad-embassies-activism.

"Attitudes towards Homosexuality." World Values Survey. 2006. Accessed April 15, 2014. http://www.worldvaluessurvey.org/WVSContents.jsp

Avery, Daniel. "IKEA Sued by Worker Fired for Posting Anti-Gay Bible Quotes, Attacking 'Promotion of Homosexuality.'" *Newsweek.* July 8, 2019. https:// www.newsweek.com/ikea-poland-lgbt-lawsuit-1447954.

Ayoub, Phillip. "Contested Norms in New-Adopter States: International Determinants of LGBT Rights Legislation." *European Journal of International Relations* 21, no. 2 (2014a): 293–322.

Ayoub, Phillip. "Cooperative Transnationalism in Contemporary Europe: European-ization and Political Opportunities for LGBT Mobilization in the European Union." *European Political Science Review* 5, no. 2 (2013): 279–310. https:// doi.org/10.1017/s1755773912000161.

Ayoub, Phillip. "Intersectional and Transnational Coalitions during Times of Crisis: The European LGBTI Movement." *Social Politics: International Studies in Gender, State & Society* 26, no. 1 (2018): 1–29. https://doi.org/10.1093/sp/jxy007.

Ayoub, Phillip M. "Protean Power in Movement: Navigating Uncertainty in the LGBT Rights Revolution." *Protean Power* 146 (2018): 79–99.

Ayoub, Phillip M. "Tensions in Rights: Navigating Emerging Contradictions in the LGBT Rights Revolution." *Contesting Human Rights* (January 2019): 43–58. https://doi.org/10.4337/9781788972864.00011.

Ayoub, Phillip. *When States Come Out: Europe's Sexual Minorities and the Politics of Visibility.* Cambridge: Cambridge University Press, 2016.

Ayoub, Phillip M. "With Arms Wide Shut: Threat Perception, Norm Reception, and Mobilized Resistance to LGBT Rights." *Journal of Human Rights* 13, no. 3 (March 2014): 337–62. https://doi.org/10.1080/14754835.2014.919213.

Badgett, M. V. Lee, Sheila Nezhad, Kees Waaldijk, and Yana van der Meulen-Rodgers. "The Relationship between LGBT Inclusion and Economic Development: An Analysis of Emerging Economies." The Williams Institute. November 2014. http://williamsinstitute.law.ucla.edu/research/international/ lgbt-incl-econ-devel-nov-2014/.

Badgett, M. V. Lee, Kees Waaldijk, and Yana Van Der Meulen-Rodgers. "The Relationship between LGBT Inclusion and Economic Development: Macro-Level Evidence." *World Development* 120 (2019): 1–14. https://doi.org/10.1016/j. worlddev.2019.03.011.

Baer, Daniel. "LiveAtState: Human Rights of Lesbian, Gay, Bisexual, and Transgender People." US Department of State. June 20, 2013. https://2009-2017.state. gov/r/pa/ime/211005.htm.

Baldez, Lisa. "Women's Movements and Democratic Transition in Chile, Brazil, East Germany, and Poland." *Comparative Politics* 35, no. 3 (2003): 253–72. https://doi.org/10.2307/4150176.

Ball, Carlos A., ed. *After Marriage Equality: The Future of LGBT Rights*. New York: New York University Press, 2019.

Ball, Carlos A. *The Queering of Corporate America: How Big Business Went from LGBT Adversary to Ally*. Boston: Beacon Press, 2019.

Bangura, Abdul Karim. *Sweden vs Apartheid: Putting Morality Ahead of Profit*. London: Routledge Press, 2017.

Baker, James, and Thomas DeFrank. *The Politics of Diplomacy: Revolution, War and Peace, 1989–1992*. New York: G.P. Putnam's Sons, 1995.

Banaszak, Lee Ann. "Inside and Outside the State: Movement Insider Status, Tactics, and Public Policy Achievements." *Routing the Opposition: Social Movements, Public Policy, and Democracy* 23 (2005): 149–76.

Banaszak, Lee Ann. *The Women's Movement inside and outside the State*. Cambridge: Cambridge University Press, 2010.

Barakat, Sultan. "Priorities and Challenges of Qatar's Humanitarian Diplomacy." *CMI Brief* 2019, no. 7 (2019). https://www.cmi.no/publications/6906-priorities-and-challenges-of-qatars-humanitarian-diplomacy.

Barcelos, Chris A., and Stephanie L. Budge. "Inequalities in Crowdfunding for Transgender Health Care." *Transgender Health* 4, no. 1 (2019): 81–88.

Barnhizer, David. *Effective Strategies for Protecting Human Rights Economic Sanctions, Use of National Courts and International Fora and Coercive Power*. London: Routledge, 2017.

Basedau, Matthias, Jonathan Fox, Jan H. Pierskalla, Georg Strüver, and Johannes Vüllers. "Does Discrimination Breed Grievances—and Do Grievances Breed Violence? New Evidence from an Analysis of Religious Minorities in Developing Countries." *Conflict Management and Peace Science* 34, no. 3 (2017): 217–39.

Basen, Wayne. "Inside Lou Engle' Anti-Gay Revival." Truth Wins Out. June 30, 2010. https://truthwinsout.org/pressrelease/2010/06/9500/.

Bashevkin, Sylvia. *Women as Foreign Policy Leaders: National Security and Gender Politics in Superpower America*. Oxford: Oxford University Press, 2018.

Baxi, Upendra. "Voices of Suffering, Fragmented Universality, and the Future of Human Rights." In *Human Rights*, edited by Robert McCorquodale, 159–214. London: Routledge, 2017.

Becker, Jo. *Campaigning for Justice: Human Rights Advocacy in Practice*. Stanford, CA: Stanford University Press, 2013.

Beer, Caroline, and Victor D. Cruz-Aceves. "Extending Rights to Marginalized Minorities: Same-Sex Relationship Recognition in Mexico and the United States." *State Politics & Policy Quarterly* 18, no. 1 (2018): 3–26.

Behravesh, Maysam. "Gender Clash: Why Is Saudi Arabia So Angry at Sweden?." *Your Middle East* (2015): 5–26.

Beittel, June S., Lauren Ploch Blanchard, and Liana Rosen. " 'Leahy Law' Human Rights Provisions and Security Assistance: Issue Overview." Congressional Research Service. January 29, 2014. https://fas.org/sgp/crs/row/R43361.pdf.

"Belarus: Amid Vicious Crackdown on Peaceful Protests, Businesses Bear Responsibility to Respect Human Rights." Amnesty International. August 21, 2020. https://www.amnesty.org/en/latest/news/2020/08/belarus-amid-vicious-crackdown-on-peaceful-protests-businesses-bear-responsibility-to-respect-human-rights/.

"Belarus Expels Swedish Ambassador after Teddy Bear Fiasco." *EU Observer*. August 3, 2012. https://euobserver.com/foreign/117154.

Ben-Moshe, Liat, and Justin J. W. Powell. "Sign of Our Times? Revis (it) ing the International Symbol of Access." *Disability & Society* 22, no. 5 (2007): 489–505.

Beresford, Alexander. "A Responsibility to Protect Africa from the West? South Africa and the NATO Intervention in Libya." *International Politics* 52, no. 3 (2015): 288–304.

Bergenfield, Rachel, and Alice M. Miller. "Queering International Development? An Examination of New LGBT Rights Rhetoric, Policy, and Programming among International Development Agencies." *LGBTQ Policy Journal* (2014). https://doi.org/10.2139/ssrn.2507515.

Bergo, Havard. "Has Foreign Aid Led to Economic Growth in Uganda?" Global Risk Insights. May 18, 2015. https://globalriskinsights.com/2015/05/has-foreign-aid-led-to-economic-growth-in-uganda/.

Berkovitch, Nitza, and Sara Helman. "Global Social Movements." *Companion to Gender Studies* (2009): 266–79.

Bew, John. *Realpolitik: A History*. Oxford: Oxford University Press, 2016.

Ingebritsen, Christine, Iver Neumann, Siegline Gstohl, and Jessica Beyer. *Small States in International Relations*. Seattle: University of Washington Press, 2006.

Biden, Joe. "Vice President Biden: LGBT Rights Integral Part of U.S. Foreign Policy Human Rights Campaign." Human Rights Campaign. March 2014. Accessed October 10, 2014. http://www.hrc.org/blog/entry/vice-president-biden-lgbt-rights-integral-part-of-u.s.-foreign-policy.

"2016 Biennial Report." US Department of Justice Office on Violence Against Women. Washington DC, 2016. https://www.justice.gov/ovw/page/file/933886/download.

Binnie, Jon, and Christian Klesse. " 'Like a Bomb in the Gasoline Station': East–West Migration and Transnational Activism around Lesbian, Gay, Bisexual, Transgender and Queer Politics in Poland." *Journal of Ethnic and Migration Studies* 39, no. 7 (2013): 1107–24.

Biryabarema, Elias. "West Can Keep Its Aid, Says Uganda amid Anti-Gay Bill Fallout." *BDlive*, African News. February 2014. Accessed October 20, 2014. http://www.bdlive.co.za/africa/africannews/2014/02/28/west-can-keep-its-aid-says-uganda-amid-anti-gay-bill-fallout.

Biryabarema, Elias, and Sven Nordenstam. "Sweden Resumes Aid to Uganda after Suspending It over Anti-Gay Law." *Reuters World News.* July 28, 2014. https://www.reuters.com/article/us-uganda-gay-idUSKBN0FX14Q20140728.

Bishop, Amie, and Anthony Adero. "Global LGBTQI Movements, Human Rights, and Health: Notes from the Frontlines." Western Washington University Fairhaven College of Interdisciplinary Studies, World Issues Forum. May 10, 2016. https://cedar.wwu.edu/fairhaven_wif/2016-2017/2016-2017/2/.

Bjola, Corneliu, and Markus Kornprobst. *Understanding International Diplomacy: Theory, Practice and Ethics.* New York: Routledge, 2018.

Björkdahl, Annika. "Ideas and Norms in Swedish Peace Policy." *Swiss Political Science Review* 19, no. 3 (2013): 322–37.

Björkdahl, Annika. "Swedish Norm Entrepreneurship in the UN." *International Peacekeeping* 14, no. 4 (2007): 538–52.

Björkdahl, Annika, Natalia Chaban, John Leslie, and Annick Masselot. "Introduction: To Take or Not to Take EU Norms? Adoption, Adaptation, Resistance and Rejection." In *Importing EU Norms*, edited by Björkdahl, Chaban, Leslie, and Masselot, 1–9. Cham: Springer, 2015.

Black, David R. "Addressing Apartheid: Lessons from Australian, Canadian and Swedish Policies in Southern Africa." In *Niche Diplomacy*, edited by Andrew F. Cooper, 100–28. London: Palgrave Macmillan, 1997.

Blackmer, Corinne E. "Pinkwashing." *Israel Studies* 24, no. 2 (2019): 171–81.

Blackwell, Marilyn Johns. *Gender and Representation in the Films of Ingmar Bergman.* New York: Camden House, 1997.

Blake, Mariah. "Meet the American Pastor behind Uganda's Anti-Gay Crackdown." *Mother Jones.* July 31, 2019. https://www.motherjones.com/politics/2014/03/scott-lively-anti-gay-law-uganda/2/.

Bob, Clifford. *The International Struggle for New Human Rights.* Philadelphia: University of Pennsylvania Press, 2010.

Bompani, Barbara. " 'For God and for My Country': Pentecostal-Charismatic Churches and the Framing of a New Political Discourse in Uganda." In *Public Religion and the Politics of Homosexuality in Africa*, edited by Adriaan van Klinken and Ezra Chitando, 19–34. London: Routledge, 2016.

Bompani, Barbara, and Caroline Valois. "Sexualizing Politics: The Anti-Homosexuality Bill, Party-Politics and the New Political Dispensation in Uganda." *Critical African Studies* 9, no. 1 (2017): 52–70.

Book, Karin, and Lena Eskilsson. "Coming Out in Copenhagen: Homo Sports Events in City Marketing." *Sport in Society* 13, no. 2 (2010): 314–28.

Boon, Hoo Tiang. *China's Global Identity: Considering the Responsibility of Great Power.* Washington, DC: Georgetown University Press, 2018.

Boswell, Louis K. "The Initial Sensitizing Event of Emotional Disorders." *Medical Hypnoanalysis Journal* 2, no. 4 (1987): 155–60. https://psycnet.apa.org/record/1988-36676-001.

Bowman, Emma. "Sweden Election: Ruling Party Scrapes A Win As Far-Right Gains Support." NPR News. September 9, 2018. https://www.npr.org/2018/09/09/ 646116493/sweden-election-ruling-party-scrapes-a-win-as-far-right-gains-support.

Brass, Jennifer N. *Allies or Adversaries: NGOs and the State in Africa.* Cambridge: Cambridge University Press, 2016.

"Breaking Its Own Rules: Amnesty's Researcher Bias and Govt Funding." Amnesty International, Australian Branch. As cited by NGO-Monitor. June 4, 2012. https://www. ngo-monitor.org/reports/breaking_its_own_rules_amnesty_s_gov_t_funding_ and_researcher_bias/.

Brennan, Jason. *When All Else Fails: The Ethics of Resistance to State Injustice.* Princeton, NJ: Princeton University Press, 2018.

Brewer, Sierra, and Lauren Dundes. "Concerned, Meet Terrified: Intersectional Feminism and the Women's March." *Women's Studies International Forum* 69 (2018): 49–55. https://doi.org/10.1016/j.wsif.2018.04.008.

"Briefing by Special Envoy for the Human Rights of LGBT Persons Randy Berry." US Department of State Office of the Spokesperson, April 20, 2016. https://2009-2017.state.gov/r/pa/prs/ps/2016/04/256425.htm.

"Briefing: Punitive Aid Cuts Disrupt Healthcare in Uganda." *The New Humanitarian.* April 2, 2014. https://www.thenewhumanitarian.org/analysis/2014/04/02/ briefing-punitive-aid-cuts-disrupt-healthcare-uganda.

Brinkerhoff, Jennifer M., and Derick W. Brinkerhoff. "Government Nonprofit Relations in Comparative Perspective: Evolution, Themes, and New Directions." *Public Administration and Development* 22 (2002): 3–18.

Brolin, Therese. "Framing the Results Agenda in Swedish Development Co-Operation." *Development Policy Review* 35, no. S2 (2017): O338-O356. https:// doi.org/10.1111/dpr.12298.

Bromley, Mark. "Building a Strategy for an LGBT-Inclusive U.S. Foreign Policy." The Council for Global Equality. November 2007. http://www.globalequality. org/storage/documents/pdf/lgbt_foreign_policy_project-discussion_paper.pdf.

Brooks, Lewis, and Felicity Daly. "A Commonwealth Toolkit for Policy Progress on LGBT Rights." The Royal Commonwealth Society. April 2016. http:// menengage.org/wp-content/uploads/2016/04/Commonwealth-Toolkit-for-Policy-Progress-on-LGBT-Rights.pdf.

Brown, Dara P. "LGBT Rights Are Human Rights: Conditioning Foreign Direct Investments on Domestic Policy Reform." *Cornell International Law Journal* 50 (2017): 611.

Brown, Anna. "5 Key Findings about LGBT Americans." *Pew Research Center.* June 13, 2017. https://www.pewresearch.org/fact-tank/2017/06/13/5-key-findings-about-lgbt-americans/.

Brown, Roderick. "Corrective Rape in South Africa: A Continuing Plight Despite an International Human Rights Response." *Annual Survey of International & Comparative Law* 18, no. 1 (2012): 45–66.

Browne, Kath. "A Party with Politics? (Re)making LGBTQ Pride Spaces in Dublin and Brighton." *Social and Cultural Geography* 8, no. 1 (2007): 63–77.

Brysk, Alison. *Global Good Samaritans: Human Rights as Foreign Policy*. Oxford: Oxford University Press, 2009.

Brysk, Alison. *The Future of Human Rights*. Cambridge, UK: Polity Press, 2018.

Burack, Cynthia. *Because We Are Human: Contesting U.S. Support for Gender and Sexuality Human Rights Abroad*. New York: State University of New York Press, 2018.

Burack, Cynthia. "Getting What 'We' Deserve: Terrorism, Tolerance, Sexuality, and the Christian Right." *New Political Science* 25, no. 3 (2003): 329–49. https://doi.org/https://doi.org/10.1080/07393140307180.

Burack, Cynthia. "Sexual Orientation and Gender Identity (SOGI) Human Rights Assistance in the Time of Trump." *Politics & Gender* 14, no. 4 (2018): 561–80. https://doi.org/10.1017/s1743923x1800065x.

Burt, J. *Political Violence and the Authoritarian State in Peru: Silencing Civil Society*. New York: Palgrave Macmillan, 2007.

Busby, Joshua W. *Moral Movements and Foreign Policy*. Cambridge: Cambridge University Press, 2010.

Cabosky, Joseph, and Rhonda Gibson. "A Longitudinal Content Analysis of the Use of Radical and Mainstream, Pro- and Anti-LGBT Organizations as Sources in the *New York Times* & the *Washington Post*." *Journal of Homosexuality* (2019): 1–24.

Calabresi, Steven G. "A Shining City on a Hill: American Exceptionalism and the Supreme Court's Practice of Relying on Foreign Law." *Boston University Law Review* 86 (2006): 1335–1416.

Callaway, Rhonda L., and Elizabeth G. Matthews. *Strategic US Foreign Assistance: The Battle between Human Rights and National Security*. New York: Routledge, 2008.

Cariati, Federika A. "How Eric Holder's Role as Attorney General Impacted the Obama Presidency." *Inquiries Journal* 7, no. 2 (2015). http://www.inquiries-journal.com/articles/994/how-eric-holders-role-as-attorney-general-impacted-the-obama-presidency.

Carrington, Daisy. "On Homosexuality: Uganda's Religious Leaders." CNN. October 16, 2014. https://www.cnn.com/2014/10/16/world/africa/on-homosexuality-ugandas-religious-leaders.

Carlson-Rainer, Elise. "Bureaucrats and Resistance: Social Movement Actors Inside the State." In National Public Radio's Academic Minute WAMC Northeast Public Radio, edited by David Hopper II, Producer. Albany, NY: *NPR Academic Minute*. April 9, 2018. http://wamc.org/programs/academic-minute.

Carlson-Rainer, Elise. "Chasing Rainbows: Some Country's LGBTI Fight Not Just for Equality, but Survival." *The Globe Post*. May 10, 2019. https://theglobepost.com/2019/05/10/lgbti-rights/.

Carlson-Rainer Elise. "Khashoggi Prompts Trump to Reconsider Human Rights in Foreign Policy." *The Hill*. October 18, 2018. https://thehill.com/opinion/

international/412058-khashoggi-prompts-trump-to-reconsider-human-rights-in-foreign-policy.

Carlson-Rainer, Elise. "LGBT Pride: Marching on the Front Lines. E-International Relations." *E-International Relations.* July 1, 2015. https://www.e-ir.info/2015/07/01/lgbt-pride-marching-on-the-front-lines/.

Carlson-Rainer, Elise. "Sweden Is a World Leader in Peace, Security and Human Rights." *World Affairs Journal* 180, no. 4 (2018): 79–85. doi:10.1177/0043820018759714.

Carlson-Rainer, Elise. "Trump's New LGBTI Policy Contradicts U.S. Human Rights Diplomacy." *Washington Diplomat*, October 31, 2018. https://washdiplomat.com/op-ed-trumps-new-lgbti-policy-contradicts-us-human-rights-diplomacy/.

Carlson-Rainer, Elise. "Will Sexual Minority Rights Be Trumped? Assessing the Policy Sustainability of LGBTI Rights Diplomacy in American Foreign Policy." *Diplomacy & Statecraft* 30, no. 1 (February 2019): 147–63. https://doi.org/10.1080/09592296.2019.1557422.

Carnegie, Allison, and Nikolay Marinov. "Foreign Aid, Human Rights, and Democracy Promotion: Evidence from a Natural Experiment." *American Journal of Political Science* 61, no. 3 (2017): 671–83. https://doi.org/10.1111/ajps.12289.

Carroll, Aengus, and Lucas P. Itaborahy. "State-Sponsored Homophobia 2015: A World Survey of Laws: Criminalization, Protection and Recognition of Same-Sex Love." Geneva: International Lesbian, Gay, Trans and Intersex Association (ILGA). 2015. http://old.ilga.org/Statehomophobia/ILGA_State_Sponsored_Homophobia_2015.pdf.

Carstensen, Martin B., and Vivien A. Schmidt. "Power through, over and in Ideas: Conceptualizing Ideational Power in Discursive Institutionalism." *Journal of European Public Policy* 23, no. 3 (2015): 318–37. https://doi.org/10.1080/13501763.2015.1115534.

Carter, Jimmy. "Speech on Humane Purposes in Foreign Policy Carter Humane Foreign Policy, 1977." Accessed November 2, 2014. http://www.thirdworldtraveler.com/Human%20Rights%20Documents/Carter_HumaneFP.html.

"Categories of Federal Civil Service Employment: A Snapshot." Congressional Research Service. March 26, 2019. https://fas.org/sgp/crs/misc/R45635.pdf.

"Centering the Rights of LGBTI Individuals in U.S. Foreign Policy: A Pathway to Effective Global Leadership." The Council for Global Equality. November 2020. http://www.globalequality.org/storage/documents/CGE_Transition_Paper.pdf.

"Challenging Tunisia's Homophobic Taboos." Amnesty International. September 30, 2015. https://www.amnesty.org/en/latest/news/2015/09/challenging-tunisias-homophobic-taboos/.

"Changing Attitudes on Gay Marriage: Attitudes on Same-Sex Marriage by Generation." *Pew Research Center*: Religion and Public Life. May 12, 2016. http://www.pewforum.org/2016/05/12/changing-attitudes-on-gay-marriage/.

Charania, Moon. "Outing the Pakistani Queer: Pride, Paranoia and Politics in US Visual Culture." *Sexualities* 20, no. 1–2 (2017): 41–64.

Charmaz, Kathy. *Constructing Grounded Theory.* Thousand Oaks, CA: Sage Press, 2014.

Chase, Anthony. "Human Rights Contestations: Sexual Orientation and Gender Identity." *The International Journal of Human Rights* 20, no. 6 (2016): 703–23.

Cheney, Kristen. "Locating Neocolonialism, 'Tradition,' and Human Rights in Uganda's 'Gay Death Penalty.'" *African Studies Review* 55, no. 2 (2012): 77–95. https://doi.org/10.1353/arw.2012.0031.

Chirot, Daniel, and Clark McCauley. *Why Not Kill Them All? The Logic and Prevention of Mass Political Murder.* Princeton, NJ: Princeton University Press, 2010.

Choi, Seung-Whan, and Patrick James. "Are US Foreign Policy Tools Effective in Improving Human Rights Conditions?" *The Chinese Journal of International Politics* 10, no. 3 (2017): 331–56. https://doi.org/10.1093/cjip/pox010.

Chong, Alan. "Small State Soft Power Strategies: Virtual Enlargement in the Cases of the Vatican City State and Singapore." *Cambridge Review of International Affairs* 23, no. 3 (2010): 383–405.

Chong, Daniel. *Debating Human Rights.* Boulder, CO: Rienner, 2014.

Clark, Ann Marie. *Diplomacy of Conscience: Amnesty International and Changing Human Rights Norms.* Princeton, NJ: Princeton University Press, 2001.

Clinton, Hillary. "Clinton's Address in Geneva on International Human Rights Day." December 6, 2011. http://translations.state.gov/st/english/texttrans/2011/12/20111206180616su0.4842885.html#ixzz3KP317fJN.

Clinton, Hillary. "Human Rights in the Twenty-First Century." Speech at Georgetown University. December 14, 2009. https://anthonyclarkarend.com/video-and-transcript-hillary-clintons-georgetown-human-rights-address-560ff7e5f924.

Clinton, Hillary. "Presidential Campaign Briefing Factsheet: 'Fighting for Full Equality for LGBT People.'" hillaryclinton.org. Accessed March 1, 2016. https://www.hillaryclinton.com/briefing/factsheets/2015/12/17/fighting-for-full-equality/.

Cohen, Roberta. "Integrating Human Rights in U.S. Foreign Policy: The History, the Challenges, and the Criteria for an Effective Policy." Speech at Brookings Foreign Service Institute. Washington, DC, 2008. http://www.brookings.edu/~/media/research/files/speeches/2008/4/human-rights-cohen/04_human_rights_cohen.pdf.

Cohan, John Alan. "Honor Killings and the Cultural Defense." *California Western International Law Journal* 40, no. 2 (2010): 178–249.

Cook-Daniels, Loree, and Michael Munson. "Transgender Older People: At Sea Far from the Sexual Rights Shore." In *Addressing the Sexual Rights of Older People*, edited by Catherine Barrett and Sharron Hinchliff, 70–83. London: Routledge, 2017.

Copeland, Lauren, Ariel Hasell, and Bruce Bimber. "Collective Action Frames, Advocacy Organizations, and Protests over Same-sex Marriage." *International Journal of Communication* 10 (2016): 3785–3807.

Conrad, Kathryn. "Queer Treasons: Homosexuality and the Irish National Identity." *Cultural Studies* 15, no. 1 (2010): 124–37. https://doi.org/10.1080/09502380010012630.

Conrad, Ryan, ed. *Against Equality: Queer Revolution, Not Mere Inclusion.* Oakland, CA: AK Press, 2014.

Conger, Kimberly H. "The Christian Right in US Politics." In *Oxford Research Encyclopedia of Politics.* Oxford: Oxford University Press, 2019.

"Congressional Budget Justification." US Department of State, Washington, DC, Fiscal Year 2020. https://www.usaid.gov/sites/default/files/documents/1868/FY_2020_CBJ.pdf.

Conzelmann, Thomas. "Beyond the Carrot and the Stick: State Reporting Procedures in the World Trade Organization and the Organization for Economic Cooperation and Development." In *International Organizations and Implementation*, edited by Jutta Joachim, Bob Reinalda, and Bertjan Verbeek, 57–69. London: Routledge, 2007.

Corbin, Juliet, and Anselm Strauss. *Basics of Qualitative Research: Techniques and Procedures for Developing Grounded Theory.* Thousand Oaks, CA: Sage Publications, 2014.

Cordell, Rebecca, K. Chad Clay, Christopher J. Fariss, Reed M. Wood, and Thorin M. Wright. "Changing Standards or Political Whim? Evaluating Changes in the Content of the US State Department Human Rights Reports." *Journal of Human Rights* 19, no. 1 (2020): 3–18. https://doi.org/10.1080/14754835.2019.1671175.

Corey-Boulet, Robbie. *Love Falls on Us: a Story of American Ideas and African LGBT Lives.* London: Zed Books, 2019.

Corey-Boulet, Robbie. "The Trump Effect." *World Policy Journal* 34, no. 3 (2017): 83–89. https://doi.org/10.1215/07402775-4280064.

Cornwall, Andrea, Jasmine Gideon, and Kalpana Wilson. "Introduction: Reclaiming Feminism: Gender and Neoliberalism." *Institute of Development Studies Bulletin* 39, no. 5 (December 2008).

Correa, Sonia. "Emerging Powers: Can It Be That Sexuality and Human Rights Is a Lateral Issue?" *SUR–International Journal on Human Rights* 11, no. 20 (2014): 167.

"2020 Country Reports on Human Rights Practices: Qatar." US Department of State Bureau of Democracy, Human Rights, and Labor. March 30, 2021. https://www.state.gov/reports/2020-country-reports-on-human-rights-practices/qatar/.

"2009 Country Reports on Human Rights Practices: Uganda." US Department of State Bureau of Democracy, Human Rights, and Labor. March 11, 2010. https://2009-2017.state.gov/j/drl/rls/hrrpt/2009/af/135982.htm.

"2009 Country Reports on Human Rights Practices." US Department of State Bureau of Democracy, Human Rights, and Labor. March 11, 2010. https://2009-2017.state.gov/j/drl/rls/hrrpt/2009/frontmatter/135936.htm.

"2018 Country Reports on Human Rights Practices." US Department of State. March 13, 2019. https://www.state.gov/reports/2018-country-reports-on-human-rights-practices/.

"Court Cases: SMUG vs. Scott Lively." Sexual Minorities Uganda. Accessed November 9, 2020. https://sexualminoritiesuganda.com/publications/court-cases/.

Cowan, Jane K., and Julie Billaud. "Between Learning and Schooling: The Politics of Human Rights Monitoring at the Universal Periodic Review." *Third World Quarterly* 36, no. 6 (2015): 1175–90.

Crawford, Gordon, and Simonida Kacarska. "Aid Sanctions and Political Conditionality: Continuity and Change." *Journal of International Relations and Development* 22, no. 1 (August 2017): 184–214. https://doi.org/10.1057/s41268-017-0099-8.

"Criminalization around the World." Human Rights Campaign. April 23, 2015. http://hrc-assets.s3-website-us-east-1.amazonaws.com//files/assets/resources/Criminalization-Map-042315.pdf.

Croome, Philippa. "Sweden Suspends Some Aid to Uganda over Anti-Gay Law." *Reuters.* March 2014. Accessed October 20, 2014. http://www.reuters.com/article/2014/03/06/us-uganda-aid-sweden-idUSBREA2509720140306.

Currier, Ashley. *Out in Africa: LGBT Organizing in Namibia and South Africa.* Minneapolis: University of Minnesota Press, 2012.

Dahlerup, Drude. "The Story of the Theory of Critical Mass." *Politics & Gender* 2, no. 4 (2006): 511–22.

D'Amico, Francine. "LGBT and (Dis) United Nations." In *Sexualities in World Politics: How LGBTQ Claims Shape International Relations*, edited by Manuela Lavinas Picq and Markus Thiel, 54–74. Abingdon, UK: Routledge, 2015.

Darian-Smith, Eve. *Laws and Societies in Global Contexts: Contemporary Approaches.* Cambridge: Cambridge University Press, 2013.

Dasandi, Niheer, and Lior Erez. "The Donor's Dilemma: International Aid and Human Rights Violations." *British Journal of Political Science* 49, no. 4 (2019): 1431–52.

Defense of Marriage Act (DOMA). H.R. 3396 (104th): 104th Congress. September 10, 1996. https://www.govtrack.us/congress/votes/104-1996/s280.

Della Porta, Donatella, and Mario Diani. *Social Movements: An Introduction.* 3rd ed. Hoboken, NJ: John Wiley & Sons, 2020.

Dellmuth, Lisa M., and Elizabeth A. Bloodgood. "Advocacy Group Effects in Global Governance: Populations, Strategies, and Political Opportunity Structures." *Interest Groups & Advocacy* 8, no. 3 (2019): 255–69.

"Development Aid Drops in 2018, Especially to Neediest Countries." Organization for Economic Co-Operation and Development. Accessed February 20, 2020. http://www.oecd.org/development/development-aid-drops-in-2018-especially-to-neediest-countries.htm.

Dicklitch-Nelson, Susan. "Are LGBTQ Human Rights in Uganda a Lost Cause?" *Georgetown Journal of International Affairs.* February 27, 2020. https://gjia.georgetown.edu/2020/02/27/are-lgbtq-human-rights-in-uganda-a-lost-cause/.

Dicklitch, Susan, Berwood Yost, and Bryan M. Dougan. "Building a Barometer of Gay Rights (BGR): A Case Study of Uganda and the Persecution of Homosexuals." *Human Rights Quarterly* 34, no. 2 (2012): 448–71. https://doi.org/10.1353/hrq.2012.0033.

Dicklitch-Nelson, Susan, Scottie Thompson Buckland, Berwood Yost, and Daniel Draguljić. "From Persecutors to Protectors: Human Rights and the F&M Global Barometer of Gay Rights TM(GBGR)." *Journal of Human Rights* 18, no. 1 (2019): 1–18. https://doi.org/10.1080.14754835.2018.1563863.

Dicklitch-Nelson, Susan, and Indira Rahman. "Joint Responsibility: LGBT Rights in a Polarized World." *The Globe Post*. April 18, 2019. https://theglobepost.com/2019/04/18/lgbt-rights/.

Diderichsen, Finn. "Market Reforms in Health Care and Sustainability of the Welfare State: Lessons from Sweden." *Health Policy* 32 (1995): 141–53.

Dietrich, Simone. "Bypass or Engage? Explaining Donor Delivery Tactics in Foreign Aid Allocation." *International Studies Quarterly* 57, no. 4 (2013): 698–712. https://doi.org/10.1111/isqu.12041.

Dietrich, Simone, and Amanda M. Murdie. "Human Rights Shaming through INGOs and Foreign Aid Delivery." *SSRN Electronic Journal*, 2015. https://doi.org/10.2139/ssrn.2641766.

Diggelmann, Oliver, and Maria Nicole Cleis. "How the Right to Privacy Became a Human Right." *Human Rights Law Review* 14, no. 3 (2014): 441–58. https://doi.org/10.1093/hrlr/ngu014.

" 'Dignity for All:' LGBTI Emergency Assistance Program." US Department of State, Bureau of Democracy, Human Rights and Labor. Accessed May 12, 2021. http://www.state.gov/globalequality/about/index.htm.

"Diplomats' Same-Sex Partners to Get Benefits." *New York Times*. May 2009. Accessed October 10, 2014. http://www.nytimes.com/2009/05/24/us/24benefit.html?_r=0.

"Disparate Trends in Permissiveness: Homosexuality and Prostitution." World Values Survey. Accessed May 18, 2016. http://www.worldvaluessurvey.org/WVSDocumentationWV5.jsp.

Dlamini, Kuseni. "Is Quiet Diplomacy an Effective Conflict Resolution Strategy?" *South African Yearbook of International Affairs* 3 (2002): 171–78.

Donnelly, Jack. *Realism and International Relations*. Cambridge: Cambridge University Press, 2014.

Donno, Daniela, and Michael Neureiter. "Can Human Rights Conditionality Reduce Repression? Examining the European Union's Economic Agreements." *Review of International Organizations* 13, no. 3 (2018): 335–57.

Dorell, Oren. "Exclusive: First Diplomat for LGBT Rights Speaks Out." *USA Today*. April 26, 2015. https://www.usatoday.com/story/news/world/2015/04/26/us-diplomat-champion-for-lgbt-people/26314885/.

Doucouliagos, Hristos, and Martin Paldam. "Conditional Aid Effectiveness: A Meta-Study." *Journal of International Development* 22, no. 4 (2010): 391–410.

Drążkiewicz-Grodzicka, Elżbieta. " 'State Bureaucrats' and 'Those NGO People':
Promoting the Idea of Civil Society, Hindering the State." *Critique of Anthropology* 36, no. 4 (2016): 341–62.

"DRL Guide to Program Monitoring and Evaluation." US Department of State
Bureau of Democracy, Human Rights, and Labor. October 2016. Accessed
September 24, 2020. https://www.state.gov/wp-content/uploads/2019/01/
DRL-Guide-to-Program-Monitoring-and-Evaluation.pdf.

"Dr. Stella Nyanzi." Front Line Defenders. Accessed October 18, 2020. https://
www.frontlinedefenders.org/en/profile/dr-stella-nyanzi.

Dueck, Colin. "The Future of Conservative Foreign Policy." *Texas National Security
Review* 2, no. 1 (2018): 171–76. https://tnsr.org/roundtable/the-future-of-
conservative-foreign-policy/.

Dunne, Tim, and Nicholas J. Wheeler. "Great Illusions or Great Transformations? Human Rights and International Relations a Hundred Years On."
International Relations 33, no. 2 (2016): 338–56. https://doi.org/10.1177/
0047117819851256.

Dunne, Peter. "Transgender Sterilisation Requirements in Europe." *Medical Law
Review* 25, no. 4 (2017): 554–81.

Duke, Sue. "The Key to Closing the Gender Gap? Putting More Women in
Charge." *World Economic Forum*. November 2, 2017. https://www.weforum.
org/agenda/2017/11/women-leaders-key-to-workplace-equality/.

Du Toit, Nadine F. Bowers. "Unapologetically Faith Based: The Nature of Donor
Engagement in the Context of South African Faith-Based Organisations."
HTS Teologiese Studies/Theological Studies 75, no. 4 (2019): a5529. https://
doi.org/10.4102/hts.v75i4.5529.

Dutta, Nabamita, and Claudia R. Williamson. "Can Foreign Aid Free the Press?"
Journal of Institutional Economics 12, no. 3 (February 2016): 603–21. https://
doi.org/10.1017/s1744137415000557.

Dzenovska, Dace. *School of Europeanness: Tolerance and Other Lessons in Political
Liberalism in Latvia*. Ithaca, NY: Cornell University Press, 2018.

Easterly, William. *The White Man's Burden: Why the West's Efforts to Aid the Rest
Have Done So Much Ill and So Little Good*. New York: Penguin Books, 2007.

Eckel, Jan, and Rachel Ward. *The Ambivalence of Good: Human Rights in International
Politics since the 1940s*. Oxford: Oxford University Press, 2019.

Edling, Margareta. "New Ombudsman Fights Discrimination on Grounds of Sexual
Orientation." Eurofound. December 27, 1999. http://www.eurofound.europa.
eu/observatories/eurwork/articles/new-ombudsman-fights-discrimination-
on-grounds-of-sexual-orientation.

"Egypt: Stop Anti-LGBT Crackdown, Intimidation. 'Rainbow Flag' Arrests Violate Privacy, Freedom of Expression." Human Rights Watch. September 30, 2017. https://
www.hrw.org/news/2017/09/30/egypt-stop-anti-lgbt-crackdown-intimidation.

Eisenstein, Hester. "The Australian Femocratic Experiment: A Feminist Case for
Bureaucracy." In *Feminist Organizations: Harvest of the New Women's Movement*,

edited by Myra Marx Ferree, 69–83. Philadelphia, PA: Temple University Press, 1995.

Ekbladh, David. *The Great American Mission: Modernization and the Construction of an American World Order.* Princeton, NJ: Princeton University Press, 2011.

Ellawala, Themal. "Legitimating Violences: The 'Gay Rights' NGO and the Disciplining of the Sri Lankan Queer Figure." *Journal of South Asian Development* 14, no. 1 (2019): 83–107.

Elliott, Thomas Alan, Edwin Amenta, and Neal Caren. "Recipes for Attention: Policy Reforms, Crises, Organizational Characteristics, and the Newspaper Coverage of the LGBT Movement, 1969–2009." *Sociological Forum* 31, no. 4 (2016): 926–47.

Elman, Amy. *Sexual Subordination and the State: Comparing Sweden and the United States.* New York: Berghahn Publishers, 1996.

El-Ojeili, Chamsy, and Dylan Taylor. "The Revaluation of All Values: Extremism, the Ultra-Left, and Revolutionary Anthropology." *International Critical Thought* 8, no. 3 (2018): 410–25.

Embassy of Sweden, Warsaw. Swedish Government Press Release: August 6, 2012. http://www.swedenabroad.com/Pages/StandardPage.aspx?id=38854&epslanguage=en-GB.

Emerson, Robert M. *Contemporary Field Research: Perspectives and Formulations.* Long Grove, IL: Waveland Press, 2001.

Encarnación, Omar G. "Clinton's Legacy on Gay Rights: From Skeptic to Supporter." *Foreign Affairs.* June 16, 2016. https://www.foreignaffairs.com/articles/2016-06-16/clintons-legacy-gay-rights/.

Encarnación, Omar G. *Out in the Periphery: Latin America's Gay Rights Revolution.* Oxford: Oxford University Press, 2016.

Encarnación, Omar G. "The Troubled Rise of Gay Rights Diplomacy." *Current History* 115, no. 777 (2016): 17–22.

Encarnación, Omar G. "Trump and Gay Rights." *Foreign Affairs.* March 31, 2017. Accessed August 14, 2018. https://www.foreignaffairs.com/chapters/2017-02-13/trump-and-gay-rights.

"Enjoyment of Human Rights by LGBT Persons." Swedish Foreign Ministry 2014. Accessed October 20, 2014. http://www.manskligarattigheter.se/en/human-rights/what-rights-are-there/enjoyment-of-human-rights-by-lgbt-persons.

Epprecht, M., and Stephen Brown. *Queer Canada?: The Harper Government and International Lesbian, Gay, Bisexual, Transgender, and Intersex Rights.* Montreal: McGill-Queen's University Press, 2017.

Erlandsson, Susanna. "Off the Record: Margaret van Kleffens and the Gendered History of Dutch World War II Diplomacy." *International Feminist Journal of Politics* 21, no. 1 (2019): 29–46.

"European Region of the International Lesbian, Gay, Bisexual, Trans and Intersex Association 2014 Annual Review: Sweden." ILGA. Accessed November 3,

2014. http://www.ilgaeurope.org/home/guide_europe/country_by_country/sweden/annual_review_2014_sweden.

Evans, Danny. "Ultra-Left Anarchists and Anti-Fascism in the Second Republic." *International Journal of Iberian Studies* 29, no. 3 (2016): 241–56.

Farnen, Russell F., ed. *Nationalism, Ethnicity, and Identity: Cross National and Comparative Perspectives*. London: Routledge, 2017.

Feder, Lester. "Homophobia Costs India an Estimated $31 Billion Annually—Should Development Institutions Care?" The Williams Institute. March 14, 2014. http://williamsinstitute.law.ucla.edu/press/homophobia-costs-india-an-estimated-31-billion-annually-should-development-institutions-care-2/.

Federman, Peter Stanley, and Nicole M. Rishel Elias. "Beyond the Lavender Scare: LGBT and Heterosexual Employees in the Federal Workplace." *Public Integrity* 19, no. 1 (2017): 22–40.

Felter, Claire, and Danielle Renwick. "Same-Sex Marriage: Global Comparisons." Council on Foreign Relations." Council on Foreign Relations. October 29, 2019. https://www.cfr.org/backgrounder/same-sex-marriage-global-comparisons.

"Feminist Foreign Policy." Swedish Ministry for Foreign Affairs. Accessed May 14, 2019.

Finnemore, Martha, and Kathryn Sikkink. "International Norm Dynamics and Political Change." *International Organization* 52, no. 4 (1998): 887–917. https://doi.org/10.1162/002081898550789.

Finnemore, Martha. *National Interests in International Society*. Ithaca, NY: Cornell University Press, 1996.

"Fiscal Year 2013 Congressional Budget Justification for Foreign Operations." US Department of State. 2013. http://www.state.gov/documents/organization/185014.pdf.

Fischer, Frank, and Herbert Gottweis. *The Argumentative Turn Revisited: Public Policy as Communicative Practice*. Durham, NC: Duke University Press, 2012.

Fitzsimmons, Tim. "Amid 'Kill the Gays' Bill Uproar, Ugandan LGBTQ Activist Is Killed." *NBC News*. October 16, 2019. https://www.nbcnews.com/feature/nbc-out/amid-kill-gays-bill-uproar-ugandan-lgbtq-activist-killed-n1067336.

Fleckenstein, Timo, and Soohyun Christine Lee. "The Politics of Postindustrial Social Policy: Family Policy Reforms in Britain, Germany, South Korea, and Sweden." *Comparative Political Studies* 47, no. 2 (2014): 601–30.

Flockhart, Trine. "Constructivism and Foreign Policy." In *Foreign Policy: Theories, Actors, Cases*, edited by Steve Smith, Amelia Hadfield, and Timothy Dunne. Oxford: Oxford University Press, 2016.

"For First Time, Majority of Americans Favor Legal Gay Marriage." Gallup Poll. May 2011. Accessed October 10, 2014. http://www.gallup.com/poll/147662/first-time-majority-americans-favor-legal-gay-marriage.aspx.

Ford, Zack. "Rick Warren: Being Gay Is Like 'Punching a Guy in the Nose' or Consuming Arsenic." ThinkProgress. November 28, 2012. https://thinkprogress.

org/rick-warren-being-gay-is-like-punching-a-guy-in-the-nose-or-consuming-arsenic-156846278109/.

Forsythe, David. *Human Rights and Comparative Foreign Policy*. Tokyo, Japan: United Nations University Press, 2000.

Forsythe, David. *Human Rights in International Relations*. Cambridge: Cambridge University Press, 2000.

Forsythe, David. *Human Rights in International Relations*. 3rd ed. Cambridge: Cambridge University Press, 2012.

France, David. *How to Survive a Plague*. IMDB. 2012. Accessed August 3, 2017. http://www.imdb.com/title/tt2124803/.

"Freedom in the World 2017—Saudi Arabia." Freedom House. Accessed May 20, 2017.

"Freedom in the World." Freedom House. Accessed May 7, 2021. https://freedomhouse.org/report/freedom-world.

Friedman, Elisabeth Jay. "Constructing 'the Same Rights with the Same Names': The Impact of Spanish Norm Diffusion on Marriage Equality in Argentina." *Latin American Politics and Society* 54, no. 4 (2012): 29–59. https://doi.org/10.1111/j.1548-2456.2012.00171.x.

Furuoka, Fumitaka. "Japan's Positive and Negative Aid Sanctions Policy toward Asian Countries: Case Studies of Thailand and Indonesia." MPRA Paper No. 6218 (2007). https://mpra.ub.uni-muenchen.de/6218/1/MPRA_paper_6218.pdf.

Gadoua, Renee K. "Mass. Pastor Scott Lively Faces Possible Fine for Harsh Anti-Gay Efforts in Uganda." *Washington Post*. October 2, 2015. https://www.washingtonpost.com/national/religion/correction-mass-pastor-scott-lively-faces-possible-fine-for-harsh-anti-gay-efforts-in-uganda/2015/10/02/304c74ea-6947-11e5-bdb6-6861f4521205_story.html.

Gadoua, Renee. "Scott Lively Could Face Fine for Anti-Gay Efforts." *Huffington Post*. October 3, 2015. https://www.huffpost.com/entry/scott-lively-anti-gay-uganda_n_560d85e6e4b0af3706dfef9c.

Gadoua, Renee. "Ugandan Priest: LGBT People Are Fleeing to Kenya." *The Christian Centural*. June 08, 2015. http://www.christiancentury.org/article/2015-06/ugandan-priest-lgbt-people-are-fleeing-kenya.

Gambrell, Jon. "Call for Responsive Governments at Dubai Summit amid Turmoil." *Daily Herald*. February 8, 2016. http://www.dailyherald.com/article/20160208/news/302089976/.

"Gay and Lesbian Rights." Gallup Poll. Accessed May 19, 2020. https://news.gallup.com/poll/1651/gay-lesbian-rights.aspx.

"Gay Sweden Democrat Backs Party's Pride Flag Decision." *The Local Sweden*. September 15, 2019. https://www.thelocal.se/20190915/gay-sweden-democrat-backs-council-vote-to-stop-flying-pride-flah.

"Gay Travel Index." Spartacus 2014. Accessed November 5, 2014. http://www.spartacusworld.com/gaytravelindex.pdf.

Gelunenko, Valeriya V., Marina V. Markhgeym, Azamat M. Shadzhe, Lyudmila A. Tkhabisimova, and Elnur E. Veliev. "Freedom of Speech in Constitutional Binds of Eastern European Countries." *Amazonia Investiga* 8, no. 19 (2019): 403–7.

Gereke, Marika, and Tanja Brühl. "Unpacking the Unequal Representation of Northern and Southern NGOs in International Climate Change Politics." *Third World Quarterly* 40, no. 5 (2019): 870–89.

Gettleman, Jeffrey. "Americans' Role Seen in Uganda Anti-Gay Push." *New York Times.* January 3, 2010. https://www.nytimes.com/2010/01/04/world/africa/04uganda.html?_r=0.

Ghoshal, Neela, and Maria Burnett. "Is It Now Legal to Be Gay in Uganda?" Human Rights Watch. September 12, 2014. https://www.hrw.org/news/2014/08/07/it-now-legal-be-gay-uganda#.

Glasius, Marlies, Jelmer Schalk, and Meta De Lange. "Illiberal Norm Diffusion: How Do Governments Learn to Restrict Nongovernmental Organizations?" *International Studies Quarterly* 64, no. 2 (2020): 453–68.

"Global Equality Fund." US Department of State Bureau of Democracy, Human Rights, and Labor. Accessed May 12, 2021. https://www.state.gov/global-equality-fund/.

"Global Barometer of Gay Rights (GBGR) and Global Barometer of Transgender Rights (GBTR)." Franklin & Marshall College. Accessed May 5, 2021. https://www.fandmglobalbarometers.org/.

"Global Gay Rights Map." International Lesbian and Gay Association (ILGA) Europe. December 2020. https://ilga.org/maps-sexual-orientation-laws.

Global Humanitarian Assistance. Accessed April 8, 2016. http://www.globalhumanitarianassistance.org/.

"Global Views on Morality." *Pew Research Center,* Global Attitudes Project. June 1, 2015. http://www.pewglobal.org/2014/04/15/global-morality/country/united-states/.

Godoy, Angelina S. *Of Medicines and Markets: Intellectual Property and Human Rights in the Free Trade Era.* Stanford, CA: Stanford University Press, 2013.

Goel, Anish, and Elise Carlson-Rainer. "India: A Microcosm of Tensions on LGBT Rights." *Foreign Policy.* December 10, 2015. https://foreignpolicy.com/2015/12/10/india-a-microcosm-of-tensions-on-lgbt-rights/.

Goldstein, Judith, and Robert Owen Keohane. *Ideas and Foreign Policy: Beliefs, Institutions, and Political Change.* Ithaca, NY: Cornell University Press, 1993.

Goodale, Mark, and Sally Engel Merry, eds. *The Practice of Human Rights: Tracking Law between the Global and the Local.* Cambridge: Cambridge University Press, 2007.

Gosine, Andil. "Rescue, and Real Love: Same-Sex Desire in International Development." In *Routledge Handbook of Queer Development Studies*, 193–208. London: Routledge, 2018.

Gracia, Enrique, and Juan Merlo. "Intimate Partner Violence against Women and the Nordic Paradox." *Social Science & Medicine* 157 (2016): 27–30. https://doi.org/10.1016/j.socscimed.2016.03.040.

Graff, Agnieszka, Ratna Kapur, and Suzanna Danuta Walters. "Introduction: Gender and the Rise of the Global Right." *Signs: Journal of Women in Culture and Society* 44, no. 3 (2019): 541–60.

Grant, Kevin Douglas. "State Department Makes Sea Change on LGBT Rights." *Global Post* 2012. Accessed October 10, 2014. http://www.globalpost.com/dispatch/news/regions/americas/united-states/120210/state-department-lgbt-rights-clinton-obama.

"Green Party Ranked 'Most Gay Friendly' in Sweden." *The Local.* July 2014. Accessed November 5, 2014. http://www.thelocal.se/20140728/swedish-green-party-most-friendly-to-lgbt.

Greenhill, Brian. *Transmitting Rights: International Organizations and the Diffusion of Human Rights Practices.* Oxford: Oxford University Press, 2016.

Gries, Peter Hays. *The Politics of American Foreign Policy: How Ideology Divides Liberals and Conservatives over Foreign Affairs.* Stanford, CA: Stanford University Press, 2014.

Grimm, Linda. "President Trump Announces Transgender Military Ban." *Historic Documents of 2017*, edited by Heather Kerrigan. London: CQ Press, 2018.

Großklaus, Mathias. "Appropriation and the Dualism of Human Rights: Understanding the Contradictory Impact of Gender Norms in Nigeria." *Third World Quarterly* 36, no. 6 (2015): 1253–67.

"Growing Up LGBT in America: View and Share Statistics." Human Rights Campaign. Accessed October 4, 2018. https://www.hrc.org/youth-report/view-and-share-statistics.

Guzzini, Stefano, and Anna Leander. *Constructivism and International Relations: Alexander Wendt and His Critics.* London: Routledge, 2011

Haász, Veronika, Jakub Jaraczewski, and Karolina Podstawa. "The FRAME Toolbox for the EU Fundamental and Human Rights Policies." FRAME. 2017. https://doi.org/20.500.11825/121.

Habib, Adam. "State-Civil Society Relations in Post-Apartheid South Africa." *Social Research* 72, no. 3 (2005): 671–92.

Hadden, Jennifer, and Lorien Jasny. "The Power of Peers: How Transnational Advocacy Networks Shape NGO Strategies On Climate Change." *British Journal of Political Science* 49, no. 2 (2019): 637–59.

Hafner-Burton, Emilie M. "Trading Human Rights: How Preferential Trade Agreements Influence Government Repression." *International Organization* 59, no. 3 (2005): 593–629. https://doi.org/10.1017/s0020818305050216.

Hafner-Burton, Emilie M., Edward D. Mansfield, and Jon C. W. Pevehouse. "Human Rights Institutions, Sovereignty Costs and Democratization." *British Journal of Political Science* 45, no. 1 (2015): 1–27.

Hammarberg, Thomas. "Human Rights and Gender Identity." Thomas Hammarberg, commissioner for human rights of the Council of Europe for the attention of the Committee of Ministers and the Parliamentary Assembly. CommDH/Issue Paper 2 (2009). July 29, 2009.

Hammarstedt, Mats, Ali M. Ahmed, and Lina Andersson. "Sexual Prejudice and Labor Market Outcomes for Gays and Lesbians: Evidence from Sweden." *Feminist Economics* 21, no. 1 (2015): 90–109.

Han, Enze, and Joseph O'Mahoney. *British Colonialism and the Criminalization of Homosexuality: Queens, Crime and Empire.* London: Routledge, 2018.

Hanley, Thomas. "Homophobia in Poland and Hungary: Assessing Its Political Motives and Influences." In *Body Politics: What's the State Got to Do with It?*, edited by Jordan A. Pino and Konstantinos Karamanakis. Boston, MA: Boston College, 2017.

Hansen, Aaron P. "US Military Assistance and Human Rights: An Examination of the Top 30 Recipients of US Military Aid between 1992–2011." PhD diss., The University of Nebraska-Lincoln, 2018.

Harding, Scott, and Kathryn Libal. "War and the Public Health Disaster in Iraq." In *War and Health: The Medical Consequences of the Wars in Iraq and Afghanistan*, edited by Catherine Lutz and Andrea Mazzarino, 111–36. New York: New York University Press, 2019.

"Has the U.S Been Committing Torture in Guantanamo?" In *Report On Torture and Cruel, Inhuman, and Degrading Treatment of Prisoners at Guantanamo Bay*, 36–39. New York: Center for Constitutional Rights, 2006.

Haskins, Susan. "The Influence of Roman Laws Regarding Same-Sex Acts on Homophobia in Africa." *African Human Rights Law Journal* 14, no. 2 (2014): 393–411. http://www.saflii.org/za/journals/AHRLJ/2014/21.html.

"HBT." Translated from Swedish by the author. Swedish Democrats. August 27, 2018. Accessed March 7, 2019. https://sd.se/our-politics/hbt/.

"Hbtq-Personers Rättigheter Omsätts I Praktisk Politik." RFSL. Translated from Swedish by the author. November 11, 2018. Accessed March 7, 2019. https://www.rfsl.se/aktuellt/debatt-sds-motstand-mot-hbtq-personers-rattigheter-omsatts-i-praktisk-politik/.

Hearn, Jeff, Sofia Strid, Lisa Husu, and Mieke Verloo. "Interrogating Violence against Women and State Violence Policy: Gendered Intersectionalities and the Quality of Policy in the Netherlands, Sweden and the UK." *Current Sociology* 64, no. 4 (2016): 551–67.

Hedenius, Ingemar. *Om Rätt Och Moral* (*On Rights and Morality*). Stockholm, Sweden: Wahlström & Widstrand, 1963.

Heidenreich, Martin. "The Renewal of Regional Capabilities: Experimental Regionalism in Germany." *Research Policy* 34, no. 5 (2005): 739–57. https://doi.org/10.1016/j.respol.2005.04.004.

Herzog, Dagmar. *Sexuality in Europe: A Twentieth-Century History.* Vol. 45. Cambridge: Cambridge University Press, 2011.

Held, Bengt. "Utrikesminister Margot Wallström (s) om HBTQ-Palestiniers Situation (Foreign Minister Margot Wallström (s) on the Situation of LGBTQ Palestinians)." Helds HBT-nyheter (Held's LGBT News). May 3, 2015. http://bengtheld.blogspot.com/2015/05/utrikesminister-margot-wallstrom-s-om.html.

Hersh, Seymour M. "Torture in Abu Ghraib." *New Yorker.* May 10, 2004. https://www.newyorker.com/magazine/2004/05/10/torture-at-abu-ghraib.

Hershey, Marjorie Randon. *Party Politics in America.* New York: Routledge, 2017.

Hines, Heather. "The LGBT Community Responds: The Lavender Scare and the Creation of Midwestern Gay and Lesbian Publications." PhD diss., Bowling Green State University, 2017.

"History." Gays and Lesbians in Foreign Affairs Agencies (GLIFAA). February 7, 2014. https://glifaa.org/archive/history-long/.

Ho, Vanessa, Sherry Sherqueshaa, and Darius Zheng. "The Forced Sterilization of Transgender and Gender Non-Conforming People in Singapore." *LGBTQ Policy Journal* 6 (2016): 53–75.

Hobson, Barbara. *Recognition Struggles and Social Movements.* Cambridge: Cambridge University Press, 2003.

Hogan, Linda. *Keeping Faith with Human Rights.* Washington, DC: Georgetown University Press, 2015.

"Hold U.S. Government Accountable." Council for Global Equality. Accessed October 9, 2019. http://www.globalequality.org/what-we-do/hold-us-government-accountable.

"Homophobia Is Defeated but Not Yet Deterred: Next Steps in the Struggle for Equality in Uganda and Beyond." Global Equality Today. May 14, 2010. https://globalequality.wordpress.com/tag/bi-sexual/.

"Homosexuality, Theology, and the Church." Focus on the Family. Accessed March 16, 2016. http://www.focusonthefamily.com/socialissues/sexuality/homosexuality-theology-and-the-church/homosexuality-theology-and-the-church.

Honkasalo, Julian. "Unfit for Parenthood? Compulsory Sterilization and Transgender Reproductive Justice in Finland." *Journal of International Women's Studies* 20, no. 1 (2018): 40–52.

Hossain, Naomi, and Nalini Khurana. "Donor Responses and Tools for Responding to Shrinking Space for Civil Society: A Desk Study." Swiss Agency for Development and Cooperation (SDC), 2019.

"How Does Sweden Compare?" In *Society at a Glance: OECD Social Indicators: A Spotlight on LGBT People.* Organization for Economic Co-operation and Development. Paris, France: OECD Publishing, 2019.

"How Gay Rights Has Become a Foreign Policy Issue." *Denver Post*. February 2014. Accessed October 10, 2014. http://www.denverpost.com/opinion/ci_25238614/how-gay-rights-has-become-foreign-policy-issue.

"How the United States Can Help Counter Violent Extremism and Support Civil Society in Kenya: Blueprint for U.S. Government Policy." Human Rights First. July 2015. Accessed February 14, 2019. http://www.humanrightsfirst.org/sites/default/files/HRF-Kenya-Blueprint-Final.pdf.

"How Can I Protect My Partners?" Centers for Disease Control and Prevention. Accessed May 7, 2021. https://www.cdc.gov/hiv/basics/livingwithhiv/protecting-others.html.

Huber, Evelyne, and John D. Stephens. *Development and Crisis of the Welfare State: Parties and Policies in Global Markets*. Chicago, IL: University of Chicago Press, 2010.

Hübinette, Tobias, and Catrin Lundström. "Sweden after the Recent Election: The Double-Binding Power of Swedish Whiteness through the Mourning of the Loss of 'Old Sweden' and the Passing of 'Good Sweden.'" *NORA—Nordic Journal of Feminist and Gender Research* 19, no. 1 (2011): 42–52.

Hudson, John. "Trump Keeps Obama's Top Gay Rights Envoy at State Department." *Foreign Policy*. February 13, 2017. Accessed March 6, 2017. http://foreignpolicy.com/2017/02/13/trump-keeps-obamas-top-gay-rights-envoy-at-state-department/.

Hudson, Valerie, and Patricia Leidl. *The Hillary Doctrine: Sex and American Foreign Policy*. New York: Columbia University Press, 2015.

Hughes, Dana. "Secretary Clinton Champions Gay Rights for State Department, Abroad." *ABC News*. November 29, 2012. Accessed October 10, 2014. http://abcnews.go.com/blogs/politics/2012/11/secretary-clinton-champions-gay-rights-for-state-department-and-abroad/.

"Human Rights." United Nations. Accessed September 6, 2019. https://www.un.org/en/sections/issues-depth/human-rights/.

"Human Rights." Council on Foreign Relations. Accessed May 12, 2021. https://www.cfr.org/human-rights.

"Human Rights." United States Institute of Peace. Accessed May 11, 2021. https://www.usip.org/issue-areas/human-rights.

"Human Rights and Democracy Fund." US Department of State Bureau of Democracy, Human Rights and Labor. Accessed April 15, 2019. https://www.state.gov/j/drl/p/.

"Human Rights Based Approach at SIDA Rights of LGBTI Persons." Swedish International Development Agency (SIDA). September 2015. Accessed May 14, 2019. https://www.sida.se/English/partners/resources-for-all-partners/methodological-materials/human-rights-based-approach-at-sida/rights-of-lgbti-persons/.

"Human Rights Campaign Local: Washington." Human Rights Campaign. Accessed November 3, 2014. http://www.hrc.org/states/washington.

"Human Rights for LGBT Persons: A Q&A with Special Envoy Randy Berry." *The Foreign Service Journal* 92, no. 5 (June 2015): 20–24. https://www.afsa.org/sites/default/files/fsj-2015-06-june.pdf.

"Human Rights Homepage." Swedish Foreign Ministry. Accessed December 15, 2015. http://manskligarattigheter.dynamaster.se/en/human-rights-in-the-world/human-rights-in-swedish-foreign-policy.

"Human Rights on LGBT Persons: Dialogue Paper on Development." Swedish International Development Agency (SIDA). 2010. http://www.globalequality.org/storage/documents/pdf/sida%20dialogue%20paper%20on%20development.pdf.

"Human Rights: The Gay Divide." *Economist*. October 9, 2014. https://www.economist.com/leaders/2014/10/09/the-gay-divide.

Humphreys, Stephen. *Human Rights and Climate Change*. Cambridge: Cambridge University Press, 2010.

Hyden, Göran, and Rwekaza Mukandala. *Agencies in Foreign Aid: Comparing China, Sweden and the United States in Tanzania*. Cham: Palgrave Macmillan, 1999.

Hysing, Erik, and Jan Olsson. "The Political Nature of Inside Activism." In *Green Inside Activism for Sustainable Development*, 47–71. London: Palgrave Macmillan, 2018.

Ibrahim, Abadir M. "LGBT Rights in Africa and the Discursive Role of International Human Rights Law." *African Human Rights Law Journal* 15, no. 2 (2015): 263–81.

"IGLHRC Demands Investigation into Killing of Ugandan LGBT Rights Defender." Outright Action International, January 27, 2010. https://outrightinternational.org/content/iglhrc-demands-investigation-killing-ugandan-lgbt-rights-defender.

"IKEA's Human Resource Policy." IKEA. Accessed March 28, 2016. https://seeacareerwithus.com/about-us/recognition/.

"In Lube in Uganda Homepage." Accessed March 1, 2018. http://www.oliverocheva.se/i-lube-uganda/.

Ingber, Rebecca. "Congressional Administration of Foreign Affairs." *Virginia Law Review* 106 (2020): 395–453. https://doi.org/10.2139/ssrn.3361299.

Ingebritsen, Christine. *Nordic States & European Unity*. Ithaca, NY: Cornell University Press, 1998.

Ingebritsen, Christine. *Scandinavia in World Politics*. Lanham, MD: Rowman and Littlefield Publishers, 2006.

"Integrated Country Strategy: Uganda." US Department of State. August 3, 2018. https://www.state.gov/wp-content/uploads/2019/01/ICS-Uganda_UNCLASS_508.pdf.

"International Child Labor & Forced Labor Reports." US Department of Labor Bureau of International Labor Affairs. 2019. https://www.dol.gov/agencies/ilab/resources/reports/child-labor.

"International Human Rights Defense Act." IHRDA. Human Rights First. 2014. Accessed October 10, 2014. http://www.humanrightsfirst.org/sites/default/files/IHRDA-Final-One-pager.pdf.

Inveen, Cooper. "Dr. Stella Nyanzi Kicks Off 11th Annual WRIHC with Powerful Keynote Address." University of Washington Department of Global Health, August 20, 2014. https://globalhealth.washington.edu/news/2014/08/20/dr-stella-nyanzi-kicks-11th-annual-wrihc-powerful-keynote-address.

Irwin, Rachel. "Sweden's Engagement in Global Health: A Historical Review." *Globalization and Health* 15, no. 1 (2019): 79. https://doi.org/10.1186/s12992-019-0499-1.

Jacobson, Adam. " 'The True Ugly Face of America': Al Qaeda's Propaganda Use of Guantanamo Bay and Implications for US Counterterrorism." Available at SSRN 2614056 (2015). http://dx.doi.org/10.2139/ssrn.2614056.

Jacobson, David. *Rights across Borders*. Baltimore, MD: Johns Hopkins University Press, 1996.

Jakobsen, Peter Viggo. "Small States, Big Influence: The Overlooked Nordic Influence on the Civilian ESDP." *JCMS: Journal of Common Market Studies* 47, no. 1 (2009): 81–102.

Janoff, Douglas. "Homophobia, Human Rights and Diplomacy." Dayton, OH: University of Dayton Human Rights Center, 2017. https://ecommons.udayton.edu/cgi/viewcontent.cgi?article=1268&context=human_rights.

Jean, Tyra. "Black Lives Matter: Police Brutality in the Era of COVID-19." Syracuse University Lerner Center for Public Health Promotion, Issue Brief no. 31, June 16, 2020. https://lernercenter.syr.edu/2020/06/16/ib-31/.

Jensen, Steven L. B. *The Making of International Human Rights: The 1960s, Decolonization, and the Reconstruction of Global Values*. Cambridge: Cambridge University Press, 2016.

Jensena, Steffen, Tobias Kelly, Morten Koch Andersen, Catrine Christiansen, and Jeevan Raj Sharma. "Torture and Ill-Treatment Under Perceived: Human Rights Documentation and the Poor." *Human Rights Quarterly* 39, no. 2 (2017): 393–415.

Jezierska, Katarzyna and Ann Towns. "Taming Feminism? The Place of Gender Equality in the 'Progressive Sweden' Brand." *Place Branding and Public Diplomacy* 14, no. 1 (2018): 55–63.

Joachim, Jutta. *Agenda Setting, the UN, and NGOs: Gender Violence and Reproductive Rights*. Washington, DC: Georgetown University Press, 2007.

Joachim, Jutta, and Birgit Locher. *Transnational Activism in the UN and the EU: A Comparative Study*. London: Routledge, 2008.

Johnson, Chris. "Dan Baer: Time for U.S. to Change Its Relationship with Saudi Arabia." *Washington Blade*. July 9, 2019. https://www.washingtonblade.com/2019/07/09/dan-baer-time-for-u-s-to-change-its-relationship-with-saudi-arabia/.

Johnson, David K. *The Lavender Scare: The Cold War Persecution of Gays and Lesbians in the Federal Government*. Chicago, IL: University of Chicago Press, 2004.

Johnson Ross, Freya. "Professional Feminists: Challenging Local Government Inside Out." *Gender, Work & Organization* 26, no. 4 (2019): 520–40.

Johnston, David. "Ruling Backs Homosexuals on Asylum." *New York Times*. June 17, 1994. https://www.nytimes.com/1994/06/17/us/ruling-backs-homosexu-als-on-asylum.html.

Jolly, Susie. *Poverty and Sexuality: What Are the Connections?* Stockholm: Swedish International Development Agency, 2010. Accessed February 17, 2019. http://www.globalequality.org/storage/documents/pdf/sida%20study%20of%20 poverty%20and%20sexuality.pdf.

Jones, Tiffany. "Researching and Working for Transgender Youth: Contexts, Problems and Solutions." *Social Sciences* 5, no. 3 (2016): 43. https://doi.org/10.3390/socsci5030043.

Jordaan, Eduard. "South Africa and Sexual Orientation Rights at the United Nations: Batting for Both Sides." *Politikon* 44, no. 2 (2017): 205–30. https://doi.org/10.1080/02589346.2017.1284469.

Jungar, Ann-Catherine. "The Sweden Democrats." In *Understanding Populist Party Organisation*, 189–219. London: Palgrave Macmillan, 2016.

Jungar, Katarina, and Salla Peltonen. "Acts of Homonationalism: Mapping Africa in the Swedish Media." *Sexualities* 20, no. 5–6 (2016): 715–37. https://doi.org/10.1177/1363460716645806.

Kagan, Robert. *Of Paradise and Power: America and Europe in the New World Order*. New York: Vintage, 2004.

Kahlina, Katja. "Local Histories, European LGBT Designs: Sexual Citizenship, Nationalism, and 'Europeanisation' in Post-Yugoslav Croatia and Serbia." In *Women's Studies International Forum* 49, 73–83. Oxford: Pergamon Press, 2015.

Kapoor, Ilan. "Foreign Aid as G(r)ift." In *The Postcolonial Politics of Development*, 76–94. London: Routledge, 2008.

Karlsson, Magnus, and Johan Vamstad. "New Deeds for New Needs: Civil Society Action against Poverty in Sweden." *VOLUNTAS: International Journal of Voluntary and Nonprofit Organizations* 31 (2018): 1025–36.

Karlsson Schaffer, Johan. "How Democracy Promotion Became a Key Aim of Sweden's Development Aid Policy." In *Do-Gooders at the End of Aid*, edited by Kristian Bjørkdahl and Antoine De Bengy Puyvallé. Cambridge: Cambridge University Press, 2019.

Katzenstein, Peter J. "Small States and Small States Revisited." *New Political Economy* 8, no. 1 (2003): 9–30.

Katzenstein, Peter J. *Small States in World Markets*. Ithaca, NY: Cornell University Press, 1985.

Katzenstein, Peter, Robert O. Keohane, and Stephen D. Krasner. "International Organization and the Study of World Politics." *International Organization* 52, no. 4 (1998): 645–85.

Keck, Margaret E., and Kathryn Sikkink. *Activists beyond Borders: Advocacy Networks in International Politics*. Ithaca, NY: Cornell University Press, 1998.

Kedo, Alexis, and Colby Goodman. "Defense Experts Highlight Effectiveness of Human Rights Conditioning." Security Assistance Monitor. Center for International Policy. December 10, 2015. https://www.securityassistance.org/blog/defense-experts-highlight-effectiveness-human-rights-conditioning.

Kehl, Katharina. " 'In Sweden, Girls Are Allowed to Kiss Girls, and Boys Are Allowed to Kiss Boys': Pride Järva and the Inclusion of the 'LGBT Other' in Swedish Nationalist Discourses." *Sexualities* 21, no. 4 (2018): 674–91.

Keles, Janroj Yilmaz. *Media, Diaspora and Conflict: Nationalism and Identity amongst Turkish and Kurdish Migrants in Europe*. London: Bloomsbury Publishing, 2015.

Kelley, Judith G. *Scorecard Diplomacy: Grading States to Influence Their Reputation and Behavior*. Cambridge: Cambridge University Press, 2017.

Keohane, Robert O. "Institutional Theory and the Realist Challenge after the Cold War." *Neorealism and Neoliberalism: The Contemporary Debate* 269 (1993): 271.

Kerry, John. "Apology for Past Discrimination toward Employees and Applicants Based on Sexual Orientation." US Department of State. Washington, DC, January 9, 2017. https://2009-2017.state.gov/secretary/remarks/2017/01/266711.htm.

Kiel, Christina, and Jamie Campbell. "Intergovernmental Organizations and LGBT Issues." In *Oxford Research Encyclopedia of Politics*. 2019. Accessed March 18, 2016.

Kim, Jim Yong. "World Bank Group President Jim Yong Kim: Discrimination by Law Carries a High Price." *World Bank News*. February 28, 2014. http://www.worldbank.org/en/news/opinion/2014/02/28/world-bank-group-president-jim-yong-kim-discrimination-law-price.

Kintu, Deborah. *The Ugandan Morality Crusade: The Brutal Campaign against Homosexuality and Pornography under Yoweri Museveni*. Jefferson, NC: McFarland & Company, Inc., Publishers, 2018.

Kinzelbach, Katrin. *The EU's Human Rights Dialogue with China: Quiet Diplomacy and Its Limits*. London: Routledge, 2016.

Kirchick, James. *The End of Europe: Dictators, Demagogues, and the Coming Dark Age*. New Haven: Yale University Press, 2017.

Kirkpatrick, Rob. *1969: The Year Everything Changed*. New York: Simon and Schuster, 2019.

Klapeer, Christine M. "Dangerous Liaisons?: (Homo) Developmentalism, Sexual Modernization and LGBTIQ Rights in Europe." In *Routledge Handbook of Queer Development Studies*, 102–18. London: Routledge, 2018.

Klímová-Alexander, Ilona. *The Romani Voice in World Politics: The United Nations and Non-State Actors*. New York: Routledge, 2017.

Klotz, Audie. *Norms in International Relations: The Struggle against Apartheid*. Ithaca, NY: Cornell University Press, 1999.

Knight, Charlotte, and Kath Wilson. "International Perspectives on the Rights and Criminalisation of LGBT People." In *Lesbian, Gay, Bisexual and Trans*

People (LGBT) and the Criminal Justice System, 207–31. London: Palgrave Macmillan, 2016.

Kollman, Kelly. "Same-Sex Unions: The Globalisation of an Idea." In *The Same-Sex Unions Revolution in Western Democracies*. Manchester: Manchester University Press, 2016.

Kollman, Kelly. *The Same-Sex Unions Revolution in Western Democracies: International Norms and Domestic Policy Change*. Manchester: Manchester University Press, 2013.

Kovács, Melinda. *Foreign Policy Discourses of the Obama Years*. London: Lexington Books, 2018.

Kronmay, Josh. "In Uganda, Push to Curb Gays Draws U.S. Guest." *New York Times*. May 2, 2010. http://www.nytimes.com/2010/05/03/world/africa/03uganda.html?_r=1.

Kronsell, Annica. "Can Small States Influence EU Norms? Insights from Sweden's Participation in the Field of Environmental Politics." *Scandinavian Studies*, 287–304. Champaign, IL: University of Illinois Press, 2002.

Kucinich, Jackie. "New Hillary Clinton Emails Detail Her State Department Battle for Gay Rights." *The Daily Beast*. July 2, 2015. http://www.thedailybeast.com/articles/2015/07/02/new-hillary-clinton-emails-detail-her-state-department-battle-for-gay-rights.html

Kuhar, Roman, and David Paternotte. *Anti-Gender Campaigns in Europe: Mobilizing against Equality*. Lanham, MD: Rowman and Littlefield International, 2017.

Kulick, D. "Introduktion (Introduction)." In *Queersverige* (*Queer Sweden*), edited by D. Kulick. Stockholm, Sweden: Natur och kultur, 2005.

Lagerman, Julia. "Queering Space in a Place within a Place?: Geographical Imaginations of Swedish Pride Festivals." Master's thesis, Uppsala University, 2018.

Lancaster, Carol. *Foreign Aid: Diplomacy, Development, Domestic Politics*. Chicago, IL: University of Chicago Press, 2008.

Landau, Elizabeth, Zain Verjee, and Antonia Mortensen. "Uganda President: Homosexuals Are 'Disgusting.'" *CNN World News*. February 25, 2014. http://www.cnn.com/2014/02/24/world/africa/uganda-homosexuality-interview/.

Lang, Sabine. "Assessing Advocacy: European Transnational Women's Networks and Gender Mainstreaming." *Social Politics* 16, no. 3 (2009): 327–57.

Lang, Sabine. *NGOs, Civil Society, and the Public Sphere*. Cambridge: Cambridge University Press, 2014.

Langlois, Anthony J. "International Relations Theory and Global Sexuality Politics." *Politics* 36, no. 4 (2016): 385–99.

Langlois, Anthony J. "Queer Rights?" *Australian Journal of International Affairs* 71, no. 3 (2017): 241–46.

Landén, Mikael, and Sune Innala. "Attitudes toward Transsexualism in a Swedish National Survey." *Archives of Sexual Behavior* 29, no. 4 (2000): 375–88.

Laskar, Pia. "The Illiberal Turn." *Lambda Nordica* 19, no. 1 (2014): 87–100.

Lavers, Michael K. "Gay U.S. Officials Travel to Jamaica." *Washington Blade.* May 30, 2015. https://www.washingtonblade.com/2015/05/30/gay-u-s-officials-travel-to-jamaica/.

Lavers, Michael K. "USAID Launches Partnership to Promote LGBT Rights." *Washington Blade.* April 9, 2013. http://www.washingtonblade.com/2013/04/09/usaid-launches-partnership-to-promote-lgbt-rights/.

Lavers, Michael K. "USAID-Supported Gay Training to Take Place in Colombia." *Washington Blade.* May 29, 2013. https://www.washingtonblade.com/2013/05/29/usaid-supported-gay-training-to-take-place-in-colombia/.

Lavers, Michael K. "Advancing Obama's LGBT Rights Agenda Abroad." *Washington Blade.* July 23, 2014. https://www.washingtonblade.com/2014/07/23/retired-u-n-official-leads-usaid-lgbt-initiatives/.

Lavers, Michael K. "LGBT Envoy Travels to Uganda." *Washington Blade.* July 21, 2015. https://www.washingtonblade.com/2015/07/21/lgbt-envoy-travels-to-uganda/.

Laviolette, Nicole. "Independent Human Rights Documentation and Sexual Minorities: An Ongoing Challenge for the Canadian Refugee Determination Process." *International Journal of Human Rights* 13, no. 2–3 (2009): 437–76. https://doi.org/10.1080/13642980902758234.

Lederman, Josh. "Trump Administration Launches Global Effort to End Criminalization of Homosexuality." *NBC News.* February 19, 2019. https://www.nbcnews.com/politics/national-security/trump-administration-launches-global-effort-end-criminalization-homosexuality-n973081.

Lee, Sook Jong, and Kyoung Sun Lee. "The Complex Relationship between Government and NGOs in International Development Cooperation: South Korea as an Emerging Donor Country." *International Review of Public Administration* 21, no. 4 (2016): 275–91.

Lewis, David. "Civil Society and the Authoritarian State: Cooperation, Contestation and Discourse." *Journal of Civil Society* 9, no. 3 (2013): 325–40.

"LGBT Community under Attack in Egypt." Human Rights First. November 2017. https://www.humanrightsfirst.org/sites/default/files/Egypt-LGBT-Factsheet.pdf.

"LGBT Community under Attack: Uganda's Anti-Homosexuality Bill." Tom Lantos Human Rights Commission, United States Congress. January 21, 2010. https://humanrightscommission.house.gov/events/hearings/lgbt-community-under-attack-ugandas-anti-homosexuality-bill.

"LGBTI Equality and Human Rights in Europe and Central Asia." ILGA Europe. Accessed December 19, 2019. http://www.ilga-europe.org/.

"LGBT Issues in the UN." Swedish Foreign Ministry 2012. Accessed October 20, 2014. http://www.government.se/sb/d/15777/a/187785.

"LGBTI Rights in 20 Years (HBTQ Frågar om 20 År)." Officer presentation. The Left Political Party (Vänsterpartiet), Stockholm, Sweden. August 2, 2017.

"LGBT Rights Issue Page." Human Rights Watch. Accessed January 14, 2020. https://www.hrw.org/topic/lgbt-rights.

Li, Yitan, and A. Cooper Drury. "Threatening Sanctions When Engagement Would Be More Effective: Attaining Better Human Rights in China." *International Studies Perspectives* 5, no. 4 (2004): 378–94. https://doi.org/10.1111/j.1528-3577. 2004.00185.x.

Liang-Fenton, Debra, ed. *Implementing US Human Rights Policy: Agendas, Policies, and Practices.* Washington, DC: US Institute of Peace Press, 2004.

Lim, Sin How, Shan-Estelle Brown, Stacey A. Shaw, Adeeba Kamarulzaman, Frederick L. Altice, and Chris Beyrer. " 'You Have to Keep Yourself Hidden': Perspectives From Malaysian Malay-Muslim Men Who Have Sex with Men On Policy, Network, Community, and Individual Influences on HIV Risk." *Journal of Homosexuality* 67, no. 1 (2020): 104–26.

"LiveAtState: Assistant Secretary of State Michael Posner on the 2011 Human Rights Report." US Department of State. June 28, 2012. https://2009-2017.state. gov/r/pa/ime/194287.htm.

Lofland, John, David Snow, Leon Anderson, and Lyn H. Lofland. *Analyzing Social Settings: A Guide to Qualitative Observation and Analysis.* New York: Wadsworth, 2006.

Loriga, Daniela Vazquez. "LGBT Rights in Russia: The 'Gay Propaganda' Law and Its Consequences in Chechnya." *Bellarmine Law Society Review* 11, no. 1 (2020): 1–14.

Loudes, Christine June. "Rights, Not Crimes: The EU's Role in Ending Criminalization of Same-Sex Acts in Third Countries." The European Region of the International Lesbian and Gay Association (ILGA-Europe). 2005. https://www.ilga-europe.org/resources/ilga-europe-reports-and-other-materials/ rights-not-crimes-april-2005.

Lubitow, Amy, and Mia Davis. "Pastel Injustice: The Corporate Use of Pinkwashing for Profit." *Environmental Justice* 4, no. 2 (2011): 139–44.

Ludmilla, Alexeeva. "In Russia, Human Rights Groups Need Western Aid More Than Ever." *Washington Post.* February 24, 2016. https://www.washingtonpost. com/opinions/in-russia-human-rights-groups-need-western-aid-more-than-ever/ 2016/02/24/b8e934d2-d1c0-11e5-b2bc-988409ee911b_story.html.

Lynch, Colum. "Republicans Join Forces with Islamic Governments against America." *Foreign Policy.* July 15, 2010. http://foreignpolicy.com/2010/07/15/republicans-join-forces-with-islamic-governments-against-america/.

Lyngaas, Sean. "LGBT Rights Becomes Pillar of U.S. Foreign Policy." *Washington Diplomat.* May 29, 2015. https://washdiplomat.com/gay-rights-becomes-pillar-of-us-foreign-policy/.

Lynöe, Niels. "Race Enhancement through Sterilization: Swedish Experiences." *International Journal of Mental Health* 36, no. 1 (2007): 17–25.

Mace, Harry J. "Emancipating Marianne: Gendering French Diplomacy and the Quai d'Orsay in European Context, 1944–1950." PhD diss., University of Kent, 2017.

Mahanty, Daniel. "Realists, Too, Can Stand for Human Rights." *National Interest.* October 9, 2013. http://nationalinterest.org/commentary/realists-too-can-stand-human-rights-9208.

Mahanty, Daniel, and Elise Carlson-Rainer. "The Importance of Human Rights Considerations in Foreign Policy." In *Homeland Security.* April 8, 2019. https://inhomelandsecurity.com/human-rights-foreign-policy/.

Mahmood, Tehmina. "Quiet Diplomacy." *Pakistan Horizon* 50, no. 4 (October 1997): 93–107. https://www.jstor.org/stable/41394635?seq=1.

Malinowski, Tom. "Human Rights in the New Approach to U.S.-Cuba Policy." US Department of State, Assistant Secretary, Bureau of Democracy, Human Rights, and Labor. As Prepared Remarks for the Senate Committee on Foreign Relations. Washington, DC. February 3, 2015. https://2009-2017.state.gov/j/drl/rls/rm/2015/237120.htm.

Malinowski, Tom. "Restoring Moral Authority: Ending Torture, Secret Detention, and the Prison at Guantanamo Bay." *The Annals of the American Academy of Political and Social Science* 618, no. 1 (2008): 148–59. doi: 10.1177/0002716208217118.

Malmedie, Lydia. "Contested Issue and Incremental Change. The Example of LGBTI in EU Foreign Policy." *Der moderne Staat* (2016): 35–50. https://doi.org/10.3224/dms.v9i1.23639.

"Map: Sexual Orientation Laws around the World, 2019." International Lesbian, Gay, Bisexual, Trans and Intersex Association (ILGA). Accessed March 20, 2019. https://ilga.org/ilga-map-sexual-orientation-laws-2019.

Matheson, Giorgia. "The Rights and Experiences of LGBTI Refugees in Europe: A Comparative Study of Procedures and Practices in Italy and Sweden." Master's thesis, Uppsala University, Disciplinary Domain of Humanities and Social Sciences, Faculty of Theology, Department of Theology, 2019.

Mayer, Hartmut. "The Challenge of Coherence and Consistency in EU Foreign Policy." In *The EU's Foreign Policy,* 123–36. London: Routledge, 2016.

Mayerfeld, Jamie. "The Democratic Legacy of the International Criminal Court." *Fletcher Forum of World Affairs* 28, no. 2 (2004): 147–56.

Mayton, Joseph. "LGBT Asylum Seekers: A Silent Revolution." *Qantara.* February 6, 2014. https://en.qantara.de/content/lgbt-asylum-seekers-a-silent-revolution.

McAdam, Doug, Sidney Tarrow, and Charles Tilly. *Dynamics of Contention.* Cambridge: Cambridge University Press, 2001.

McCammon, Holly J., and Amanda J. Brockman. "Feminist Institutional Activists: Venue Shifting, Strategic Adaptation, and Winning the Pregnancy Discrimination Act." *Sociological Forum* 34, no. 1 (2019): 5–26.

McCarthy, John, D., and N. Zald Mayer. "Resource Mobilization and Social Movements: A Partial Theory." In *Social Movements in an Organizational Society*, 15–42. London: Routledge, 2017.

McCarthy, Niall. "Global Humanitarian Assistance: Who Are the Biggest Contributors?" *Forbes*. July 21, 2015. http://www.forbes.com/sites/niallmccarthy/2015/07/21/global-humanitarian-assistance-who-are-the-biggest-contributors-infographic/#7f1b6a6769af.

McCartney, Danielle. "Monitoring the World Society: LGBT Human Rights in Russia and Sweden." *Advances in Gender Research* 24 (2017): 309–32.

McClendon, Gwyneth. *Envy in Politics: How Envy, Spite, and the Pursuit of Admiration Influence Politics*. Princeton, NJ: Princeton University Press, 2018.

McClintock, Michael. "Counter-Terrorism and Human Rights since 9/11." In *The Ashgate Research Companion to Political Violence*, edited by Marie Breen-Smyth, 411–42. Burlington, VT: Ashgate, 2012.

McWilliams, Carey. *Mask for Privilege: Anti-Semitism in America*. London: Routledge, 2018.

Mearsheimer, John J. "A Realist Reply." *International Security* 20, no. 1 (1995): 82–93.

Mercer, Jonathan. *Reputation and International Politics*. Ithaca, NY: Cornell University Press, 1996.

Mearsheimer, J. J. *The Tragedy of Great Power Politics*. New York: W.W. Norton & Company, 2001.

"Meet Randy Berry, the First U.S. Diplomat for LGBT Rights." *Huffington Post*. April 29, 2015. https://www.huffpost.com/entry/randy-berry-lgbt-rights-diplomat_n_7173328.

Mertus, Julie A. *Bait and Switch Human Rights and US Foreign Policy*. New York: Routledge, 2008.

Meyer, David. *The Politics of Protest: Social Movements in America*. Oxford: Oxford University Press, 2015.

Michaelson, Jay. "Trump's Proposed Transgender Military Ban Aims to Sever the T from LGBT." *The Daily Beast*. July 27, 2017. https://www.thedailybeast.com/trumps-proposed-transgender-military-ban-aims-to-sever-the-t-from-lgbt.

Micheletti, Michele. *Civil Society and State Relations in Sweden*. London: Routledge, 2019.

"Milestones in the American Gay Rights Movement." Public Broadcasting Service, *The American Experience*. Accessed November 25, 2019. http://www.pbs.org/wgbh/americanexperience/features/stonewall-milestones-american-gay-rights-movemet/.

Miller, Robin, M. S. Kavanagh, and G. Block. "Stepping off the Curb: How Stonewall Kickstarted the Gay Revolution." Thesis, American University, 2016.

"Mills Replies David Cameron; You Can't Threaten Us with Gay Aid!" *Ghana Joy News*. August 2011. Accessed November 11, 2013. http://edition.myjoyonline.com/pages/news/201111/75813.php.

Milne, Richard. "Sweden: Why the 'Moral Superpower' Dissented over COVID-19." *Los Angeles Times*. October 16, 2020. https://www.latimes.com/world-nation/story/2020-10-16/sweden-why-the-moral-superpower-dissented-over-covid-19.

"Mission Strategic Plan." US Department of State and USAID Strategic Plan. Accessed April 15, 2019. http://www.state.gov/s/d/rm/rls/dosstrat/2014/.

Mitchell, Lincoln. "Supporting Democracy Abroad U.S. Country Report." Freedom House. 2014. https://freedomhouse.org/report/democracysupport/united-states#.VpP5MVm6Rj8.

Mogire, Edward. "Refugees and the Terrorist Threat." In *Victims as Security Threats*, 147–62. London: Routledge, 2016.

Moller, Tommy. *Political Party Dynamics and Democracy in Sweden: Developments since the "Golden Age."* London: Routledge, 2020.

Montinola, Gabriella R. "When Does Aid Conditionality Work?" *Studies in Comparative International Development* 45, no. 3 (2010): 358–82.

Moon, Kyoung-Hee, Kyung-Ock Chun, Mi-Sung Kim, and Eun-Kyung Kim. "A Comparative Study of Electoral Gender Quotas in Sweden, Germany, and South Korea." *Asian Women* 28, no. 1 (2008): 75–100. https://doi.org/10.14431/aw.2008.03.24.1.75.

Moreau, Julie. "Political Science and the Study of LGBT Social Movements in the Global South." In *LGBTQ Politics: A Critical Reader*, edited by Marla Brettschneider, Susan Burgess, and Christine Keating, 439–57. New York: New York University Press, 2017.

Moreau, Julie. "Trump in Transnational Perspective: Insights from Global LGBT Politics." *Politics & Gender* 14, no. 4 (2018): 619–48.

Moreau, Julie, and Ashley Currier. "Queer Dilemmas: LGBT Activism and International Funding." In *Routledge Handbook of Queer Development Studies*, edited by Corinne L. Mason, 223–38. New York: Routledge, 2018.

Morgan, Joe. "Gay Uganda's Plea: 'Don't Cut Aid, You'll Make It Worse.'" *Gay Star News*. February 26, 2014. https://www.gaystarnews.com/article/gay-ugandas-plea-dont-cut-aid-youll-make-it-worse260214/.

Morrison, Carlos, and Jacqueline Trimble. "Still Work to Be Done: The Million Man March and the 50th Anniversary Commemoration Selma to Montgomery March as Mythoform and Visual Rhetoric." *Howard Journal of Communications* 28, no. 2 (2017): 132–43.

Morsink, Johannes. *The Universal Declaration of Human Rights and the Holocaust: An Endangered Connection*. Washington, DC: Georgetown University Press, 2019.

Mos, Martijn. "Conflicted Normative Power Europe: The European Union and Sexual Minority Rights." *Journal of Contemporary European Research* 9, no. 1 (2013): 78–93.

Moss, Kevin. "Split Europe: Homonationalism and Homophobia in Croatia." In *LGBT Activism and the Making of Europe*, 212–32. London: Palgrave Macmillan, 2014.

Mowery, David C., and Carol Lancaster. "Aid's Purposes: A Brief History." In *Foreign Aid: Diplomacy, Development, Domestic Politics*, 25–61. Chicago, IL: University of Chicago Press, 2006.

Moyn, Samuel. *Not Enough: Human Rights in an Unequal World*. Cambridge, MA: Harvard University Press, 2018.

Mugisha, Frank. "India and the Global Fight for LGBT Rights." *Foreign Policy*. January 22, 2019. https://foreignpolicy.com/gt-essay/india-and-the-global-fight-for-lgbt-rights/.

Mulford, David C., US ambassador to India. "Issue of Gujarat Chief Minister Narendra Modi's Visa Status." US Embassy, New Delhi. March 21, 2005. https://2001-2009.state.gov/p/sca/rls/rm/2005/43701.htm.

Müllerson, Rein. *Human Rights Diplomacy*. London: Routledge, 1997.

Müllerson, Rein. *Human Rights Diplomacy*. 2nd ed. London: Routledge, 2014.

Murdie, Amanda, and Dursun Peksen. "Women's Rights INGO Shaming and the Government Respect for Women's Rights." *Review of International Organizations* 10, no. 1 (2015): 1–22.

Murray, Sofia. "Framing a Climate Crisis: A Descriptive Framing Analysis of How Greta Thunberg Inspired the Masses to Take to the Streets." Bachelor's thesis, Uppsala University, 2020.

Mustola, Kati, and Jens Rydström. *Criminally Queer: Homosexuality and Criminal Law in Scandinavia, 1842–1999*. Amsterdam: Aksant, 2007.

Myers, Joe. "Foreign Aid: These Countries Are the Most Generous." *World Economic Forum*. August 19, 2016. https://www.weforum.org/agenda/2016/08/foreign-aid-these-countries-are-the-most-generous/.

Myers, Steven Lee, and Helene Cooper. "U.S. Backs Gay Rights Abroad, Obama and Clinton Say." *New York Times*. December 6, 2011. http://www.nytimes.com/2011/12/07/world/united-states-to-use-aid-to-promote-gay-rights-abroad.html?pagewanted=all&_r=0.

Myrdal, Alva. *Nation and Family: The Swedish Experiment in Democratic Family and Population Policy*. Cambridge, MA: MIT Press, 1944 (1968 in English).

Naim, Moises. "What Is a GONGO? How Government-Sponsored Groups Masquerade as Civil Society." *Foreign Policy*. October 13, 2009. http://foreignpolicy.com/2009/10/13/what-is-a-gongo/.

Najjar, Jihan. "The Experiences of Iranian Sexual Minority Refugees and Asylum Seekers: A Phenomenological Study." PhD diss., The University of Nebraska-Lincoln, 2020.

Nanda, Ved P. *Global Human Rights: Public Policies, Comparative Measures, and NGO Strategies*. London: Routledge, 2019.

Nardi, Dominic J., Jr. "Can NGOs Change the Constitution? Civil Society and the Indonesian Constitutional Court." *Contemporary Southeast Asia* 40, no. 2 (2018): 247–78.

Narrain, Arvind, Adrian Jjuuko, Monica Tabengwa, Gary Kinsman, Amar Wahab, Pere DeRoy, Namela Baynes Henry, et al. *Envisioning Global LGBT Human Rights: (Neo) Colonialism, Neoliberalism, Resistance and Hope.* London: University of London Press, 2018.

Nauert, Heather. "Department Press Briefing." US Department of State. August 23, 2017. Accessed October 12, 2019. https://www.state.gov/briefings/department-press-briefing-august-23-2017/#EGYPT.

Nicholson, Helene Coley. "After the Visits . . ." *Jamaica Observer.* December 30, 2015. http://m.jamaicaobserver.com/columns/After-the-visits_47377.

Nielsen, Richard A. "Rewarding Human Rights? Selective Aid Sanctions against Repressive States." *International Studies Quarterly* 57, no. 4 (2013): 791–803. https://doi.org/10.1111/isqu.12049.

Niklasson, Birgitta. "The Gendered Networking of Diplomats." *Hague Journal of Diplomacy* 15, no. 1–2 (2020): 13–42. https://doi.org/10.1163/1871191X-BJA10005.

Nilsson, Annika, and Jessica Rothman. "Evaluation of the Sida Supported RFSL Projects 'LGBT Voices' and 'Rainbow Leaders.'" Sida. 2017. Accessed August 3, 2018. https://www.sida.se/contentassets/a09863bdac41467ea541a12e-2160caf5/22051.pdf.

Nilsson, Annika, Klara Lundholm, and Erik Vagberg. "Study on SIDA's Work on Human Rights of Lesbian, Gay, Bisexual, Transgender and Intersex Persons." Swedish International Development Agency (Sida). November 2013. http://www.sida.se/contentassets/e68f76aa89ca48cab8a17788fe9afe36/study-on-sida8217s-work-on-human-rights-of-lesbian-gay-bisexual-transgender-and-intersex-persons_3728.pdf.

Nogueira, Maria B. B. "The Promotion of LGBT Rights as International Human Rights Norms: Explaining Brazil's Diplomatic Leadership." *Global Governance* 23, no. 4 (2017): 545–63. https://doi.org/10.1163/19426720-02304003.

Nordberg, Jenny. "Who's Afraid of a Feminist Foreign Policy?" *New Yorker.* April 15, 2015. http://www.newyorker.com/news/news-desk/swedens-feminist-foreign-minister.

Norocel, Ov Cristian. ""Give Us Back Sweden!" A Feminist Reading of the (Re) Interpretations of the Folkhem Conceptual Metaphor in Swedish Radical Right Populist Discourse." *NORA-Nordic Journal of Feminist and Gender Research* 21, no. 1 (2013): 4–20.

Nossiter, Adam. "Senegal Cheers Its President for Standing Up to Obama on Same-Sex Marriage." *New York Times.* June 28, 2013. https://www.nytimes.com/2013/06/29/world/africa/senegal-cheers-its-president-for-standing-up-to-obama-on-same-sex-marriage.html.

Novak, Andrew. "Using International and Foreign Law in Human Rights Litigation: The Decriminalization of Homosexuality in Belize." *Journal of Human Rights Practice* 10, no. 2 (2018): 346–54.

Nuñez-Mietz, Fernando G. "Resisting Human Rights through Securitization: Russia and Hungary against LGBT Rights." *Journal of Human Rights* 18, no. 5 (2019): 543–63.

Nuñez-Mietz, Fernando G., and Lucrecia García Iommi. "Can Transnational Norm Advocacy Undermine Internalization? Explaining Immunization against LGBT Rights in Uganda." *International Studies Quarterly* 61, no. 1 (2017): 196–209. https://doi.org/10.1093/isq/sqx011.

Obama, Barack. "Presidential Memorandum: International Initiatives to Advance the Human Rights of Lesbian, Gay, Bisexual, and Transgender Persons." Office of the Press Secretary, December 6, 2011. https://obamawhitehouse.archives.gov/the-press-office/2011/12/06/presidential-memorandum-international-initiatives-advance-human-rights-l.

O'Connell, Annie. "Why Sweden Is a Leader in Foreign Aid." The Borgen Project. August 20, 2019. https://borgenproject.org/sweden-is-a-leader-in-foreign-aid/.

O'Dwyer, Conor. "The Benefits of Backlash: EU Accession and the Organization of LGBT Activism in Postcommunist Poland and the Czech Republic." *East European Politics and Societies* 32, no. 4 (2018): 892–923.

O'Dwyer, Conor, and Katrina Z. S. Schwartz. "Minority Rights after EU Enlargement: A Comparison of Antigay Politics in Poland and Latvia." *Comparative European Politics* 8, no. 2 (2010): 220–43. https://doi.org/10.1057/cep.2008.31.

"Office of the Special Envoy to Monitor and Combat Anti-Semitism." US Department of State Secretary for Civilian Security, Democracy, and Human Rights. Accessed April 24, 2020. https://www.state.gov/bureaus-offices/under-secretary-for-civilian-security-democracy-and-human-rights/office-of-the-special-envoy-to-monitor-and-combat-anti-semitism/.

Oleszek, Walter J., Mark J. Oleszek, Elizabeth Rybicki, and Bill Heniff. *Congressional Procedures and the Policy Process*. Thousand Oaks, CA: CQ Press, 1978.

Oliver, Marcia. "Transnational Sex Politics, Conservative Christianity, and Antigay Activism in Uganda." *Studies in Social Justice* 7, no. 1 (2012): 83–105. https://doi.org/10.26522/ssj.v7i1.1056.

Olsson, Jan, and Erik Hysing. "Theorizing inside Activism: Understanding Policymaking and Policy Change from Below." *Planning Theory & Practice* 13, no. 2 (2012): 257–73. https://doi.org/10.1080/14649357.2012.677123.

O'Mahoney, Joseph. "How Britain's Colonial Legacy Still Affects LGBT Politics around the World." *The Conversation*. April 16, 2019. https://theconversation.com/how-britains-colonial-legacy-still-affects-lgbt-politics-around-the-world-95799.

Onapajo, Hakeem, and Christopher Isike. "The Global Politics of Gay Rights: The Straining Relations between the West and Africa." *Journal of Global Analysis* 6, no. 1 (2013): 21–45. https://therestjournal.com/wp-content/uploads/2019/03/JGA_Vol.6_No.1_A_2.pdf.

Onyulo, Tonny. "Uganda's Other Refugee Crisis: Discrimination Forces Many LGBT Ugandans to Seek Asylum." *Public Radio International*. July 13, 2017.

https://www.usatoday.com/story/news/world/2017/07/13/uganda-other-refugee-crisis-lgbt-ugandanss/475353001.

Örum, Oscar. "The Swedish Democrats Are Expelled from the Pride Festival." *Dagens Opinion.* July 18, 2014. http://dagensopinion.se/artikel/sverigedemokraterna-portas-fran-pridefestivalen/.

Ott, Dana. *Small Is Democratic: An Examination of State Size and Democratic Development.* London: Routledge, 2018.

"Our Model for LGBTIQ Human Rights Change." Outright Action International. Accessed April 15, 2019. https://www.outrightinternational.org/how-we-work.

Padden, Brian. "US Foreign Policy on Gay Rights Sparks Debate." *Voice of America News.* July 16, 2011. Accessed October 10, 2014. http://www.voanews.com/content/us-foreign-policy-gay-rights-sparks-debate/1703238.html.

Palladino, Robert J. "Implementation of Phases Two and Three of Brunei's Sharia Penal Code." US Department of State Office of the Spokesperson. April 2, 2019. https://www.state.gov/r/pa/prs/ps/2019/04/290840.htm.

Pandith, Farah Anwar. "Conversations with America: U.S. Engagement with Muslim Communities." US Department of State. July 9, 2010. https://2009-2017.state.gov/s/srmc/144398.htm.

Patashnik, Eric. "After the Public Interest Prevails: The Political Sustainability of Policy Reform." *Governance* 16, no. 2 (2003): 203–34.

Paternotte, David, and Phillip Ayoub, eds. *LGBT Activism and the Making of Europe: A Rainbow Europe?"* New York: Springer, 2014.

Paternotte, David, and H. Seckinelgin. " 'Lesbian and Gay Rights Are Human Rights': Multiple Globalizations and LGBTI Activism." In *The Ashgate Research Companion to Lesbian and Gay Activism,* 209–23. Burlington, VT: Ashgate, 2015.

Pauly, Louis W., and Bruce W. Jentleson, eds. *Power in a Complex Global System.* London: Routledge, 2014.

Payne, Jenny Gunnarsson, and Theo Erbenius. "Conceptions of Transgender Parenthood in Fertility Care and Family Planning in Sweden: From Reproductive Rights to Concrete Practices." *Anthropology & Medicine* 25, no. 3 (2018): 329–43.

"Peace and Development." Stockholm International Peace Research Institute. Accessed September 24, 2020. https://www.sipri.org/research/peace-and-development.

Pease, Kelly-Kate S. *Human Rights and Humanitarian Diplomacy: Negotiating for Human Rights Protection and Humanitarian Access.* Oxford: Oxford University Press, 2016.

Peck, James. *Ideal Illusions: How the US Government Co-opted Human Rights.* New York: Metropolitan Books, 2011.

Peleg, Ilan. *The Legacy of George W. Bush's Foreign Policy: Moving beyond Neoconservatism.* New York: Routledge, 2018.

Persson Tholin, Jenny, and Linus Broström. "Transgender and Gender Diverse People's Experience of Non-Transition-Related Health Care in Sweden." *International Journal of Transgenderism* 19, no. 4 (2018): 424–35.

Peterson, Abby, and Mattias Wahlström. "Between Politics and Party." In *Pride Parades and LGBT Movements*, 211–26. London: Routledge, 2018.

Peterson, Abby, Mattias Wahlström, and Magnus Wennerhag. " 'Normalized' Pride? Pride Parade Participants in Six European countries." *Sexualities* 21, no. 7 (2018): 1146–69.

Peterson, Abby, Mattias Wahlström, and Magnus Wennerhag. "The Histories of Pride." In *Pride Parades and LGBT Movements*, 18–70. London: Routledge, 2018.

Peterson, Timothy M., Amanda Murdie, and Victor Asal. "Human Rights, NGO Shaming and the Exports of Abusive States." *British Journal of Political Science* 48, no. 3 (2016): 767–86. https://doi.org/10.1017/s0007123416000065.

Petersson, Stig-Åke. "Svensk Biståndspolitik Och Homosexuellas Mänskliga Rättigheter." Stockholm, Sweden: RFSL, 2000.

Petrikova, I. "Promoting 'Good Behaviour' through Aid: Do 'New' Donors Differ From the 'Old' Ones?" *Journal of International Relations and Development* 19, no. 1 (2016): 153–92.

Pettinicchio, David. "Institutional Activism: Reconsidering the Insider/Outsider Dichotomy." *Sociology Compass* 6, no. 6 (2012): 499–510. https://doi.org/10.1111/j.1751-9020.2012.00465.x.

Pfitsch, Hollis V. "Homosexuality in Asylum and Constitutional Law: Rhetoric of Acts and Identity." *Law & Sexuality: A Review of Lesbian, Gay, Bisexual, and Transgender Legal Issues* 15 (2006): 59–89.

Piccone, Ted. "China's Long Game on Human Rights at the United Nations." *Foreign Policy at Brookings*. September 2018. https://www.brookings.edu/wp-content/uploads/2018/09/FP_20181009_china_human_rights.pdf#:~:text=CHINA%E2%80%99S%20LONG%20GAME%20ON%20HUMAN%20RIGHTS%20AT%20THE,pivotal%20player%20in%20the%20international%20human%20rights%20system.

Picq, Manuela Lavinas, and Markus Thiel. *Sexualities in World Politics: How LGBTQ Claims Shape International Relations*. New York: Routledge, 2015.

Pierson, Paul. "The Study of Policy Development." *Journal of Policy History* 17, no. 1 (2005): 34–51. https://doi.org/10.1353/jph.2005.0006.

Pinfold, Corinne. "28 Arrested after Protesters Throw Eggs at Baltic Pride." *Pink News*. July 27, 2013. http://www.pinknews.co.uk/2013/07/27/28-arrested-after-protesters-throw-eggs-at-baltic-pride/.

"Policy Issue: Democracy and Human Rights." US Department of State. Accessed May 22, 2019. https://www.state.gov/policy-issues/human-rights-and-democracy/.

Posner, Michael. "Reflections on the Obama Administration's Human Rights Policies and the Way Forward." Council on Foreign Relations. March 4, 2013. https://www.cfr.org/event/reflections-obama-administrations-human-rights-policies-and-way-forward.

Power, Samantha. *A Problem from Hell: America and the Age of Genocide*. New York: Basic Books, 2012.

Power, Samantha. *The Education of an Idealist*. New York: HarperCollins Books, 2019.

"President Obama Joins President Kenyatta of Kenya in a Joint Press Conference." The White House, Office of the Press Secretary. July 25, 2015. https://obamawhitehouse.archives.gov/the-press-office/2015/07/25/remarks-president-obama-and-president-kenyatta-kenya-press-conference.

"Presidential Memorandum—International Initiatives to Advance the Human Rights of Lesbian, Gay, Bisexual, and Transgender Persons." The White House, Office of the Press Secretary. December 6, 2011. https://obamawhitehouse.archives.gov/the-press-office/2011/12/06/presidential-memorandum-international-initiatives-advance-human-rights-l.

"Preventing and Responding to Gender-Based Violence." US Agency for International Development. May 7, 2019. https://www.usaid.gov/gbv.

Puar, Jasbir K. *Terrorist Assemblages: Homonationalism in Queer Times*. Durham, NC: Duke University Press, 2018.

Quine, Oscar. "Frank Mugisha: Uganda's Most Outspoken Gay Rights Activist on Changing People's Attitudes, Coming Out, and the Threat of Being Attacked." *Independent*. August 22, 2014. https://www.independent.co.uk/news/people/profiles/frank-mugisha-uganda-s-most-outspoken-gay-rights-activist-changing-people-s-attitudes-coming-out-and-threat-being-attacked-9681476.html.

Raghavan, Gautam. "Best Practices in Engaging the LGBT Community on the Affordable Care Act." White House. August 1, 2014. https://www.whitehouse.gov/blog/2014/08/01/best-practices-engaging-lgbt-community-affordable-care-act.

Rahman, Momin. "Sexual Diversity." In *Routledge International Handbook of Diversity Studies,* edited by Steven Vertovec, 75–82. New York: Routledge, 2014.

"Rainbow Academy." RFSL. November 15, 2016. https://www.rfsl.se/en/organisation/international/rainbow-academy/.

Rainer, Elise C. "When Fundamentalists Come to Power, Women Lose." *Modern Diplomacy*. October 17, 2020. https://moderndiplomacy.eu/2020/10/17/when-fundamentalists-come-to-power-women-lose/.

Rainer, Elise C., and Anish Goel. "Myanmar's Military Is Only Hurting Itself." *Foreign Policy*. November 8, 2019. https://foreignpolicy.com/2019/11/08/myanmar-military-rohingya/.

Rajagopal, Balakrishnan. *International Law from Below: Development, Social Movements and Third World Resistance*. Cambridge: Cambridge University Press, 2004.

Rajan, S. Irydaya, and Jolin Joseph. "Migrant Domestic Workers in the GCC: Negotiating Contested Politics and Contradictory Policies." In *Asianization of Migrant Workers in the Gulf Countries*, 233–46. Singapore: Springer, 2020.

Ramirez, Mario Hugo. "The Fate of Many, the Brutality of Others: Human Rights Documentation and the Margins of Subjectivity in El Salvador." PhD diss., University of California, Los Angeles, 2017.

Rathore, Khushi Singh. "Where Are the Women in Indian Diplomacy?" *The Diplomat.* November 12, 2020. https://thediplomat.com/2020/11/where-are-the-women-in-indian-diplomacy/.

Reardon, Betty, and Asha Hans. *The Gender Imperative: Human Security vs State Security.* London: Routledge, 2019.

"Recommendation 1117 (1989) on the Condition of Transsexuals." European Parliament Resolution. September 12, 1989.

"Reducing Poverty through Growth." Millennium Challenge Corporation. Accessed December 19, 2019. https://www.mcc.gov/.

"Reflections on the Obama Administration's Human Rights Policies and the Way Forward." Council on Foreign Relations. March 4, 2013. https://www.cfr.org/event/reflections-obama-administrations-human-rights-policies-and-way-forward.

Reich, Rob. *Just Giving: Why Philanthropy Is Failing Democracy and How It Can Do Better.* Princeton, NJ: Princeton University Press, 2018.

Reisser, Wesley. "Human Rights Speakers Series—LGBT Rights Abroad." Outright Action International. June 7, 2016. https://www.youtube.com/watch?v=flrAPcZx0Gc.

"Remarks by John Kerry Announcing the Appointment of Special Envoy for the Human Rights of LGBT Persons, Randy Berry." US Department of State. February 23, 2015. http://www.state.gov/secretary/remarks/2015/02/237772.htm.

"Remarks by the President at Signing of Executive Order on LGBT Workplace Discrimination." The White House Office of the Press Secretary. July 21, 2014. https://www.whitehouse.gov/the-press-office/2014/07/21/remarks-president-signing-executive-order-lgbt-workplace-discrimination.

"Remarks from President Obama and President Sall of Senegal Joint Press Conference." White House Press Office. June 27, 2013. https://www.whitehouse.gov/the-press-office/2013/06/27/remarks-president-obama-and-president-sall-republic-senegal-joint-press-.

Renouard, Joe. *Human Rights in American Foreign Policy: From the 1960s to the Soviet Collapse.* Philadelphia: University of Pennsylvania Press, 2016.

"Report: Brazil Human Rights Practices, 1993." US Department of State. January 31, 1994. http://dosfan.lib.uic.edu/ERC/democracy/1993_hrp_report/93hrp_report_ara/Brazil.html.

"Report of the Commission on Unalienable Rights." US Department Commission on Unalienable Rights. August 26, 2020. https://www.state.gov/report-of-the-commission-on-unalienable-rights/.

"Report on International Prison Conditions." US Department of State Bureau of Democracy, Human Rights, and Labor, Washington DC, March 22, 2013. https://2009-2017.state.gov/j/drl/rls/209944.htm.

"2018 Report on International Religious Freedom." US Department of State. June 21, 2019. https://www.state.gov/reports/2018-report-on-international-religious-freedom/.

"Reported Hate Crimes 2016." Swedish government Bureau of Statistics. Accessed February 26, 2019. https://www.bra.se/bra-in-english/home/crime-and-statistics/crime-statistics/reported-hate-crimes.html.

"2016 Republican Facts." Human Rights Campaign. Accessed March 1, 2016. http://www.hrc.org/2016RepublicanFacts/donald-trump.

Reveron, Derek. *Exporting Security: International Engagement, Security Cooperation, and the Changing Face of the US Military*. Washington, DC: Georgetown University Press, 2016.

Rexed, B. "Sweden and the World Health Organization over 40 Years (Sverige och WHO i 40 år)." Stockholm, Sweden: Socialdepartementet, Socialstyreslen & Allmänna Förlaget, 1988.

Reynolds, Andrew. "Representation and Rights: The Impact of LGBT Legislators in Comparative Perspective." *American Political Science Review* 107, no. 2 (2013): 259–74.

"RFSL Support Service." RFSL Areas of Work. April 8, 2020. https://www.rfsl.se/en/organisation/rfsl-stodmottagning/.

Rheindorf, Markus, and Ruth Wodak. "Borders, Fences, and Limits—Protecting Austria from Refugees: Metadiscursive Negotiation of Meaning in the Current Refugee Crisis." *Journal of Immigrant & Refugee Studies* 16, no. 1–2 (2018): 15–38.

Rice, Susan. "U.S. Will Press for a Major UN Vote to Restore Language in a Resolution on Extrajudicial Killings." *Global Equality Today*. December 10, 2010. https://globalequality.wordpress.com/2010/12/10/u-s-will-press-for-a-major-un-vote-to-restore-language-in-a-resolution-on-extrajudicial-killings/.

Richards, Jacob. "From One to Windsor: Sixty Years of the Movement for LGBT Rights." *GPSolo* 31 (2014): 35.

Rimmer, Susan Harris. "Women as Maker of International Law: Towards Feminist Diplomacy." In *Research Handbook on Feminist Engagement with International Law*, edited by Susan Harris Rimmer and Kate Ogg, 26–43. Cheltenham, UK: Edward Elgar, 2019.

Ring, Trudy. "Secretary of State Rex Tillerson Recognizes Transgender Day of Remembrance." *Advocate*. November 20, 2017. https://www.advocate.com/transgender/2017/11/20/secretary-state-rex-tillerson-recognizes-transgender-day-remembrance.

Ritchie, Jason. "Pinkwashing, Homonationalism, and Israel–Palestine: The Conceits of Queer Theory and the Politics of the Ordinary." *Antipode* 47, no. 3 (2015): 616–34.

Ritzman, Thomas A. "Importance of Identifying the Initial Sensitizing Event." *Medical Hypnoanalysis Journal* 7, no. 3 (1992): 98–104. https://psycnet.apa.org/record/1993-14760-001.

Rodriguez, S. M. *The Economies of Queer Inclusion: Transnational Organizing for LGBTI Rights in Uganda*. London: Lexington Books, 2018.

Roggeband, Conny, and Anna van der Vleuten. *Gender Equality Norms in Regional Governance: Transnational Dynamics in Europe, South America and Southern Africa.* London: Palgrave Macmillan, 2014.

Rohrich, Kyle James. "Human Rights Diplomacy amidst "World War LGBT": Re-examining Western Promotion of LGBT Rights in Light of the "Traditional Values" Discourse." In *Transatlantic Perspectives on Diplomacy and Diversity,* edited by Anthony Chase, 69–96. New York: Humanity in Action Press, 2015.

Rosén Sundström, Malena, and Ole Elgström. "Praise or Critique? Sweden's Feminist Foreign Policy in the Eyes of Its Fellow EU Members." *European Politics and Society* 21, no. 4 (2019): 418–33.

Rosenberg, Lena, Anders Kottorp, and Karin Johansson. "LGBQ-Specific Elderly Housing as a "Sparkling Sanctuary": Boundary Work on LGBQ Identity and Community in Relationship to Potential LGBQ-Specific Elderly Housing in Sweden." *Journal of Homosexuality* 65, no. 11 (2018): 1484–1506.

Rosenthal, Hannah, special envoy to monitor and combat anti-Semitism. "Combating Anti-Semitism: Protecting Human Rights." US Department of State. April 14, 2010. https://2009-2017.state.gov/j/drl/rls/rm/2010/140284.htm.

Rosling, Hans, O. Rosling, and A. R. Rönnlund. *Factfulness: Ten Reasons We're Wrong about the World—and Why Things Are Better Than You Think.* New York: Flatiron Books, 2018.

Rothschild, Nathalie. "Lawyers Open First Office Focused on Assisting LGBT Asylum Seekers." *Sveriges Radio.* November 10, 2017. https://sverigesradio.se/sida/artikel.aspx?programid=2054&artikel=6819364.

Rowlands, Sam, and Jean-Jacques Amy. "Preserving the Reproductive Potential of Transgender and Intersex People." *European Journal of Contraception & Reproductive Health Care* 23, no. 1 (2018): 58–63.

Rumelili, Bahar, and Rahime Suleymanoglu-Kurum. "Women and Gender in Turkish Diplomacy: Historical Legacies and Current Patterns." In *Gendering Diplomacy and International Negotiation,* 87–106. Cham: Palgrave Macmillan, 2018.

Rundquist, Solveig. "Stockholm Pride Bars Sweden Democrats." *The Local Sweden.* July 29, 2014. https://www.thelocal.se/20140729/sweden-democrats-barred-from-stockholm-pride.

Rutsch, Poncie. "Guess How Much of Uncle Sam's Money Goes to Foreign Aid. Guess Again!" NPR. February 10, 2015. http://www.npr.org/sections/goatsandsoda/2015/02/10/383875581/guess-how-much-of-uncle-sams-money-goes-to-foreign-aid-guess-again.

Rydgren, Jens. "Immigration Sceptics, Xenophobes Or Racists? Radical Right-Wing Voting in Six West European Countries." *European Journal of Political Research* 47, no. 6 (2008): 737–65.

Rydström Jens. *Odd Couples: A History of Gay Marriage in Scandinavia.* Amsterdam: Aksant, 2011.

Saiya, N., T. Zaihra, and J. Fidler. "Testing the Hillary Doctrine: Women's Rights and Anti-American Terrorism." *Political Research Quarterly* 70, no. 2 (2017): 421–32. https://doi.org/10.1177/1065912917698046.

Samelius, Lotta, and Erik Wågberg. "Sexual Orientation and Gender Identity Issues in Development." Sida Department for Democracy and Social Development. November 2005. https://tandis.odihr.pl/bitstream/20.500.12389/19549/1/02220.pdf.

Sandberg, Maria. "To Fund or Not to Fund? How and Why Governments Support—and Do Not Support—Civil Society in Different Policy Sectors." MA thesis, Göteborgs Universitet, 2018.

Sandelind, Clara. "Constructions of Identity, Belonging and Exclusion in the Democratic Welfare State." *National Identities* 20, no. 2 (2018): 197–218.

Sandell, Richard. *Museums, Moralities and Human Rights.* London: Routledge, 2017.

Sanders, Rebecca. "Norm Proxy War and Resistance through Outsourcing: The Dynamics of Transnational Human Rights Contestation." *Human Rights Review* 17, no. 2 (2016): 165–91.

Sandholtz, Wayne. "United States Military Assistance and Human Rights." *Human Rights Quarterly* 38, no. 4 (2016): 1070–1101. https://doi.org/10.1353/hrq.2016.0057).

Sandlin, Evan W. "Competing Concerns: Balancing Human Rights and National Security in US Economic Aid Allocation." *Human Rights Review* 17, no. 4 (2016): 439–62. https://doi.org/10.1007/s12142-016-0426-2.

Sands, Philippe. *Lawless World: The Making and Breaking of Global Rules.* London: Allen Lane, 2005.

Sani, Giulia Maria Dotti. "Undoing Gender in Housework? Participation in Domestic Chores by Italian Fathers and Children of Different Ages." *Sex Roles* 74, no. 9–10 (2016): 411–21.

Saul, Heather. "Sweden Announces Aid Cuts over Uganda Anti-Gay Bill." *Independent.* March 6, 2014. http://www.independent.co.uk/news/world/europe/sweden-announces-aid-cuts-over-uganda-anti-gay-bill-9173189.html.

Schattschneider, E. E. *Politics, Pressures, and the Tariff.* New York: Prentice-Hall, 1935.

Scheinin, Martin. "Impact of Post-9/11 Counter-Terrorism Measures on All Human Rights." In *Using Human Rights to Counter Terrorism,* edited by Manfred Nowak and Anne Charbord, 92–124. Cheltenham, UK: Edward Elgar Publishing, 2018.

Scheingold, Stuart. *The Politics of Rights: Lawyers, Public Policy, and Political Change.* New Haven: Yale University Press, 1974.

Schmidt, Vivien A. "Taking Ideas and Discourse Seriously: Explaining Change through Discursive Institutionalism as the Fourth 'New Institutionalism.'" *European Political Science Review* 2, no. 1 (2010): 1–25.

Schmitz, David F., and Vanessa Walker. "Jimmy Carter and the Foreign Policy of Human Rights: The Development of a Post-Cold War Foreign Policy." *Diplomatic History* 28, no. 1 (2004): 113–43.

Schrama, Reini, and Asya Zhelyazkova. " 'You Can't Have One without the Other': The Differential Impact of Civil Society Strength on the Implementation of EU Policy." *Journal of European Public Policy* 25, no. 7 (2018): 1029–48.

Schur, Edwin M. *The Family and the Sexual Revolution; Selected Readings.* Bloomington, IN: Indiana University Press, 1964.

Seckinelgin, Hakan. "Same-Sex Lives between the Language of International LGBT Rights, International Aid, and Anti-Homosexuality." *Global Social Policy* 18, no. 3 (2018): 284–303. https://doi.org/10.1177/1468018118795989.

"Security Clearance Frequently Asked Questions." Clearance Jobs. Accessed October 20, 2020. https://www.clearancejobs.com/security-clearance-faqs.

Sejersen, Mikkel. "Democratic Sanctions Meet Black Knight Support: Revisiting the Belarusian Case." *Democratization* 26, no. 3 (2019): 502–20.

Selbervik, Hilde. "Aid and Conditionality." The Organisation for Economic Co-operation and Development (OECD). July 1999. https://www.oecd.org/countries/tanzania/35178610.pdf.

Semenova, Nataliya S., Ekaterina V. Kiseleva, Marianna V. Ilyashevich, and Ekaterina S. Alisievich. "Traditional Values and Human Rights of LGBT under the Contemporary International Law." *Mediterranean Journal of Social Sciences* 6, no. 5 (2015): 305–12. https://doi.org/10.5901/mjss.2015.v6n5p305.

Sexual Minorities Uganda. May 2, 2021. https://sexualminoritiesuganda.com/.

"Shared Responsibility: Sweden's Policy for Global Development." Government bill 2002/03:122. Ministry for Foreign Affairs. May 15, 2003. https://www.government.se/legal-documents/2003/05/200203122/.

Sharlet, Jeff. "Letter from Kampala: Straight Man's Burden." *Harper's Magazine.* September 2010. https://harpers.org/archive/2010/09/straight-mans-burden/.

Shattuck, John, Harold Hongju Koh, David J. Kramer, Michael Posner, and Tom Malinowski. "The Pandemic and Human Rights: State Department CUR Is Not the Cure." *The Hill.* May 14, 2020. https://thehill.com/opinion/civil-rights/497309-the-pandemic-and-human-rights-state-departments-cur-is-not-the-cure.

Shawar, Yusra Ribhi, and Jennifer Prah Ruger. "The Politics of Global Health Inequalities." In *The Oxford Handbook of Global Health Politics*, edited by Colin McInnes, Kelley Lee, and Jeremy Youde, 59–84. Oxford: Oxford University Press, 2020.

Shippers, Birgit, ed. *Critical Perspectives on Human Rights.* Lanham, MD: Rowman & Littlefield International, 2018.

Shule, Lucy. "Uganda: A Mix of Strategies for Soft Power Goals." In *Diplomatic Strategies of Nations in the Global South*, 239–62. New York: Palgrave Macmillan, 2016.

Sides, John. *Identity Crisis: The 2016 Presidential Campaign and the Battle for the Meaning of America*. Princeton, NJ: Princeton University Press, 2018.

Sieczkowski, Cavan. "Ikea Pulls Lesbian Couple Feature from Russian Magazine." *Huffington Post*. November 21, 2013. http://www.huffingtonpost.com/2013/11/21/ikea-pulls-lesbian-couple_n_4316669.html.

Sikkink, Kathryn. *Mixed Signals: US Human Rights Policy and Latin America*. Ithaca, NY: Cornell University Press, 2018.

Sikkink, Kathryn. "Patterns of Dynamic Multilevel Governance and the Insider-Outsider Coalition." In *Transnational Protest and Global Activism*, 151–73. Lanham, MD: Rowman and Littlefield Publishers, 2004.

Sikkink, Kathryn. *The Justice Cascade: How Human Rights Prosecutions Are Changing World Politics*. New York: W.W. Norton Publishers, 2011.

Silva, Simon Kaijser da (Director). *Don't Ever Wipe Tears without Gloves* (Swedish: *Torka aldrig tårar utan handskar*). Written by Jonas Gardell. SVT1, 2012.

Simeon, James C., Patricia Tuitt, Julia Kienast, Barbara Kőhalmi, Anita Rozália Nagy-Nádasdi, and Selina March. "Terrorism and Asylum: Introduction." School of Advanced Study University of London RLI Working Paper Series Mini-Volume, 2019. https://sas-space.sas.ac.uk/9204/1/RLI_Working_Papers_No.31–36.pdf.

Simon, Scott. "All Our Relations: Indigenous Rights Movements in Contemporary Taiwan." In *Taiwan's Social Movements under Ma Ying-Jeou*, 236–57. London: Routledge, 2017.

Simonyi, András, and Nathaniel Hojnacki. "IKEA's Dead Wrong Decision on LGBT Rights in Russia: Don't Make Our Recent Purchase Our Last." *Huffington Post*. November 25, 2013. https://www.huffpost.com/entry/ikea-russia-magazine_b_4337223.

Slaughter, Anne-Marie. *A New World Order*. Princeton, NJ: Princeton University Press, 2005.

Smith, Haviland. "Idealist vs. Realist Foreign Policy." American Diplomacy: Foreign Service Dispatches and Periodic Reports. April 2011. Accessed November 2, 2014. http://www.unc.edu/depts/diplomat/item/2011/0104/oped/op_smith_idealism.html.

Smith, Julia, Christoforos Mallouris, Kelley Lee, and Tobias Alfvén. "The Role of Civil Society Organizations in Monitoring the Global AIDS Response." *AIDS and Behavior* 21, no. 1 (2017): 44–50.

Smith, Leanne M. "Implementing International Human Rights Law in Post Conflict Settings—Backlash without Buy-in: Lessons from Afghanistan." *Muslim World Journal of Human Rights* 5, no. 1 (2009).

Smith, Miriam. "Homonationalism and the Comparative Politics of LGBTQ Rights." In *LGBTQ Politics: A Critical Reader*, edited by Marla Brettschneider, Susan Burgess, and Christine Keating, 458–76. New York: New York University Press, 2017.

Smith, Steve, Amelia Hadfield, and Timothy Dunne, eds. *Foreign Policy: Theories, Actors, Cases.* Oxford: Oxford University Press, 2016.

Smith, Tom, Jaesok Son, and Jibum Kim. "Public Attitudes towards Homosexuality and Gay Rights across Time and Countries." The Williams Institute, UCLA School of Law. November 2014. https://williamsinstitute.law.ucla.edu/research/international/public-attitudes-nov-2014/.

Snyder, Sarah B. *From Selma to Moscow: How Human Rights Activists Transformed US Foreign Policy.* New York: Columbia University Press, 2018.

Söderström, G., ed. *Sympatiens hemlighetsfulla makt: Stockholms homosexuella 1860–1960*, 630–77. Stockholm, Sweden: Stockholmia, 1999.

Somerville, Ian, and Sahla Aroussi. "Campaigning for 'Women, Peace and Security': Transnational Advocacy Networks at the United Nations Security Council." In *Gender and Public Relations*, 172–92. London: Routledge, 2013.

Sörberg, Anna-Maria. *Homonationalism.* Stockholm, Sweden: Leopard förlag, 2017.

"Speech by the Minister for Foreign Affairs Margot Wallström at the Seminar about #femdefenders, Arranged by Women to Women International (Kvinna till Kvinna)." Sweden Ministry for Foreign Affairs. November 28, 2014. https://www.government.se/speeches/2014/11/speech-by-the-minister-for-foreign-affairs-margot-wallstrom-at-the-seminar-about-femdefenders-arranged-by-kvinna-till-kvinna/.

Spierings, Niels. "Homonationalism and Voting for the Populist Radical Right: Addressing Unanswered Questions by Zooming in on the Dutch Case." *International Journal of Public Opinion Research* (2020): edaa005. https://doi.org/10.1093/ijpor/edaa005.

Spierings, Niels, Marcel Lubbers, and Andrej Zaslove. " 'Sexually Modern Nativist Voters': Do They Exist and Do They Vote for the Populist Radical Right?" *Gender and Education* 29, no. 2 (2017): 216–37.

Sriram, Chandra Lekha, Olga Martin-Ortega, and Johanna Herman. *War, Conflict and Human Rights: Theory and Practice.* London: Routledge, 2017.

Staggers-Hakim, Raja. "The Nation's Unprotected Children and the Ghost of Mike Brown, or the Impact of National Police Killings on the Health and Social Development of African American Boys." *Journal of Human Behavior in the Social Environment* 26, no. 3–4 (2016): 390–99. https://doi.org/10.1080/10911359.2015.1132864.

Stapleton, AnneClaire. "Brunei's New Anti-Gay Law Goes into Effect This Week. Here's How the World Is Reacting." CNN. March 31, 2019. https://www.cnn.com/2019/03/30/asia/brunei-lgbt-death-penalty-intl/index.html.

Stassen, Kristien, Roel Smolders, and Pieter Leroy. "Sensitizing Events as Trigger for Discursive Renewal and Institutional Change in Flanders' Environmental Health Approach, 1970s–1990s." *Environmental Health* 12, no. 1 (2013): 46. https://doi.org10.1186/1476-069X-12-46.

"State Department Issues Guidance on How to Implement New Rules for Foreign Service Officers with Same-Sex Partners." Family Equality. January 11, 2010. https://www.familyequality.org/2010/01/11/state-department-issues-guidance-on-how-to-implement-new-rules-for-foreign-service-officers-with-same-sex-partners/.

"Statement by NSC Spokesperson Caitlin Hayden on the Response to Uganda's Enactment of the Anti-Homosexuality Act." The White House Office of the Press Secretary. June 19, 2014. https://www.whitehouse.gov/the-press-office/2014/06/19/statement-nsc-spokesperson-caitlin-hayden-response-uganda-s-enactment-an.

Steenkamp, Jan-Benedict. "Corporate Social Responsibility." In *Global Brand Strategy*, 209–38. London: Palgrave Macmillan, 2017.

Stein, Marc. "Theoretical Politics, Local Communities: The Making of US LGBT Historiography." *GLQ: A Journal of Lesbian and Gay Studies* 11, no. 4 (2005): 605–25.

Steinmetz, Katy. "Why It's a Big Deal That Obama Said 'Transgender.'" *Time Magazine*. January 21, 2015. http://time.com/3676881/state-of-the-union-2015-barack-obama-transgender/.

Stephenson, Elise. "Domestic Challenges and International Leadership: A Case Study of Women in Australian International Affairs." *Australian Journal of International Affairs* 73, no. 3 (2019): 234–53. https://doi.org/10.1080/10357718.2019.1588224.

Stephenson, Elise. "Invisible while Visible: An Australian Perspective on Queer Women Leaders in International Affairs." *European Journal of Politics and Gender* 3, no. 3 (2020): 427–43. https://doi.org/10.1332/251510820X15880614774555.

Stern, Jessica. "Human Rights Speakers Series—LGBT Rights Abroad." OutRight Action International. June 7, 2016. https://www.youtube.com/watch?v=flrAPcZx0Gc.

Stewart, Andrew. "A Journal for Manly Culture: An Exploration of the World's First Gay Periodical." *Papers of the Bibliographical Society of Canada/Cahiers de la Société bibliographique du Canada* 57 (2019): 85–105.

Stewart, Colin. "N.Y. Times under Continued Attack for Anti-LGBTI Article." *76 Crimes*. December 29, 2015. https://76crimes.com/2015/12/29/n-y-times-under-continued-attack-for-anti-lgbti-article/.

"Stockholm Pride." Swedish Ministry of Foreign Affairs. Accessed January 26, 2016. http://www.government.se/government-of-sweden/ministry-for-foreign-affairs/diplomatic-portal/stockholm-pride-2015/.

Stokes, Ethan, and Rebecca Schewe. "Framing from the Pulpit: A Content Analysis of American Conservative Evangelical Protestant Sermon Rhetoric Discussing LGBT Couples and Marriage." *Journal of Communication & Religion* 39, no. 3 (2016): 59–75.

Stoum, Tina Maria Sæteraas. "Sexually (Dis) Orientated?: Conceptualizing the Norwegian Ministry of Foreign Affairs' Promotion of LGBT Rights." Master's thesis, Norges teknisk-naturvitenskapelige universitet, Det humanistiske fakultet, Institutt for tverrfaglige kulturstudier, 2012.

Strand, Cecilia. "The Rise and Fall of a Contentious Social Policy Option—Narratives around the Ugandan Anti-Homosexuality Bill in the Domestic Press." *Journal of African Media Studies* 5, no. 3 (2013): 275–94. https://doi.org/10.1386/jams.5.3.275_1.

Strand, Sanna, and Katharina Kehl. " 'A Country to Fall in Love With/In': Gender and Sexuality in Swedish Armed Forces' Marketing Campaigns." *International Feminist Journal of Politics* 21, no. 2 (2019): 295–314.

Stubley, Peter. "Sweden Democrats: Anti-immigration Party with Neo-Nazi roots on Course to Become Second Biggest in General Election." *Independent.* September 5, 2018. https://www.independent.co.uk/news/world/europe/sweden-democrats-election-poll-results-nationalist-populist-party-immigration-a8524181.html.

Sullivan, Andrew. "The First Gay President." *Newsweek.* May 21, 2012. http://www.newsweek.com/andrew-sullivan-barack-obamas-gay-marriage-evolution-65067.

Sullivan, Patricia L., Leo J. Blanken, and Ian C. Rice. "Arming the Peace: Foreign Security Assistance and Human Rights Conditions in Post-Conflict Countries." *Defence and Peace Economics* 31, no. 2 (2020): 177–200.

Sundevall, Fia, and Alma Persson. "LGBT in the Military: Policy Development in Sweden 1944–2014." *Sexuality Research and Social Policy* 13, no. 2 (2016): 119–29.

"Sweden and Gender Equality." Swedish government. April 10, 2019. https://sweden.se/society/gender-equality-in-sweden/.

"Sweden and Human Rights." Swedish government. October 2, 2018. https://sweden.se/society/sweden-and-human-rights/.

"Sweden Democrats Tap into Immigration Fears." *BBC News.* September 25, 2018. https://www.bbc.com/news/world-europe-29202793.

"Sweden Is Taking a Proactive Role in International LGBT Efforts." Swedish Ministry of Foreign Affairs 2013. Accessed October 12, 2014. http://www.government.se/sb/d/17191/a/221203.

"Sweden Population: Live." Worldometer. February 20, 2020. https://www.worldometers.info/world-population/sweden-population/.

"Sweden Reconsidering Aid to Uganda." *Swedish Radio (Sveriges Radio).* February 24, 2014. https://sverigesradio.se/artikel/5793295.

"Swedish Christian Democrat Leader Attends Pride for First Time." *SverigesRadio.* August 1, 2016. https://sverigesradio.se/sida/artikel.aspx?artikel=6485455.

Swedish Migration Agency. Accessed April 4, 2021. https://www.migrationsverket.se/English/About-the-Migration-Agency/Statistics.html.

"Swedish Minister Meets Ugandan Gay Activists." *The Local Sweden.* February 25, 2014. https://www.thelocal.se/20140225/swedish-minister-meets-ugandan-gay-activists-anders-borg-lgbt-homosexuality.

Swiebel, Joke. "Lesbian, Gay, Bisexual and Transgender Human Rights: The Search for an International Strategy." *Contemporary Politics* 15, no. 1 (2009): 19–35.

Swimelar, Safia. "Nationalism and Europeanization in LGBT Rights and Politics: A Comparative Study of Croatia and Serbia." *East European Politics and Societies* 33, no. 3 (2019): 603–30.

Symons, Jonathan, and Dennis Altman. "International Norm Polarization: Sexuality as a Subject of Human Rights Protection." *International Theory* 7, no. 1 (2015): 61–95.

Tailor, Adam. "Sweden Stood Up for Human Rights in Saudi Arabia. This Is How Saudi Arabia Is Punishing Sweden." *Washington Post.* March 20, 2015. https://www.washingtonpost.com/news/worldviews/wp/2015/03/20/sweden-stood-up-for-human-rights-in-saudi-arabia-this-is-how-saudi-arabia-is-punishing-sweden/.

Takao, Yasuo. "The Politics of LGBT Policy Adoption: Shibuya Ward's Same-Sex Partnership Certificates in the Japanese Context." *Pacific Affairs* 90, no. 1 (2017): 7–27.

Tan, Avianne. "North Carolina's Controversial 'Anti-LGBT' Bill Explained." *ABC News.* March 24, 2016. http://abcnews.go.com/US/north-carolinas-controversial-anti-lgbt-bill-explained/story?id=37898153.

Tarrow, Sidney G. *Power in Movement Social Movements and Contentious Politics.* 3rd ed. Cambridge: Cambridge University Press, 2011.

Tatchell, Peter. "Has LGBT Pride Lost Its Way?" Peter Tatchell Foundation. July 6, 2017. www.petertatchellfoundation.org/has-lgbt-pride-lost-its-way/.

Teets, Jessica C. *Civil Society under Authoritarianism: The China Model.* Cambridge: Cambridge University Press, 2014.

Terkel, Amanda. "Sweden Cutting Aid to Uganda over 'Appalling' Anti-Homosexuality Bill." ThinkProgress. December 3, 2009. https://archive.thinkprogress.org/sweden-cutting-aid-to-uganda-over-appalling-anti-homosexuality-bill-7c99e3fbbf89/.

Thakur, Ramesh. *The United Nations, Peace and Security: From Collective Security to the Responsibility to Protect.* Cambridge: Cambridge University Press, 2016.

Thapa, Saurav Jung. "LGBT Uganda Today: Continuing Danger Despite Nullification of Anti-Homosexuality Act." Human Rights Campaign Global Spotlight. September 2015. https://assets2.hrc.org/files/assets/resources/Global_Spotlight_Uganda__designed_version__September_25__2015.pdf.

Tharoor, Ishaan. "Gambia's President Threatens to Slit the Throats of Gay Men." *Washington Post.* May 12, 2015. https://www.washingtonpost.com/news/worldviews/wp/2015/05/12/gambias-president-threatens-to-slit-the-throats-of-gay-men/.

"The American-Western European Values Gap: American Exceptionalism Subsides." Global Attitudes Project. *Pew Research Center.* February 29, 2012. http://www.pewglobal.org/2011/11/17/the-american-western-european-values-gap/#homosexuality.

"The Anti-Homosexuality Act." Ugandan government. 2014. https://www.ref-world.org/pdfid/530c4bc64.pdf?fbclid=IwAR0r_ZCq2az0HsiSbQmm9wy JMc3Vj33bZZ22y_cWtlaN_U8GirNeCoa6sw8,%201-11%20(2014).

"The Biden Plan to Advance LGBTQ+ Equality in America and around the World." Biden for President Campaign. Accessed November 9, 2020. https://joebiden.com/lgbtq-policy/.

"The Bush Global Gag Rule: Endangering Women's Health, Free Speech and Democracy." Center for Reproductive Rights. July 1, 2003. https://reproductiverights.org/document/the-bush-global-gag-rule-endangering-womens-health-free-speech-and-democracy.

"The Department of State's Accomplishments Promoting the Human Rights of Lesbian, Gay, Bisexual and Transgender People." US Department of State Office of the Spokesperson, Washington, DC, December 6, 2011. https://2009-2017.state.gov/r/pa/prs/ps/2011/12/178341.htm.

"The Europride Parade Stockholm Broke All Records." EuroPride. August 5, 2018. Accessed March 4, 2019. http://europride2018.com/2018/08/05/pride-parade-broke-all-records/.

"The Global Divide on Homosexuality: Greater Acceptance in More Secular and Affluent Countries." Global Attitudes Project. *Pew Research Center*. 2013. Accessed June 5, 2015. http://www.pewglobal.org/2013/06/04/the-global-divide-on-homosexuality/.

"The Government's Statement of Foreign Policy." Swedish Foreign Ministry. February 2019. https://www.government.se/.

"Thematic Programming Priorities." US Department of State Bureau of Democracy, Human Rights and Labor. Accessed May 7, 2021. https://www.state.gov/key-topics-bureau-of-democracy-human-rights-and-labor/programs/thematic-programming-priorities/.

"The New Anti-Gay Bill Proposed by the Ugandan Parliament." *Huffington Post*. December 1, 2014. Updated February 2, 2016. https://www.huffpost.com/entry/the-new-antigay-bill-prop_b_6236390.

"The Occupation of the National Board of Health and Welfare." [SocialStyrelson] Swedish Radio P3 Documentary. Broadcasted on March 22, 2009. https://sverigesradio.se/sida/avsnitt/83613?programid=2519.

"The Swedish Women's Lobby's Index: 'Member Organizations.'" The Swedish Women's Lobby. Accessed August 19, 2015. http://sverigeskvinnolobby.se/en/members/.

"The Universal Declaration of Human Rights (UDHR)." United Nations. December 10, 1948. http://www.un.org/en/documents/udhr/.

"The Yogyakarta Principles: Principles on the Application of International Human Rights Law in Relation to Sexual Orientation and Gender Identity." International Commission of Jurists. 2006. http://www.yogyakartaprinciples.org/.

Thiel, Markus. "Theorizing the EU's International Promotion of LGBTI Rights Policies in the Global South." In *EU Development Policies*, 35–53. Cham: Palgrave Macmillan, 2019. https://doi.org/10.1007/978-3-030-01307-3_3.

Thoreson, Ryan R. *Transnational LGBT Activism Working for Sexual Rights Worldwide.* Minneapolis: University of Minnesota Press, 2014.

Tillerson, Rex. "Transgender Day of Remembrance." US Department of State, Washington, DC, November 20, 2017. https://uy.usembassy.gov/rex-w-tillerson-statement-transgender-day-remembrance/.

Tilly, Charles. *Social Movements 1768–2008.* 2nd ed. Boulder, CO: Paradigm, 2009.

Tilly, Charles, and Sidney Tarrow. *Contentious Politics.* Oxford: Oxford University Press, 2007.

Tilly, Charles, and Lesley Wood. *Social Movements 1768–2012.* 3rd ed. Boulder, CO: Paradigm, 2013.

"Timeline: Iraq War." *BBC News.* July 5, 2016. https://www.bbc.com/news/magazine-36702957.

Tingsten, Herbert. *The Swedish Social Democrats; Their Ideological Development.* Totowa, NJ: Bedminster Press, 1973.

Tomson, Danielle Lee. "The Rise of Sweden Democrats: Islam, Populism and the End of Swedish Exceptionalism." The Brookings Institution. March 25, 2020. https://www.brookings.edu/research/the-rise-of-sweden-democrats-and-the-end-of-swedish-exceptionalism/.

Toops, Jessica. "The Lavender Scare: Persecution of Lesbianism during the Cold War." *Western Illinois Historical Review* 5 (2013): 91–107.

Topel, Kimberly D. "So, What Should I Ask Him to Prove That He's Gay: How Sincerity, and Not Stereotype, Should Dictate the Outcome of an LGB Asylum Claim in the United States." *Iowa Law Review* 102 (2017): 2357–84.

Towns, Ann E. " 'Diplomacy Is a Feminine Art': Feminised Figurations of the Diplomat." *Review of International Studies* (2020): 1–21.

Towns, Ann, and Birgitta Niklasson. "Gender, International Status, and Ambassador Appointments." *Foreign Policy Analysis* 13, no. 3 (2016): 521–40.

Towns, Ann E., and Karin Aggestam, eds. *Gendering Diplomacy and International Negotiation.* London: Palgrave Macmillan, 2018.

Trägårdh Lars. *State and Civil Society in Northern Europe: The Swedish Model Reconsidered.* New York: Berghahn Books, 2007.

Traub, James. "The Death of the Most Generous Nation on Earth." *Foreign Policy.* February 10, 2016. http://foreignpolicy.com/2016/02/10/the-death-of-the-most-generous-nation-on-earth-sweden-syria-refugee-europe/.

"2019 Trafficking in Persons Report." US Department of State. June 20, 2019. https://www.state.gov/trafficking-in-persons-report-2019/.

Tremblay, M., D. Paternotte, and C. Johnson. *The Lesbian and Gay Movement and the State: Comparative Insights into a Transformed Relationship.* Burlington, VT: Ashgate Publishing Company, 2011.

Tsai, Robert L. "Obama's Conversion on Same-Sex Marriage: The Social Foundations of Individual Rights." *Connecticut Law Review* 50, no. 1 (2018): 1–59.

"Uganda's Anti-Gay Bill Puts U.S. Aid at Risk." Inter Press Service. February 2014. Accessed October 20, 2014. http://www.ipsnews.net/2014/02/ugandas-anti-gay-bill-puts-u-s-aid-risk/.

"Uganda Anti-Gay Timeline." Gay & Lesbian Advocates and Defenders. May 6, 2014. https://www.glad.org/wp-content/uploads/2014/05/uganda-timeline.pdf.

"Uganda: Parliament Must Reject Bill Imposing Death Penalty for Gay Sex." Amnesty International. October 11, 2019. https://www.amnesty.org/en/latest/news/2019/10/uganda-parliament-must-reject-bill-imposing-death-penalty-for-gay-sex/.

"Uganda Threatens to Re-introduce 'Anti-Homosexuality Act.'" OutRight Action International. October 10, 2019. https://outrightinternational.org/content/uganda-plans-re-introduce-anti-homosexuality-act.

"UN and Regional Mechanisms." OutRight Action International. Accessed June 10, 2019. https://www.outrightinternational.org/region/un-and-regional-mechanisms.

UN General Assembly. "University Declaration of Human Rights." 217 (III) A. Paris, 1948, Accessed October 7, 2020. https://www.un.org/en/universal-declaration-human-rights/.

"UN: General Assembly Statement Affirms Rights for All: 66 States Condemn Violations Based on Sexual Orientation and Gender Identity." Human Rights Watch. December 18, 2008, https://www.hrw.org/news/2008/12/18/un-general-assembly-statement-affirms-rights-all.

"United Nations Economic and Social Council (ECOSOC)." Accessed May 17, 2016. https://www.un.org/ecosoc/en/home.

"UN Resolution 1325: Landmark Resolution on Women, Peace and Security." UN Office of the Special Adviser on Gender Issues and Advancement of Women, October 31, 2000. https://www.un.org/womenwatch/osagi/wps/.

"USAID Annual Budget Request to U.S. Congress." USAID. Accessed January 6, 2016. https://www.usaid.gov/results-and-data/budget-spending.

US Department of State Bureau of Democracy, Human Rights and Labor. Accessed May 5, 2021. http://www.state.gov/j/drl/.

"U.S. Looking to Make LGBT Rights a Foreign Policy Priority." Inter Press Service. June 2014. Accessed October 10, 2014. http://www.ipsnews.net/2014/06/u-s-looking-make-lgbt-rights-foreign-policy-priority/.

"U.S. President's Emergency Plan for AIDS Relief (PEPFAR)." http://www.pepfar.gov/.

Valentinavicius, Vytautas. "Protesters Try to Disrupt Lithuania Gay Pride." *Omaha World-Herald.* July 27, 2013. https://www.omaha.com/news/protesters-try-to-disrupt-lithuania-gay-pride/article_25531d13-c436-520a-be88-55cc9144cb23.html.

Van den Berg, Mariecke. "Rings for the Rainbow Family: Religious Opposition to the Introduction of Same-Sex Marriage in Sweden." *Theology and Sexuality* 23, no. 3 (2017): 229–44.

Van Der Toorn, Jojanneke, John T. Jost, Dominic J. Packer, Sharareh Noorbaloochi, and Jay J. Van Bavel. "In Defense of Tradition: Religiosity, Conservatism, and Opposition to Same-Sex Marriage in North America." *Personality and Social Psychology Bulletin* 43, no. 10 (2017): 1455–68.

Van Klinken, A. "Sexual Orientation, (Anti-) Discrimination and Human Rights in a 'Christian Nation': The Politicization of Homosexuality in Zambia." *Critical African Studies* 9, no. 1 (2017): 9–31.

Varga, Bretton A., Terence A. Beck, and Stephen J. Thornton. "Celebrating Stonewall at 50: A Culturally Geographic Approach to Introducing LGBT Themes." *The Social Studies* 110, no. 1 (2019): 33–42.

Vasilev, George. "LGBT Recognition in EU Accession States: How Identification with Europe Enhances the Transformative Power of Discourse." *Review of International Studies* 42, no. 4 (2016): 748–72. https://doi.org/10.1017/s0260210515000522.

Velasco, Kristopher. "A Growing Queer Divide: The Divergence between Transnational Advocacy Networks and Foreign Aid in Diffusing LGBT Policies." *International Studies Quarterly* 64, no. 1 (2020): 120–32.

Velasco, Kristopher. "Human Rights INGOs, LGBT INGOs, and LGBT Policy Diffusion, 1991–2015." *Social Forces* 97, no. 1 (2018): 377–404.

Velte, Kyle. "Fueling the Terrorist Fires: How Discrimination against LGBT Americans in the Name of Religious Liberty Threatens National Security." *Brooklyn Law Review* 82 (2017). https://ssrn.com/abstract=2794691.

Verloo, M. ed. *Varieties of Opposition to Gender Equality in Europe.* New York: Routledge, 2018.

"Views on Gay Rights by Political Affiliation in the U.S." Gallup Statista. 2015. http://www.statista.com/statistics/226165/views-on-gay-rights-by-political-affiliation-in-the-us/.

"Violence against the Transgender Community in 2020." Human Rights Campaign. Accessed May 19, 2020. https://www.hrc.org/resources/violence-against-the-trans-and-gender-non-conforming-community-in-2020.

Vogelgesang, Sandy. "Diplomacy of Human Rights." *International Studies Quarterly* 23, no. 2 (1979): 216–45. https://doi.org/10.2307/2600243.

Wabyanga, Robert Kuloba. "The Destruction of Sodom and Gomorrah Revisited: Military and Political Reflections." *Old Testament Essays* 28, no. 3 (2015): 847–73.

Wahab, Amar. " 'Homosexuality/Homophobia Is Un-African?:' Un-Mapping Transnational Discourses in the Context of Uganda's Anti-Homosexuality Bill/Act."

Journal of Homosexuality 63, no. 5 (2016): 685–718. https://doi.org/10.108 0/00918369.2015.1111105.

Wahl, Alice, and Lars Jonsson. "Kartläggning av nationella undersökningar gällande homofobi, bifobi och transfobi, samt identifiering av andra länders nationella mål och uppföljningssystem för hbtq-personers rättigheter" (2017).

Waites, Matthew. "LGBT and Queer Politics in the Commonwealth." In *Oxford Research Encyclopedia of Politics*, edited by D. Haider-Markel. Oxford: Oxford University Press, 2019.

Walek, Czeslaw, chairman, Prague Pride and Board member for Alturi. "Human Rights Speakers Series—LGBT Rights Abroad." OutRight Action International, June 7, 2016. https://www.youtube.com/watch?v=flrAPcZx0Gc.

Waltman, Max. "Prohibiting Sex Purchasing and Ending Trafficking: The Swedish Prostitution Law." *Michigan Journal of International Law* 33, no. 1 (2011): 133–57.

Warburton, Timothy Ryan. "From AIDS to Assimilation: Representations of Male Homosexuality in Swedish Literature." PhD diss., University of Washington, Department of Scandinavian Studies, 2014.

Warner, Gregory. "Uganda Passes Anti-Gay Bill That Includes Life in Prison." NPR, December 20, 2013. https://www.npr.org/sections/parallels/2013/12/20/ 255825383/uganda-passes-anti-gay-bill-that-includes-life-in-prison.

Weber, Cynthia. *Queer International Relations: Sovereignty, Sexuality and the Will to Knowledge.* Oxford: Oxford University Press, 2016.

"We Defend LGBTI Rights." European Parliament's LGBTI Intergroup. Accessed December 10, 2019. https://lgbti-ep.eu/.

Weeks, Jeffrey. *The World We Have Won: The Remaking of Erotic and Intimate Life.* London: Routledge Press, 2007.

Weiss, Thomas G. "Sanctions as a Foreign Policy Tool: Weighing Humanitarian Impulses." *Journal of Peace Research* 36, no. 5 (1999): 499–509. https://doi. org/10.1177/0022343399036005001.

Weldon, Laurel. *When Protest Makes Policy: How Social Movements Represent Disadvantaged Groups.* Ann Arbor, MI: University of Michigan Press, 2012.

Wellman, James, and Clark Lombardi. *Religion and Human Security: A Global Perspective.* Oxford: Oxford University Press, 2012.

Wennerhag, Magnus. "Pride anländer till Sverige: En resa i två etapper." In *Civilsamhället i det transnationella*, edited by F. Wijkström, M. Reuter, and A. Emami, 33–61. Stockholm, Sweden: European Civil Society Press, 2017.

Westcott, Ben. "Brunei to Punish Gay Sex and Adultery with Death by Stoning." CNN. March 30, 2019. https://www.cnn.com/2019/03/27/asia/brunei-anti-lgbt-stoning-law-intl/index.html.

Westcott, Lucy. "Kenyan Leaders Respond to Obama's Support for LGBT Rights." *Newsweek.* July 25, 2015. http://www.newsweek.com/kenyan-leaders-respond-obamas-support-lgbt-rights-357563.

"Western Donors Cut Aid to Uganda in Response to Anti-Gay Law." *Reuters*. February 2014. Accessed October 10, 2014. http://www.trust.org/item/2014 0226160032-td4jl/.

"What We Do." United States Institution for Peace. Accessed September 24, 2020. https://www.usip.org/.

White House Press Statement, "President Biden Announces U.S. Special Envoy to Advance the Human Rights of LGBTQI+ Persons," June 25, 2021, https://www. whitehouse.gov/briefing-room/statements-releases/2021/06/25/president-biden-announces-u-s-special-envoy-to-advance-the-human-rights-of-lgbtqi-persons/.

"Who We Are." Amnesty International. Accessed April 5, 2021. http://www.amnestyusa.org/about-us/who-we-are.

Wirtz, Andrea L., Tonia C. Poteat, Mannat Malik, and Nancy Glass. "Gender-Based Violence against Transgender People in the United States: A Call for Research and Programming." *Trauma, Violence, & Abuse* 21, no. 2 (2020): 227–41.

Wiering, M. A., and B. J. M. Arts. "Discursive Shifts in Dutch River Management: 'Deep' Institutional Change or Adaptation Strategy?" In *Living Rivers: Trends and Challenges in Science and Management*, 327–38. Dordrecht: Springer, 2006.

Wilcox, Clyde. *Onward Christian Soldiers?: The Religious Right in American Politics*. London: Routledge, 2018.

Williams, Christopher. "Assessing South Africa's Ambivalent SOGI Diplomacy in Africa." *South African Journal of International Affairs* 24, no. 3 (2017): 375–94.

Williams, Roger Ross. *God Loves Uganda*. New York: First-Run Features. October 11, 2013.

Wilson, Angelia R. *Why Europe Is Lesbian and Gay Friendly (and Why America Never Will Be)*. Albany, NY: State University of New York Press, 2014.

"Working for a Gay-Friendly Sweden." Swedish Ministry for Foreign Affairs. Accessed May 19, 2016. https://sweden.se/society/working-for-a-gay-and-equal-sweden/.

"Working for the Rights of Lesbian, Gay, Bisexual, Trans and Intersex people in the European Parliament." European Parliament's LGBTI Intergroup. Accessed December 19, 2019. https://lgbti-ep.eu/.

"World Prison Brief: Prison Population Total." Institute for Crime & Justice Policy Research. Birkbeck, University of London, November 2018. Accessed October 12, 2019. https://www.prisonstudies.org/highest-to-lowest/prison-population-total?field_region_taxonomy_tid=All.

Wright, Joseph. "How Foreign Aid Can Foster Democratization in Authoritarian Regimes." *American Journal of Political Science* 53, no. 3 (2009): 552–71. https://doi.org/10.1111/j.1540-5907.2009.00386.x.

Wright, Katherine Fairfax, and Malika Zouhali-Worrall. *Call Me Kuchu*. Germany. September 17, 2012.

Xavier-Brier, Marik. "Red, White, and Gay?: American Identity, White Savior Complex, and Pink Policing." PhD diss., Georgia State University, 2016. https://scholarworks.gsu.edu/sociology_diss/87.

Yamin, Alicia Ely, Neil Datta, and Ximena Andion. "Behind the Drama: The Roles of Transnational Actors in Legal Mobilization over Sexual and Reproductive Rights." *Georgetown Journal of Gender and the Law* 19 (2017): 533–69.

Young, Iris Marion. "Five Faces of Oppression." In *The Community Development Reader*, edited by Susan Saegert and James DeFilippis, 346–55. London: Routledge, 2012.

Youssef, Lisa. "Reflections on the Ideological Evolution of the Sweden Democrats Party: A Qualitative Analysis of Party Programs over Time." Bachelor's thesis, Linnaeus University, 2020.

Yulius, Hendri, Shawna Tang, and Baden Offord. "The Globalization of LGBT Identity and Same-Sex Marriage as a Catalyst of Neo-Institutional Values: Singapore and Indonesia in Focus." In *Global Perspectives on Same-Sex Marriage*, 171–96. Cham: Palgrave Macmillan, 2018. https://doi.org/10.1007/978-3-319-62764-9_9.

Zajak, Sabrina, Niklas Egels-Zandén, and Nicola Piper. "Networks of Labour Activism: Collective Action across Asia and Beyond. An Introduction to the Debate." *Development and Change* 48, no. 5 (2017): 899–921. https://doi.org/10.1111/dech.12336.

Zappulla, Antonio. "The Simple Reason Why So Many Businesses Support LGBT Rights." World Economic Forum. January 14, 2017. https://www.weforum.org/agenda/2017/01/why-so-many-businesses-support-lgbt-rights/.

Zayani, Mohamed. *The Al Jazeera Phenomenon: Critical Perspectives on New Arab Media*. New York: Routledge, 2005.

Zayas, Alfred de. "UN Independent Expert Reports on World Bank and IMF Human Rights Performance." Brettonwoods Project. September 27, 2017. https://www.brettonwoodsproject.org/2017/09/un-independent-expert-reports-world-bank-imf-human-rights-performance/.

Zeidan, Tarek. "For LGBTI People in Lebanon, They Go through Their Own Stonewall Everyday." *Gay Star News*. January 8, 2019. https://www.gaystarnews.com/article/for-lgbti-people-in-lebanon-they-go-through-their-own-stonewall-everyday/#gs.84y79b.

Zekos, Georgios. "Asylum: The Vehicle for Channeling Economic Immigrants into Countries for 'Politico-Economic' Reasons." SSRN 3386059 (2019).

Zhao, Suisheng. *Chinese Foreign Policy: Pragmatism and Strategic Behavior*. London: Routledge, 2016.

Zuckerman, Phil. *Society without God: What the Least Religious Nations Can Tell Us about Contentment*. New York: New York University Press, 2008.

Index

Abu Ghraib, 81

activism: collective, 184; discrimination, violence, and repression in US, 52; to end racial and gender discrimination, 132; evangelical, 141; international, 146; NGO advocacy and, 44; political, 37, 57; to protest federal policies, 53–54; from Swedish civil society organizations, 100–19, 128–33; training programs, 96; transnational, 44, 62, 128, 143, 150, 171; from US-based civil society organizations, 56–58, 63–73, 76–79; youth, 88

Adero, Anthony, 201

advocacy: domestic, 79, 143; in foreign policy institutions, 25; for human rights and democratic freedoms, xiii; institutional, 15, 23, 25, 28–29, 34, 44, 58–63, 80, 84, 87, 100–6, 183–84, 197; international, 51, 128; intersectional, 183; in Latin America, 12; NGO, 3, 13, 15–16, 23, 28–29, 43–44, 52, 80, 86, 100–13, 132, 177, 183, 196, 203; organizations, 146; public, 29, 34, 106–13, 132, 205; Swedish LGBTI, 100–13; transgender, 105; transnational, 35, 143, 171, 207; US LGBTI, 58–63

Afghanistan, 67, 168

Africa, xiv, 6, 8, 22, 24, 32, 71, 142, 204

African leaders, 161

African LGBTI Out and Proud Diamond group, 149

agenda-setting, 156, 184, 194

Aggestam, Karin, 91, 93, 190

Agius, Christine, 121, 180

aid: allocation to civil society, 149; bilateral, 19, 142, 149, 157–58, 190; conditioning, 7, 24, 30, 133, 137–38, 148–49, 154, 157–59, 181, 210–11, 215; foreign, 29, 32–33, 37, 51, 80, 84, 88, 92, 101, 120, 131, 136–38, 142, 147–49, 151–53, 157, 159, 161, 170, 173, 211–12, 215; gay, 138; health-care-related, 159; humanitarian, xvi, 3, 7, 20, 30, 51, 58, 101, 126, 207, 215; international, 2, 6, 13–14, 19, 29, 31–32, 47, 85, 88, 95, 138, 159–60, 182, 188, 193, 203, 208, 212; suspension, 161

Åkesson, Jimmie, 91, 118

Al-Jazeera, 169

Algeria, 36

Aliki, Silas, 99

allyship, 110, 119–25, 184

American Journal of Political Science, 211

www.ingramcontent.com/pod-product-compliance
Lightning Source LLC
Chambersburg PA
CBHW030858270326
41929CB00008B/477

* 9 7 8 1 4 3 8 4 8 5 7 8 2 *